HELPING BEYOND THE 50-MINUTE HOUR

0 6 MAY 2022

"Slacktivism" is a term that has been coined to cynically describe the token efforts that people devote to some causes, without long-term or meaningful impact. We wear colored wristbands, pins, or ribbons proclaiming support for a particular organization. We might post something on social network sites or send messages to friends about causes dear to our hearts. We might even volunteer our time to work on behalf of marginalized, oppressed, or neglected groups—or donate money to a charity. Yet the key feature of significant social action is follow-through—continuing efforts over a period of time so as to build meaningful relationships, provide adequate support, and conduct evaluations to measure results and make needed adjustments that make programs even more responsive.

This book is intended as an inspiration for practicing psychotherapists and counselors, as well as students, to become *actively* involved in a meaningful effort. The editors have searched far and wide to identify practitioners representing different disciplines, helping professions, geographic regions, and social action projects, all of whom have been involved in social justice efforts for some time, whether in their own communities or in far-flung regions of the world. Each of them has an amazing story to tell that reveals the challenges they've faced, the incredible satisfactions they've experienced, and the lessons they've learned along the way. Each story represents a gem of wisdom, revealing both questions of faith, as well as of sustained action. The authors have been encouraged to dig deeply in order to talk about the honest realities of their work. After reading their stories, you will be ready to pick a cause that speaks to you and begin your own work.

Jeffrey A. Kottler, PhD, is Professor of Counseling at California State University, Fullerton, and the author of over 80 books. He is the founder and CEO of the Empower Nepali Girls foundation.

Matt Englar-Carlson, PhD, is Professor of Counseling and the Co-Director of the Center for Boys and Men at California State University, Fullerton.

Jon Carlson, PsyD, EdD, is Distinguished Professor of Psychology and Counseling at Governors State University, University Park, Illinois and a psychologist with the Wellness Clinic in Lake Geneva, Wisconsin.

HELPING BEYOND THE 50-MINUTE HOUR

Therapists Involved in Meaningful Social Action

Edited by Jeffrey A. Kottler,
Matt Englar-Carlson, and Jon Carlson

 Routledge
Taylor & Francis Group

NEW YORK AND LONDON

First published 2013
by Routledge
711 Third Avenue, New York, NY 10017

Simultaneously published in the UK
by Routledge
27 Church Road, Hove, East Sussex BN3 2FA

Routledge is an imprint of the Taylor & Francis Group, an informa business

Library of Congress Cataloging in Publication Data
    Helping beyond the fifty minute hour : therapists involved in
    meaningful social action / [edited by] Jeffrey Kottler,
    Matt Englar-Carlson, and Jon Carlson.
        p. cm.
    Includes bibliographical references and index.
    1. Social action. 2. Social justice. 3. Social change.
    I. Kottler, Jeffrey A. II. Englar-Carlson, Matt III. Carlson, Jon.
    HM831.H454 2013
    303.4–dc23
    2012029737

ISBN: 978–0–415–66096–9 (hbk)
ISBN: 978–0–415–89630–6 (pbk)
ISBN: 978–0–203–80708–8 (ebk)

Typeset in Bembo
by Swales & Willis Ltd, Exeter, Devon

Printed and bound in the United States of America by Sheridan Books, Inc. (a Sheridan Group Company).

CONTENTS

PREFACE

Just what you need: another book about advocacy and social action. Our ethical codes mandate that clinicians take a stand for social justice and make it a priority in our work. Professional conferences frequently select topics of global human rights, advocacy, and social action as their predominant themes. More and more books and articles are being published about making a difference in the larger world—and with good reason. After all, helping professionals have a moral obligation not only to work on behalf of our own clients, but also on behalf of those who have been neglected and ignored. Even more significantly, we have particular skills, backgrounds, and commitments that are especially well suited for advocacy work in the community or on a global scale. Our training in systemic interventions, group dynamics, cultural competencies, relationship skills, and therapeutic interventions make us perfect candidates to help facilitate constructive changes with marginalized groups that would otherwise not have access to our (or anyone else's) services.

Unfortunately, therapists usually have relatively little visibility in their own communities. Codes of ethics call for privacy and many therapists interpret that literally, leading to secret lives and practices that are far too private indeed. Therapists have an important voice and skill sets, and need to be actively involved in living their values as well as teaching them to others. Therapists can be models for their clients and practice generosity while still adhering to the highest standards of professional practice. Yet we also recognize that such admonishments are all too common in public forums, without as much follow through in real, sustained action.

"Slacktivism" is a term that has been coined to cynically describe the token efforts that people devote to causes, without long-term or meaningful impact.

We wear colored wristbands, pins, or ribbons proclaiming support for a particular organization. We might post something on social network sites or send messages to friends about causes dear to our hearts. We might even volunteer our time to work on behalf of marginalized, oppressed, or neglected groups—or donate money to a charity. Yet the key feature of significant social action is follow through—continuing efforts over a period of time so as to build meaningful relationships, provide adequate support, and conduct evaluations to measure results and adjust programs to make them more responsive.

This book is intended to inspire practicing psychotherapists and counselors, as well as students, to become *actively* involved in a meaningful effort. Pick a cause—*any* cause—that speaks to you, and begin. Collaborate with friends and colleagues who share your interest and who can support you through the inevitably challenging times ahead. We tend to romanticize such work as noble and laudable, but often gloss over the price paid for such efforts. There are sacrifices to be made—of time, energy, resources, even one's health. The work is often accompanied by a fair degree of frustration, even despair and hopelessness, given some of the intractable conditions that are faced and the roadblocks along the way. It is incredibly difficult work, gratifying for sure, but it also takes a bit out of your soul. That may explain why it is so challenging to maintain our efforts over time, to stick with projects for years, decades, or even a lifetime.

We have searched far and wide to identify practitioners representing different disciplines, helping professions, geographic regions, and social action projects, all of whom have been involved in social justice efforts, whether in their own communities or in far-flung regions of the world. Our authors represent tremendous diversity, not only in their ethnic, religious, and cultural backgrounds, but in their professional orientations and work settings. You will notice differences in language and titles in which psychologists, social workers, counselors, family therapists, psychiatrists, religious leaders, community activists, and even a student or two, talk about their roles and responsibilities in different ways. Social justice and advocacy are defined very differently by the contributors, reflecting the unique ways that they view themselves as change agents, facilitators, advocates, activists, community leaders, psychologists, systemic interventionists, or simply participants in a collective process. Each author dug deeply in order to talk about the honest realities of their work. The stories reveal the challenges faced, the incredible satisfactions experienced, and the lessons learned along the way. Each story represents a gem of wisdom, revealing both questions of faith, as well as of sustained action.

The primary focus of this book is to inspire students and practitioners alike to become more actively involved in making a difference beyond their own practices, whether in the local community or around the world.

Overview of the Stories

Each of the contributors to this volume was asked to address a series of questions that were intended to provide a loose structure to discuss their experiences in the field as social activists.

- What led you to undertake this work, both personally and professionally? Be honest and transparent.
- What have been your greatest satisfactions, growth, and development as a result of this work?
- What is one vivid example of a piece of work you did that really moved you, or perhaps transformed you in some way?
- What are some of the greatest frustrations, challenges, and obstacles you've faced? How have you addressed them?
- What keeps you going in the face of these problems?
- What advice do you have for other therapists about how they can get more *actively* involved in social justice projects and service, especially in an ongoing, sustained effort?

Many of the authors use the beginning of their contribution to explain how the chapter you are about to read came into being, while others just give a brief overview of how activism, outreach, involvement, and advocacy became central aspects of their lives. Above all, we asked the authors to tell the narrative of their work in a way that was not limited to the common boundaried style and tone of scholarly articles. Rather, the story of each author should come through in the best way possible. To bring the reader further into each story, we also encouraged authors to submit photographs that represented their action.

The book is organized into five parts so that the stories and reach flow out in concentric circles from the self of the individual counselor to global action. In Part One, Re-Visioning Clinical Practice, the contributors offer a broad perspective on how our lives as clinicians are often limited and suggest potential ways to broaden our work and professional roles. Jeffrey begins the book with his own powerful account of how his professional life has changed radically in the past 15 years as a result of his work with lower-caste girls in Nepal. William Doherty redefines the role of the modern "therapist" and examines how being a "citizen-therapist" enriches the lives of clients and whole communities. Both chapters effectively serve as a manifesto to the influence of social action on the therapists themselves, and to the ways that a single person can truly make a meaningful difference.

Part Two of the book, The Dreamers: What Change Could Be, presents the stories of experienced, novice, and future professionals who are finding their way and exploring the different avenues social action can take in our daily and future lives. Sari Gold gives voice to the yearning that many professionals have to find a greater meaning in their work. Leah Brew recalls her own feelings of marginalization and finds an unanticipated avenue for change as a social justice advocate for professional identity via the legislative process. Josselyn Sheer shares her students experiences in India and vividly recalls the watershed moment when she realized how she wanted to spend her future professional life. Henry Sibbing examines his life of integrating social justice into his first career as a lawyer and municipal judge and his second career as a professional counselor. Taken together, these accounts illustrate the yearnings, urges, and desires to be a part of something greater than oneself—to feel as if one is part of and making a contribution to the social welfare surrounding all of us.

Part Three, Community Action, locates social action and social justice work domestically—in the communities where we work or reside. Each of these stories recounts the efforts of recognizing a need and then working to find a way to help better the community. Stan Bosch and Joseph Cervantes write about their work with gang-affiliated youth in Southern California. They describe their efforts to provide meaning and voice to the lives of young boys' and girls' lives in communities ravaged by violence, poverty, and hopelessness. Gerald Monk shares his experience in San Diego, learning from his students and the local community that real community mental health efforts must reside, be a part of, and learn from the communities in which they are located. Byron Waller shares his efforts in Chicago to navigate racialized communities and create common understanding—and recounts how difficult this work can be. Dallas and Debbie Stout recall how their lives became grounded in community action around gun control issues and public policy. Loretta Pyles writes about her efforts in upstate New York in community organizing with women survivors of domestic violence. She speaks of the ways in which professionals can move outside their offices and help build strong, healthy communities. Selma Yznaga provides a revealing portrayal of how she learned that wanting to offer help to the Buena Vida community in Brownsville, Texas was not enough—rather she had to become a *student* of community, and then a *member* of that community, to understand how to contribute. Sharon Bethea examines her career of giving service to and advocating for youth and their families in inner city communities. She shares her experiences with the African-centered Oakland Freedom Schools project. Social justice work with African-descended people in New York City is the focus of Jamila Codrington's chapter, which describes her work to help people displaced by the 2010 earthquake in Haiti. A veteran of he Army, Cyrus Ellis examines his own drive to help returning Army veterans adjust to life outside of the military in suburban Chicago. This section closes with Fred Bemak's provocative account of how he has mobilized domestic and international crisis counseling services in the aftermath of natural disasters. He challenges the reader to look within and take the risk to go where help is most needed.

Part Four, Global Outreach, addresses the undertaking of social action in international settings. Beginning in Thailand, Tipawadee Emavardhana explores her lifelong commitment to social action and explains why it is so critical to give to others. In many families, social action and consciousness is considered a family value. The work of father and daughter Keith Edwards and Rebecca Rodriquez illustrates this emphasis. Together they document their own efforts serving internationally and finish by looking at their work providing care to other activists working around the world. Kathryn Norsworthy and Ouyporn Khuankaew are women with vastly different backgrounds, yet their commitment to feminist activism brought them together. However shared beliefs do not immediately lead to cohesive connections, and Kathryn and Ouyporn share how they worked to develop a truly egalitarian relationship while engaged in social action across Southeast Asia. When Haiti experienced the devastating 2010 earthquake, Chante DeLoach immediately went to help. Her chapter chronicles the intensity of being in a location where the acute needs vastly outnumber the available assistance. A central question of this book is how do professionals navigate more traditional careers and engage in social action. Cirecie A. West-Olatunji explores that very question and how she has learned to integrate domestic and global social justice into her life to the point where they are one and the same. Heather Guay focuses on the way that her involvement in Nepal has transformed her life to the point where social action now *is* her life.

Part Five, Closure and Reflection, is where we consider some of the take-home messages and commonalities of the stories. Further, we look to locate our own work in the context of the stories and experiences of the contributors. Jeffrey asks himself why he does what he does, and how his motivation is derived from multiple sources. Jon contemplates his professional life and how contributing to the welfare of others has been a driving force. In the last chapter, Matt works to make sense of all the stories, of his own connection to this book, and of where we as a profession go next.

Together, we are really proud of this project—not because of our efforts, but because we feel that the authors, their stories, and the work they all do stand alone as the heroes. We are certain that others will find something that inspires them, and we hope the next step becomes clear—turn that inspiration into action and *do something*.

Jeffrey A. Kottler
Huntington Beach, California

Matt Englar–Carlson
Huntington Beach, California

Jon Carlson
Lake Geneva, Wisconsin

ABOUT THE EDITORS

Jeffrey A. Kottler is one of the most prolific authors in the fields of psychology and education. He has written 80 books on a wide range of subjects during the past 35 years. He has authored a dozen texts for counselors and therapists that are used in universities around the world, and a dozen books each for practicing therapists and educators.

Some of his most highly regarded works include: *On Being a Therapist, The Client Who Changed Me, The Assassin and the Therapist*, and *Making Changes Last.* He has also authored several highly successful books for the public that describe rather complex phenomena in highly accessible prose (*Beyond Blame, Travel That Can Change Your Life, Divine Madness, Private Moments, Secret Selves, The Language of Tears*, and *The Last Victim: Inside the Minds of Serial Killers*).

Jeffrey has worked as a teacher, counselor, and therapist in preschools, middle schools, mental health centers, crisis centers, universities, community colleges, and private practice settings. He has served as a Fulbright Scholar and Senior Lecturer in Peru (1980) and Iceland (2000), and has worked as a Visiting Professor in New Zealand, Australia, Hong Kong, Singapore, and Nepal. Jeffrey is Professor of Counseling at California State University, Fullerton and President of Empower Nepali Girls (www.EmpowerNepaliGirls.org), which provides educational scholarships for at-risk children in Nepal.

Matt Englar-Carlson is Professor of Counseling and the Co-Director of the Center for Boys and Men at California State University, Fullerton. He is a fellow of the American Psychological Association (APA). As a scholar, teacher, and clinician, Matt has been an innovator and professionally passionate about training and teaching clinicians to work more effectively with their male clients. He has over 30 publications and 50 national and international presentations, most of which are focused on men and masculinity and diversity issues in psychological training and practice. Matt co-edited the books *In the Room With Men: A Casebook of Therapeutic Change* and *Counseling Troubled Boys: A Guidebook for Professionals*, and was featured in the 2010 APA-produced DVD *Engaging Men in Psychotherapy*. Further, he is the Series Editor (with Jon) of the APA's 24-volume *Theories of Psychotherapy* book series. In 2007 he was named the Researcher of the Year by the Society for the Psychological Study of Men and Masculinity. He is also a member of the APA Working Group to Develop Guidelines for Psychological Practice with Boys and Men. As a clinician, he has worked with children, adults, and families in schools, communities, and university mental health settings. He lives with his wife Alison and his two children, Jackson and Beatrix, in Huntington Beach, CA. In his spare time, he rides his bike with Jeffrey and others, and seeks the perfect cup of coffee and donut.

Jon Carlson is Distinguished Professor of Psychology and Counseling at Governors State University, University Park, Illinois and a psychologist with the Wellness Clinic in Lake Geneva, Wisconsin. In addition to serving as the longtime editor of *The Family Journal*, Jon is the author of 50 books in the areas of family therapy, marital enrichment, consultation, and Adlerian psychology. Some of his best-known works include: *Adlerian Therapy, Never Be Lonely Again, Inclusive Cultural Empathy,* and *Time for a Better Marriage.* Jon has also produced 250 video programs that feature the most prominent leaders in the field (including the professionals featured in this book) demonstrating their theories in action. These videos are used to train the next generation of practitioners.

Together, Jeffrey and Jon have collaborated on several other books, including *Bad Therapy, The Mummy at the Dining Room Table, The Client Who Changed Me, American Shaman, Their Finest Hour, Moved By The Spirit, Creative Breakthroughs in Therapy* and *Duped: Lies and Deception in Psychotherapy.*

ABOUT THE CONTRIBUTORS

Fred Bemak is a Professor in the Graduate School of Education and the Director of the Diversity Research and Action Center at George Mason University. He is also the Founder and Director of Counselors Without Borders. Fred has previously held administrative and faculty appointments at Johns Hopkins University and Ohio State University, as well as visiting faculty appointments at the Federal University of Rio Grande do Sul (Brazil), the University of Queensland (Australia), and National Taiwan Normal University. Prior to his university work, Fred directed federal- and state-funded programs serving youth and families and was Clinical Director of a National Institute of Mental Health-funded training consortium based at the University of Massachusetts Medical School. Fred has done extensive consultation, training, invited presentations, and supervision with mental health professionals and organizations throughout the United States and in over 50 countries. His work has focused on cross-cultural counseling, refugee and immigrant mental health, social justice, counseling at-risk youth, and post-disaster counseling, with extensive publications in these areas. Fred is a former Fulbright Scholar and Fulbright Specialist, World Rehabilitation Fund Fellow, Kellogg International Fellow, and American Psychological Association Visiting Psychologist.

Sharon Bethea, PhD, is an Assistant Professor in Counselor Education, Inner City Studies, and African/African American Studies at Northeastern Illinois University in Chicago. She earned a PhD in Educational Psychology from the University of Missouri at Columbia. Her research interests include the psychosocial and intellectual development of inner city youth, community youth programs, alternative therapeutic paradigms for the psychological well-being of African Americans throughout the diaspora, and counselor identity development. She is the Immediate Past President of the Association of Black Psychologists' Chicago Chapter. She has been a counseling professional for over 25 years and has held leadership positions in schools, community programs, and community organizations that serve primarily inner city communities. She is also a mom, family member, fictive relative, partner, community advocate, and mentor.

Stan Bosch, PsyD, has worked for more than 20 years with men (particularly men of color) and spiritual issues. He has ministered to Los Angeles's gang-involved youth for several years. Dr. Bosch's work with inner city youth was featured in the National Geographic documentary *Inside LA Gang Wars*. Dr. Bosch recently completed his doctoral studies in clinical psychology at the Chicago School of Professional Psychology. Along with his psychological work with Latino and African American youth, he also administers to them spiritually as a Roman Catholic priest.

Leah Brew, PhD, is the Department Chair and Associate Professor in the Department of Counseling at California State University-Fullerton. Her teaching and research interests include pedagogy in counselor education, and diversity awareness and sensitivity. She has published books, book chapters, and journal articles in the areas of basic counseling skills, teaching counseling and culture, and inter-cultural parenting. Highlights of her relevant professional service activities include: Student Representative on the Association for Counselor Education and Supervision Board, Secretary and Past President of Western Association of Counselor Education and Supervision, Board Member of the California Coalition for Counselor Licensure, Vice President and President of the California Association for Licensed Professional Clinical Counselors, and Subject Expert for the California Board of Behavioral Science.

Joseph M. Cervantes, PhD, ABPP, received his PhD in Community-Clinical Psychology from the University of Nebraska-Lincoln. He is a Professor in the Department of Counseling, School of Health and Human Development at California State University-Fullerton and maintains an independent forensic practice in child, adolescent, and family psychology. He holds Diplomates in both Clinical and Couple and Family Psychology from the American Board of Professional Psychology and is licensed in California and Hawaii. Dr. Cervantes' research interests are in the relatedness of cultural diversity and indigenous spirituality, and immigration issues, a subject on which he has conducted numerous immigration evaluations and appeared in court on multiple occasions as an expert witness. He has served as a Consulting Editor for the journal *Professional Psychology: Research and Practice*, and is currently a Consulting Editor for the journals *Cultural Diversity and Ethnic Minority Psychology* and *Family Psychology*. Dr. Cervantes has served as the Ethics Chair for the Orange County Psychological Association, and is past President of the National Latina/o Psychological Association and past Chair,

Committee on Ethnic Minority Affairs, APA. He has Fellow status with Division 45 and 12 of the APA.

Jamila Codrington, PhD, is a New York-licensed Psychologist specializing in children, adolescents, and families. She is a Clinical Supervisor and Therapist at Astor Services for Children and Families, a community-based outpatient mental health clinic in the Bronx. Dr. Codrington is the Immediate Past President of the New York Association of Black Psychologists and has served on the Board of Directors for several years. She was awarded the 2010–2011 distinguished Bobby E. Wright Award by the Association of Black Psychologists for her exemplary commitment to community service and empowerment. Through public forums, consultations, guest lectures, radio interviews, and partnerships with grassroots organizations, Dr. Codrington has provided numerous presentations on a wide array of mental health, education, and social justice issues affecting individuals and communities of African descent. She earned her PhD in Counseling Psychology at the University of Maryland at College Park and received specialized postdoctoral training in the evaluation and treatment of court-involved/incorrigible youth. Her clinical and research interests include the treatment of trauma in children and adolescents, coping and resilience, mental health issues among the juvenile justice population, racial identity development, culturally relevant and holistic therapeutic interventions, and African-centered healing practices. Dr. Codrington has published in professional journals including the *Journal of Multicultural Counseling and Development*, *Psych Discourse*, and *Dreaming*, and has presented at annual conventions for the Association of Black Psychologists, APA, Diversity Challenge Conference, Teachers College Winter Roundtable, and the American Counseling Association.

William J. Doherty, PhD, is Professor of Family Social Science and Director of the Citizen Professional Center at the University of Minnesota. He has led or coached more than a dozen public engagement projects since 1999. His work focuses on re-envisioning the role of professionals as catalytic leaders in working with communities.

Chante DeLoach, PsyD, is a Licensed Clinical Psychologist in private practice and an Associate Professor of Clinical Psychology at the Chicago School of Professional Psychology. She sees individuals, couples, and families and specializes in issues of race and trauma. A staunch advocate for using one's social capital, training, and privilege for the benefit of others, Dr. DeLoach has engaged in clinical and humanitarian work in numerous countries including Ethiopia, Zambia, Ecuador, Mexico, Brazil, and Haiti.

Keith Edwards, PhD, is Professor of Psychology at Rosemead School of Psychology, Biola University, where he teaches courses in couples therapy, individual therapy, and research methods. He held faculty positions at Rutgers University and Johns Hopkins University before joining the Rosemead faculty in 1973. Dr. Edwards is a Licensed Clinical Psychologist and a certified Emotion-Focused Couples Therapist (EFT) and has Level 2 training in EFT for individuals. His research interests include emotions, relationship functioning, and spirituality that integrates Christian theology, attachment theory, and interpersonal neurobiology. He is a Staff Associate of the Narramore Christian Foundation and has conducted seminars on marriage and missionary member care in Europe, Africa, Asia, and South America. He lives in Hacienda Heights, CA with his wife, Ginny, who is a retired elementary school teacher. The Edwards have been married since 1966 and have three married children and six grandchildren. His education includes a BEd in Mathematics from the University of Wisconsin-Whitewater, an MA and PhD in Quantitative and Research Methods from New Mexico State University (1969), and a PhD in Clinical and Social Psychology from the University of Southern California (1984).

Cyrus Marcellus Ellis, PhD, is an Associate Professor of Counselor Education at Governors State University. Dr. Ellis earned his Doctorate in Counselor Education from The Curry School of Education at The University of Virginia. Dr. Ellis is a 20-year veteran of the US Army, US Army Reserve, and the New Jersey National Guard. He is the recipient of the OHANA award from Counselors for Social Justice and is a past Chair of the Human Rights Committee for the American Counseling Association. Dr. Ellis is a board member of VetNet, a nonprofit organization serving veterans in the Chicago area.

Tipawadee Emavardhana, PhD, is currently the Director of the Thai Adlerian Parenting Network and a former Associate Professor in the Psychology program at Thammasat University. She holds a BA in Psychology with honors from Thammasat University, Thailand, M. Psych. in Clinical Psychology from Flinders University of South Australia, and a PhD in Counseling Psychology from the University of Missouri-Columbia. She currently works as a trainer and consultant in personal growth, transformation, and behavioral change using a combination of Buddhist and Adlerian psychologies.

Sari Gold, MD, was born in Finland. She received her BA in Psychology from CUNY-Hunter College, New York. She graduated from the Albert Einstein College of Medicine, New York, in 1998 and did her Psychiatry residency training at Long Island Jewish Medical Center, Zucker Hillside Hospital, followed by a Psychosomatic Fellowship, also at Long Island Jewish Medical Center, Glen Oaks, NY. Currently, she works for Brownsville Multi-Service Family Health Center in Brooklyn, NY and has a part-time private practice.

Heather A. Guay is an educator and therapist from Southern California. She is the President and Co-Founder of Namaste Nepal-Helping Himalayan Children.

She first visited Nepal in December 2007 to deliver educational scholarships to underprivileged girls and keep them from being sold into human trafficking. This experience initiated a deep desire and commitment to help and support children and educators in Nepal in a variety of ways. Heather enjoys reading, teaching, and sharing about her experiences in Nepal. She believes that each person has the power to change the world.

Ouyporn Khuankaew is the Founder and Director of International Women's Partnership for Peace and Justice as well as a freelance activist. She works with women's organizations, community peace groups, governmental and non-governmental organizations, and grassroots activists within Thailand and internationally in the South and Southeast Asia regions and the West on a variety of peace and justice projects.

Gerald Monk is a Professor in the Department of Counseling and School Psychology at San Diego State University and the Director of Community Engagement in a multi-ethnic, multi-lingual inner city suburb of San Diego. Gerald is a practicing Marriage and Family Therapist in California and a mediator and trainer in health care and organizational contexts. Gerald worked as a Psychologist and mediator in New Zealand for 15 years prior to moving to the United States in 2000. He has a strong interest in promoting constructionist theories in family and organizational systems work. His main professional commitment lies in the development and application of narrative mediation. Gerald has taught numerous workshops all over the world. He was a recipient of the Fred J. Hansen Grant for Peace Studies to conduct bi-communal workshops in the buffer zone in Nicosia, Cyprus and recently provided training with ethnic leaders in Myanmar. His expertise includes developing, articulating, and implementing culturally sensitive and socially just educational and mediation practices, and he has co-authored six books in this area, including *Narrative Therapy in Practice: The Archaeology of Hope* (1997), *Narrative Mediation: A New Approach to Conflict Resolution* (2000), *Narrative Counseling in the Schools* (2007), *New Horizons in Multicultural Counseling* (2008), and *Practicing Narrative Mediation: Loosening the Grip of Conflict* (2008).

Kathryn L. Norsworthy is an activist, Counseling Psychologist, and Professor of Graduate Studies in Counseling at Rollins College, Winter Park, Florida. She regularly travels to Thailand and other parts of South and Southeast Asia to collaborate with local partners on peace and justice projects. She also works in central Florida and at the state level to secure full civil rights for the gay, lesbian, bisexual, and transgender communities.

Loretta Pyles, PhD, is Associate Professor at the School of Social Welfare and faculty affiliate in the Department of Women's Studies at the University at Albany, State University of New York. Her scholarship is concerned with how individuals, organizations, and communities resist and respond to poverty, violence, and disasters in a policy context of neoliberal globalization and social welfare retrenchment. Her sensibility about transformative social change was formed during her time working in a women's collective at a community-based domestic violence program in Lawrence, Kansas. After Hurricane Katrina in 2005, Pyles conducted extensive community-based research in New Orleans, where she was a faculty member at Tulane University until 2008. She has been conducting participatory action research with rural peasant associations in Haiti since the 2010 earthquake there. She is currently conducting a comparative study funded by the National Science Foundation called: "Dynamics between Local and Foreign Actors: Influences on Capabilities in Post-Earthquake Rural Haiti and Hurricane Impacted Rural Gulf Coast." She is the author of *Progressive Community Organizing: A Critical Approach for a Globalizing World* (2009) and serves on the Editorial Board for *International Social Work*. She currently teaches yoga part time.

Rebecca Rodriguez majored in Intercultural Studies at Biola University and later went on to earn her elementary teaching credential. She taught for four years and has been a stay-at-home mom for the past 11 years. Rebecca and her husband, Osvaldo, served as cross-cultural workers with HCJB Global and Hospital Vozandes in Quito, Ecuador for nearly three years with their two sons, E.J. and Andrew. She is fluent in Spanish, has visited more than 15 countries, and has also lived in Germany, Mexico, and Costa Rica. Rebecca is a graduate student in Counseling at California State University-Fullerton.

Josselyn Sheer completed her undergraduate studies at The University of Maryland, College Park and is currently a graduate student in Social Work at Smith College. She explored her passion for service while taking a course on altruism and social justice onboard Semester at Sea, circling the globe and stopping in a half a dozen different countries to work in schools, orphanages, and health agencies. From an early age, Josselyn not only knew that helping others was her vocation in life, but that this was the career path for her to pursue. She is excited to continue this path of study with the hope of affecting other people's lives and one day running her own practice.

Henry Sibbing, JD, received a Bachelor's in Philosophy from the University of Southern California, a JD from the Southwestern School of Law in Los Angeles, and a Master's in Counselor Education from the University of Wisconsin-Whitewater. He was a practicing trial lawyer in Southeast Wisconsin for 35 years in the fields of Family Law and Criminal Defense. Since his retirement from the law, he serves clients as a Licensed Mental Health Counselor in both Wisconsin and Florida, dividing his time between states while continuing his part-time Municipal Court duties in Lake Geneva, Wisconsin. He and his wife Mary have six adult children and enjoy spending time with their six grandchildren.

Dallas Stout, PsyD, has worked in the nonprofit community in Southern California for over 20 years, including many years leading Orange County's largest adolescent residential drug rehab and high school. He has volunteered on the Board of Directors and Advisory Boards of a variety of local, countywide and statewide programs for troubled youth and related issues. His latest volunteer project is serving as President of the California Chapters of the Brady Campaign to Prevent Gun Violence and the California Brady Political Action Committee in Sacramento. He is on the faculty at California State University-Fullerton and the University of the Rockies. He uses his experience to assist a variety of nonprofit programs in Southern California through Doctors Consulting, which he founded with his wife Dr. Debra Stout in 2004. Because of his visible commitment to and involvement in the fields of troubled youth, violence, and gang prevention, and the prevention and treatment of substance abuse, Dallas is widely regarded as a respected leader in these causes.

Debbie Stout, PsyD, left a lucrative management career in the Southern California teen retail clothing industry to earn her Doctorate in Psychology and has since worked to establish herself as an advocate for youth in Southern California. Debbie spent many years working for the Orange County Department of Education's alcohol, tobacco, and other drug use and violence prevention programs. In that capacity, she coordinated a nationally acclaimed gang prevention and intervention program in conjunction with the Boys and Girls Club of Westminster. Debbie served as Co-Chair of the Violence Prevention Coalition of Orange County from 2002 to 2010. Debbie continues to serve on the Advisory Boards of La Calle News, Inc., a program aimed at keeping young women out of gangs, and the Orange County Safe From the Start Coalition, which works to reduce children's exposure to violence. Two years ago Debbie was invited to join the Orange County United Way's Basic Needs Community Impact Council, where she has a vote in determining how nearly 10 million dollars is spent each year in the county. She is a also faculty member at California State University-Fullerton.

Selma de Leon-Yznaga, PhD, is an Associate Professor in the Counseling and Guidance Master's program at the University of Texas at Brownsville. She has held numerous positions in state and national professional counseling organizations, and in 2007 founded the Texas Counselors for Social Justice, a division of the Texas Counseling Association. Her research interests include ethnic identity development, acculturation distress, racial discrimination, and issues surrounding Mexican immigration. Selma is an active community volunteer, providing pro bono counseling and community outreach services to those who need them the most.

Byron Waller, PhD, is an Associate Professor of Counseling at Governors State University. He earned his Associates degree from Moody Bible Institute, Bachelor's from Grace College, Master's in Counseling from Chicago State

University, and his Doctorate in Counseling Psychology from Loyola University Chicago. He has been teaching and counseling individuals, couples, groups, families, children, adolescents, and adults in a variety of settings for more than 18 years. He has worked with individuals and communities in the areas of racial and ethnic reconciliation, social justice, relationship and intimacy development, life adjustment and transition, multiculturalism, math and academic achievement, academic self-efficacy, career counseling, Christian counseling, and African American issues. He has supervised hundreds of counselors in the area and continues to provide clinical supervision for counselors seeking licensure.

Cirecie A. West-Olatunji, PhD, serves as associate professor/coordinator of the Counseling Program and director of the Center for Traumatic Stress Research at the University of Cincinnati and is president-elect of the American Counseling Association (ACA). Nationally, Dr. West-Olatunji has initiated several clinical research projects that focus on culture-centered community collaborations designed to address issues rooted in systemic oppression, such as transgenerational trauma and traumatic stress. Cirecie West-Olatunji has conducted commissioned research under the auspices of the: National Science Foundation, ACA, Kellogg Foundation, federal Witness Assistance Program, Spencer Foundation, the American Educational Research Association, and the African American Success Foundation. Her publications include two co-authored books, several book chapters, and numerous articles in peer-reviewed journals. In addition to national presentations, Dr. West-Oiatunji has delivered research papers in Brazil, Botswana, Canada, China, Ghana, Japan, Malaysia, Singapore, and South Africa. Additionally, she provided consultation in a PBS initiative to create a children's television show focusing on diversity through KCET-TV in Los Angeles, CA ("Puzzle Place"). Dr. West-Olatunji has also provided consultation to the Center for American Education in Singapore and to the Buraku Liberation Organization in Japan to enhance their early childhood and counseling initiatives. More recently, coordinated disaster mental health outreach projects in post-Katrina New Orleans, southern Africa, and Haiti.

PART I

Re-Visioning Clinical Practice

1

THE POWER OF TRANSCENDENT EMPATHY

Empowering Lower-Caste Girls in Nepal

Jeffrey A. Kottler

I had been working as a therapist on and off for almost 30 years when the trajectory of my life and work abruptly shifted. Through the years I've worked in a variety of settings, beginning with my first jobs in a crisis center and community college. After an internship in a psychiatric unit in a teaching hospital, I supervised therapists in a community mental health center and then in an outpatient psychiatric clinic. Although I have spent a fair bit of time training and supervising therapists in various countries around the world, most of my clinical work has been in private practice, with mostly affluent professionals.

It isn't that I haven't found my work as a therapist satisfying and fulfilling, but rather that I feel replaceable: many others could do my job with equal (or superior) effectiveness. There have been times when I would listen to my privileged clients complain about their troubles and I found it hard to remain compassionate. During other periods, those complaints began to sound like incessant whining, and the critical voice inside my head would scream: "You've got everything anyone would want in life, and still it is not enough for you!" It took me awhile to figure out I was speaking to myself as much as to my clients.

I stopped practicing therapy altogether for a period of time, concentrating instead on my teaching, research, and supervision. I had become burned out and found it difficult to listen to my clients anymore. They all began to sound the same. I found it more and more challenging to remain present with them. I became bored not only with them, but also with myself—I was tired of listening to my own stories.

Then I gradually selected new clients very carefully, choosing only to work with those who presented novel or interesting challenges. After all, I felt like a hypocrite teaching and writing about a profession that I was no longer actively practicing. With a very small practice, I once again found myself energized and intrigued with my work, yet something was still missing. I suppose this feeling might be inevitable and familiar to those of you who have been in the field for many years—it is hard to keep things fresh and exciting, the way it felt during the early stages. I have seen enough other therapists as clients to know that I was not alone. This is the context of what was going on in my life when everything changed for me.

What Would YOU Do?

It had always been one of my life's dreams to travel to Nepal and trek in the Himalayas. I am an avid hiker, climber, cyclist, and adventurer who has used travel as a way to stimulate me when my work felt stale and repetitive. There are courses I've taught over 100 times, and conversations I've had with students and clients that often felt predictable. The times I've been in therapy as a client, sought supervision, attended workshops, or read books couldn't affect me nearly as dramatically as some of my adventures abroad (Kottler, 1997; Kottler & Marriner, 2009). I've spent months working in Australia, New Zealand, Iceland, Peru, and on Semester at Sea, and have always returned a profoundly different person than the one who departed. Yet none of these experiences prepared me for what occurred during my first visit to South Asia.

One of my Doctoral students, Kiran, was an obstetrician in Nepal who was researching childbirth experiences in remote regions. She wanted to learn qualitative research methodology to investigate why her country's maternal mortality rate is among the highest in the world. Kiran invited me to follow her on her rounds to isolated villages in order to teach her qualitative interviewing and grounded-theory analysis. What a perfect excuse for me to do some trekking!

It was during our visit to a remote village along the Indian border that I first learned about girls who were disappearing. While Kiran was examining her patients as the only doctor who ever visited that district a few times each year, I spent time in the school working with the children and teachers. I kept hearing rumors about certain girls who were "disappeared," but couldn't quite get a handle on what that meant.

"I don't understand what this means," I finally pressed the school principal, although he seemed to pretend he hadn't heard me.

When I asked again, the principal stared at me for a minute, as if deciding how he would respond. Finally, he shook his head and pointed to a girl of about 12 years old who was talking with some friends. "Do you see that girl? She will be disappeared next."

What a strange thing to say, as if she were a performer on stage with a magician who would wave a magic wand and she would vanish. What I learned instead is that "disappeared" meant that this girl would likely not be around much longer because her family was too poor to keep her in school.

"But where will she go?" I pressed. "What will happen to her?"

The principal shrugged, and that's all I got out of him. But it was enough to pique my curiosity. Eventually I learned that all families have to pay to attend public school, and when they have multiple children and limited resources, they often allow the boys to attend school and keep the girls at home. Since they can't afford to feed them all, the girls end up being married off as early as age 12; the unfortunate ones end up being sold and smuggled across the border, where they end up as sex slaves in brothels.

Upon further investigation, I learned that each year 12,000 Nepali girls end up stolen, kidnapped, or sold into slavery—some as young as eight years old. I don't know about you, but this is just about the most horrifying thing I'd ever heard.

So imagine yourself standing on the school grounds, staring at a vibrant young girl with tremendous academic potential, but who lives in such poverty that she has no future other than as a child sex slave. In addition, some Indian men who frequent the brothels of Mumbai are HIV positive and believe that having sex with a virgin will cure their disease. That is why young virgins are in such demand, especially innocent Nepali girls who have no rights or recourse. What would *you* do if you encountered this situation?

"So," I asked the principal, "how much would it cost to keep this girl in school for a year?"

"Oh, sir, it is very, very expensive." As he said this, he rubbed his fingers together.

"Yeah? Well, how much are we talking about exactly?"

"It would cost many rupees. She needs to pay her school feels. She needs books and supplies. And of course her uniforms—she needs one for Winter and one for Spring. Then there are other ..."

"Okay," I interrupted, "how much are we talking about?"

The principal did the mental calculations in his head. "I'd say about 3,000 rupees."

"3,000 rupees? That's like $50. Are you saying that for $50 Inu could stay in school and wouldn't be disappeared?"

The principal shrugged and wiggled his head in the characteristic Nepali way of signaling ascent.

I don't know about you, but the thought that for $50 I could save a girl's life was irresistible. Without considering the consequences of my action, I reached in my pocket and pulled out some money and put it in the principal's hand. "This is for her. She stays in school. And I'm coming back next year to make sure that she's okay."

I walked away from that encounter as if walking on a cloud. I had this huge grin on my face. It felt like that was the single most meaningful and important thing I'd ever done in my life. I'd spent the previous decades doing all kinds of things to be helpful to others: volunteering my time to causes, working pro bono for clients who couldn't afford my services, and working for universities in which the vast majority of my students were minority and first-generation immigrants. Yet it always seemed to me that if I weren't there, somebody else would be—who could do the job as well as I could. But this was a case in which if I didn't intervene, then nobody else would. I felt as if my whole life had been redeemed in that moment, that if I did nothing else, this single effort was my most important legacy. Forget the books I'd written and the other lives I'd touched—*this* was what mattered most.

My student, Kiran, watched this whole episode and saw the tears in my eyes. "Well, Jeffrey," she said gently, "that was a good thing you did."

"Yes, it was, wasn't it?"

I was feeling so damn proud of myself. I couldn't believe that for $50, for the cost of a good meal, I'd just saved a girl's life. Even more meaningful, this was a girl I'd actually met; I could see with my own eyes what a difference it would make in her life.

"So," Kiran continued, "what will you do now?"

"What do you mean?" I answered, a bit surprised. Wasn't this enough? I mean, give me a break—I just saved this girl.

"That is a very good thing you did, Jeffrey. What I wonder is what will you do now? There are thousands of other girls like her. What will you do about *them*?"

I had no idea when I reached in my pocket and pulled out a bit of money how this would change my life, my commitments, my priorities, my very life path. I went home soon after that and resumed my usual duties—teaching students, seeing a few clients, writing more books about therapy—but I frequently found myself thinking about the girl and wondering how she was doing. Since she lived

PHOTO 1.1 Jeffrey Kottler spending time with some of the scholarship girls in the Everest region. Empower Nepali Girls provides scholarship for at-risk girls who would otherwise not be allowed to attend school.

in a place without electricity, without even an address that could receive mail, the only way I could check on her was to return to her village. I immediately made plans to do so, as well as to plan with Kiran ways we might identify other academically gifted girls who were at greatest risk of being sold.

Kiran's research study was groundbreaking; it revolutionized obstetric care in Southern Nepal (Regmi & Kottler, 2009). She discovered from her interviews that the main reason why so many women were dying in childbirth was not only because 90% of the country had no access to health care whatsoever, but also because even when it was available, women refused to avail themselves of the services. One reason was because lower-caste women were treated like animals by the male doctors, who humiliated them, touched their private parts, and put "snakes in their arms." The latter refers to inserting intravenous tubes without explaining what they were for—or for that matter, without talking to the patients at all. The few women who did go to the hospital for complicated pregnancies returned to their villages and warned their neighbors never to go to that place where they were treated so poorly.

As disturbing as these stories were, nothing prepared us to learn that the other reason pregnant women did not seek help was because their mothers-in-law would not permit it. Their husbands' mothers believed that if their daughters-in-law were having a difficult labor, it was because they did something to anger the gods, and that it would be better for them to die so that their sons could find stronger wives. Even Kiran was shocked by this finding; it led her to train other doctors to involve mothers-in-law as part of the medical team so they would become allies rather than adversaries.

Kiran and I decided to pool our own funds to support more girls in school. For a few hundred dollars each year, we could provide scholarships for a handful of other girls. I began thinking about all the ways that I fritter away money on superfluous indulgences: $50 for a good meal—that's the cost of a girl's life; $150 for a pair of shoes I don't really need—that's three girls who could be saved; $500 for a new chair—that's 10 girls! These were the calculations I began doing in my head every time I spent money. Now, don't get me wrong—I really enjoy spending money on gadgets, clothes, trips, and other things. It wasn't so much guilt that was motivating me as a newfound understanding of ways I could spend my own money and time.

The next year, I returned to Nepal to check on the girl and distribute scholarships to three other girls in her village. The year after that we expanded to another village, then another, then another, each in a different district. Before we knew it, we were supporting dozens of lower-caste girls, all of whom had great potential but few resources. Kiran and I had this audacious vision that we might grow the next generation of women doctors who could save other women at risk.

I've heard the term "grassroots," but was never sure what it actually meant in practice. So far, we had funded our project solely from our own pockets, so we had no paperwork to keep track of and no bureaucracy. We knew each of our girls personally and could monitor their progress carefully, and make sure that all funds were spent solely to support them. In a region where corruption was so rampant we wanted to be as careful as possible with how our money was spent. In addition, I was skeptical about the ways in which big charities and organizations operated. I had read that in many of these operations less than 20% of the donated money actually gets to those who are supposed to be helped. I'd seen representatives from the well-known charities staying in 5-star hotels and driving around in Range Rovers, receiving six-figure salaries. Because we had so little money in our budget, I wanted to make sure we could stretch the funds as far as possible.

Friends, colleagues, family members, and students learned about what I was doing and asked if they could help. Sure, why not? I began to collect donations that made it possible to double, then triple the number of girls we were helping—20 the next year, then 60, and now well over 150 children in nine villages around the country.

It became necessary to register as a charitable organization in the United States, as well as in Nepal. But I was still determined that we would remain solely volunteers. We would have minimal overhead, no office, no paid staff, so that almost all of the donations would go directly to support the girls.

About this time, someone who had been thinking about making a donation said, "How do I know what happens to this money? I've never heard of you. How do I know that the money goes where you said it will?"

I suppose there is a theme of impulsivity that runs throughout my story, because my immediate response was, "Why don't you come with us on the next trip and see for yourself? Why don't you meet the girls and their families yourself and see what is happening? That way, you can act as a witness for anyone else who wonders about what is really going on." That's how the next stage of this project evolved into a kind of reciprocal exchange process, in which our volunteers have been affected almost as much as our girls.

As a psychologist, I've long been frustrated by how long it sometimes takes therapy to work, and how the effects are often short lived. I've long had fantasies of being a travel agent, planning the kinds of trips for people that would transform them dramatically in a relatively short period of time—with enduring effects. As I mentioned earlier, such travel experiences have been the most powerful change experiences in my own life. I once made a study of people who had changed their lives while on particular kinds of trips, and catalogued the factors that were most associated with such effects, especially those that were most enduring.

I found some interesting results that helped shape the way I planned to take volunteers with me to Nepal. First of all, adversity seemed to have the greatest impact on people. When travelers become lost, when they find themselves in novel environments in which they must meet their needs in new ways, when they must develop new resources to face challenges, or when their most cherished assumptions are challenged—that's when the real action takes place. The lessons are most enduring when there is high emotional involvement.

Keeping these principles in mind, I wanted to design experiences for our volunteers that not only maximized their commitment to our cause but also exposed them to the kinds of things that have been so influential in my life. It is just amazing to spend time with people who, even though they have so little (most don't even have shoes and eat one meal a day), are so spectacularly happy. I don't mean to over-idealize their plight, but so many Nepalese people we meet along the way greet us with "Namaste" and the most glorious smiles you can imagine. They have nothing but the clothes on their backs, but their Buddhist/Hindu beliefs guide them to appreciate whatever small gifts that life might offer them. It is both exhilarating and disturbing to encounter people who have so little and yet appear so content, especially for those of us who have so much and always hunger for more. Team members often return from our visits completely disoriented about what they have discovered, and determined to put into practice what they have learned from our children.

I have long been a fan of the idea that our clients are our best teachers, and so it has been with our scholarship children and their families: they help us as much as we help them.

It has now been 13 years since we began our project. Our very first girl is the first in her village to pursue higher education. She received a full scholarship to attend an elite university and has been followed by dozens of others.

It just amazes me what is possible with (relatively) so little money and effort. Yet if I've made this enterprise sound like an easy, fun adventure, I've left a lot out. What began as a lark, an impulsive gesture, has now taken over my life.

I already have several other jobs, so I don't exactly have the time and energy for another. It's easy to *launch* a service project: it really is as simple as finding somewhere to make a difference and then following through. It only cost me 50 bucks to get started. But, alas, the *follow through* is the killer. All these lives now hang in the balance of my being able to continue raising money and recruiting volunteers. There are so many other girls who need help, and I feel so frustrated sometimes that I can't do nearly as much as I want.

I face many other problems that are so overwhelming and dispiriting. After having taken over 100 team members with me over the years, less than a handful have stuck with the project after they return (see Heather Guay's Chapter 22 as a notable exception). Most carry on with their lives, perhaps haunted by what they've seen but not enough to keep them involved. Meanwhile, all those girls who once cost $50 per year to support in school now cost $125; those entering university or medical school cost several thousand dollars each per year. Where will I find the money to support so many children? How can I recruit more help as we continue to expand?

Then there are the logistical and physical problems that I must frequently contend with. It takes three planes, a bus trip, and several days' walk in the Himalayas to get to some of our villages. Last year it took me seven weeks just to visit all our girls, who are spread across the country; in some cases, it took me a week to get to one of the villages and return.

The cultural misunderstandings and political shenanigans I experience are exhausting. After all, we are attempting to change the culture of the country so that girls become more valued and are afforded opportunities that are ordinarily closed to them. I have to rely on my Nepalese partners to implement our strategies, but often a lot is lost in translation. We are constantly battling an entrenched system in which the village elders, all men, resent the fact that we are assisting lower-caste "untouchable" girls. Why aren't we helping the Brahman boys, the highest caste? Many of them need help too.

In my more calm moments, I find all of this so interesting. It is actually fun to figure out ways to address the challenges we face in bridging the differences in our cultural values. All these years I have been teaching diversity and multi-cultural issues, and now I get to put some of these principles into action. When elders in one village started working to sabotage our efforts, we pacified them by agreeing to donate school equipment and supplies for all the children in the school. Although our organization's charter specifies that we only spend money on scholarships for girls, we now consider it part of our overhead to donate used computers, books, sports equipment, and teaching resources to the schools. This approach has reduced that particular problem for now, but there are so many others that I can't yet begin to understand.

The Girl in the Turquoise Scarf

I can barely catch my breath. For the past half hour, we have been snaking our way up a narrow trail leading to a *stupa*, a Buddhist shrine, perched high over a Himalayan village. I turn and look downward, noticing with relief that I'm not the only one who stopped to rest: there are 55 girls strung out behind and ahead of me, the youngest 10 years old and the eldest in her late teens. They have all been transported here from their villages across Nepal, each of them supported by a scholarship to keep them in school.

We have spent the previous week conducting home visits, consulting with parents and teachers, awarding new scholarships, and providing supplies and resources for the children. We have been mentoring them and helping them to support one another, given the challenges they face with poverty, catastrophic illness in their families, and often an abandoned parent. For many of the girls, this is the first time they've left their village; some traveled for three days to arrive at our location. The girls from the plains or jungle have been mostly terrified by the strange environment of the mountains. They are climbing the steep incline in flip-flops or plastic shoes. Despite our efforts to help girls from the various groups interact with one another, they are mostly staying close to their friends.

As I try to breathe deeply and gather my energy for the climb to the summit, I think about the morning's activities. We had arranged the girls into small groups, each from a different village. They had been asked to share something in their lives about which they felt pride, as well as share a difficult struggle they were facing. Since most of the girls are from the "untouchable" caste, it was not surprising that many shared economic hardships. Most of them lived in small huts in which their families slept together on the floor. I also knew about the challenges they faced as girls in a country in which women have few opportunities for advancement, especially in such remote areas. But I was surprised by how many of the girls had lost parents, some from disease, many from abandonment, and one father was eaten by a tiger! Others had fathers who were alcoholics or incapacitated. As they were telling their stories, the girls were trying to hold back tears. Me too. I was just so amazed by their courage and resilience.

I continue up the steep trail and notice a girl sitting on a rock, shivering. She is quite striking, although very quiet; in the time I've known her we have barely spoken. I recognize her as one of the girls from a jungle village. I ask her name, *"Timro nam ke ho?"* but she only gives me a shy smile and looks away.

I sit next to her on a rock and offer her my jacket to cover her shoulders, but she shakes her head. She is obviously embarrassed by the attention. I notice that another dozen girls further along the path are watching us carefully. Like I feel so often in these situations in a strange land, I wonder if what I am doing is culturally appropriate. "Please," I insist, "you must wear this jacket." I cover her and she meets my eyes for the first time. I then notice how carefully, almost compulsively, she keeps rearranging her turquoise scarf to cover the right side of her face, almost as if she were hiding something.

Once we both gather our strength, we continue walking up to the top of the hill and I lose track of her for awhile. The girls are running around, screaming and yelling, fascinated most of all by the pine needles hanging from the trees.

PHOTO 1.2   One-third of the lower-caste girls supported by scholarships, mentoring, and guidance

The Himalayan peaks were stretched across the horizon, but the tree branches commanded the most attention; the girls placed them on their heads as makeshift hats.

While descending to the bottom, I notice that the girl with the turquoise scarf is still holding the garment across her face. Finally my curiosity gets the best of me, and I ask her if she would mind removing the scarf so I could see her face. I can tell immediately that she is mortified by my request, and the other girls start to gather around us. I feel like I have no choice but to proceed with the request. "Please, " I insist, "could I see your face? "

Slowly, reluctantly, the girl allows the scarf to unravel. I am horrified to see that her cheek is completely swollen and filled with pus of all kinds of nasty colors. My first reaction is that someone had struck her, but she explains to me that it is a skin infection that had been getting worse over time. It is clear to me that without intervention, this girl would not only become permanently disfigured, but might very well die.

I call over her teacher, as well as other adults who had been helping to chaperone the children. "Look at her face," I call out to them. "We have to do something!" They look concerned, but just shrug. What could be done? In a country in which 90% of the population has no access to regular health care, most injuries and diseases had to run their course—or heal on their own.

I insist that the girl receive medical care, that she be taken to doctor, a dermatologist, who could lance the wound and provide antibiotics to kill the infection. But they tell me it is much too expensive, especially to consult with a specialist. Then there are the transportation costs and the money for the drugs. Another shrug.

"What would all that cost?" I ask. "I will pay for it. We must get her some help."

I am told this would cost as much as 10,000 rupees, which may sound like a lot until you do the calculations: this is about $14. For less than the price of a single meal back home, I could save this girl's face, if not her life!

"You are a god," the girl whispers to me with awe.

I don't know what to say to that, other than to shake my head.

"You are *my* god," she repeats. I could tell she meant it. This was no idle compliment.

I walk away. I flee. I don't want her to see me crying. Once alone, I just completely lose control, sobbing in a hoarse voice I barely recognize as my own. I was scaring myself with the raw power of my emotions. I've done a lot of good things in my life. I've helped a lot of people as a therapist or teacher or supervisor. I look for opportunities every chance I get to help little old ladies cross the street, help lost tourists find their destinations, or help anyone else I meet find what they're looking for. But of everything I've ever done, nothing seemed to come close to what I could do to help a young girl just by noticing that she kept covering her face.

So, what's the moral of this story, the theme that I'm exploring way beyond a single gesture of altruism? This isn't just about throwing money at causes, or simply making financial donations. I'm cynical enough to know that because of the corruption in the developing world, and the high cost of overhead and operating expenses, only a small fraction of charitable gifts ever reaches those they were designed to assist. The money our organization provides to support the education of at-risk girls in Nepal is absolutely crucial to their survival and welfare, but the relationships we develop with each of the girls and their families are just as important. Most of our scholarship recipients never dreamed it was possible for them to become anything other than wives of farmers, that is, until they met professional women from around the world who showed them what was possible. That's the thing about "transcendent empathy:" the influence flows in both directions. Most of our volunteers and team members never dreamed it was possible to be so happy and content with life while having so little. We come home from our visits to Nepal determined to devote ourselves to things that matter so much more than mere ambition and achievement—friendships, family, creative pursuits, and yes, service to others.

Although I still do therapy on a small scale, and continue my work as a professor, supervisor, and researcher, I must say that I now think of my main job as advocating for girls in Nepal. I still find the visits there to be exhilarating, but also exhausting and overwhelming. I make time to go trekking each trip; I'm still in love with the mountains. And I must say that one of my favorite things in life is to bring friends and colleagues with me to meet the wonderful children and experience the Himalayas up close and personal.

It has been fascinating to use my skills as a therapist to make a difference on a larger (or at least a different) scale. I am aware, for instance, that throwing money at causes is not nearly enough without adequate and ongoing support, outcome evaluation, and personal contact. The mentoring the girls receive from our volunteers during our visits is at least as important as the scholarships. Most of the girls have never before met women who work as professionals; most of them never dreamed that they could ever do anything other than be a wife and mother.

Based on what we know and understand about systemic change, our teams visit the homes of every one of our girls to honor them in front of their families and neighbors. We've been concerned that once we leave, our financial support alone wouldn't be enough to sustain the children in an environment that is somewhat less than encouraging. But with our public ceremonies, the families would lose too much face if they married or sold their daughters; even though they are at the bottom of the caste system, being selected as scholars with great potential gives them a certain status. Many of the places we visit have never had visitors from abroad before, and our donors and volunteers come from all over the United States, Canada, Australia, New Zealand, Spain, and Hong Kong, among other countries.

All of this began with just one girl who needed help. It is truly amazing what you can do once you get out of your office and into your own community—or to other parts of the world. There is an ancient Jewish expression that by saving one life, you save the world. I truly believe that's also how we save ourselves.

For further information: www.EmpowerNepaliGirls.org

References

Kottler, J.A. (1997). *Travel That Can Change Your Life*. San Francisco: Jossey-Bass.

Kottler, J.A. & Marriner, M. (2009). *Changing People's Lives While Transforming Your Own: Paths to Social Justice and Global Human Rights*. New York: Wiley.

Regmi, K. & Kottler, J. (2009). An epidemiologist learns grounded theory. In V. Minichiello & J. Kottler (eds.), *Qualitative Journeys: Student and Mentor Experiences with Research*. Thousand Oaks, CA: Sage.

2

THE CITIZEN-THERAPIST AND SOCIAL CHANGE[1]

William J. Doherty

As I think back to the US presidential contests of my adulthood, it's clear that I've placed too much importance on who gets elected. With many of my therapist friends, I've been on a bipolar ride between idealization and cynicism, sometimes reversing affectively within a given administration, and always hoping that the next election cycle will bring the great new leader. But as with any idealization, it's a setup: these leaders will always disappoint because we expect them to do work that only we can do for ourselves. Too much is at stake these days for us to take refuge in our practices when things don't go well in our communities and nation. It's time to create a new professional role for ourselves: the citizen-therapist for the 21st century—an agent of change, not just a critic of what isn't changing. Unfortunately, our training has done little to prepare us for this role.

Like most therapists, I went into this profession not just to help my own clients, but to make the world a better place. When I trained in the 1970s, I thought therapy was the number one untapped source of social improvement. I believed in a kind of "trickle up" psychological dynamic, whereby therapy would make enough people healthier to tilt the social order toward justice and harmony. Yes, I actually believed this when we sang "All You Need Is Love" under the moonlight in Bethel, Maine, during summer encounter groups. I even entertained the idea that national transformation would begin when everyone in Congress and the White House got into therapy—or at least a good personal-growth group.

In my own journey since then, I've moved from unrealistic hope to unnecessary despair—and in the last decade or so, to learning a way to work as a local citizen-therapist, no matter who's running the government in Washington or in my state. I believe that the challenge for us who profess the possibilities of change is to re-imagine ourselves as citizen-therapists while keeping our day jobs, and not to abandon our families for long junkets to distressed regions of the world.

When considering the role models I know who do this type of work, I think of my friend and colleague Bill Allen, who, after seeing too many African American children placed outside their families, began building relationships with Minnesota state officials so as to influence policy about foster-home placements. He has credibility with these policymakers—and with others in the community who care about children—not because he majored in public policy, but because, as a family therapist, he knows firsthand what happens to these children, and he knows that many families can stay together with the right kind of professional and community support.

I think of psychologist and family therapist Jack Saul, who works in the aftermath of war, torture, and political violence in his backyard of New York City. What makes him part of the new breed of citizen-therapists is how he uses public testimony, media, and performance arts to engage community members as healers.

When it comes to bridging social divisions, I think of Boston family therapist Laura Chasin and her colleagues at the Public Conversations Project. After being disgusted by a televised shouting match on abortion, Laura decided to bring the principles of respectful dialogue to the public sphere, beginning with a discussion about abortion and moving on to many other polarizing issues of our time.

These citizen-therapists use their relational and systems skills in broader environments. But unlike previous generations that tended to see their mission as bringing powerful professional know-how to under-resourced communities, today's citizen-therapists believe deeply in the capacities of communities to change and heal themselves. Such therapists are catalysts more than direct-change agents—facilitators more than teachers. They differ from an earlier generation of preventive mental health professionals, who disdained therapy as a Band-Aid. Today's citizen-therapists practice the healing art of therapy in their offices, but they don't believe that we're going to treat our way out of the social problems affecting our communities and nation: they know we must be actors on a bigger stage than that offered by our practices or clinics, and that our clinical knowledge and skills carry over to community work, even if we aren't the most important actors on that stage.

There's one other difference. The new breed of citizen-therapists operates with a 21st-century consciousness of nuance and collaboration, instead of the 1960s consciousness, which saw the world starkly in terms of oppressors and victims, with classes of people assigned to each category. In a more complicated century, the '60s perspective offers two dead-end paths to community solutions: the "confessional approach," in which oppressors admit their privilege and guilt (which they aren't inclined to do outside of diversity workshops and graduate school courses), and the "advocacy approach," in which professional elites lobby political elites on behalf of non-elites. But now, as we invite everyone to the work of public problem solving without ideological litmus tests, may the '60s—a decade of activism that accomplished major social changes and started a needed cultural revolution in our field—rest in peace.

I consider myself a member of the small, but growing, community of committed citizen-therapists, and I've begun training others. Perhaps the following pointers from my experience will help you on your own journey.

Discover Your Passion and Connect it to the Larger Picture

The reason we therapists are so well situated to be change agents is that we hear real stories of personal pain in a troubled world. We don't get our material secondhand from newspapers and academic research articles. So the first step to getting involved is to ask yourself which clinical issues in your practice grab your interest most, and then start seeing the personal problems you treat within their larger social context—what C. Wright Mills called the public dimensions of personal discontents.

For example, the problem of "overindulgent parenting" can be viewed strictly as a matter of personal habits and parenting skills, or as part of a larger social issue—in this case, a generation of educated but anxious parents who are worried about their children's success in a competitive world. Depression in an immigrant African community is more than a clinical problem: it's connected to the perennial challenges of immigration and the enduring impact of war and trauma—events that the community can't speak about. Eating disorders and self-image problems among young women go beyond DSM diagnostic categories into the social fabric of modern commercial societies.

As you think about the issues raised in your practice, here's an axiom to remember: all clinical problems treated by therapists are thoroughly interconnected with larger public issues—all of them. But the public dimensions of psychological problems, and the civic action that could be appropriate to take, don't appear in our treatment manuals.

My own first foray into community activism emerged from my concern that we're turning middle-class childhood into a rat race of over-scheduling and over-achievement, and that parents have come to see themselves as service providers to their children. I saw this disturbing development in my practice and everywhere in my local community. The desire to get involved came when I began to see this problem as not just a particular family's issue, but as organically connected to larger social forces (the invasion of competitive, market-driven individualism) and community institutions (the sports leagues and ballet schools that have increasingly taken over children's lives). Once we look outside our windows, it's easy to see how the problems we treat in our offices are integrally connected to broader community issues.

Connect with Fellow Therapists

Once you've identified an issue you care deeply about and have connected it with the public sphere, you're ready to join a community. The first community I recommend is at least one fellow therapist with whom you can share your journey. Start conversations on what each of you feels passionate about, and see whether you get charged up about the same issues.

For me, this process began with a series of conversations with my colleague Patrick Dougherty. Over numerous lunches at a local café, we brooded, brainstormed, and hatched ideas about how to engage with the world outside our offices. Patrick then introduced me to two political scholars and community organizers: Harry Boyte and Nan Kari, who became my mentors. Eventually, I pulled together several colleagues and students into an ongoing group for mutual support and mentoring. Like most therapists, I'm not a good Lone Ranger: I do community work only with buddies behind or alongside me.

Connect with a Community

The next step is pivotal: finding a community to work with outside your professional world. This isn't as hard as it sounds. Ask yourself what communities you're already connected to. It might be the neighborhood you work in, the schools your kids attend and where you've given talks to PTA groups, or your faith community.

For me, finding a community was initially difficult because of my assumption, common among therapists, that community work is needed only in low-income neighborhoods. As I saw it, my problem was that most of my contacts were in middle-class communities, so it was mostly suburban and well-off urban folks who invited me to speak on my favorite topic—overscheduled kids and reclaiming family time. People in struggling urban neighborhoods didn't seem to have overscheduled kids. Feeling stymied, I felt tempted to revert to save-the-world strategy number one: stay in your office and support the best candidates and causes, venturing forth every four years to get out the vote.

I finally realized that the suburbs have plenty of troubles of their own. My work could start with whichever community cared about the issue I cared about and was open to working with me. (It's a little like how you operate when you're a new therapist: you don't so much choose your clients as feel grateful that they'll see you.) An opportunity emerged soon afterward. I was invited to give a talk to a group of parents in Wayzata, Minnesota, a middle-class suburb of Minneapolis-St. Paul, on reclaiming family time. Following my talk, many parents spoke up about feeling out of control regarding their kids' schedules and feeling they were unable to restore a semblance of family life. Afterward, a middle-school principal confided in me, "We school leaders are part of this problem: we offer so many activities to kids that if parents agree to even half of them, they're not going to have much family life left." This brief exchange both startled and energized me. It drove home the reality that overscheduling wasn't just an individual family issue. In a hypercompetitive world, in which parenting has become a form of product development, family time is a public issue.

PHOTO 2.1 At a party store for kids, where I was scouting out the aisle displaying expensive birthday party gear for kids as young as one year. One of my citizen-parent projects was addressing out-of-control kids' birthday parties

Listen for Public Stories

With my newfound insight into the public dimensions of this problem, I moved to the next essential task of the citizen-therapist: talking with people in the community about the issue. Whenever I expressed curiosity about hockey schedules and missed family dinners and traveling leagues and cutthroat competitive dance, I was flooded with stories from exhausted, discouraged parents. When I asked my clients about their daily schedules (a topic I'd previously avoided as "too superficial"), they told me at length about their harried lives.

I learned to start conversations with parents in my community by passing on stories from previous conversations, which elicited vigorous nods and even more outrageous stories to pass on—like the four year olds who practiced hockey at 5:00 am on nursery school days (true story). Whenever I got myself invited to speak to PTA groups and church forums, I asked for more stories and invited attendees to reflect together on what's happened in our culture to bring this craziness upon us. Virtually every parent I talked to was eager to engage with this as a public issue.

Link the Personal to the Communal—in Public

It's relatively easy to get people talking about problems that bedevil their own families; it's a bigger challenge to help them connect their own stories to that of the community and to the work that lies ahead. At a town meeting in Wayzata for the launching of the Putting Family First project, I decided to address this challenge head-on. I put four questions to the 80-some parents, school board members, and community officials present: "Is this problem we're talking about here—overscheduled kids and underconnected families—only an individual family problem? Or is it also a community problem? Are the solutions only individual family solutions? Or are they also community solutions? Do you think this community is ready to take action? What actions should we take?"

The group was charged up, shouting out answers to the first three questions: "Yes, it's a community problem! Yes, the solutions must come at the community level as well as the family level! Yes, we're ready to take action!" The noise level grew intense as people discussed the final question in small groups. When they all reassembled, hands flew in the air as people vied to speak. Parents said they were fed up with the rat race, and they were thrilled that we were going to do something about it. One mother stood up and said: "I could use something like a Good Housekeeping Seal of Approval for organizations I'm signing my kids up with—something that would show me that this organization will work with me in my efforts to have a balanced family life."

The Putting Family First leadership group came into being that night. A dozen parents, representing a wide swath of the community, went on to develop a Putting Family First Seal of Approval for local organizations that offer activities for kids, and a Consumer's Guide to Kids' Activities, a handbook that rates all the community and school sports programs on the family friendliness of their schedules. The key to launching this initiative was the public event that captured the energy of the community and got them working together creatively.

Use Your Clinical Skills

During the night of the public launch event for Putting Family First, I learned how to combine my skills as a therapist with my new citizen-professional role in a public forum. When the discussion veered toward bashing coaches and community leaders, I interrupted with the speed of a family therapist witnessing a session heading south. "I don't think anybody is setting out to hurt kids," I said, "and I know that there are a lot of competitive pressures on coaches and parents alike. In my view, we're all part of this problem, and we can all be part of the solution." This made sense to most parents and became a mantra for the Putting Family First initiative: no villains.

Another key moment for a quick intervention came when two parents uttered a couple of classic energy deflators for a public meeting. A woman sitting in the front declared self-righteously, "This is all well and good, but we're preaching to the choir. It's the parents who *aren't* here who are the problem." Then somebody added, "There should have been three times as many people here tonight." As I watched heads nodding, my heart sank momentarily.

As a family therapist, I'm used to working with families when somebody in the room gets anxious and tries to pull the plug on a moment of courage or connection. I responded, "I think it was Margaret Mead who said that it only takes a small group of committed people to change the world, and indeed that it's never been changed in any other way." After letting this sink in, I piggybacked on the language of the first speaker. "Every social movement begins with a choir," I said. "And we have a lot of people already in this choir." I saw people sit up straighter in their chairs, and I could feel the energy flowing back into the room. Then I brought it home: "If only 12 people with the passion and energy I see in this room had shown up here, I'd have been happy."

Later, I began teaching citizen-professionals and parent-leaders how to anticipate deflating lines in public gatherings and how to counteract them. Part of my job as a citizen-therapist is to work with my colleagues, Tai Mendenhall and Jerica Berge, to help other citizens learn public skills.

Invite Recipients of Services to Become Citizen-Activists

I got involved with the FATHER Project in Minneapolis when its staff leaders heard about my community work. It's a program that helps low-income, mostly minority, single fathers reconnect with their children, land jobs, and get right with child support. Like most human services agencies, the FATHER Project had no role for successful "graduates," the people who were doing well now and no longer needed services.

The executive director, Andrew Freeberg, asked me to coach him and his colleague Guy Bowling in how to involve the successful men as citizens with a larger mission. I met several times with them to develop criteria for which men we'd invite to deliberate with us about whether this was an attractive and feasible project. This small group then generated a larger list, and we began to meet as the Citizen Father Project.

These men, mostly low-income and African American, are the kind of people that Reagan-era conservatives scapegoated as the purveyors of social breakdown and that '60s liberals viewed as victims of forces beyond their control. But these men see themselves as neither scapegoats nor victims. They know they once weren't good fathers, but now they're committed to their children and invested in improving their community through a mission "to support, educate, and develop healthy, active fathers and to rebuild family and community values." I've documented the group's work and the powerful ideas and language that come up in our conversations: "We have no 'father backbone' from our own fathers."

"I am tired of being a statistic; I want to be part of the solution." "We are citizen fathers, and what we do will live after us in our community."

These men are no strangers to the enduring legacy of racism in America, but they see no benefit to being angry victims. They hold themselves morally responsible for lapses with their children, and for getting right by them and the children's mothers. Our meetings are intense, sometimes rambling, often warm and funny, and always proud. Coached by citizen-professionals, these men are doing community outreach to make a difference in a problem that they see as holding their community back. Andrew and Guy, the process leaders, are learning the craft of citizen-professional work: how to guide the men as they go deeply into a personal and public issue and then develop strategic actions. Together they have brought a second generation of citizen fathers into the program, and are spreading this way of working to sibling agencies.

Go with the Flow

Once you get involved with community concerns that overlap with your clinical concerns, you'll find yourself drawn to new issues that you couldn't have envisioned at the outset. Kids' birthday parties weren't on my radar screen as a national problem, but the Birthdays Without Pressure project came my way via two converging paths. As a new grandfather, I was paying attention to the pressure that my daughter Elizabeth was experiencing to become a hyperparent—specifically, to hold a big bash for her son William's first birthday. Having inherited her mother's practical streak, Elizabeth would respond to her friends, "Why would I throw a big party for him at age one? He doesn't even know he exists!" Then I visited a party store, where I found an aisle devoted to one-year-old birthday paraphernalia. While there, I overheard a young boy telling his mother that he liked a party product in a nearby aisle and receiving this rebuke: "That's not your color scheme." Clueless boy.

I was on the hunt, then, to find out whether other parents were feeling pressure about birthday parties. I asked every parent I knew, including my clients, and brought up the question when I gave talks to parents about other topics. If I mention an issue and individual parents say "Oh, yes!" I begin to think it's a pressure point that parents might organize around. When I bring it up during community talks about other issues and the audience responds with a collective "whoo!" it's another sign of a community pressure point. In this case, parents and audiences were oh-yessing and whooing all over town. They were telling me stories of parties with limos and hired entertainers, of 30 guests at two-year-olds' parties, of entitled little ones complaining that the take-home party bags weren't up to expectations, and of "starlet" parties at the Libby Lu party store, where six-year-old girls get tarted up and dance in public like Britney Spears.

Earlier in my career, I would have seen this as an individual parent problem, but now I see it mainly as a cultural problem: average parents responding to a competitive and supersizing culture by upping the standards for birthday celebrations. Once the arms race takes off, it's exceedingly hard for most parents to pull back. We raise our children in packs or herds, and herds generally aren't changed one member at a time. What's needed is a leader of the pack to start the countertrend. One day, I received an e-mail from a parent-educator colleague who'd heard me talk about out-of-control birthday parties and knew that I was looking for a lead parent to co-organize a project. He said he thought he had the parent: Linda Zwicky, who'd lit up a parent class by saying she wanted to start a boycott of party bags, those junky gifts that every guest must be awarded for showing up.

Linda, her parent-educator colleague, and I had coffee. We invited others to the next coffee, and then to a couple of house meetings. Before long, we'd organized Birthdays Without Pressure, which had a mission to start a local and national conversation about out-of-control birthday parties and to offer alternatives based on parents' experiences. We did the one-to-one interviews in the community with parents, professionals, and even party-store owners. I talked to my media connections from the overscheduled kids project and found quite a lot of interest. After a year of meeting every two to three weeks to analyze the problem and develop our message, we held a public rally in January 2007, which was attended by 180 parents and covered by *USA Today*, ABC, and local media. We launched our website that day too.

The response was so strong that our server had to be upgraded to handle the volume. For the next month, the parents and I did hundreds of media interviews with journalists and TV and radio shows all over North America and three other continents. We were on message and furthering our mission to raise awareness and pass on strategies that worked for real parents who wanted to resist today's competitive culture of childrearing. When it was over, we had a small party and ended our project, which now consists of a website where parents can get information and contribute to the message board. And we still do a media interview or two each week. Even the *Tehran Times* in Iran ran a story about out-of-control birthday parties and our citizen parent project in Minnesota.

Projects like Birthdays Without Pressure have an afterlife through the development of citizen-leaders—again, a classic principle of community organizing. Linda Zwicky and her fellow parent-activist Julie Printz from the birthday group went on to start a project dealing with the problem of the sexualization of young children in today's culture. For this project, which went public in 2009, I coached my citizen-professional colleague Shonda Craft to lead the process to address what's happening to our kids in a Bratz Dolls and Sexy Fairy Halloween world. Among other things, the group is developing a code of ethics for corporations.

The Path Ahead

Now that I've learned to do this citizen-therapist work, my mission is to teach other therapists (and like-minded professionals) to become involved in their local communities. It requires focused effort and coaching, but it's a lot easier than learning to be a therapist in the first place.

The Citizen Professional Center at the University of Minnesota is supervising professionals in more than a dozen projects on health care issues (diabetes, smoking, depression), cultural change (over-sexualization and the excesses that lead to childhood obesity), war trauma in an immigrant community, and even loss of spiritual values in raising children in the face of rampant consumerism. Wherever there's a social pressure point in a community, there's the making of citizen initiatives catalyzed by a citizen-professional.

This work doesn't require the therapist to have expert knowledge of the problem area being addressed, at least at the outset, because his or her expertise is primarily in bringing to bear a process and working style. I knew less about diabetes than anyone else in the room when I began my diabetes work, and my kids were raised in the era before traveling soccer teams. But I learned as we went. I knew nothing about the experiences of sub-Saharan African immigrants, but I could still coach local professionals, African and non-African, to catalyze a community initiative that accesses the knowledge, wisdom, and experience of the African community.

A downside of this work is that it rarely involves financial compensation for the citizen-therapist in the early stages, although funding has come at some point for more than half of our projects. For instance, the Family Education Diabetes Series with the American Indian community has been supported by grants for a number of years.

On the upside, citizen-therapist work doesn't require a large time commitment; it can be done in about six to eight hours per month over an extended period of time. Working much harder than that means you're overfunctioning and doing things that other citizens should be doing. Many therapists contribute this amount of time to community service work or pro bono therapy, and could shift their time to citizen-professional work.

I've learned that, to be successful, community engagement must meet the needs of therapists as well as communities. When this kind of public practice outside the office fits within therapists' values and vision, therapists experience an expanded sense of professional contribution and enjoy a much closer relationship to their community. They take on a new identity—citizen-therapist—and feel part of something larger: the movement toward a renewal of our democracy.

As parent Jael Weere from Ghana said in a meeting, "Back in Africa, we knew about pseudodemocracy; what I am seeing here is real, empowered democracy." Her citizen-action group, led by a marriage and family therapist, is tackling the challenge of the ongoing impact of war and trauma on children and families in the Liberian community of Northwest Hennepin County, Minnesota. Their chosen path is to break the silence via theater performances that involve youth enacting real stories and elders narrating the larger arc of their people's history. This is followed by community conversations to break the silence about war and trauma. This is not something that therapists would dream up in their offices!

Citizen-therapist work calls on our professional heritage of sensitivity to complex human needs and our ability to connect with people. Though I believe that any kind of therapist can learn to do this work, systems-trained therapists have special advantages at the outset. They know how to work with groups. They know how to connect with people who often begin with different needs and agendas, and have the skills to forge a common purpose across diverging viewpoints. They know how to create processes in which everyone has a voice and powerful individuals don't dominate the dialogue. They know how to be central to the process when it's necessary to keep it productive, and how to be peripheral when they're getting in the way. They know how to inspire and be inspired.

All therapists who are committed to this great profession believe deeply in the human capacity for self-healing and constructive change. The world needs this faith and set of skills to bring renewed life into the public sphere, not just into the private sphere. The renewal of our commonwealth won't come from supporting a candidate and waiting for miracles. Nor, I might add, will it come from '60s-style polarizations between us good guys and the purveyors of "isms" that oppress people. We have to invent a new breed of public actor with great interpersonal skills: citizen-therapists for a new century. I'm betting we can do it.

Note

1   Updated and adapted from Doherty, W. J. (2008). Beyond the consulting room: Therapists as catalysts for social change. *Psychotherapy Networker*, November/December, 28–35.

PART II

The Dreamers

What Change Could Be

3

WHEN WORK IS NOT ENOUGH

Searching for Greater Satisfaction and Meaning

Sari Gold

This story began when I was perusing the websites of professional conferences in the field of psychiatry. I was looking for motivation and inspiration—a change of some sort. I was feeling antsy professionally, despite the satisfaction I received every day in my work as a staff psychiatrist at a homeless women's shelter, and in my private practice. Stagnation was the word that often kept coming to my mind, and I was looking to expand my repertoire of therapies and skills in the field of couple's therapy, my newfound area of interest. I found the keynote speakers and topics at a brief therapy conference to be particularly interesting, and since the timing and location seemed just right, I signed up.

In retrospect, I believe this story began, in some ways, the day I began meditating in earnest, several months prior. I had found myself gravitating for a while to any media involving "change," "new direction," or "new life": movies, articles, books—any direction to find a more meaningful way of living. I needed to explore what was holding me back from pursuing what I knew I wanted to do: get involved with giving back. I didn't seem to be able to just go and do it. I certainly didn't know exactly what it was I wanted, just that I needed "it." I had felt the need for "it" for many years, ever since the sudden loss of my younger brother in a tragic and traumatic accident in 2002. My feelings of grief over him had been severe and the loss extremely profound; it took the members of my whole family a long time just to catch our breath, but it also left me in a place where life felt suddenly short. Within me I felt an urgency to experience life now—not tomorrow, not later. I had been in therapy in the past, as most of us in the field have, but returning to therapy didn't seem the right way at this time. I had been interested in meditation for a long time, but in the past I couldn't seem to get started. At this point I had practiced yoga for many years with increasing frequency, and had finally gotten to a regular daily practice. The jump to meditation seemed to follow naturally. It certainly seemed easier to start meditating than to start a new project or to find a particular cause to get involved in. So I found myself going into daily early morning quietness and becoming more mindful and seeing the benefits of it: calmer demeanor, more focused at work, more available to my family and friends, better sleep, and an overall improved sense of well-being. This was something I really connected with. A dear Buddhist friend of mine encouraged me to attend a Buddhist event, and there I briefly practiced meditation and mindfulness. I had grown interested in trying different techniques, and what seemed to be particularly helpful was focusing a certain amount of time each day on noting what I was thankful for and asking for specific things I felt I needed. I had been asking for new opportunities and the ability to really listen to my own intuition for a change in the direction of my life, and it now seemed like it was coming to fruition.

If I am honest with myself, it seems that maybe this story really began about five years ago, the day I received an e-mail from a previous supervisor from my Psychosomatic Fellowship, about two months after the completion of the program. It was a simple e-mail he forwarded to me about an available job that might be of interest: working part time conducting psychiatric assessments at a homeless women's shelter. I was fresh out of training and looking for part-time work to supplement my income while starting a private practice, and this seemed like something I might enjoy. On impulse I decided to apply. Two months later I found myself starting my new part-time job. And now, more than five years later, I still love my job. I find it stimulating every day and have grown to really appreciate what I get back from each client I see: a deep appreciation for what I have. I think that was the day this story was really born, as it changed my career path and landed me where I am now: trying to start a project in that community, the shelter, and writing about that process.

And this brings me back to my attendance at the therapy conference. The teachings were inspiring and stimulating, just as I had hoped. On the final day of the conference, on impulse, I decided to switch gears and went to hear a talk about how to transform your own life as a therapist. I was very moved by this presentation, as it seemed to address exactly what I had been thinking about for years. I followed my instinct and engaged in conversations after the presentation, talking primarily about my work at the shelter and how I was hoping to begin a project there. Suddenly, I found myself being asked to consider contributing to a book on the topic of therapists who make a difference by contributing locally or globally in community projects. I was taken aback by that request. I wasn't *really* contributing now, just thinking about it. But it was suggested that I consider writing about the process of beginning or attempting to launch a new project. Maybe that would be a different kind of chapter, a new interesting angle, in the book. I was intrigued for sure. I had never done anything like that. But as you can see, one thing leads to another and here I was, with a whole new potential path laid ahead of me, after only a brief conversation. I was focusing in my meditation

PHOTO 3.1   The Help Women's Shelter

on following my intuition; following my instincts had led me to this workshop and allowed me to receive exactly what I was looking for: an opportunity for change.

From Thought to Action

Now I was faced with a huge challenge. Should I follow through with all these new incredible opportunities, just the change I had looked for in both my internal quest with meditation and with my external quest in coming to this conference, or should I let myself remain passive, letting inaction continue to leave me partly unfulfilled and empty? In many ways, the path of least resistance is very appealing, and I had so many wonderful things in my life already. From anyone else's perspective, I was certainly living a full, rewarding, and interesting life. Yet when this opportunity arose, I felt a new powerful wave of excitement come over me that I hadn't experienced in a long time. So despite my doubts, I started writing the first notes on this chapter that same day, during my long-delayed flight back home.

   As a therapist, I encourage my patients to take risks and try new things, but somehow I did not apply the same rule to myself. It is important to me that I genuinely live what I teach to others. Here was my opportunity to try it in action.

This would be a real test of an assumption that I had held for a long time about myself: that I was more of a follower, good at doing what was asked of me, but not necessarily creative, and certainly not a leader. I thought about it for a few more days, but decided to go for it and challenge myself.

In order to go forward, I relied on some of the techniques that I use with patients. I wrote down my future goals and let my imagination go wild to access even the most grandiose images of the future. I listed the disadvantages, and the fears and obstacles I had let stop me before. I let myself maintain the feeling of excitement and really allowed myself to feel the propelling motion and energy of it. I also spoke to my loved ones, specifically those who knew about my search for a change. Finally, I decided to trust my own instinct that this was the right thing to do.

The Inspiration

During those days of processing these new ideas, a recent experience at the shelter kept coming back to me and truly inspired me to get moving. I had met a client from one of the Caribbean Islands a few months back, and her story really moved me. She was in her late 50s and had lived in the United States for 20 years or so, and had left her children back home to be raised by other relatives, as is so commonly done in that part of the world. She had come to the United States to make a better living and provide for her children, and was working as a live-in home health aide. After her last client passed away, she ended up in the shelter. He was an elderly man who treated her terribly, even spitting at her, yet she had stayed for about five years, and stated: "I just didn't pay no mind to it. I love helping people." After the man suddenly died, his family asked her to leave immediately. They provided no additional help or monetary support, and she had no place to go but to the shelter.

As we talked more, I learned that most of her salary had gone back to her family, and in reality, she was supporting not just several of her now-adult children, but was also paying for the private education of several nephews and nieces. She had also purchased a home in which many relatives lived, and she continued to pay the mortgage. There were many people who depended on her continued income. I asked what was left for her, and she responded, "not much, just enough to get by." There were no savings for a rainy day. When I lamented about how she helped everyone and had nothing left for herself, she sheepishly told me how she also sends small donations to seven different churches every month from her meager leftovers. This just astonished me. She looked so happy, perfectly content to be staying in a homeless shelter, feeling blessed for the opportunity to help so many people: "my life's work," as she put it. Remaining optimistic and confident about the future, she said "I know things will work out for me in the end." Needless to say, my assessment of her did not uncover any mood, anxiety, or other psychiatric disorders. Her story stayed with me.

Zeroing In

I had already been brainstorming for several months about a particular project at the shelter. I had even run the idea by my husband for some feedback, and he seemed to think it was a worthwhile idea. Many of the women I see for an assessment are frustrated by the lack of activities at the shelter. These are typically women who have been living a structured life, working and being productive. For various reasons, they have lost their jobs and homes, and the familiar safe structure of daily living. The residents often come from other areas of the city or from other parts of the country, sometimes even from abroad, and the local area is rather unfamiliar to them. Add to that the severe financial problems, and access to any activities seems impossible. So I wanted to create a program to offer activities that would foster improved physical and emotional well-being and provide some new coping skills for the future.

What if such a program was readily available and free for all who are interested? This could potentially make a big difference in the shelter experience for many of these women. I even envisioned that through shared positive experiences, this program could foster friendships for women who are isolated and feeling alone, yet in many ways are in very similar circumstances. Also, as a therapist, I know that building up the positive in life, and engaging in activities that help a person feel good, can improve self-esteem and motivate other positive life changes. The passivity and disengagement I see so often can be more infectious than the positive energy and sense of motivation. Perhaps this program would provide another necessary tool for some of these women, who so desperately need to keep fighting for survival and opportunities. Maybe some of them would be able to attempt an activity they had heard about before but never had an opportunity to try. Perhaps the most motivated women would inspire others less motivated to try as well, thereby spreading positivity. I had some grandiose ideas about this project, but at the end of the day, even the least far-fetched goal was acceptable in my mind: maybe a particular class or activity would just make the women happier for a moment, and start the day on a better note.

Developing a Plan

So how would I start a program like that? This shelter is an assessment shelter, and women from all walks of life find their way here. In order to receive help with housing, all clients are required to submit to a medical and psychiatric evaluation; if any additional needs are identified, clients can begin the appropriate treatment and can then be referred to subspecialty shelters. The goal is for the clients to stay no more than 21 days in order to complete this and other assessments, and to then be transferred to either some form of housing, or to another, more permanent shelter. In practice, however, many clients remain in the shelter longer than this. Such delays can be caused by a client's procrastination, a lack of bed space in the receiving shelter, or for a host of other reasons.

The shelter subcontracts all their medical services from a nonprofit multi-disciplinary health system in the community, which is my employer. Therefore, I am somewhat removed from the shelter itself, although I work within the facility. In my daily work, I am typically in contact with the medical office staff and case managers for the shelter clients, but I am not involved in the daily goings-on. This may have kept me somewhat uninformed about the shelter client's typical day for all this time. So to begin the process, I met with my supervisor at the shelter to bring up my ideas for this new program. Her initial reaction was positive, and we discussed what kinds of activities might be helpful, how to find out what activities or groups already exist, and possible past trials of other activities that were successful or not, and why not.

Positive Reinforcement

This seemed like a good start. I felt energized and optimistic, and I had ideas now to go forward with. I had thought about providing the clients with activities similar to those I found helpful personally, namely yoga, meditation, Zumba dancing, nutritional counseling, psychoeducation, and perhaps others. Next I contacted the shelter activities director, who informed me of current activities and told me that previous attempts at physical activities were stopped due to liability issues, specifically concerns about injuries. But she also described the enthusiastic reaction to meditation events that were irregularly provided. She confirmed that space and scheduling would not be a problem. The director of social work was quite helpful as well, suggesting the possibility of free bus transportation to local community centers that offer either free or very low cost activities. Our volunteer coordinator, in turn, suggested the possibility of adding cooking events and perhaps combining them with a nutrition program. She also explained that there were procedures that the potential volunteers would have to go through first, but that the process could be simplified to accommodate an easy transition. For example, I could be the go-between with paperwork and could organize the group orientation. By now I noticed my notes becoming long and copious, and my energy and motivation soaring!

I went back to my supervisor with all these new ideas and suggestions. We discussed conducting a survey of interest among clients and how to approach any funding issues. Likely, we would have to start with volunteer teachers. We discussed the issue of liability and she seemed confident we could work around those issues by getting medical clearances and having clients sign waivers before any physical activities. (She also let me know that a medical staff member at the shelter could provide sessions in Reiki healing.) She then arranged to meet with the shelter director in order to present all these ideas to her. Surprisingly, she called me later the same day with the exciting news that the shelter director not only liked all the ideas, but would also provide yoga mats once we were ready to go ahead with classes. She also wanted to provide similar classes for the shelter staff as well!

Nitty Gritty

This wonderful reaction was very exciting, and despite the time it had taken to get this process rolling—two months—it all seemed to be moving along quite quickly now, and the response had been only positive. Now it was time to get into the actual detail work. The survey results indicated that most clients would participate in all of the proposed activities. The clients even suggested additional activities we had not even thought about. This confirmed my suspicion that a lot of these clients would eagerly take advantage of any opportunities to feel better if given the chance.

I contacted the health system grant writer, who informed me of the possibility of tagging this project onto another major health initiative in the future. This idea was not terribly promising, but it was something to think about. At least now I knew that we would have to get this started on a volunteer basis, as no financial compensation was available for the teachers. I also contacted the operations manager for the health system and found out that it was possible to get private donations to support this particular program directly. This would give me an opportunity to perhaps do some fundraising in the yoga community in the future, specifically as a means to provide a small salary for the teachers in the shelter. This might increase interest and possibly the number of classes being offered weekly.

I contacted my own yoga teachers to see if there was any interest in teaching classes at the shelter. Sure enough, true to the yoga community spirit, my teachers were enthusiastic about the possibility of bringing yoga to these women in need and suggested forming a group of alternating teachers who might each volunteer once a month to teach a class. In addition, I reached out to the owner of a local Zumba studio. I knew that she was involved with many local charities and when I presented my idea to her, she was very interested in participating. She also offered to connect me to other teachers. It seemed that things were falling into place.

By now I was about four months into this project. It seemed like I was working hard and getting few results, but as I was trying to work this out, I was also working at the same time, getting involved with another charity, and trying to keep up with my usual family and social activities. It seemed like a lot of work and responsibilities, but my biggest hindrance to this project remained my natural tendency to be passive. I needed to work every day in my meditation to find the motivation to keep sending the e-mails, to keep making the phone calls, and to keep talking to my family and friends about this project. At times I felt I was fighting against my own nature. But at the same time, whenever I took another step, as another task was finished, I felt a sense of accomplishment and deep satisfaction that motivated me to keep going. I also kept my focus on the end goal: I am working to set up a program that is sustainable for the long term, and I know it is not reasonable to expect it to be done in a hurry. I also kept in mind that I am new to this. All these administrative issues, organizing and contacting people, and going from one step to the next, are foreign to me, and learning a new system and language requires time and patience. So I continued to remind myself to be realistic with my expectations.

Deflation

Suddenly, after months of slow but seamlessly smooth progress, things took a turn that I didn't expect. I was still feeling excited about the prospect of getting things moving and starting to bring the teachers in to run classes, to organize the busing, etc, when things stalled. Meetings were cancelled, e-mails were left unanswered, and vacations slowed the flow of communication; weeks seemed to go by in which nothing happened. It was difficult not to get discouraged. One particular event really crystallized in my mind how the energy in one's immediate environment can shift things rapidly and drastically. I was putting together ideas about arranging fundraising events for the new charity that my family had just gotten involved with. I was quite excited about it and spoke with some friends about my ideas. They were wonderfully supportive and felt my ideas were reasonable.

I then approached my sister, with whom I am very close. She is a go-getter, a really productive and efficient person. I was hoping she would be my partner in realizing these goals. Her reaction was a completely unexpected solid wall of resistance that caught me off guard. She went silent as I was enthusiastically describing my plans over the phone. As I was getting unnerved and somewhat anxiously chattering on, trying to really hype things up to get a reaction out of her, she suddenly interrupted and began tersely listing all the reasons why she could not be a part of this. She was busy, she was really not the type to get into these kinds of things, she did not like organizations, and no one can really trust that the money really gets where it is supposed to go because there are too many people abusing the system and monies are spent willy-nilly. On and on she went. It wasn't just her list of reasons, but more her tone of voice and her conviction that this was a waste of time that really got to me. I felt all the excitement drain out of me and was completely deflated after I hung up the phone. I soon became convinced that my plans for these fundraisers were not going to amount to anything. I also began to believe that my ambitious plan to set up a whole new program at the shelter was going to go nowhere, fast. Who did I think I was to have such a grandiose plan? It took a few days, several corrective conversations with other family, friends, and mentors, and a lot of meditation, before I approached her about that phone call. When I expressed to her the effect that her words and attitude had had on me, she felt terrible. We discussed it at length, and it became clear that it was she who had an issue that she was struggling with, one that had set me back into a state of immobilization. Once the air was cleared, however, I noticed my hopefulness and excitement return immediately.

Things were not progressing in reality, however, and I found my attention becoming focused on things that were actually going somewhere, things that were producing results. These were enjoyable things, such as my own physical activities, organizing the fundraising events for the charity my family was now involved with, planning summer travels, and work-related seminars and training. Of course I also noticed that the less I did for this program, the more discouraged I began to feel. I often thought this plan would not see daylight. And again, true to my nature, I began talking about it less and allowing it to fall onto the back burner. The one thing that kept me from giving up was my meditation. Interestingly, I noticed a parallel between the two: I found it hard to meditate consistently when I was struggling to keep my motivation going. Similarly, maintaining a daily meditation routine helped me stick with my plan, even when it was on the back burner. Finally, after weeks of procrastinating, I made a phone call that seemed to get things back on track, reminding me that sometimes it takes just one simple act to get things going.

The Results are In

So now here I am, a year later, reporting on the current status of my project. At this time, it is still far from being actualized. We will soon begin the bus transportation to the community centers, and I have started teaching a bi-weekly psychoeducation group and it has become quite popular. In addition, regular Reiki healing sessions have begun, and the nutritionist from the health system appears to be interested in adding some time for a regular group meeting at the shelter. The sticking points at this time are the activities I am most eager to start: meditation, yoga, and Zumba. I recently received word from the administration that all approvals have gone through, and I could rally yoga teachers to get involved. I reached out to all the local yoga studios with an urgently worded e-mail asking for volunteer teachers, and was humbled by the numerous responses from generous teachers eager to donate their time. I now have a group of teachers waiting to begin our first weekly yoga and meditation class. Having come up with such a successful strategy, I may reach out to local Zumba teachers in the future with a similar e-mail once the yoga class is up and running.

There are more challenges ahead, as I am expecting to be involved in the future with possible fundraising for the monies needed to compensate teachers; I may also have to apply for grants for further funding. This will again challenge me: I am not a salesperson by nature. It is difficult for me to even promote my own private practice. In my idealistic world, all I have to do is ask, but I know it is not that simple. Many people are suffering financially, and it will take the skill of persuasion and a real belief in this cause to gather the support I need.

Growing by Doing

I knew from the beginning that there was a possibility that I might not be able to end this chapter with a description of a successful and smoothly running operation. What I was hoping to achieve is what I actually discovered: that I am capable of pushing through my own self-imposed limits to do things I had not even imagined. While trying to organize this program, I became involved with a wonderful charity and arranged two fundraising events abroad, and one locally. I motivated my family to get involved, and hopefully I am teaching my teenage daughter a valuable lesson as she watches my ongoing learning process. Each part of the project spawned new ideas and interests, and the results allayed my previous fears of becoming overwhelmed and lost.

On the contrary, I have more confidence in myself than before. Also, I met many inspirational people who have started unique and successful community projects. I learned to identify people who can help me, not only in practical ways, but also those who can encourage me to keep going. And I recognize now that it is essential to ask for help. One cannot do it alone. I learned to motivate people into action, and my sister ended up becoming the most actively involved in the fundraising efforts! I also learned to trust my own instincts more, and to really open my mouth when it is important to do so. I cultivated patience and persistence as I dealt with large organizations, in which the wheels turn slowly. In addition, all these experiences have energized and enhanced my existing work, as I feel more connected to and invested in the community I work in. And I realized I can deal with rejection and disappointment and still keep going. I have always known that I am a daydreamer, and this process has taught me to believe in what my grandfather always said: "In life, you have to have dreams for the future." How else can you choose a path to follow?

My advice to anyone who is thinking about starting a project in the community is to just do it! Surround yourself with people who inspire you, and people who believe in you and your project. Identify your weak links and enlist help from people who possess those strengths. Get feedback for your ideas from people whose opinion you trust. Most importantly, find something that you really believe is important, because you'll need to maintain your conviction in the face of many obstacles. Keep your mind open to opportunities that are offered to you, and trust your instincts. Sometimes a series of seemingly unrelated events leads you to where you were supposed to find yourself all along.

4

MARGINALIZED NO MORE

Leah Brew

The year is 2008. I am sitting in the balcony of the Senate room at the State Capitol in Sacramento, California. On the short plane ride here, I was eagerly anticipating presenting before the Senate Business and Professions Committee; I thought it was such an honor to be part of the political process. I am not feeling that way now. While one senator is presenting a bill, the others are working on their computers or walking around talking with each other. I am unable to find a single person who is listening to the senator who is presenting. Then it is time to vote. The vote goes precisely down party lines, or so my lobbyist tells me. We watch a few more bills get voted on, and my stomach churns watching this not-very-democratic process repeat over and over again, with few exceptions. Finally, like a teacher scolding elementary school students, the Pro Tempore bangs his gavel and asks everyone to quiet down and pay attention. I hope that the subcommittee meeting will be better.

In the subcommittee meeting, we are scheduled to go last. We wait hours for our bill to be called. We hope there is still time to present before 5:00 pm so that we do not have to return tomorrow; I also have a plane to catch and don't want to change my flight. Finally, it is our turn to present arguments for our bill. We are seeking the Licensed Professional Clinical Counselor credential; California is the only state that does not acknowledge this license. This is our second bill. The first one did not get enough votes to pass or fail; it simply died. We are starting again. Despite hundreds of letters sent by students, colleagues, and me to many senators—and despite meeting face to face with politicians or their representatives—the bill dies again. The few senators' offices I visited told me they felt confident their politician would support the bill. However, they did not. We were told that the chair of this committee, a psychologist, might be against this bill and that he held a lot of power. As predicted, he voted against the bill, and we were told that he likely influenced others to do the same.

I wonder to myself: why am I here? I have a baby who needs me. I am the new chair of my department, and I am ignoring about 15 e-mails per hour to be here. I have papers to grade waiting in my office. Why am I spending my time and energy as an advocate? Apparently all those letters and meetings with legislators were a waste of my precious time, since meeting with senators had little to no influence. But the question is rhetorical, really. I have spent my life being marginalized as a multi-ethnic Asian-American woman, and I will no longer tolerate it. I feel compelled to fight.

Marginalized in Many Ways

My experiences with feeling marginalized have been related to different aspects of my identity. My first experiences were related to racism. I grew up in a small, racist town in Texas as the only ethnic minority in my school. I was teased and bullied in elementary school while teachers stood back and watched. As a young adult, my husband at the time (who is Thai) and I would not get seated in restaurants, or worse, get seated but never served after hours of waiting.

Later, the reason for my marginalization morphed into another aspect of my identity. Working in a white-collar job in corporate America, I was discriminated against not just because of my ethnicity, but also because of my gender. I was told by the "good 'ole boys" that I was intimidating and needed to be more conciliatory. The other supervisors with whom I worked and my direct reports did not perceive me in this way, which I discovered in an anonymous survey while doing Steven Covey training. Only the executives of the company felt I was intimidating. The underlying message was that women should not assert their opinions. My greatest solace was that I was working on my Master's degree in counseling at the time to escape the suffocating corporate environment.

During my Master's program, I learned how counselors were the stepchildren of the mental health profession. The psychiatrists were gods, the psychologists were demi-gods, and the social workers were just above us counselors in terms of rights and respect. I did not experience marginalization directly at this point, but I was prepped and ready to find it. Despite hearing about the low status of counselors, at least I felt safe from racism in the academic world. My sense of safety was naive, though. An African American man once told me point blank that my experience as an Asian-American woman was nothing compared to his experience. He asserted that as a "model minority" I had no right to complain about my experiences with racism. I found this horribly disturbing since, as a self-proclaimed expert in multi-culturalism and as a counselor educator, he completely denied my experiences.

All of these different experiences of feeling devalued and marginalized led me to realize that I would have to work harder and smarter to minimize further marginalization, even if my minority status might give me extra points in the hiring process. I went above and beyond minimum requirements in completing my Master's and Doctoral degrees. I obtained my Licensed Professional Counselor credential in Texas, which I thought would help if states allowed reciprocity when it was time to find a job. I took extra courses during my Master's and Doctoral degrees, sat for the National Counselor Exam (which was used in about half of the states at that time) and was willing to move almost anywhere for a faculty position. I ended up finding a job in California. I was hopeful that I would not be marginalized there. As I walked across campus toward my interview, I saw many Asian students, Latino students, Black students, and other ethnic and religious groups of students among the White faces. The students seemed to be gathering by major, I was guessing, not by skin color. As I listened to the Asian students talking, I noticed they had American accents and were not international students like at my alma mater. I felt I belonged here. The people were liberal like me, they looked like me, and they sounded like me. As an only child in a multi-ethnic family, the experience of belonging was quite unfamiliar to me. This initial feeling turned out to be true. Once I started to teach, I met students and faculty members who were not only multi-ethnic Asian-Americans, they were specifically Japanese-American like me. For the first time, I felt at home. I was so relieved to be "normal."

The relief of not being marginalized was short lived when I decided to seek licensure. I discovered that the only license available in California with my training was the Licensed Marriage and Family Therapy (LMFT) credential. However, once the state board reviewed my application, I was informed that I was not eligible to sit for the exam because my degree did not have a family systems course in it. I thought this was strange since I was preparing students to become LMFTs, so I asked if I could simply take a family class. The board refused, stating that I needed to have the identity of a marriage and family therapist and would need another Master's degree that was systems focused. I felt indignant about this absurd perspective. After all, only one marriage and family therapist taught in our program; all other faculty members were psychologists and counselor educators. I concurrently felt helpless, as I had many times before, and acquiesced like the good Asian girl I was raised to be. Shortly after learning this, I was recruited by a group of counselors who formed an organization, the California Coalition for Counselor Licensure (CCCL). I was invited to participate in this coalition that was full of counselors representing a variety of organizations who were qualified to provide therapy in many other states. Finding a little hope, I quickly joined.

After meeting the other board members, I realized I was not alone. There seemed to be hundreds of counselors who were underemployed or unemployed and longed to provide therapy. This project was bigger than just my need for a license. This project reflected the marginalization of counselors that I had often heard about during my graduate training, and I had to make a difference. I was tired of feeling oppressed and was ready to direct all that pain into this project.

"I'm Just a Bill"

You might be asking yourself, "Leah, how does this story fit in a social justice book?" I asked myself the same question. As I read through some of the other draft chapters in this book, I was moved to learn about the impact others make in their own communities or in communities of other nations. The stories are poignant, honest, and impressively altruistic. My story is different in that I am advocating for a profession. However, my story is also like the others in that I long to overcome the oppression of others, regardless of its form. I recognized that by participating in this project, I was not only helping myself, but I was also helping potentially hundreds of counselors who could not get licensed in the state and by extension, helping potential clients get mental health services.

And so my journey to advocate for the counseling profession began. As a faculty member, part of my job was (and is) to perform service work in my profession; participating in CCCL met that expectation. However, I had another motivation. I was deeply in debt from my Doctoral education, and the cost of living was three times higher in California than in my home state of Texas; I needed additional income. My assumption had been that I would be able to carry a few clients each week to help bridge the gap. My inability to earn additional income propelled me swiftly into this cause, especially when I felt overwhelmed by my heavy teaching load combined with the work required by being on the board. However, each time I considered giving up and stepping down from the board, I would be contacted by counselors from other states who asked for my help in getting licensed. Being aware of others who were unable to earn an income grounded me in the process.

At first, the commitment was fairly easy. The board consisted of about 20 people who would be invited to monthly conference calls for two-hour meetings. In time, though, the two hours led to two and a half or three hours; the conference calls became more intense, and when we were getting close to submitting a bill, we would meet every other week in subcommittee meetings as well. We would often come to consensus about what the requirements should be, but a few times, the discussions were contentious and voting was necessary. The leader of CCCL was gifted at managing this process.

Once we had a bill and had found a lobbyist, we had to learn how to get a bill passed. For those of you old enough to remember the Schoolhouse Rock song "I'm Just a Bill," the words do not tell you half of the story. We went through the process three times before we got it right. Each attempt took more than a full year.

The first year, our lobbyist had to find a politician to author our bill, which was difficult because no one knew what a counselor was or why this licensure was needed. We waited for months biting our nails before we got our final decision of support, because without it, we could not submit the bill at all. We had no idea how to navigate the politics in the political system; the learning curve was huge.

Consequently, the bill died in committee. I felt disappointed because I knew we had to fight for another year, and yet I also felt relieved since I didn't think the requirements were rigorous enough. At least we all learned a lot about how to proceed the next year. So we pulled up our bootstraps and tried again.

The second time, we were able to secure an author more quickly since it had been authored before. We corrected all the mistakes we'd made in our previous attempt, but the bill still died in committee. This was the point where I started my story, and I was devastated. We were sure that our bill was strong and that our cause was just. But politics is, sadly, more about politics than justice. I felt helpless, hopeless, and defeated. I was angry for days. When this second bill died, I was taken back to my childhood experiences of feeling like I was being bullied without anyone to protect me. I was ready to give up, but our fearless leader cheered us on. We had done too much work to give up now. And so we persisted.

The third time, we had a fiercely rigorous bill. We knew how to navigate the politics and made it clear that we would continue to pursue this bill indefinitely. We had a few more weapons in our arsenal, which gave us more support and far more power. This time it worked: the bill passed all the way through the committees, the Senate, the Assembly, and the governor's desk! I was at a counselor education conference in San Diego the week the bill was signed, and was delighted to announce this success at the opening reception. I felt like all the incidences of

PHOTO 4.1   Leah Brew and Dean Porter at the Capitol in a subcommittee meeting

oppression and marginalization were somehow vindicated with this one success. I felt strong, useful, and optimistic.

One might think the story would end here. Instead the intensity increased and the content of the work changed. We still had to advocate for counselors as certain decisions were made about the processes of grandparenting. During an 18-month period, we evolved CCCL from a coalition of counseling organizations to a membership organization, the California Association for Licensed Professional Clinical Counselors (CALPCC). Then, once the applications were released, our workload doubled. I could feel some underlying resentment growing because I was on sabbatical trying to focus on writing, but was losing 10–15 hours per week continuing this work. By this time, I was elected president of CALPCC, and we now had over 200 e-mails per week asking questions about the application for grandparenting. We discovered why.

I was shocked, appalled, and, ironically, flattered that the regulating board had a note on their website referring all questions to our CALPCC website. We attempted to reduce the e-mails by getting more information out to counselors. In a two-week period, I presented to the school counselor association in California, to the alumni from my institution, and created a webinar with the executive director that we hoped would answer most questions. We created an FAQ page that was elaborate and organized to help mediate e-mails, but the questions kept coming. As department chair, I consulted with our department administrative assistant often on how to complete the forms for our alumni who were applying for the license.

I handled this while trying to complete my own application, which included taking 90 hours of continuing education credits. I found myself tired, cranky, and frustrated that so much of my time was still dedicated to this. I was forgetting the higher purpose of helping not only a profession, but also the counselors and clients who would benefit. Once the grandparenting period was over, the workload reduced, and I regained my perspective that I was not just doing this for my own benefit, but to advocate for the profession and for the counselors and clients they would see. I am pleased about the work we have done so far, relieved that my presidency is almost over, and satisfied that I persevered through the challenges.

Frustrations, Challenges, and Obstacles

Some challenges stand out more than others for me in the process to obtain licensure. Up until recently, I often felt like I did not belong when I participated in groups. I believe this was in part due to my experiences in elementary school with bullying. Being involved in this group process was scary in and of itself. I was terrified of feeling rejected. I wondered how much I should assert my beliefs versus how much I should stay quiet and go with the "group think" to avoid rejection. Sadly, I am no good at holding my peace. I wondered if anyone would respect me as a new faculty member fresh out of school with only a couple of years of clinical experience. These feelings emerged at the onset of my participation, and they were replaced by another challenge once I was steeped in the process: handling interpersonal conflict.

As mentioned before, CCCL met at least monthly, and often bi-monthly via conference call. We were about 20 counselors from different generations, different educations, and different specialties trying to agree on a cohesive path to licensure. And as with any group, we had different personalities to negotiate on our conference calls. Some members spoke too much and others not at all, some were detailed and others preferred only the big picture, some were charismatic and others were monotone, and finally, some members did most of the work and others participated only minimally. During my 10 years on this committee, we met in person only once. So trying to participate in phone meetings with slightly different agendas, very different personalities, and not really knowing each other well was particularly overwhelming for me. I am an only child raised in a family in which feelings were not expressed, my parents intentionally never disagreed in front of me, and my dad was always right and everyone else was wrong. I had to manually and consciously learn the skills of negotiating differences rather than asserting my self-righteousness like my dad. Fortunately, I learned to handle myself better from my counseling training. But I was a neophyte with conflict, and I feared disagreements within the organization. In order to deal with these long and sometimes stressful phone calls, I would often clean the house while on the phone, which is my favorite coping mechanism to minimize frustrations. Thankfully, I managed to avoid burning any bridges throughout the process.

Ten years is a long time, and I had personal challenges as well while participating in this coalition. My first responsibility was as a tenure-track professor, trying to earn high teaching evaluations while publishing, presenting at conferences, and participating in committees both on and off campus. During one two-year period, I became involved in a new relationship, got married, earned tenure, had a baby, and was elected chair of my department. These events happened between the second and third bills we submitted. During the third attempt, I started the chair position with a six-month old baby and the 2008 budget cuts with layoffs, 10% furloughs, and increased workloads. I felt quite exhausted and helpless in so many aspects of my life. The time and effort required for me to be on this coalition cost me dearly. I barely met the publication requirements to get tenure. I spent very little time with my new husband and subsequently, with my new baby. The biggest price I paid was my peace of mind. The roller coaster ride of this process has wreaked havoc on my stress levels and my ability to have patience with my colleagues, with my students, with my daughter, and (probably more than anyone) with my husband. I could have easily let this service activity go, but I held on tightly. I had to find a way to persevere.

Privilege Keeps Me Going

I was asked just last week how I manage to juggle so many different responsibilities. The answer is simply: privilege. Personally, I am privileged to have a family that supports me both emotionally and financially, when needed. Even though I am my child's primary caregiver, my husband supports me as much as he can while balancing his own intense workload. We earn a good enough income that I can have my daughter in our university childcare facility, which is more like a school than a daycare. This childcare facility also allows incredible flexibility to match my teaching and meeting schedules. I have made friends through the childcare center who are also professors with similar values, and we watch each other's kids when we have extra meetings or excessive work. I am also aware of my privilege that my daughter does not have special needs that would require more time and energy from me. I have the privilege of a full community to support me, and that keeps me going.

I am professionally privileged as well. As a professor, I am expected to participate in service activities. So when I have to travel to Sacramento or attend meetings, my schedule is much more flexible than if I had a private practice. Furthermore, I get paid the same whether I participate or not; private practitioners lose income when they volunteer outside the office. My colleagues have consistently supported this endeavor, and we get along well, which I know is not true in many academic departments. We have worked together to make sure our program meets the requirements for this new license; I am grateful for their support. As I write this, I have the privilege of being on sabbatical to take the time to work on service and writing projects like this. Even without sabbatical, I truly love the work that I do, which is most definitely a privilege. With the support of my colleagues, I know that advocating for the counseling profession will benefit our students and the clients they see, and that most definitely keeps me going.

Throughout the legislative process, I have had the privilege to work with a remarkable group of counselors in this coalition. When I felt hopeless, they persevered, and vice versa. They have mentored me in how to lead this type of process, which was always respectful, inclusive, open, and with a dash of optimism. I was impressed by so many individuals who made the most of their strengths so that collectively, all the work was completed. I was privileged to be informally mentored by so many different people who I genuinely like, which contributed to my staying part of this process.

Intrapersonally, my Japanese mother and military father taught me to be organized, disciplined, and efficient. In the past, I felt my ethnicity and upbringing were barriers to my happiness. Now I see that these life challenges gave me the skills and perseverance to overcome. As a result, I have to say that my experiences of being marginalized and oppressed have given me the fortitude, the interest, and the desire to participate in the huge task of participating in a political process to obtain licensure. I feel that my privileges now outnumber my experiences with marginalization. Instead of walking into a new situation and automatically feeling marginalized, I now feel confident and strong.

How to Become an Advocate for Social Justice

I could give some behavioral advice on becoming a social justice advocate, such as: get organized, manage time constructively, work efficiently, and take care of yourself. Instead I feel compelled to provide a counselor-type of answer. I think the first and most important task is that you must feel inspired to do the work. If I had believed that I had to participate on this task force simply because it was the right thing to do or it was my responsibility as a professional, I would have burned out long ago. My drive to make a difference in the world that is measurable and concrete propels me forward when obstacles arise. Furthermore, the complete disregard for my profession by the state board and legislators resonated to the other types of injustices I had experienced in my life. These factors facilitated my passion. Passion is not something that can be learned or created; it has to emerge organically, and advocacy requires hard work that can only be sustained with passion.

I also believe that my ability to capitalize on my strengths facilitated my ongoing participation. The trend in strength-based psychology exists for a reason: using strengths builds confidence and increases success. In my case, I am a good administrator. I felt less confident talking with legislators, so I only did that a few times. In contrast, I took roles that required organizing information, establishing structure, and facilitating action. Therefore, the type of advocacy is only one aspect of social justice. Choosing your role in that advocacy is equally important.

Finally, I had many privileges that afforded me the time and support to advocate for my profession. I have many interests and passions. I do not have the time to pursue them all, so I have to make choices about what I can do. I say this for two reasons. The first reason is that life is too busy for most people, and adding more responsibility has consequences. I recommend assessing the benefits and your ability to participate with the consequences before starting new endeavors. Sometimes, it's simply not worth it. Second, I can be more judgmental that I would like to admit, and I was occasionally disappointed and perturbed by the number of people who committed to participate and then did little or nothing. Yes, life gets in the way at times, but when you choose to participate in a project in which others depend upon you, either do the work or resign from it. Please. The counseling profession is smaller than one might realize, and when individuals are not dependable, that information can ripple through the counseling community with unanticipated negative outcomes. By choosing advocacy projects wisely, counselors have the ability to affect a greater impact on the clients or institutions they serve.

I have had many experiences of feeling marginalized, not good enough, and inadequate. Through a combination of my own strength, some luck, and the support of good people, I have shifted into a position of privilege in most areas of my life. I feel fortunate that I could participate in the process to obtain counselor licensure in California. It has been a privilege to convert all that experience into the enormous task of advocating for my profession in a very concrete way. We counselors still have work to do in California, and we still have work to do nationally, but we have made significant strides that will build an even stronger profession for the future.

5

A WANNABE THERAPIST'S
JOURNEY TO MAKE A DIFFERENCE

Josselyn Sheer

I'd lost complete control. What was supposed to be an organized game of musical chairs and dancing ended up being complete and utter turmoil. There were children surrounding me, clinging onto every part of my body and holding my hands. Boys were climbing on top of the chairs. Girls were refusing to get up at all. They were jumping up and down, furiously demanding every ounce of my attention. My body heat radiated against the children as we danced to the music. It wasn't until I felt myself being pulled, literally, from opposite sides of my body, that I knew how out of control things were getting. I felt helpless. What had I gotten myself into? I thought I wanted to be a therapist, to work with children, to help save the world. But at that moment, all I could think of was how to save myself.

Jumping In, with Both Feet, But Eyes Closed Shut

Throughout my life, I have flirted with the idea of being a therapist. "What does it mean to truly help someone," I continue to ask myself. "How will I really know if I've helped someone?" About a year ago, I signed up to travel around the world to invest myself in service projects and figure out if this is really what I wanted for my life's work. I volunteered at a school in Ghana, a community-wide cultural project in Brazil, a Chinese center for homeless children, a village in Brazil, an orphanage in Taiwan, and now this, a school in India for lower-caste children who could not attend school without charitable support.

I understand the world cannot be saved by just a few months of service, but I learned what I *can* do: save the fate of one, two, five, or 10 children by teaching them, believing in them, and reaffirming them.

My plan to help others was going pretty well thus far; in fact, better than I had expected. Yet now, in this remote village in Southern India, I was seriously

questioning my own sanity, much less my misguided intention to make a difference. Maybe I didn't want to be a therapist after all; at this point, working as a
barista in a coffee shop was sounding pretty good an as alternative. At least the
caffeinated patrons wouldn't start jumping all over the chairs.

With my assigned children, I had no agenda, no lesson plan, and no real idea of
what "music/dance" meant, which is what I signed up to teach for the afternoon.
For me, it seemed natural to volunteer for dance because I used to be a dancer, and I
love music; other subjects like science, math, and geography did not call out to me.
Yet now I stood in silence for a few seconds, looking around the room in horror at
the chaos that was unfolding. Eventually, I took a deep breath and reminded myself
that this was what I asked for, so it was time to make the best of the situation.

My first instinct was to provide the children with some guidelines and ground
rules about how our dance and music session would continue. Typically, I would
start by announcing that everyone must respect one another and that all ideas
would be welcomed. I have worked with children on many different occasions
back at home, so it felt natural and familiar to be back in this setting. What I've
never had experience with, though, is working with children who have yet to be
exposed to the idea of "free expression." The children at this school called me
"Ma'am," and were praised by their teachers and elders only when they used their
manners, politely saying "please" and "thank you" at the beginning and end of
each sentence. They dressed for school each morning in a uniform; the boys had
their hair perfectly combed and the girls had double braided pigtails that were tied
with two navy blue bows. Each day, they would sit in one classroom while different teachers would come in and instruct them. When a teacher asked a question,
the boys and girls would respond in unison, singing the answer and waiting for
any sort of approval from their instructor. It reminded me of a scene from *Matilda*
when Miss Trunchbull would ask Miss Honey's class if they understood her, and
in one droned-out harmony, the students would respond, "Yes Miss Trunchbull." At school, order and respect were of the utmost importance.

I quickly realized that maybe more than anything else, these kids needed creative expression. They were begging for some sort of openness, and in their own
way they were surely showing it to me. So instead of doing what felt comfortable
for me (as the adult), and what surely felt comfortable for the students (who were
trained to behave for the adults in their lives), I deviated away from my own rules;
instead, I followed the no-rule rule. For 30 minutes, I jumped up and down so
many times that sweat poured off of my body incessantly.

I held hands with a child on my left and a child on my right, using my arms and
hips to demonstrate what "freedom of expression" meant. I jumped and touched
the sky and wiggled to the ground, touching my toes, and the children imitated
the exact same thing. I thought to myself, "They're getting it! They're totally getting it!" I smiled and could not contain my laughter as I made eye contact with
each child I danced with, each one smiling and laughing back at me. It was the
most fun I've had in awhile.

PHOTO 5.1   Working with students in Southern India.

Musical Chairs

About an hour later, I decided to play a game with the kids. "Everyone listen up! We are going to play MUSICAL CHAIRS!" I said in my most excited, high-pitched squeal. Now, reflecting back on this, I realize how culturally inappropriate the game was for the young boys and girls that surrounded me. After all, they were living in Southern India, where cooperation is valued over competition, especially in school.

So I tried again, this time much louder. "Everybody, listen up: eyes on me." I don't think there was a single child who stopped what they were doing and looked up at me. What looked like a classroom when we first entered was suddenly transformed into a dance floor with desks and chairs surrounding the perimeter of the open grounds. Second-grade boys and girls continued to jump up and down to the music. With this new freedom that they were given, the children began to love it and take ownership over it. Thirty minutes earlier, I had all of the power in the room. Suddenly, with no control and a hoarse voice, I was powerless.

I was determined to play Musical Chairs. Two rows of chairs had now been arranged, back to back, and the stage was set for the game. Two students demonstrated how to play, and soon after, the music started and the dancing around the chairs began. All was going well until I noticed out of the corner of my eye two young girls fighting in the corner. I had a feeling that something bad might have happened, and as soon as I looked over and watched what was going on, about three or four of the children realized that my attention was no longer directed on them and their game of Musical Chairs. Without warning, all of my energy and attention was focused on the conflict in the corner.

My First Attempt at Cross-Cultural Conflict Resolution

Quietly, I parted hands with the young boys and walked over.

"What's going on?" I asked one of the girls softly.

She hit me!" Yasmen told me, pointing to a frowning girl just inches away from her.

"It's true, Ma'am," the other girl said softly, looking up at me, holding her belly and frowning. "She hit me and I don't know why, Ma'am."

I bent down to the level of both of young girls and asked them if they would come outside the classroom with me. I took both of their hands, Yasmen on my left hand and Akshaya on my right, and we walked off to a shady corner far away from the musical chairs.

Earlier, I had spent time learning about the role that spirituality plays at this rather unique school. Each day, the students participate in a number of activities such as karate, meditation, and yoga. I made friends with the yoga instructor and gained some insight into the importance of these activities; I learned that each student at the school was required to take yoga. Their training aimed to improve their bodily postures, health and relaxation, and breath control. I found this fascinating.

Yasmen and Akshaya sat down and I sat in front of both of them, facing them with my legs crossed and my arms by my side. So many thoughts raced through my mind. I wanted to repair the damage that was done between these two young children. My goal was to make this better—but how? It suddenly occurred to me that I had no real history with conflict resolution for second graders. I had to make some decisions, and I had to act fast. I had a daunting assignment before me.

"Before we talk," I addressed the girls in my most grave voice, "I want all three of us to take a few deep breaths in and out together, okay?" I looked them both in the eyes, praying that I would get some nod of approval or any kind of recognition. The day before, the yoga instructor asked if I would lead the group of children in their yoga class that afternoon. I knew that these children were spiritual believers, so if this didn't work, then I would have seriously started to doubt myself.

"Okay Ma'am," they chimed.

"Okay, take a nice long inhale in through your nose, hold it, and let it out through your mouth."

The girls followed me, holding their breath as long as I did, letting it out through their mouths and releasing their bellies, sinking further into the shaded corner in which we sat.

"And once more, breathe in, hold, and let it out," I sang.

We did this three more times. Once we were finished, I turned my focus to the girl on my left and said, "Okay Yasmen, you tell me your story first, and then Akshaya can share her side." In my head I thought, 'I have to start somewhere, right?'

Yasmen immediately started crying as soon as I called on her. She sank down and put her head in her hands, rocking her body side to side. I sat in disbelief and silence that lasted for about 10 seconds. Finally, after what felt like five full minutes, she sat up, tucked her hair behind her ears, and took a long breath in.

"Ma'am," she sniffled, "I was playing the game that you taught us … the musical … uh …"

"Musical chairs,'" I chimed in.

"Yes, yes, I was playing musical chairs," she continued, "and the music stopped and I sat down on an open seat."

I nodded to let her know that I was following, and she continued on.

"And then she pushed me, Ma'am. She pushed me right out of the chair, and she hurt me Ma'am."

Akshaya sat in silence, shedding silent tears and waiting patiently for her turn to talk.

"Okay. Why don't you tell your side now," I said, turning my attention over to Akshaya.

I looked directly into her eyes, faced her completely, and waited patiently. She was silent as tears flowed down both of her cheeks, staring at the shady pavement with a blank look on her face. After a few seconds, I said, "I need your help understanding what happened. Can you help me understand?" The young girl looked up at me, sniffled, and gained a sense of self-control before speaking.

Finally, she said, "I didn't hit her, Ma'am." Shaking her head from side to side, more tears streamed down the sides of her cheeks. I could not believe how distraught both of the girls were over the fight. I tried my best to remain impartial, not giving one child more attention than the other. I nodded slowly, trying to interpret the musical chair fiasco, but the two stories I had heard did not seem to match up.

I Didn't Sign up for This

It occurred to me that without seeing the incident with my own eyes, I was in no position to decide who was the victim in this case. "I didn't sign up for this," I thought to myself. Frustration began to take over my body, until suddenly, I realized something: maybe I *did* not sign up for this. I could not control what was going on, I could not control the fact that I felt out of place, uncomfortable, and unsure of myself. What I could control, though, was my ability to make things better. "I can help here. I can help them make things better," I thought to myself, encouragingly.

I scooted forward, moving closer to the girls, and took a long inhale through my nose. The two girls took my lead and for the second time, followed my breathing. It was remarkable.

"Okay," I said, looking at one girl and then the other. "At school, we are all friends. We don't use hitting to solve problems. If we have an issue with a friend, we use our words to express what is going on. If we hit a friend instead of using our words, then it becomes an even bigger problem, and people's feelings get hurt. And do we want our friends' feelings to get hurt?"

The girls stared back at me. Silence.

"Is that what we want?" I repeated.

"No Ma'am," the two said in unison.

"I don't want that either. I want to have fun with you two! I miss seeing you smile. Wouldn't it be great if we could go back inside and have fun playing and dancing and smiling together?"

"Yes Ma'am," they said together.

"Okay. But before we can do anything, I need you two to shake hands and apologize for what happened. I need you both to apologize for making one another feel sad. Can you do that for me?"

With no hesitation, the two responded, "Yes Ma'am." Yasmen, who was sitting on my left, sat crossed legged with her arms folded across her chest. She sat up, moved her body towards her former enemy, and turned her frown into a smile.

"I am sorry for making you cry," she sniffled, and stuck out her right hand. Akshaya slid her hand against Yasmen's with no uncertainty, and locked eyes with her foe.

"I am sorry for making you cry," Akshaya repeated. The two stared at one another, locking eyes.

"Okay. Now are we ready to go back inside and have some more fun?" I said to the two.

"Yes Ma'am," they said. I stood up, and both girls stood on opposite sides of me, taking my hands into theirs and walking beside me back into the classroom.

"I did it!" I thought. I sat and cooled off in the classroom as the two girls rejoined the game of musical chairs, which was now narrowed down to only a few students. I drank water in the corner and reflected on what had just happened. It went unnoticed that the three of us went missing from the classroom; rather, when we re-entered, it was as if we'd been to the bathroom or taking a walk. Not one person in the room knew what had really happened. Even I didn't understand what had happened. And that's when it hit me: I have got to learn more about this stuff.

So That's What Doing Therapy is Like!

"I had my first therapy session today," I thought to myself as the day came to an end. Mediating Yasmen and Akshaya to resolve their problems seemed to come naturally to me. From a distance, I saw myself in the eyes of two second-grade Indian girls. I remember what it was like to feel jealous of a friend, insignificant, and unnoticed at school. I remember my teacher not intervening in the feud between a friend and me. At this school, I intervened as a result of my training, intuition, and experience. But as I sit here and reflect further, I ask myself how I knew to step in and take charge. Was it solely because of my experiences as a young girl? Did I feel overlooked as a child, and therefore feel a need to make up for this? I think this is part of the reason, but I also think that the idea of turning something that was so bad into something good intrigued me. It took little to no effort to make my way from one side of the room to the other. In just a few minutes, the three of us sat in the shape of a triangle and took turns talking. We communicated, listening to one another and processing our thoughts. In just a few minutes, we put trust in one another. In just a few minutes, the girls were open minded enough to put the past behind them and apologize. There was a mutual respect that filled the air. It was so *easy* to help them.

Taking It All In

A little after the incident I just described, I headed out to the playground to help supervise the children. I played with the boys in the back field for about two hours. We played catch with a rubber ball that was slit down the middle. They introduced me to the rest of their friends, one of whom in particular stood out to me. He looked similar to the rest of the group, but he sounded very different. Unable to pronounce any vowel sounds, the boy muttered with his mouth open, trying with all of his might to communicate with me the best he could.

"I'm sorry, " I said, "could you say that one more time?" It was hard enough to understand the children with their Indian accents, but with this boy, I had no clue what he was saying.

Finally one of the boys seemed to understand what he was saying and translated for me. "He said 'Hello Ma'am,' and that he welcomes you to our school."

"Oh," I said. I felt my cheeks immediately turn red. I wanted to travel back in time and somehow take back what had just happened. I bent down to the child's level, squinting from the sunlight hitting my eyes and said, "Hi. Thank you so much for your warm welcome. I am so happy to be here. We are going to have such a wonderful time." He smiled at me and extended his hand, placing it into mine, gripping my five fingers while looking, staring back at me.

I could not understand the disabled child's mumbling, and I felt ashamed because of that. I learned, though, that the boy was deaf. So in reality, since I was new, there was no way I could have understood him. Despite this, I quickly realized that the boy's friends translated for him as a form of guidance and love. They translated his message because they respected him, because they wanted to help him. They normalized his behavior and supported him. Not once did they make fun of him. Never did they laugh or point or make him feel like an outsider. Instead, they listened to him. And without question, they looked up at me, a complete stranger, and interpreted the message to me. It was an experience that has touched me and will stay with me forever. It was so beautiful, and I walked away from the cricket game with tears in my eyes.

It became clear to me why I was at the school. More than anything, these kids needed nurturance and guidance. They were screaming for attention and love. All they wanted to do was to play with me, hold my hand, show me things, learn from me. The day before, after I had finished with my impromptu yoga class, I stood by the door with my hands by my chest, quietly saying "Namaste" to each child that exited the room, honoring them in the most respectful way possible. I would lower my upper body and face, bowing down to each child, and they would mirror me, doing the same thing. I will never forget when the first child released his hands from prayer position and suddenly wrapped his arms around my body. He held it no longer than five seconds. The next child came just seconds later. This child, however, was not in line to bow down to me or to thank me with her words. She stood in line simply to receive a hug. She wrapped her arms around me and I did the same to her, and we locked eyes as we let go of one another.

The next thing I knew, there was a line to the back of the room of children waiting, patiently, for a hug from their new yoga instructor. I felt so full of love by the time I hugged each child. I felt like this is what I needed to be doing, helping children who needed it the most. I locked eyes with each child that said goodbye to me, wanting to remember everything about each of them, but knowing deep down how quickly memories fade. I felt a rush of emotions fill me as I wrapped my arms around the kids, children who were strangers to me just three days before. It is a moment I will never forget.

Goodbyes

Saying goodbye to the children was one of the most difficult things I've had to do. Three girls wrote notes for me to read once I had left. One read, "I miss you, Jas. Please come. I love you. I love you. I love you, Jas." I cried when I read her note. The sense of reciprocity that took over the school was so overwhelming. The children that I got to know had every reason to be sad and upset, given their life circumstances of poverty and extreme deprivation. I learned that many of them came from very dark backgrounds of abuse and neglect. Some lived with extended family members because their parents passed away from a major tsunami years ago. The school was a special place that will stay with me forever. I cannot stop thinking about the children who are now a part of me. They expressed their gratitude and appreciation to me, and said thank you over and over again. On the inside, though, I was the one who was thanking them for what they taught me. I learned about the power of kindness

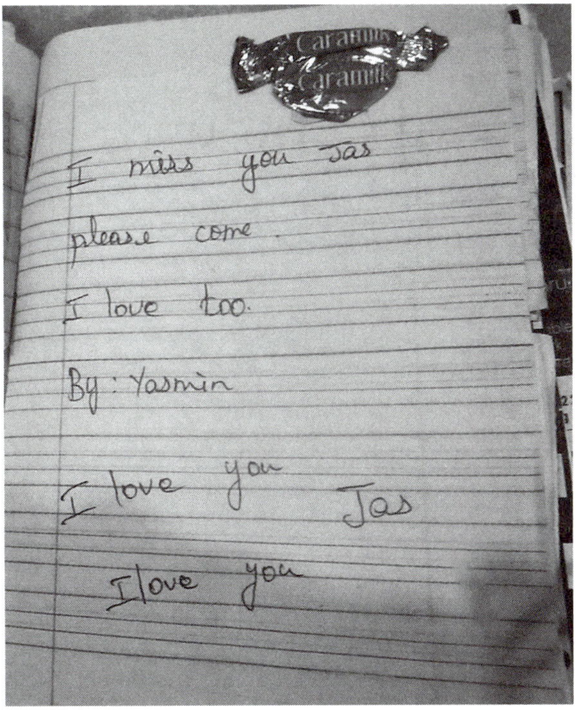

PHOTO 5.2   A letter of goodbye from one of the girls

and compassion, and how little it takes to make a difference in the lives of some people who have so little in the first place.

Love Grows by Giving

Although I am a student and a beginner, a wannabe therapist if you will, these are some of the things that I learned. By challenging myself to step outside of my normal routine, growth occurred in so many unexpected ways. I broke down my usual barriers and ventured way from what is familiar and comfortable. I faced adversity and felt a sense of guilt and shame because of the privileges that I enjoy, from which so many others are excluded. Yet I left feeling a greater simplicity about my life. I know much more than I give myself credit for, and I learned how easy it is to do good. While playing with the children, I received just as much love as I gave.

For me, it's the little things that add up to some really big things. Holding people, metaphorically and literally, makes a difference. It is possible to do a lot in a very short amount of time. This is so easy to do: anywhere, any time, any place. All you need to do is show up, open your heart, ask people what they need most, ask them to teach you, and be fully present.

6

SOCIAL JUSTICE—THE WAY LESS TRAVELED

Henry Sibbing

All religions seem to be based on social justice. During my religious training it was evident that Christianity certainly espouses concepts of social justice. It seems to me that Jesus spoke of social justice when he said, "Amen, I say to you, whatever you did for one of these least brothers of mine, you did for me." Under John Wesley's direction, Methodists became leaders in many social justice issues of the day, including prison reform and abolitionism movements. The Buddha speaks of compassion and reminds us that others are full of suffering. *The Quran* contains numerous references to elements of social justice. One of Islam's Five Pillars is *Zakat*, or alms giving. Charity and assistance to the poor—concepts central to social justice—are important parts of the Islamic faith.

I believe that the term "social justice" encompasses a thought process that includes making changes in the world that uplift and "make better" the plight of those less fortunate. I make note of this since I believe that most, if not all, human beings have a notion of "social justice" within their psyche, if only from their religious experience. I feel fortunate to have my religious training, but the skills and insights from my counseling training also help me in my day-to-day interactions with neighbors, associates, employees, or the world outside the clinic. I have used all of these tools as a City Attorney to better solve problems at the local City Council meetings, collective bargaining meetings, and other secular encounters in which societal problems are being discussed and solutions sought. In these places, many of us can bring our spiritual selves into daily living. This chapter explores how I apply my legal and counseling training to social justice in my community.

My Way Less Traveled

I was brought up as a Catholic and went to Catholic parochial grade and high school, both of which were taught by nuns of the Order Sisters of Charity. Even their name spoke of social justice. I then attended Marquette University, a Jesuit institution. The Jesuits were founded by St. Ignatius of Loyola in 1540 and espouse much of his Catholic religious teaching, philosophy, and intellectual curiosity. My parochial educational background perhaps explains why I have always felt the concept of social justice to be a part of my philosophical and psychosocial fabric. Many people feel an inner need to "make the world a better place" or "fulfill their purpose" and wonder about the etiology of those yearnings. It could be the "natural law" of Thomas Aquinas poking its way through the crust of modern economic and material indoctrination within my innermost spirit. I majored in philosophy and did my final thesis on the natural law as seen by Aquinas. He taught that there was a natural law in the universe that guided our basic understanding of right and wrong. Or it could simply be a manifestation of my social and religious training from my parents during childhood. In either case, there seems to be a sense of justice and fairness in me that I carry into my professional roles as a therapist, lawyer, and judge.

The story of my social justice work outside the clinical setting was greatly influenced by my friend/mentor in the counseling field. The two of us have shared so much of our personal lives with each other, raising our children and pursuing our respective careers and being neighbors in the same small town in southern Wisconsin. Ironically enough, we started our professional relationship by exchanging clients. As a lawyer I represented men and women in the courtroom that were going through bitter divorce actions that often involved child custody issues. My friend would often be called in to give a professional opinion on custody/placement for my court presentations or see clients when trouble entered their life. He would refer clients to me when his formidable skills in the field of marriage and family counseling were not enough to save the marriage. Over a period of 20 years, I repeatedly found myself trying to use in my legal practice counseling skills I learned from my friend to try to either save the marriage or at the very least instill in the parties the need to develop post-divorce parenting skills to ensure that children received loving and competent attention from both parents. Post-divorce childrearing/placement issues have always been daunting and often nasty, but they are an extremely important task in the field of marriage and family law.

Over time, I found myself more interested in developing the skills of a counselor rather than those of a lawyer. My spirit and soul were much more comfortable with the healing profession. I soon discovered, to my chagrin, that the legal profession is not one of healing.

There are certain watershed moments that direct the path of each person's life. It is not unusual for several such events to present themselves over a lifetime. I can identify five turning points that defined the course of my journey.

What I was Born Into

The first occurred when I was born into a family that valued religious beliefs, education, and a strong work ethic. Those three attributes formed the basis for most important decisions I have made in my life. In addition I knew my parents, who provided an intact family throughout my youth, loved me unconditionally. I was also born into the world with an e-ticket (i.e., I mean the original one from the early years of Disneyland, where the admission fee came with three e-tickets to the best rides in the park). My e-ticket was the fact that I was born a white male in America—a heritage that gave me great privileges, all explicitly unknown to me until my counselor education provided an awareness of the gifts of my social position. I was, and continue to be, clearly advantaged in a country that rewards and favors those with an enhanced social position, economic independence, and political influence. As I have grown older, I have become aware of social justice principles and issues that identify unfairness and injustice for those who are seriously marginalized from birth with respect to these unearned gifts.

Early Marriage and Becoming a Family Man

The second major event was my early marriage and starting a family while I was an undergraduate. This was a turning point, since I began my adult life at age 19 with serious responsibility and economic challenge. My task from that time on was to continue my education and earn enough money to provide the necessities for a family of two adults and four children. This struggle led to becoming a lawyer, since it seemed like the only real skills I possessed had to do with reading, writing, and talking—the skills that defined the profession.

At age 20 I began working in a paper mill in southern Ohio, working the third shift and going to classes in the morning at Miami University of Ohio. When a job in the sales department opened up I was transferred along with my family to Los Angeles. I worked days and completed my undergraduate work at the University of Southern California at night. Corporate politics required me to become a "yes" man—which I never was very good at. There was always a compass inside of me that let me know when I was heading in the wrong direction, as well as a voice inside of me that required me to speak out when I saw what I felt was injustice. This combination was not conducive to being a good corporate team player, at least in the 1960s. So I decided to apply to a law school that allowed me to work days and go to classes at night.

Loss of My Father and New Direction

Not long after I began my law school studies, two memorable events occurred: my father's early death (age 59) of cancer and starting a job with Xerox Corporation. I was 27 years old and in my second year of law school. My father was a special man—quite spiritual and a good man, in every sense of the word. He and I were very close, but because he and my mother lived in Ohio and I in Los Angeles we were not able to spend much time together in the 5–6 years prior to his passing. I always thought there would be time for us to finally "catch up" —sort of a *Cats in the Cradle* situation that was very sad for me. He worked for a large corporation that frankly treated him quite unfairly it seemed, as he gave seven days a week as manager of their shoe stores—very underpaid with no pension. I left his funeral with much bitterness and anger. I vowed to repay him for instilling his great social values in me. I thought being a lawyer would allow me to bring a bit of social justice to the world!

Before completing my law school studies, however, I faced a major decision. The paper company decided they wanted me back in Ohio, but I could not return, as I was already two years into my law school studies. I gave the paper company my notice, looked for a new job, and unexpectedly landed a job with Xerox as a paper specialist.

I graduated from law school in 1975 and passed the California bar in June that year; I was 31 years old. However, my working days and going to school nights took a toll on my marriage. It was the 1970s: "Women's Lib" was in full bloom, and my wife quite rightfully identified with the basic tenets of the movement. She began to feel her life purpose was somewhere outside of the home. We went our separate ways—I wanted to take responsibility for the children, so I was awarded physical custody of four children aged 5–12: two boys and two girls. I left California to return to the Midwest, where I thought I would have a better chance of raising four children as a single parent.

I began working 10–12 hours per day as a sole practitioner in my new law office as the City Attorney of a small community in the Midwest. I shortly thereafter met a woman who was also a single parent who shared many of my values. She was willing to take on the responsibilities of four children, and I certainly needed help with my parental duties. We moved in together and were living as a blended family. There was fun, hard work, and a bright future for all until my new wife's young child was tragically killed in a school bus accident a block from our home. This was the third major event that changed the course of my life—all of our lives—as our innocence was gone forever. The world would never be a safe place after that loss. It took my wife eight years to learn to laugh again. I was 41 when this happened. Many marriages do not survive such an event due to the extreme grief that besets parents, but I was determined to make our marriage work and dedicated my time to doing all I could to support her during this terrible time. We were able to think clearly enough to come to a decision to have another child, and this child proved to be the healing salve that allowed us to begin our lives anew.

Heart Problems, Another Change of Direction, and a New Heart

At age 46 I suffered a major heart attack and was left with significant heart muscle damage (ejection fraction less than 20). My cardiologists described me as a four-engine airplane that could still fly, just not as high as before. I was also told that I had to keep what was left of my heart muscle as strong as possible—exercise and a healthy diet was mandatory. A friend came to my aid by buying me a pair of running shoes and telling me, "We are going to run a marathon this spring." It was slow going for a while. The old saying "you have to crawl before you run" was never truer than in my case. At the beginning I was afraid to walk to the Post Office, which was a block from my home, for fear I would have another heart attack and die on the street. My friend and I walked a block at a time for weeks until I was walking a mile, then by myself, then running a block—and so on until I was able to run 5 miles. We did eight Lake Geneva marathons together from 1992 to 2000.

During this time I realized that working as an attorney was having a negative impact on my life. I managed to provide for a large family's material needs, but my work did not nourish my heart. It was killing me. I began my studies in the counselor education program in the fall of 2001 when I was 55 years old. I had planned on completing my program in two years, and pushed hard to get in as many classes as possible while working full time as a lawyer and part time as Municipal Judge. I pushed too hard, and while attending the first meeting of my Appraisals class I had a sudden cardiac death experience and was paddled back to life by the campus police with their newly acquired portable defibrillators. I survived this and was able to complete the Master's program when I was 59 years old. The following year I became a Licensed Professional Counselor in the State of Wisconsin. A few months later I suffered my second and most serious heart attack while at work at a dual-diagnosis clinic in Milwaukee. I was just about to begin the Monday morning group session when my chest once again felt like it had a giant rubber band squeezing it. I knew what was happening and had the receptionist drive me to the nearest hospital. That was the last straw—the damage now was so extensive that I developed congestive heart failure to the extent that breathing was nearly impossible. A heart transplant was the only solution if I was to be able to continue my work as a therapist. On Halloween Eve and the morning of All Saints Day in 2002, I received the gift of life from a 35-year-old man who died from meningitis. Words cannot express this experience. It has been nine years now, and it is only this past year that I have been able to fully reap the benefits of this gift.

Social Justice in the Courtroom

My main work—the judgeship—has become the source of my opportunities to practice social justice. The duties of a Municipal Judge include presiding over Juvenile Court. This is a time set aside each month to hear cases brought against children under the age of 17. These are violations of the law that include truancy, drug possession, underage alcohol use, disorderly conduct, curfew violations, etc. It is a chance for me to interact with the students and young people in my community who are struggling with meeting the expectations of teachers, parents, and the law about their behavior. These students are from a variety of ethnic and economic backgrounds. They have made decisions to engage in certain socially unacceptable conduct or are not fully participating in the academic programs for a variety of reasons. In court, the reasons for their behavior come together with my counselor training and my judicial duties as I perceive them. It is my duty as a judge to be fair and just, yet it is also my training as a counselor to be empathic, compassionate, sincere, authentic, and insightful—and to be a source of hope. When you think about it, are these not the qualities a good judge should have as well?

There are a number of aspects of my counselor training and education that provided helpful skills for carrying out the duties and responsibilities of a judge. As I progressed through graduate school, I formed an opinion that every judge should be given a mini-counseling education course along with their judicial college courses. There is a lot more to being a judge than knowing the law. Judges are asked to evaluate individuals as to their rehabilitative needs and abilities. This means knowing the whys and roots of their behavior. Counseling skills are incredibly valuable in unearthing the causes of the misbehavior that has resulted in law violations. Social service workers provide pre-sentence investigations to the Circuit Court Judges in criminal matters. These adjunct tools are not available to Municipal Judges, as we deal with civil infractions (ordinance violations, or first offenders if you will). Yet it is the Municipal Judge who sees the youthful offender for the first time. Youthful offenders in my court are aged 10

PHOTO 6.1 Justice Henry Sibbing

(middle school) to 17 (high school age), and it is the initial appearance in court for that young person and his family. I believe it is the ideal time to make an early intervention into the thinking, attitude, and behavior before conduct results in serious criminal offenses and a criminal record that seriously damages lives. I see time after time the downward spiral of youthful offenders who, once they get into the criminal justice system, have a hard time getting free of it. Therefore I see the role of Municipal Judges as very special and unique to the entire spectrum of criminal justice: we have a unique opportunity to really make a difference in a young person's life.

It has long been my mission statement to do all I can to prevent the child before me and their parents from continuing to engage in conduct that will lead them into the criminal justice system and eventually jail. However, recidivism rates are high. The criminal justice system is relatively easy to get into, and very hard to get out of. Once an individual is in the criminal system, a record is created that is often a difficult burden to carry and still be successful in a society that places a great emphasis on clean records for employment, schooling, and even public service volunteer work. Therefore a part of my work in the Juvenile Court is to impress upon those who appear before me the seriousness of the fact that they are in a court of law.

How I Work to Create Real Change

I begin the court sessions with a 15-minute introduction, which includes the fact that this is a serious matter now that they are before a judge in a court of law. I explain the possible consequences of their actions if they are found guilty of the charges against them, including the loss of driving privileges—now I really have their attention.

Then I begin to explain that my mission statement in this court is to develop new skills, attitudes, and goals that will enable them to avoid the criminal justice system. I explain to both the student and their parents that I am going to suggest new ways of doing things that may alter their current outlook on school, life, and their future. I reiterate that my main objective is to see them succeed! At this point the student is often perplexed, as this is certainly not what they expected. Many juveniles come into court expecting to be yelled at and punished for doing something wrong—treated the same they have always been treated both at home and at school: scolded, punished, demeaned, warned, intimidated, not listened to, rejected as a failure, as incompetents—viewed as perhaps even incorrigible. I don't see them that way; instead, I choose to see their potential.

As a judge in the Municipal Court, I may be the last stopgap prior to an extended anti-social and/or criminal behavior lifestyle that results in incarceration in a penal institution. It is for this reason that I willingly use every skill and asset at my disposal to prevent these young people from going further down the path of self-destruction. I see my counseling education as my most important and effective tool in turning perhaps a few of these young lives around. While my legal education gives me knowledge of the law, my counselor education helps me understand and evaluate the students as individuals, not merely as perpetrators. In such an evaluation process I can apply certain counseling benefits by using active listening, genuine caring, and providing a sense of hope to those who are able to benefit from my lectures from the bench.

Of course, one thing that a judge gets to do is lecture, though I do try to make my lectures more egalitarian. There are ethical guidelines that every judge must follow when speaking to defendants about the case. Respect, civility, compassion, and truthfulness are just a few of the qualities a judge must exhibit when addressing a person who is receiving a sentence. A proactive judge can also impart some bits of wisdom to young people who seem to be in need of direction. I use this time to share some of the wisdom I have acquired over the 68 years of my life. I often self-disclose as a way to build a bridge between us. For the student who feels that smoking cigarettes is cool, I share my story of being addicted to nicotine for over 20 years, only to be rocked by a heart attack at age 46—a condition directly related to smoking that led to an eventual heart transplant. I review with admitted gang members the evidence that most gang members end up in prison within a few years after high school. I examine the lifestyle of students who choose to violate the school rules and fail to take advantage of the many activities available to them at the multi-million dollar state-of-the-art high school the community has provided for them. I share my own story: that I was not especially enamored with the scholastic rigors of high school, but I really enjoyed going to school so that I could have fun with my friends, play sports, and meet girls. I explain that I went to school to have fun. Along the way I had to earn decent grades in order to have this fun, and ironically, when I did get good grades that itself turned out to be more fun—my parents were more permissive and the teachers patted me on that back, which felt good as well. I note that school is also a good business decision—students with high school diplomas make a lot more money than inmates in jail! The point of all this is to "reframe" their experience. To be clear, while doing my judging/counseling, I am also imposing a certain amount of financial burden in the way of fines and loss of privileges. However, I give students a chance to do community service to work off fines and often will reduce fines or eliminate them altogether if they attain a B average on their next report card or successfully complete a counseling program.

The traditional method of dealing with youthful offenders has been a bit of "accountability" with a serious amount of punishment thrown in: a "spare the rod and spoil the child" mentality. I have always been an advocate of accountability. However, punishment in the form of physical pain or incarceration has limited and short-term success. It seems suited in cases that require protecting the community from violent or destructive behavior. Yet that approach often exacerbates a mental or emotional problem that leads to more misconduct followed by more punishment—a never-ending spiral of dysfunction ensues. I employ the concepts of accountability and reformation in my courtroom when addressing youth offenders who are found guilty of non-violent minor offenses (i.e., possession of marijuana, underage use of alcohol, and truancy). Accountability comes in the form of a monetary penalty (fine/forfeiture) that can be paid in cash or worked off by doing community service. I have partnered with our local street department and fire department, and they accept referrals from my court to offer offenders the opportunity to work off their obligations to the city by doing community service for the city. I see this as a form of restorative justice, meaning simply that the offenders are asked to give back to society in a constructive way that results in repaying or restoring the "victim" (in this case the community) to a suitable wholeness. This contribution of community service is also a form of social justice, in the sense that offenders of relatively minor offenses are dealt with in a human-istic manner that emphasizes the restoration of their well-being in concert with the social welfare of the community. Adler refers to this as social interest. I believe that many in my courtroom have been given the message that they are useless and cannot be part of the community, and that punitive approaches embitter—rather than empower—the offender. My work is about bringing people back to the community, not pushing them further away.

I spend a great deal of time and energy talking to students who are before me for truancy about why they are failing to take advantage of the many opportuni-ties for fun and personal growth by attending school. We have a conversation about what obstacles are preventing them from enjoying the pleasure that results from achievement. I effectively listen to what they say and often ask if they are afraid to go to school. They are surprised that a judge would ask such a question. I ask because often children do not go to school because they are fearful for one reason or another while at school. From time to time I hear stories of bully-ing—stories they have thus far been afraid to tell. I have the school liaison officers with me, which allows for investigations and resolution of these bullying issues. I am always hopeful that bullying situations will be addressed in a professional, expeditious, and compassionate manner.

As part of the "sentence," I have developed a "hold open" program in truancy cases, which allows students to earn back the $450.00 fine that is imposed. For every day the student is at school they earn $7.00 towards repaying that fine. This program is intended to work as an incentive for the students to change their behavior by increasing their motivation.

What I See: A Typical Night

Most of the young people who come before me in Juvenile Court have serious mental health issues that have been neglected or overlooked. Many come from disadvantaged homes in one way or another, or homes in which there are unad-dressed psychosocial issues. I often see low-income single parents with many financial obligations, and they seem unable to provide the time and effort it takes to meet all of the child's material and psychological needs. I see married couples going through difficult times in their own lives (e.g., illness, unemployment, divorce, drug or alcohol addictions) and they are unable to meet their children's needs for guidance, encouragement, spiritual guidance, and a hopeful anticipation of a future. Schools are not able to address these types of circumstantial or situational problems. They do not have the financial or personnel resources to provide the essentials of social and educational training/upbringing that some children fail to obtain at home. Role models of acceptable and positive behavior are absent from some children's lives, through no fault of their own. As a result, children from homes with insufficient human and financial resources are the most likely to fail to meet the standards expected of them in both school and the broader community.

Last evening, I held Student Court and there were three cases. The first case involved a 14-year-old Hispanic boy who has been on my court docket every month for a year. I am getting familiar with him. He is a freshman in high school, but simply cannot seem to get into the school/education mode. His life is somewhat representative of other young Hispanic males who are living in a home in which both parents speak little or no English, and they each work two jobs in order to make ends meet. His parents are seldom home to provide structure or discipline. He is left to fend for himself, and frankly, he has done okay in terms of self-preservation. Yet he spends time with groups of similarly situated children, and they are repeatedly the subject of police contact for minor offenses (e.g., trespassing, smoking, underage alcohol, truancy, etc). This particular young man is good looking, intelligent, personable, and respectful in court. He has over $500 in fines sitting over his head that I have allowed him to work off with community service, but he just refuses to put forth the required effort to meet this obligation, and every month he comes to court with the same excuse: "I don't know why—just didn't have time." He comes to court by himself, saying each time his parents can't come because they are working. Interestingly, this young man has never missed a court appearance. He seems to enjoy the colloquy that we have about his life. Upon reflection, it seems as if he is purposefully not completing his community service so that he can come into court and have a conversation with me. Maybe I'm the only adult who listens to him and is available to have a conversation with him? Maybe these court appearances are the only meaningful efforts of his month? I will keep that in mind the next time we meet—once again I gave him another 60 days to complete his community service, and I wouldn't be surprised if he has another habitual truancy ticket by the next court date. I once again told him that I liked him and had confidence he could succeed in school and community service if he tried; he smiled in agreement and as he left, saying he would improve by next time—we'll see.

The next situation involved a young woman who was sighted for disorderly conduct involving a fight. She sat in front of me with an expression that told me that she would fight me if I said the wrong thing to her. Interestingly, her father had a similar expression and seemed to be just waiting to pounce on me if I said anything about his daughter that displeased him. Their body language told me there were anger management issues going on in this family. I knew immediately to tread lightly if I was to keep a lid on the emotions of this father/daughter duo. I quizzed the young lady on why she chose to fight the other girl. She explained that the girl was saying disparaging remarks about her mother, accusing her of being a prostitute and a slut. So she just grabbed her and began striking and choking her—not letting up until a vice-principal had to physically break it up by pulling her off. I inquired about her past and asked if this was the first fight she had ever been in, and her reply was no. There were several other times, all of which occurred when someone said something to her that appeared to be insulting or pejorative. The father seemed surprised at this revelation of prior incidents. I suggested that there was a pattern developing, and that attention should be given to this apparent lack of social skills in handling unpleasant or threatening remarks from friends or fellow students. I suggested anger management counseling for the student and family counseling to the father, and he agreed that this would be a good idea. I sensed that this young lady's narcissistic tendency might soon change to a more social interest outlook as she learned more about her ability to communicate her feelings rather than just express her anger through fighting. I felt comfortable that my counseling training and courtroom intervention would result in a positive counseling experience with a qualified clinic and a much happier school experience for her. I suspect the father may have learned something about his own reaction to people who annoyed or threatened him. As I saw him nod his head in agreement with what I was saying to his daughter, I sensed that he was learning something about his own attitude as well. A family intervention disguised as a court appearance! Go figure!

The last case involved a young man who appeared in court with both parents: a pleasant-looking husband and wife flanking a tall, muscular, quiet young man wearing a sad and forlorn expression. The school liaison officer explained that the young man had not attended school for almost two semesters now—especially noticeable after being made ineligible to play baseball due to poor grades last spring. I questioned the young man regarding this coincidence, and he explained that his dad had coached him in baseball ever since he was a small boy in various leagues. It was apparent that the baseball aspect defined the father-son bond to a very large degree. I sensed a deep sadness that I thought might have developed as he felt he had let his father down by becoming ineligible to play baseball. The depression increased as the truancy continued, since the school rules required passing grades to play sports, and a true dilemma had developed. The boy saw no way out of this dilemma—and no point in going to school if he was not allowed to play baseball. The school liaison officer came to the rescue by suggesting several programs that the student could enter that would allow him to recoup his good standing in school in time to restore his eligibility by next spring's practice, when he would be a junior. I asked him, "Imagine you were playing baseball next spring. How would your life be different, and what would you be doing?" We talked a bit about this potential future. Upon hearing that there were options out of this dilemma, his entire demeanor changed and a huge smile appeared on his face. It was awesome to see the immediate transformation when the young man was given hope. The parents walked out of the courtroom with a "thank you" and smiles on their faces. This was indeed a case in which pushing or punishing a child when he was down was not the best or appropriate way to get positive behavior change. I was able to create a possible solution that was similar to what a solution-focused therapist might do.

Frustrations, Challenges, and Obstacles

Not all who observe my work in the courtroom are pleased by my approach. There are some in the law enforcement community who have criticized my work as being "soft" on criminals and too "touchy feely." Some in law enforcement overtly supported a candidate against me in the last election who ran on a platform of judicial toughness. This opponent publicly professed that jail was the appropriate punishment for teen miscreants. I maintained my independence on this issue, and fortunately I won the election by 14 votes (out of several thousand)! I was pleased that the community chose a judge who was trying to help teens overcome difficulties over one who felt that jail was the best behavior modification tool.

The closeness in this last election points to the fact that many believe jail is the best and only way to effectively deal with those who break the rules. This attitude has permeated the criminal justice field for over 30 years now, to the extent that most jails are bulging and taxpayer coffers are barren. Society can no longer afford more jails, or the assets needed to run and manage them. Our local county has emphatically stated that they will not build a new two million dollar addition to the new jail facility that was built only 10 years ago. They are now looking at alternatives to sentencing that include intensive counseling in drug and alcohol courts as a part of the sentence. There is a growing awareness that society can no longer afford to merely warehouse violators of the law. There must be a more enlightened way to address our growing prison population.

There are other obstacles that arise in my work that are disappointing. One obstacle remains the resistance of law enforcement to adopting a policy of cooperation with the court's efforts to change behavior rather than a policy that emphasizes punishment. An example of this is the failure to support a home detention program I am trying to use to enforce my efforts to get students to attend school. When a student refuses to cooperate with my suggestions, I inform them that I have the ability to order a home detention period of confinement—perhaps two to three weeks until I see an improvement in grades. The program requires an officer to check on the student's home from time to time to ensure compliance. The police department has been reluctant to commit officers to this program, citing budget problems. This detention program is nothing more than the old-fashioned school detention or parental "grounding" imposition that was a part of my childhood. It seems like a powerful incentive to compliance. Schools no longer have the ability to provide after-school detention, and some parents cannot enforce home rules with their children due to lack of resolve or fear. So the court has the ability to resurrect this form of encouragement, but is faced with budget constraints.

Not Done Yet

A few years ago I was thinking of retiring. I was about to advise the city of my non-candidacy, when I literally "bumped" into a lady in a parking lot. When she recognized who I was, she quickly thanked me profusely for the work I did with her son in the courtroom. She explained that he took my words of encouragement seriously, finished high school and was now serving in the Army overseas— she was very proud of her son's accomplishments. I decided on the spot that my place in the universe was in this courtroom, helping one child at a time.

Just a week ago, an older man stopped me on the street and thanked me for the work I had done for his son when he was charged with drug possession as teenager. A component of the counseling effort I give the students has an option of participating in an Alcohol and Other Drug Abuse assessment and follow-up program, which includes enrolling in a Community College Drug Awareness course. If successfully completed, I dismiss the citation, leaving the student with a clear record. The man proudly reported to me that his son was a senior at a local university and doing very well, but most importantly, he felt his son was drug-free.

There is not a court session in which I am unable to provide some counseling-type interventions that address inherent psychosocial issues that, once addressed, improve school behavior and instill hope for a positive school and family experience. In so many cases, children who are failing in school just need someone who believes in them and is willing and able in some way to say to the student: "I genuinely care about you." Being a counselor has taught me the importance of conveying that compassion and care. I always walk out of the courthouse with a feeling of accomplishment that I very seldom felt as a lawyer. With these success stories appearing as often as they do, I will continue my work as a counselor/judge for as long as I am able—it is a part of my life's purpose.

PART III
Community Action

7

SACRED ADVOCACY

Helping At-Risk Boys and Girls Find Meaning in Violent, Unjust Communities

Stan Bosch and Joseph M. Cervantes

Gang intervention with at-risk youth has been a sizeable topic that has had numerous cited references over the last half century. That writing has primarily been found in the disciplines of sociology, social work, and gang intervention. As authors of this chapter, we have viewed mental health practice with this disempowered group of adolescents as both a professional and a spiritual calling. This calling that we now name *sacred advocacy* refers to the intrinsic relationship that exists with children and adolescents who have experienced daily threats and incidents of violence (i.e., micro & macro-aggressions) and subsequently, a deterioration of the soul. The impact of these continuous ravages of one's personhood has contributed to the need for psychological intervention and the innate wisdom of spirituality, given that the majority of "at-risk youth" in inner city programs continues to be Latina/o and African American (Cervantes & Parham, 2005).

In order to understand the context of our involvement with at-risk youth, I (Stan) as program director will briefly describe the intervention vehicle. The Gang Reduction and Youth Development Program (GRYD) of the City of Los Angeles is part of an intensive effort to foster youth development and reduce the influence of street gangs in the lives of our youth. There are 12 targeted zones where we focus our efforts and provide both intervention and prevention services. I (Stan) work with Soledad Enrichment Action, Inc. (SEA), which consists of 19 charter schools and intervention programs that target "at-risk" and gang-involved youth. SEA serves as the lead agency in six of the 12 GRYD zones, providing community-based gang intervention and individualized services. The core of its overarching strategy is to build and maintain a "Peace Infrastructure" throughout the Los Angeles area. This Peace Infrastructure is defined as systemic relationships that prevent, stop, or minimize gang violence. The staff of this program provides a variety of violence prevention and peace maintenance services, and offers individualized services to help adolescents exit gang life. The services include: street-based intervention, school-based intervention, neighborhood interfacing, and community engagement. Individualized service provisions attend to as many as 50 gang members (14–25 years old) in each of the six GRYD areas. Elements include: a) clinical case management designed to help participating students create an individualized life plan that defines the problems locking them into gang life and the support that will facilitate their liberation from a violent lifestyle; b) psychotherapy and mentoring to provide grief relief counseling for PTSD and complex trauma, chemical recovery, parenting effectiveness, family violence, trauma relief, behavioral changes, etc; and c) job training and placement, job finding and maintenance skills, resume writing, interview skills, workplace decorum, and problem solving.

This comprehensive approach is intent on changing conditions that have fueled nearly 400 gangs and 41,000 active gang members by supporting its core mission of establishing safe, clearly identified places where at-risk youth and their families can receive unconditional support, services, and counseling. Targeting communities with high levels of gang crime with a strategy that is as tough on crime as it is on the root causes of crime, the innovative approach complements suppression with data-driven prevention and intervention services that aim to end cycles of gang violence for healing and peace.

Our experiences with this distinctive yet vulnerable group of adolescents, who have been targeted almost from birth to struggle with life, will be discussed within two interwoven voices. The first author (Stan) is a program director, and the second author (Jose) is a consultant with significant prior experience with this population. We have been humbled by the challenges that have typically defined these adolescents involving poverty, gang membership or affiliation, often marginal or homeless existence, preponderance of illegal drugs in the neighborhood, and chronic failure in academic performance. Our discussion of these experience is divided into the following sections that highlight primary aspects of sacred advocacy practice: initiation and gangster affiliation; union, recovery, and healing; reaffirmation in a loving Jesus: encounters of spirituality and psychological first aid; developing mindfulness and peace in a violence-prone world; and implications for social justice counseling.

Personal and Professional Interests

As a Catholic priest (Stan) and pastor of two churches in Compton, CA (a neighbor of Watts and South Los Angeles) for 12 years, I found myself fatigued, frustrated, and increasingly depressed by the numbers of young gang-involved boys and girls that I would visit in trauma units who had been wounded in neighborhood violence. I lost count of how many teenagers I have buried as a result of the gang wars. Furthermore, I could not continue to maintain an ecclesial infrastructure and attempt to awaken a local community that lives with complacency and

PHOTO 7.1   Good friends Stan Bosch and José Cervantes lean on each other in their difficult work

in the paralysis of anxiety and dread: afraid of their own neighbors, and terrified by their own children.

I experienced a deep inner call to shift my energies from maintaining communities in a church structure to facilitating a sacred therapeutic space where young gang-involved kids could begin to discover what had been hidden and repressed: the capacity to experience and give life in the midst of violence. It has been a journey in solidarity with those who experience extreme trauma, having had to continue to work through my sister's violent death when we were in high school, and growing up with a mentally retarded adopted brother while my mother shut down emotionally. In therapy, it is about awakening the unconscious resources of the soul (psyche) for justice's sake, not about escaping into a world of denial in fear.

Having accompanied a myriad of families who have mourned the death of their young to gang violence, I was compelled to begin Doctoral studies in psychology as a holy and healing endeavor. My return to school convinced me of the need to contextualize my lived personal experience of violence and destruction within solid research and theory. It became something of an archetype of initiation (re-initiation) into the study and practice of healing the psyche that I had begun with a Master's degree in Clinical Psychology before my graduate theology studies years ago. These past several years as a psychotherapist working with gang members and their families reflects the belief and the experience that there is hope in creating holding communities with previously broken families, and certainly in a therapeutic relationship in which young men and women may learn to express their emotions and discover unnamed longings and dreams in order to act with confidence in a violence-free future. I have witnessed the beginning of transformation in the lives of numerous adolescents, because of the therapeutic alliance and in partnership with intervention workers and wraparound relationships in case management that I never experienced, even as a leader, in organized religion.

I (Jose) have long been invested in understanding and assisting adolescents who have difficulties with the court system and have involved themselves in group affiliations or gang activity. I had two older half brothers who were leaders of Latino gangs in the 1950s who were grooming me for similar participation as a young child. Active family of origin involvement and my own determination to go beyond the stereotyped and prejudicial attitudes of my elementary school teachers were critical saving graces for me. A salient aspect of my own developmental trajectory moved me to study for the Catholic priesthood for several years; I eventually left and completed graduate school in psychology. My interest has always been in helping children who are less fortunate, particularly at-risk children and teenagers who have experienced less than a foundational start in their lives. Involvement in the current program stems from a long history of being watchful, self-aware, and feeling the pull of social justice participation with this vulnerable population. Wanting to make a difference in the lives of these adolescents, despite the dangers, has complemented a long ingrained social responsibility, now renamed sacred advocacy, to our neighborhoods and communities.

Initiation and Gangster Affiliation

Psychological practice with at-risk youth, particularly adolescents who have hit the bottom of the barrel relative to the available support system, has been a particular challenge in our experience. A primary psychological mindset we have witnessed with these juveniles has been a lack of self-value or self-confirmation, which has contributed to delinquent behaviors or motivated them to form gang affiliations, given that other gang members provide them with recognition. In addition, we have learned that many of these adolescent behaviors have been prompted by negative self-perceptions that have been socialized through parental neglect or abuse. My experience (Stan), in particular, after involvement with this level of at-risk youth for over 25 years, has found that gangs often provide these kids with the opportunity to obtain respect, power, recognition, affiliation, and love. Consequently, these young people are continuously searching for a sense of self by joining a gang, which helps support a developing identity primarily influenced by an emotional space that needs mending from the onslaught of familial and neighborhood violence.

We have also noticed that these castaway youth have a strong need for a rite of passage: a ritual or event to acknowledge their transition from childhood to adulthood. For example, present-day rites of passage include graduation, obtaining a drivers license, or perhaps playing on a team sport. However, it has become obvious to us that for youth who do not have access to these activities, gangs typically fulfill this need by offering a transitional portal that is both unique and exciting, yet filled with danger.

The rites of passage issue is an important developmental process for anyone who wants to work with gangs to understand, as there are parallels between puberty rites that are found in traditional societies and the urban practices of street gangs. For example, in traditional societies, puberty rites may involve tattooing, scarification, acquiring a new name, leaving the parental home, living with same-age peers, or undertaking a spiritual journey as a test of manhood. In contrast, street gang members typically revere their elders (called original gangsters or "OGs"), have a period of separation from their family of origin, and maintain a sacred place referred to as a territory or section of a community. In addition, we have found that youth involved in gangs typically experience a symbolic death; new members take new identities with a street name and new fashion of dress, and undergo the initiation rites of a particular gang.

We have learned that the issue of proving one's manhood is an important aspect of gangs, in which promoting aggression and destructive behavior towards others is highly valued as a means to secure a reputation. Attempting to undo this negative imprint of affirmed violence is at the core of our practice in sacred advocacy, which includes renovated rites of passage embedded within a group therapeutic process. As a psychotherapist and Catholic priest (Stan), I have encountered many poor, unrealized opportunities of ineffective male/father bonding on the streets and neighborhoods of South Los Angeles, which is notorious for its gang violence, ubiquitous poverty, and scarcity of role models for African American and Latino youth. The absent father, in the vast majority of our youth's lives, leaves adolescents vulnerable to the seductive invitations by older veteran "homies" to belong to a reality greater than themselves, and offers the possibility of becoming a part of a surrogate family. This reality often traps youngsters into doing "missions" that consequently leave them imprisoned behind walls of stigma and shame that are projected onto other susceptible peers as acts of violence.

Experiences of Gang Affiliation

Clinical interviews, casual conversations, and group therapeutic intervention have provided us direct experiences for peering into the lives of this vulnerable population and appreciating the various challenges they have learned to inherit out of necessity. Many of these challenges have included negative parental role modeling, older siblings who have exhibited antisocial behavior, and often, absent parents. Other risk factors that we have witnessed are violent neighborhood environments where social attachment is low, the presence of active socialization from gang members, poverty, disorganization in one's day-to-day activities, the absence of meaningful employment, and the availability of illegal drugs. More specific assessments of family of origin issues have included low parental attachment and supervision, incest, broken homes, domestic violence, child abuse, alcoholism and drug addiction, and repetitive familial problems with the police.

The frequent overt and internalized negativity of youth in this population has made it very difficult for us to maintain confidence in and support for our work. It is disheartening to see kids who have very low expectation of themselves at school, poor attachment to teachers and to their school progress, and very low educational aspirations. One-on-one interaction, however, has sensitized us to their emotional neediness and fragility; our awareness of their fatalistic worldview has increased our tolerance and reinforced our motivation to engage in this world. This aspect of fatalism has proven to be a highly charged emotional attitude that often places a teen in a high-risk, high-danger situation. The day-to-day risks that our population is forced to endure include "watching your back," as the preoccupation with the safe "route" to take to school or the market, crossing enemy neighborhoods, becomes a stressful obsession. Drug usage represents a coping strategy and defense against chronic depression and anxiety. It is common conventional wisdom that young gang-affiliated adolescents believe that there is no promising future for them; their goal is to live past 21 years old.

Having to deal with intense anxiety, danger, and self-protection often results in limited language to describe what has occurred to one's personhood. The term *alexithymia* helps to define the experiences of those who are exposed to multiple health risks, substance abuse, domestic violence, and child abuse, as well as a matrix of inexplicable personal tragedy.

Alexithymia

In the past 25 years as researchers and clinicians, we have "witnessed" the odious efforts of at-risk youth in their awkward, and at times desperate, search to find the means and the medium (via the words) to experience liberation in their challenging, oppressive, and destructive environments. There is a lived poverty and palpable experience of abandonment in the unconscious hunger to be heard and understood. Their propensity is to turn to the underground world of drug use and gang involvement as forced attempts to find avenues of escape and respite from the inner prison of isolation. Finding words to express deep inner emotions is the ultimate path to the psyche's quest for wholeness, yet is essentially a world away from desperate adolescents who are just tying to stay alive.

Our experience as therapists—facilitating group, individual, and family therapy—values meaningful dialogue and awareness of one's greater purpose as mechanisms for determining useful responses to events, as opposed to unpremeditated or unconscious acting out. In other words, the therapeutic relationship, and the sacredness of its undertone, facilitates a movement away from self-destructive behavior toward holding a consciousness about alternative choices with the support of group members.

Recent examples of therapeutic group experiences of youth from this population include Anthony and Karla. Anthony, a 15-year-old African American 83 Crip gang-involved teenager, expressed an extremely volatile emotional state in a session with seven other African American teens. His cousin had recently been killed in a drive-by payback incident. Anthony virtually screamed through a litany of violent retaliatory acts that he was going to unleash on his enemies. "Payback," retaliation for violent acts against an enemy gang, is ubiquitous in this inner city world. As his diatribe subsided, the group held his distressed affect in silence for what appeared to be a long, agonizing minute. The group became reliably established in the transference as an attuned, accepting, and affect-articulating presence. Anthony's psychosomatic symptoms seemed to recede as an apparent product of the opportunity to have a "group-witness" experience. Recognizing that there was an intimate relationship between what Anthony and our group was feeling, as if he could really imagine enacting his hatred to such an extreme, he responded with an antithetical, despondent affect, saying, "Naw … I could really never ever kill anyone."

I (Stan) recognized that what I/the group was feeling helped Anthony understand what he was feeling. I have seen the very youth in the therapy room that day take part in senseless acts of vengeance before they were offered the opportunity to find words to put to their confused emotional state (alexithymia). The group therapeutic process became an essential attuned, nonintrusive presence, which created the emotional safety necessary for an "at-risk" or gang-involved adolescent's "true self" to emerge. The pain is at times intolerable, and the tragic fact that Anthony died playing Russian roulette with his "homies" reveals the nature of a nihilist worldview that beseeches transformation.

Karla, one of the program's student participants, is another "familiar face" in the gang world. She landed at the SEA charter school and Gang Intervention Program after a dizzying descent into alcohol abuse, crystal meth addiction, and affiliation with a local gang. The start of a group process of 10–12 students, including Karla, typically begins with the following introductory comments within the confines of an otherwise austere school, in which the walls are lined only with gray lockers. The decor seems as incongruous as the mission.

"What is the purpose of what we do here?" I always ask at the beginning of group sessions, together with the recitation of exceptions to confidentiality.

"Get stuff out," a 17-year-old named Charles volunteers. "So it don't burn inside you."

"Beautiful," is my response.

Karla's story represents a characteristic young person for our healing work. Her mother raised four children without child support, working as a floral arranger for quinceañera celebrations. Rent money ran short, and the family was forced to move time and again. Unsupervised and lonely, Karla fell into the wrong crowd, was jumped into the "Playboys," a South-Central LA gang; she began drinking, then smoking pot, and spent almost two years addicted to crystal meth. Recently, she has kicked her addiction and boosted her grades. Much of her journey, she publically declares, has come because of these sessions.

"Around here, we don't talk about our stuff," she said. "I used to cry every day. I can't explain the relief." Karla and I both know that her problems have hardly vanished. There is rarely food in the house, Karla declares. A woman who lives down the street gives Karla a bit of money to get by. This adolescent is a talented artist, and she earns a few dollars by selling pencil drawings, mostly portraits, to her friends.

She still has to fight her way through the neighborhood; a classmate recently punched her in the face in a dispute over whose turn it was to use a computer. On days like that, she said, she draws only for herself—self-portraits, typically, showing how she looked before she shaved her head, with long hair that would cover her face and hide her from the world.

During one recent session, Karla also told the group that she and her girlfriend had recently broken up, leaving her deeply wounded. (In general, she said, her sexual orientation has rarely been an issue at home or school.)

"Are you discovering anything about yourself?" I asked her.

"That I'm weak. I thought I was hard. I'm not."

"That must be liberating."

"I guess."

"Loneliness is a part of life," another voice in the group told her. "We never escape it completely."

Union, Recovery, and Healing

My work (Stan) with at-risk youth has involved a community-based program in which students interface with one another about elements relevant to their daily survival. This dialogue has provided the opportunity to intervene within the classroom setting or to share more salient issues regarding critical events in group counseling that occurs on a weekly basis, often 2–3 times per week. The therapeutic encounter is based on the practicing ideal that we are all children of a higher order in which there must be mutual respect, understanding, and learning from one another. This process involves managing difficult life histories that include drug-abusing parents, physical beatings, domestic violence, drive-by shootings, and learning how to navigate gang affiliation. There have been many occasions in which these disclosures during group encounters have revealed a recent involvement in a drive-by shooting that has left some of the group members with significant anxiety, fear, and preoccupation for their lives and families.

Some of our principle dilemmas have involved how to safely manage the disclosure of secretive and emotionally destructive information that involves hurting and killing other human beings without losing sight of daily survival and some semblance of personal dignity. The healing process has been challenged by having kids recognize some of their own nightmares and emotional struggles, and admitting that their lives have been misaligned in highly destructive ways. In addition, the ethical quandary for us as mental health professionals has been to recognize that any disclosure, even within the confines of a confidential group, can result in personal injury and threats to family members of some of these youth. We continue to struggle with this quandary of balancing the confidential rights of the group, their physical well-being, and the need to protect the broader community.

Psychotherapeutic healing involves the "self-object experience of witness." Witnessing, as a special form of therapeutic participation, validates the relevance of lived experiences between one another. We believe, as cited by Alice Miller (1990), that healing trauma and violence requires the presence of someone in the child's life who witnesses, and thus gives the child the opportunity and ability to experience the pain. We have come to believe, and ultimately testify to the fact, that the specificity of witnessing in the therapeutic alliance is the recognition of the horror, the mistreatment, and the pain that otherwise cannot become fully conscious experience. We confirm and acknowledge, after bearing witness to the spiritual poverty of many of these youth, that the rawness of the pain in the presence of others creates a shared awareness and solidarity that acts as a healing ointment on an open wound.

Reaffirmation in a Loving Jesus: Encounters of Spirituality and Psychological First Aid

So we have come to appreciate the therapeutic understanding of sacred advocacy has special meaning with these young people. In the absence of a healthy and whole (holy) role model, gang-involved and at-risk youth are vulnerable and easily "give their hearts" in the search for a reality greater than themselves. Gang membership becomes the violent and viable alternative in the absence of a solid community model—a life-giving option to be human in the world. We hold that humans are the very mystery that, from the Christian tradition, denotes "a reality whose meaning can never be fully exhausted." In other words, there is a surplus of meaning in human existence and its relationships (Parabola, 2008).

Our professional work has incorporated the principle that these youths' lives are a mystery in this sense with depth and profound meaning; this is the "psychological first aid" that can initiate the movement into healing wholeness. This acknowledgement implies being in a relationship, walking with, and embracing youth in their search for meaning, and the discovery of one's life as a mystery, the very likeness of God. Our experience with this youth population has shown that they are isolated and alienated from one another, and segregated and estranged from mainstream society—and certainly from our worshiping communities. The stigma of "gang member" ostensibly inculcates fear in people and excludes their membership and participation in a loving community where safety, hope, and belief in oneself can be secured.

Sacred Advocacy is not limited to court-imposed participation in a psychotherapeutic alliance. This understanding of advocacy is the invitation, if not the mandate, for all caring and willing individuals to seek, to encounter, and to engage our youth with the confidence and the desire to know them by name. Acknowledging, giving names to traumatic experiences, and recognizing the true face of these teens, person by person, has provided us a valuable key to help young at-risk discover, literally "dis-cover" the goodness, the gift, and the mystery of their human life that has been "covered over" by shame and abandonment (Constantine, Hage, Kindaichi, & Bryant, 2007).

Developing Mindfulness and Peace in a Violence-Prone World

Gang intervention is a practice that has been historically relegated primarily to social work and socially conscious individuals who are invested in assisting at-risk youth, and has typically been invisible to mainstream society. Our work, primarily through Stan, has been to provide a spiritual backdrop to working with at-risk youth, with the union of psychotherapy and spirituality as a delicate, yet powerful force with this vulnerable, violent population.

Our very semantics and metaphors implicitly marry psychology with spirituality. Therefore our mission becomes the art of service, or healing of the soul. Spirituality is about Spirit. The word for Spirit in Hebrew (*Ruach*) and Sanskrit connotes "breath." Therefore, our breath is Spirit within. The fact is that no informed educator can tell us where breath comes from, but can only describe the process in the circulatory and respiratory systems of our bodies after we breathe. The mystery is that breath is a gift and a miracle, and to the extent that we become aware and mindful of breath, our breathing and our life changes ... the awareness is transformative. We breathe intentionally with our clients and are "inspired" by the awareness that emerges in our therapeutic relationships, which are essentially "spiritual." An outcome of this process is the development of mindfulness (Hanh, 1976).

A significant influence in our professional practice with at-risk youth has been Kornfield (2008), who described mindfulness as an attention that incorporates a non-judging and respectful awareness. In the Christian tradition, the Rhineland mystic Meister Eckhart maintained that all spirituality is about "waking up" and becoming aware. The human dynamic, in the face of pain and suffering, is to go to sleep, to become unconscious. The youth in the program continue to teach us about how deep psychic pain is experienced; it frequently remains underground until the next traumatic episode. Mindfulness practices foster the development of a sacred space in which to differentiate cognitive perceptions from the affective states of emotion; it becomes the space in which to reflect upon personal existential experiences as self and oneself in relation to others. This practice facilitates the withdrawal of unconscious projections onto those (enemy gang members and others) who represent the threat of re-traumatization. This work is sacred and holy, and facilitates a rite of passage in which the eventual healing experiences allow for a temporary relief from psychic and soul wounding in the gathering of a loving community.

The practice of mindfulness begins with an intention to simply pay more attention to what is going on inside us. For our work, mindfulness is about helping young at-risk individuals to face their pain and discover words for painful emotions. When one feels tension, anger, or discomfort of any kind, one can briefly pause and check in to see what is going on. Recognizing that we are suffering is the first step of mindful transformation. The principles of recognition, acceptance, investigation, and non-identification form the essential structure of the therapeutic group experience.

The non-identification stage is especially significant because individuals learn that their identities are separate from their experiences. Identifying oneself with one's experience creates dependence and anxiety. One learns that experience is tentative. In this stage, one is able to let go of identification and rest in awareness, which Buddhism refers to as true peace or nirvana. In our work, we understand this sacred process as the reaffirmation of a loving Jesus in the hearts of these young people, a confession of some of their darkest secrets, and the beginning of their belief in their true personhood.

Implications for Social Justice Counseling

We have learned several lessons from working with youth in South Los Angeles. Some of these salient observations have included very human and tangible insights:

- *There is a very real human need to be recognized, to be known.* At the heart of the graffiti phenomena, or "tagging," is a hunger for one's name and neighborhood to be seen and acknowledged. As so many gang-involved youth have described their addiction to tagging … "I just want people to see me … my name!" And many youth risk their lives in order to see their name on a wall. As mentioned earlier in this chapter, there is real power in knowing our young people by name! Furthermore, when neighbors know one another by name, and recognize and engage their youth on the block as individuals, listening to their experiences and their hurts and dreams, violence against people and property diminishes.

- *Humans have an existential need for attachment.* In the absence of a healthy mother or father, another adult figure who is concerned about and consistently present for the youth can be a matter of life and death for a high percentage of at-risk youth. A devoted godparent, uncle, teacher, or athletic coach can make a difference by being a model of care and affection—and ultimately a loving way of living and a peaceful alternative to gang life.

- *In a world of violent inner cities where abuse is ubiquitous, its reality has to be taught.* Abuse is normalized in the vast majority of families of at-risk youth. Many relationships are sexualized; emotional abandonment is real, and physical cruelty becomes an accepted reaction to frustration and miscommunication in our experience. Abuse needs to be recognized and reported. As professional counselors, we say that "we act out what we don't talk out!" Our therapy offices, school classrooms, and church sanctuaries can be the starting places and spaces for confronting abuse in all its forms as a step toward healing (Nilsson, Schale, & Khamphakdy-Brown, 2011).
- *Depression is at epidemic levels with at-risk youth and their families.* The anxiety that is triggered by having to "watch your back" simply to walk to school or to the market leaves our youth vulnerable and threatened daily. Smoking marijuana and using pharmaceutical and other drugs becomes a compulsion to relieve and release some of the tension and stress faced by our inner city youth. Access to mental health services is virtually non-existent in our experience with this population. Furthermore, most African American and Latino families teach a code of silence that prohibits revealing any family business outside the home. However, we have learned that a person's emotional need to be acknowledged and listened to is a deep human longing. Acknowledging the frequency of micro- and macro-aggressions, and their contribution to the psychological vulnerability of these youth, can build salient milestones of connection and instill hope.
- *Remember to ask genuinely "how are you doing"?* Most people are so preoccupied with their own repetitive thoughts and concerns that mindful presence to another becomes the exception. Most at-risk youth have been shamed on a daily basis throughout their lives. Shame is different than guilt. Guilt is the recognition that I have made a mistake. Shame, on the other hand, is the belief that "I am a mistake"! The daily trauma of shaming is real for our youth, who are told by parents, police, and teachers that they are mistakes. When are they asked about the traumatic experiences of the previous night witnessing a friend die on the street; or the stress of having to imagine a "route" through neighbors' yards and hopping fences to arrive safely to school; or the pressure to do a violent "mission" by the OG's from their neighborhood? We have learned that the very human offer of one's time and care—by asking "how do you feel?"—makes a difference. We have learned that the power of "being curious" about their feelings and experiences in genuine a way can awaken one's positive sense of self and empower at-risk youth to be authentically aware and concerned about their family members, peers, and others.
- *There is a power in presence.* For an adult to be present at a school function or celebration can have eternal consequences. When our youth face the tragedy

of death or hospitalization because of a violent encounter, the presence of people who care does not go unnoticed. And your presence in the life of a young person models the kind of caring relationship that holds the power to transform the world by its contagion.

- *Give yourself time to pray, reflect, and grieve.* The need for inner silence, grieving of the mind, is mandatory—particularly when helping at-risk youth with a karma of violence trailing them. The importance of rejuvenating and re-grounding in the healing landscape of the earth cannot be underlined enough (Parabola, 2007). Meditating or offering prayer are meaningful processes to help us re-connect and remember the essence of sacred advocacy in ourselves and in the lives of those we serve.

The streets of many communities across the country, particularly where low income people reside, are far from being liberated. In fact, entire families, neighborhoods—even cities—are being held hostage by desperate youth with a deep longing to belong. However, our lessons learned from day-to-day contact with gang-involved young people and the therapeutic healing that we experience gives us great hope. These children are our children by legacy; they are literally dying in wait of alternative relationships for liberation, healing, and justice. Our community participation in their lives is the hope!

References

Cervantes, J.M. & Parham. T. (2005). Towards a meaningful spirituality for people of color: Lessons for the Counseling Professional. *Cultural Diversity and Ethnic Minority Psychology, 11*, 69–81.

Constantine, M.G., Hage, S.M., Kindaichi, M.M., & Bryant, R.M. (2007). Social justice and multicultural issues: Implications for the practice and training of counselors and counseling psychologists. *Journal of Counseling and Development, 85*, 24–29.

Hanh, T.N. (1976). *The Miracle of Mindfulness: A Manual on Meditation.* Boston: Beacon Press.

Kornfield, J. (2008). *The Buddha Is Still Teaching: Contemporary Buddhist Wisdom.* New York: Bantam Books.

Miller, A. (1990). *Breaking Down the Walls of Silence.* New York: Dutton/Penguin Books.

Nilsson, J.E., Schale, C.L., & Khamphakdy-Brown, S. (2011). Facilitating trainees' multicultural development and social justice advocacy through a refugee/immigrant mental health program. *Journal of Counseling and Development, 89*, 413–422.

Parabola. (Summer 2008). *God.* New York: Parabola.

Parabola. (Fall 2007). *HolyEarth.* New York: Parabola.

8

REAL-LIFE SOCIAL ACTION IN THE COMMUNITY

Byron Waller

Social justice has always been a part of my life and a major influence in the way I view the world. As a professional therapist, professor, and community counselor, I have always looked for opportunities to get involved with my community and work with people where they live their lives. I grew up in Chicago during the 1960s, when social concerns were primary for our nation and in my neighborhood. "Civil rights, racial equality, and fairness" was a cry I heard over and over again from my family, friends, school, community, and church. Social justice has been the most significant factor that has led me to the helping and counseling profession. Although I often work within the 50-minute hour as a therapist, most of my passion and motivation comes from the early experiences I had in my community. These experiences included being a part of community activism, and pioneering racial and ethnic interactions. These kinds of activities outside of the office have been a part of my calling in the helping profession.

My Social Justice Beginnings

Growing up poor in an urban city, I was always searching for ways to make it out, and to help other people in the process, knowing that other people were working hard for me to change a system that limited my chances for success. Personally, I was trying to catch the "American dream" and to just be a part of the mainstream. Struggling and striving while believing that the dream was within reach, I recognized that there were obstacles, structures, perceptions, and individuals who stood in the way of attaining my dreams. At the same time, I knew there were many people, programs, and movements going on that created opportunities if I was willing to work hard, and to fight for fairness for myself and others who could not fight for themselves. The Civil Rights Movement and social change agents were significant in creating an environment in which it could be possible for me as a black child to integrate into the mainstream and be a part of my own and Martin Luther King's dream.

In this vein, my experience as a Christian and my involvement in organizations gave me other experiences to learn from. I learned how to navigate my way through many of my environmental challenges and how to gain access to the skills I needed to manage my life. The environment provided me with the structure I needed for consistency, the discipline for persistence, and the work ethic for goal planning and attainment. Just add family support, intelligence, luck, an education, and opportunity, and you have a person who is able to get out of an environment pitted with ways to fail. My progress was not totally dependent on myself. There were White and Black people giving of themselves so that others could have the opportunity to improve their lives. My faith and the support of both Black and White created a small youth center that became an oasis in the community for young Black people to come and change their lives. This is the context I came from: social justice and social action were indelibly part of my process to progress, and racial conflict was an unmistakable obstacle to overcome.

From an early age, I was involved in Christian organizations and ministries as a consumer and participant. The people in the organizations were loving and supportive, but they were always led and operated by White people. All of the instructors, directors, and staff were also White. Initially, all of the people who made the decisions were white. I did not see a person who looked like me in a position of leadership in the organization. This issue was significant in my personal development. This later signaled for me an area of needed growth: to see Black people in leadership and social justice activities.

Over time, I recognized that the Christian organizations were missions in the Black neighborhood. They were there to help acculturate the Black youth into their belief system, which in the long run was very helpful. However, when Black people began to become active in the leadership of the organizations, the White leadership gave very clear instructions about the content and process of their involvement. There were clear struggles in sharing the power, integrating Black culture, and collaborating on influencing the Black youth and programs. When the Black leadership began to gain influence with the Black youth, the White leaders and funding for the programs slowly began to disappear. The number of White people began to decrease, and the programs and services left with them. Although the Black leadership was willing to negotiate to maintain funding, the funds and the White people disappeared. I later noticed that the integration and sharing of power, civil rights, equality, and fairness were issues even then between White and Black people. This struggle became a professional theme for my activism and a common personal life experience.

My Real Social Justice Story

Shortly after I got married and we had our first child, I felt the need to have a more permanent place to raise him. My primary concern was my child and having a safe place and a good caretaker for him. My wife and I agreed that we would have her grandmother as the sitter and we wanted to live in a safe, clean neighborhood. We agreed to look with two goals in mind: to live close to my wife's grandmother for daycare and near public transportation for my job. We found a place that worked and we liked the neighborhood, so a couple of years later we decided to purchase a house. We found a place in a working-class neighborhood with small bungalows and Cape Cod houses. The make-up of the neighborhood was white and suburban, and met our needs as a young couple with another child on the way. We were very happy and interacted frequently with our immediate neighbors. However, within a year, our distal neighbors began posting signs in their windows stating, "We are staying!" The signs did not initially bother us, because we thought: "Good, we want you to stay." But the neighbors did not stay.

As time continued, "White flight" occurred quickly, and the neighborhood changed from a primarily White, connected working-class neighborhood to a half-White, half-Black, ever-changing, disconnected neighborhood. At first this was not a problem for us. Our children and neighborhood continued to progress and our family had a great experience in an integrated neighborhood. People in the neighborhood continued to interact and share the area. Then it seemed to change as the percentage of Blacks overtook the percentage of Whites, and community services like street cleaning and garbage collection began to decrease. The taxes increased, school funding for our children decreased, and school performance declined. Our neighborhood and our relationships with all of our neighbors began to erode. The great, integrated neighborhood we enjoyed disappeared, along with its resources. This experience was profound for me because it connected me to the experience I had when I was growing up at the youth center. The message seemed to be that there is something wrong with sharing power and resources with Black people, and that there is something about Black people to avoid and run away from. We did not believe this but saw that many White people did, even our friends. We decided to stay in the neighborhood for a while until our children grew to a certain age and the services did not meet our needs. We moved away when our children entered junior high and the educational resources began to change. I am sure that many people have had this experience when living in a changing and transitioning environment. But I felt that I could not just leave without doing something about this phenomenon. This event was the experience I needed to motivate me to do something about social justice and to take action.

During this time, I began to develop my social justice competencies and to prepare myself for social action. Although I had experiences and training as a multi-cultural counselor, I wanted to be sure that I understood what it meant to be a competent, socially active counselor. The preparation I sought required me to become more aware of my social viewpoints; take action to eliminate educational inequalities; be aware of institutional barriers; gain knowledge of the potential biases in instruments, procedures, and the interpretation of findings; work to eliminate biases, prejudices, and discrimination; and become sensitive to the issues of oppression, sexism, heterosexism, elitism, and racism (Sue, Arredondo, & McDavis, 1992) on a larger level. I also worked on my advocacy competencies on the individual level by helping to identify external barriers, negotiate relevant services and education, develop action plans, analyze the sources of political power and social influence, seek out potential allies, and support existing alliances. My intent was to help transform my neighborhood and the world.

Throughout this process, I learned that social justice and social action were very difficult undertakings, and that changing one's own and someone else's mindset and belief system took effort and time. This is even more challenging when considering larger systemic and policy changes. Promoting change may cost something of the socially active counselor because it involves risks; but since I wanted change, I needed to learn to understand resistance and the process of promoting change. Much of my social action training was informal and involved the skills that Goodman, Liang, Helm, Latta, Sparks, and Weintraub (2004) outlined in their training program: (a) continued self-reflection and examination, (b) learning how to share power, (c) developing your own voice through critical thinking, (d) how to facilitate consensus, (e) how to build on strengths, and (f) how to empower and develop skills in others who stay in the area. Below is an example of how I applied some of these social justice and social action skills.

My Real Social Action Story

My early experiences shaped my professional outlook and involvement as a professional therapist, professor, and community counselor. Many of my activities have been within one or two communities. I have now been working and living in this suburban community for more than 25 years. Many of the issues remain the same, but some of the challenges have become more intense and ingrained in the community. The need for more social justice and social action is evident. My social justice actions are not only directly with the clients I work with, but also in the community where they live. I observed many of the same issues I saw years ago, but the intensity and frequency of the problems had increased. The residents have access to fewer resources, and are living in a more unstable and dangerous environment. Working outside the 50-minute hour gives me the chance to move outside the office and into the community to affect the lives of the people we work with every day. This opportunity could not only promote individual change but also community and systemic change. Progressive change is definitely needed in this area. Children, youth, adults, and the elderly are searching for change, fairness, justice, and opportunity in these communities. I have been involved in many areas of work over the years as a parent, community member, professional, consultant, and volunteer.

It is personally satisfying to represent people who cannot represent themselves and to help them gain access to resources and stabilize their lives. I am specifically drawn towards helping individuals and communities stabilize during transitions. Whether the transition is career related or relationship connected, I am focused on helping people to be resilient in these difficult times and to find a way to get their footing so they can walk on their own. People and communities need individuals who can help them get up again and move ahead, especially after a change has occurred. Another part of the enjoyment is actually dealing with difficult racial and ethnic issues by identifying and discussing issues and attempting to resolve them so that both parties can feel that they are being heard and that some level of justice is explored and chosen from both perspectives. Racial conflicts are one of the more challenging issues because no one wants to be accused of being a racist, yet at the same time some do not want to acknowledge that racism still exists in our structures and in ourselves.

One of the pieces of work in social justice and racial reconciliation that moved me was when I worked with a private practice and was consulted by a local Christian school to help manage a racial conflict. I was the only Black therapist in the practice, but everyone in the practice was concerned about the obvious racial tensions in our community. This incident involved a racial uproar; many parents threatened to remove their children from the all-White high school in which several Black students recently enrolled. Several of the Black female students complained to the administration about multiple racial harassments situations from the White male students. When a Black male student was harassed, he responded physically and was suspended by the school's administration. The White male students who were involved were also later suspended. The parents of the White students complained, and the parents of the Black student threatened to remove their son from the school because they did not want him to be a "pioneer" to integrate a school in which he is not wanted. Other parents of Black students also threatened to remove their children. Information and debates about the racial conflict moved to local churches and community pastors, primarily the White ones. The congregants began to discuss what to do with the school's situation, and ultimately with the changing racial make-up of the community. The same pattern I had experienced earlier in another suburb appeared again. My colleague and I were asked to come into the school to help resolve and manage the conflict. My work focused on three levels: directly with some of the Black parents, with the school's administration, and with the local pastors and churches who supported the Christian school. The work with the parents was initially emotional and heated, which was good because I wanted to allow them to express their feelings of frustration and anger related to what they perceived as injustice and unfairness. After which, I wanted to make a plan of action so we could clearly communicate to the administration, other parents, and the church community that supports the school their viewpoint and the actions they wanted—and possibly enact policy and systemic changes. The Black parents were clear about their outrage: it was "the 21st century and we are still dealing with the same stuff even in the Christian church." They believed that as Christians, beliefs of unfairness and hatred should change and everyone should become brothers and sisters in fairness and love, as Jesus taught. This upset them because they believed that the white kids got their attitudes from their parents, who professed Christianity.

The school's administration was led by an open and experienced principal, who seemed to be multi-culturally aware, since in the past he was a missionary in a Central American country. He had recommended that the school board consult with me and my colleague to help manage the issue, which allowed me to assess his level of cultural awareness. It was generally good; however, he was not aware of some of the issues African Americans experience in America, or of the perceptions that are typical of a transitioning environment. I was able to discuss with him the viewpoints of the school board, administration, teachers, and the overall student body. Most of the people in the school were hesitant to directly address the racial issue, although the general attitude was not positive toward integration. I directly asked him his viewpoint, which he answered without hesitation. He said, "every one of God's creations is equal and should be loved equally. The Lord told us to love Him and our neighbors as ourselves. We need to deal with this issue directly. The children need to see us deal with this racial issue fairly." He also spoke of his experiences in Central America. I asked him about the similarities and differences between this situation and his experiences abroad. He admitted that the differences here were racial attitudes. I was encouraged, since he seemed willing to make decisions based on principles, rather than fear.

We met with the school's administration, teachers, some of the parents, and the local pastors. Each group's concerns were different. The administration wanted to settle the conflict, the teachers were not sure how to handle the situation, the White parents wanted things the way they were, and the Black parents did not want their children to be harassed or in a environment that was harmful to them. Each of their concerns was listened to and taken into consideration. I learned that some of the White parents had experienced a changing environment when they were growing up in the city, and many of them moved here to escape a similar situation. Their concerns focused on their children and maintaining their community and the institution they had established. Therefore, the one major concern was not to destroy the community support and the existence of the school, but to promote change in the system and policies.

My colleague and I decided to meet with the local pastors separately and privately in order to get their view of the situation. We understood that this racial challenge was systemic, encompassing one's social, moral, and spiritual areas. Many of the pastors openly expressed their ideal of racial harmony and God's love of all people. At the same time, they spoke of the fears and viewpoints of their congregations and churches, which consist of the people who had supported the school for many years. Many of them were not happy with the integration of the school, or the suspension of the kids. Many believed that they were "just being kids." The discussions were often thoughtful, honest, and theological, but were rather frustrating for me. I was often able to express my viewpoint as a person, an African American, and a Christian, but sometimes I wanted to say some things that I know they were not ready for, which would be too controversial, and maybe distracting. So I focused on the idea that I should love the Lord God with all of my heart, soul, mind, and strength, and that I should love my neighbor as I love myself, and that I ought to be an example of what Jesus did when he encountered someone who was of a different gender and race: he was very accepting and clear. These ideas kept me grounded and open during these discussions. I am not sure what focused anyone else during this time, but the priorities of some participants were obvious. Many pastors were afraid to make bold moves because they had to answer to their congregations. Many of them could be easily voted out and removed. Most people in this situation knew the fair thing to do, but were not willing to pay the price of justice. Just like in social justice, we might want to change the damage of racial inequalities, but we may not want to give up some of our privileges that maintain the injustice. At times that was true for me, for when I sat in on some of the meetings, I was afraid to make direct comments. At other times I made indirect comments about the need to stand up for what was right, just like Jesus did. So I understood the fears of the pastors because I did not want to negatively affect the practice. Over time I found myself able to challenge my own fears and many of the group's beliefs and policies.

The outcome of this racial situation was unresolved. The effort to deal with these complicated racial issues became difficult. The most challenging dilemma was navigating how to maintain the stability, support, and confidence of the old way of doing, perceiving, and receiving things while being just and fair and integrating the new ways. One of the sticking points was how to deal with losing something that we have worked hard to attain and have grown comfortable with—and letting someone else receive it. I think justice and Jesus would call that the art of giving and receiving: an unselfish, spiritual process. That being said, each of us has our own process and time, confrontation, work, and effort; changing these elements is the catalyst for real social justice to occur.

I continue to work in this community, and a good portion of my work surrounds racial reconciliation. However I no longer primarily focus on racial resolution and reconciliation in the community. Much of my work has evolved to work with the people who stay as the neighborhood transitions from White to Black, and as the resources transition from available to scarce. Most of the racial change has already taken place. The concept of transition is now one of my callings. I am always open to evolving in my work, profession, and self. All I know is that social justice and fairness will continue to be part of my work outside of the 50-minute hour. I now volunteer for a community agency as a board member, volunteer, and supervisor. I want to continue to do some of the direct work with people in the community but also realize the importance of administrative, policy, and decision-making involvement. In order to remove institutional and structural barriers, social justice workers must be involved at every level of society and the community. My area of growth continues to be in this area. Leadership that promotes change must be done at every level, including at the top. The 50-minute hour gives me a chance to work directly with people to promote change in their lives; outside the 50-minute hour, I can help change other levels of the community, which also indirectly promotes change in the lives of this community. Social action and social justice require both levels.

My Challenges and Obstacles to Social Justice and Action

The greatest obstacles I face when working outside of the 50-minute hour are my own fear and frustration. I am afraid of what might happen to me as I stand for social justice and become involved in social action in my community. When I work for change, there are others who want to maintain the status quo because it is working very well for them. So, there is the potential for harm and there is some risk to getting involved. There is also the potential you will be labeled a troublemaker, and others may avoid you because of your participation in social justice and action. As a result, some of your personal privileges may be at risk (i.e., you may not get the promotion or the job you wanted because of your involvement and reputation in social justice and social action). In these situations, I first remember the commitment I made to social justice and social action for the welfare of all oppressed people and to be an agent for systemic change. Some have even suggested that there is a "moral imperative" for each of us to be committed to social justice and action. A second way I deal with the fear is by becoming as smart and thoughtful as possible about my involvement in social justice and action. What I mean by this is that I make decisions about my involvement by working as part of a group rather than by myself. I try to work with others who have as much or more experience within social justice as me, and I attempt to mentor those who do not. Working as part of a team produces shared responsibility and shared support. Finally, I tend to focus primarily on systemic and community change, not just individual change. My social justice action tends to focus on changing policies within a system that impact the community rather than just an individual, although what happens to an individual may be a sign of the overall system. Social justice is multi-dimensional (affective, intellectual, and pragmatic) and I must be ready to become involved wisely on each of the levels.

One of the challenges to involvement in social justice and action is managing the risk of participation. I admit that in some situations I could have been more active, but I was not due to fear of the consequences of my involvement. I have often chosen the old adage to "choose my battle so I could win the war." So I have been wise in my activities, but at the same time I have had to deal with the results of my actions. I had to remember that first, there is clearly a cost to being involved, and second, there are many challenges. I used the steps that Gainor (2005) developed as a model for professionals to follow in order to manage the risks and challenges of becoming involved in social justice and action: 1) develop a passionate sense of moral outrage and allow it to motivate you through the fears and challenges to help others who are oppressed; 2) move of loss to strength: let the recognition of the losses of the oppressed move you toward a commitment to help others; 3) gain competence in your own social justice and social action skills; 4) although the situation may seem to be uncertain and scary, focus on the change you are working to produce: this will keep you moving forward; and 5) use the resources around you to promote systemic and social change. These steps have helped me continue my work outside of the 50-minute hour.

Implications for My Continued Social Justice and Action

Social justice and social action have been an essential part of my upbringing and my consciousness as a helping professional. Although I initially started in the religious realm as a social change agent, I soon began to realize that one could help individuals in many areas and on many levels. Based on my early experiences, ethnic and racial social justice was my primary area of involvement. For a period of time I worked within my office and the duties as prescribed by my positions, but getting outside of the 50-minute hour and into the community required me to expand my areas of involvement so that all oppressed people could receive the help they need to gain access, to be empowered, and to receive the support needed to change the system more broadly. Ethnic and racial issues continue to be my primary areas of involvement, but now I work not only in the religious arena but also in the community at large as an agent of change. I can now affect people's lives through my teaching, training, and workshops in university and community settings.

Expanding my perspective and areas of involvement has increased my influence in promoting change. I can now directly affect others' lives through my teaching and encourage them to become agents of change. Being an agent that looks to change—and even transform—situations and communities could be very scary and challenging. However, following some basic guidelines can help. Working as part of a team and empowering the groups we work with can help us manage the challenges and obstacles that come with our community goals. Mentoring other change and transformation agents is another new way I can contribute to the overall goal of representing and empowering the oppressed to break down and eliminate institutional and social obstacles.

I now live in an area where I do not have to be so vigilant about safety and I no longer have the American dream as my goal, but I continue to want to help others improve their quality of life as a counselor, professor, and a community change agent in and outside of the 50-minute hour. I now see the 50-minute hour as a good place to start one's training to impact others, but I understand that for real change (and for systemic change and even transformation) to take place, I have to be willing to get out of the office and get involved with the community. For me, the community includes where I live and where people with whom I come into contact live. It becomes vital for me to face my own fears, to be willing to manage risk, and to transform people's lives on a variety of levels. I continue to teach, train, and advocate for systemic change, but I also see the importance of promoting change in the lives of students and clients so they can become change agents in their communities. The 50-minute hour within the class or session is important, but affecting others beyond that time and space becomes the ultimate goal, just like the Civil Rights Movement that influenced me. I could now influence others in that way.

References

Gainor, K.A. (2005). Social justice: The moral imperative of vocational psychology. *The Counseling Psychologist, 33(2)*, 180–188.

Goodman, L.A., Liang, B., Helms, J.E., Latta, R.E. Sparks, E., & Weintraub, S. R. (2004). Training counseling psychologists as social justice agents: Feminist and multicultural principles in action. *The Counseling Psychologist, 32(6)*, 793–837.

Sue, D.W., Arredondo, P., & McDavis, R.J. (1992). Multicultural competencies and standards: A call to the profession. *Journal of Counseling and Development, 70*, 477–486.

9

WALKING THE TIGHTROPE OF CHANGE

Building Trust and Effective Practice in a Diverse Multi-Stressed Urban Community

Gerald Monk

Jose, an intern I am supervising, is feeling overwhelmed with some of his clients and their issues. His 18-year-old client (we will call him Manuel) is struggling to finish high school. It is not because Manuel is having trouble with his Algebra or is in conflict with his English teacher and is feeling unsupported. His troubles are in a different category. He recently learned that his uncle, who is a hit man for a drug syndicate, murdered a man in Juarez; the story was that his uncle cut off his victim's head, arms, and legs, and they found the poor man's torso in a dumpster. The head was wrapped up in a UPS-type robust cardboard box and mailed to the victim's family. Now Manuel is living in fear because the opposing gang syndicate is pursuing his uncle's syndicate. The retaliation is fierce when a senior drug cartel lieutenant is murdered. Manuel says the gang's reach is far when it is in full retaliation mode. The uncle who was responsible for this gruesome murder has disappeared. The family hasn't heard from him in quite a few weeks. Manuel is struggling to attend school. Not only is he frightened about his family's safety, he wakes up with terrors that he will be tortured and murdered like he presumes was his uncle's fate. This traumatized student is struggling to tell Jose, his counselor, the burdens and fears he is experiencing, and his family loyalty prohibits him from disclosing his family's secrets about being involved in the drug wars at the border.

It's difficult working in a multi-stressed community. Manuel's story highlights some of the clinical challenges of being a professor supervising trainees and interns working at the Center for Community Counseling. This center, funded by San Diego State University, is located in City Heights, an inner city neighborhood in San Diego, California. Manuel's case is not unique; there are several challenges that stretch the preparedness of mental health professionals. Let me share two other stories that showcase why therapists must build trust and then work actively with such a culturally diverse client group as the inhabitants of City Heights.

Another intern, Jessica, is seeking guidance from me on how to counsel a family. Her 16-year-old female client, Louise, has difficulty concentrating in her classes and seems to get periodically depressed. Her father and their family of four kids got evicted from the rental home they were residing in two months ago. Apparently the landlord got fed up with the mangled mess from a couple of broken vehicles in the backyard and her father was getting behind in paying the rent. Louise is distressed. She and her family have been living with a distant cousin in a two-bedroom apartment with 15 people. It is a chaotic, crazy living environment. Her dad has started abusing alcohol, methamphetamines, and marijuana. Now Louise is looking after her two younger brothers and sister as her father is depressed and generally unavailable.

Louise's mother has been trapped in Hermosillo after visiting her own dying mother; now Louise's mother can't get back to the United States. The mother is undocumented and has already been caught at the Mexican-US border for attempting to cross back to be with her family in City Heights. Louise got so fed up a month ago that she posted an advertisement on *Craigslist* to try to locate a one-bedroom apartment for her brothers and sister. She said she was walking around the streets of City Heights looking for a place and found one a few weeks ago. Her aunt paid the deposit and they just signed the lease. Louise worries about where the next month's rent will come from. She is really trying to stay in school. She is also scared that her father will go too far with his drunken rants and that she and her siblings will be taken out of the house and placed in foster care. My intern, Jessica, wants to explore meeting with the father to engage him about the stress her client is experiencing and to encourage him to take on more parenting responsibility in the household. The client is afraid that if the therapist contacts her father he will verbally attack her for sharing family secrets with a stranger.

This final story relates to my intern's experiences supporting a grant I am involved in within City Heights. As part of this grant, I work closely with the police on projects in the local schools and in the community. Police officers are engaged in community policing, and strive to build good relationships with the community to promote safety and enhance community connectedness. It is a privilege to work with such a dedicated police force. I was distressed to discover that a local police officer I had worked with was assassinated in City Heights last week (at the time of writing). The officer had just bought food at McDonald's and was heading to the station for lunch. He died while sitting at a red traffic light in his patrol car when a young man pulled up beside him, wound down his window, and shot him with a shotgun at point-blank range. The turnout for his memorial was quite extraordinary. Three-quarters of our internship class participated in the candlelight vigil, along with 600 people from at least 15 different ethnic communities who were there to commemorate this young officer's courage, dedication, and service to the community. It was very moving to see the whole community rally around, even though many of the families are very afraid of the cops because of the associations they have with police brutality south of the US border. The young man who shot the officer immediately drove to his house, where he engaged police in a gun battle two streets from our counseling clinic. He died quickly in the fiery exchange. A group of our interns went to the young man's memorial; we were the only outsiders present. Our team attended because one of our interns from this community knew his family. This prior relationship created an opportunity for us to make progress on what has become a crucial mission: to build bridges with our disenfranchised and alienated population in this City Height's community.

These three stories are a sample of the wide array of events and experiences that go on every day in City Heights. Typically, the stories are a combination of tragedy and despair sprinkled with hope, courage, and resiliency—and sometimes even heroism. No matter what the stories are, I often have the feeling that I'm walking on a tightrope that straddles a canyon, with fear and alarm all around. This chapter seeks to tell part of the story of my journey on this tightrope with my colleagues and students in our efforts to promote trust and confidence in a community that is so easily drawn to the path of unpredictability and mistrust. The chapter also outlines some strategies and lessons learned to help make working in a multi-stressed community so gratifying.

Our trainees and interns, and the faculty that teaches them, are a very dedicated and community-minded bunch. I am proud of what they do and have done to serve the families of City Heights. They are demonstrating the new directions our Center for Community Counseling is evolving into. They are honoring the recent change of our center's name from the Center for Community Counseling to the Center for Community Counseling and Engagement. That is exactly what we are doing—working at *engaging* the community. It is a difficult job.

Therapy and Community Work in City Heights

I have learned that working so closely in this community is not always teetering on the edge of hopelessness and discouragement. The breakthrough acts of courage and inspiration of its citizenry helps us all be resilient in our respective duties. I am involved in this work mostly due to a serendipitous accident. Also, maybe partly, I spend so many hours of my life here because I feel guilty about all of the unearned privileges I have in my life compared to many others around me, and this work gives me an opportunity to give back a little. My teacher friend often reminds me of the biblical quote: "For everyone to whom much is given, of him shall much be required" (Luke 12:48). Let me describe how our team, which is made up of professors Linda Terry, Brent Taylor, Pilar Hernandez (and more recently Soh-Leong Lim and Jan Ewing) along with our Community-based Block and Counseling and School Psychology Colleagues, started our community project in City Heights and why I say it was a serendipitous accident.

In 2001, our team was given an unexpected opportunity to transform the way we provide clinical services to people seeking mental health services in San Diego, California. San Diego State University (SDSU) was short of office space and the dean of our College of Education came up with a proposal that was too good to be true: replace our antiquated and inaccessible university counseling clinic by building a new facility in a location that could provide much-needed mental health services to a multi-stressed inner city community. This chance opportunity led us to build the clinic in the inner city community of City Heights.

The SDSU community-based counseling clinic was originally located in our campus building and had been providing counseling services since the late 1970s. We had 10 one-way mirror booths from which the professors could observe the graduate students at work. While the rooms were adequate for the purposes for which they were designed, the facilities were effectively out of reach of the community. Clients had terrible problems finding the location, which was embedded in old 1940s vintage bunker-like structures in a remote part of the campus. There was poor parking and difficult entry because of stringent security arrangements. It was difficult to recruit clients, and students would often have to get friends of friends to come to the clinic as clients. The ethnic composition of both clients and trainees then was predominantly middle-class Euro-American. Implicit in this arrangement was the dynamic that clients had to overcome all kinds of obstacles to access our counseling resources, instead of us removing help-seeking barriers to be more available to the people who could have benefitted from what we had to offer. The events that were about to occur were to change all of this.

In exchange for giving up our clinical space on the SDSU campus we were offered an opportunity to relocate the clinic in a neighborhood that suffers from numerous social, economic, and health care concerns. Our brand new clinic was opened in the fall of 2002. Located in a large two-story structure housed next to a range of SDSU offices, we were now in the heart of City Heights on a street (according to the Mid-City police) occupied by the most vicious Van Dyke gang. Our new clinic was set up with a small waiting room, administrative offices, two seminar rooms that could be used for conducting group work, and 12 counseling offices with one-way mirrors. This was a significant and exciting period for the faculty and trainees. We were about to work with real challenges that multi-stressed clients and their families were being subjected to. Now we could provide mental health services to the community in City Heights, which has a population of approximately 90,000 people (Population and Housing Estimates, 2010).

The Community of City Heights

City Heights has an unparalleled ethnic and cultural diversity due to the presence of multiple immigrant and refugee populations from Southeast Asia, East Africa,

Mexico, South America, and the Middle East. The 2000 census showed that 44% of City Heights' population emigrated from more than 60 countries. More than 40 different languages and dialects are spoken in City Heights (2000 Census of Population and Housing).

Many families living in this community deal with serious day-to-day struggles such as compromised housing situations, unemployment, or over-employment, with many parents working two, even three, jobs. Single parents make up more than one-third of families in the area, and close to a majority of residents over 25 years old have not graduated from high school. There is a significant presence of prostitution, alcohol, and guns as well as an active drug trade; all of which attracts gang and criminal activity. This is a challenging environment for many growing up in this neighborhood. City Heights promised to be a great opportunity for neophyte therapists to hone their skills with families that might really benefit from their contributions.

The Challenges

Bringing our program into an inner city ethnically diverse community raised enormous challenges for a majority white, middle-class MFT student body and a largely white professional faculty. This move to City Heights confronted us head-on with the extraordinary mismatch between the mental health needs of an ethnically diverse population and the mental health services to be provided by a largely homogenous Euro-American group of MFT trainees with limited culturally responsive training. We have not been alone in grappling with this mismatch of background in providing culturally competent and culturally responsive services.

To provide some perspective of the magnitude of this challenge, 10 years ago the majority of California's population identified itself as non-White. According to Lok and Chapman's (2009) research, in 2000 roughly 53% of California's population was non-White and within six years, this proportion had grown to approximately 57%. Population projections based on this trend suggest that by 2030, 66% of California's population will be non-White. Over 90% of this population growth is anticipated to be within California's Latino (75%) and Asian (17%) populations.

In contrast to a diverse ethnic majority of 57% in California and a minority Euro-American population, survey results in 1998 by the California Association of Marriage and Family Therapy showed that 94% of the 12,900 family therapists surveyed were European-American, whereas 66% of their clients were from other racial groups (Green, 1998). The profile of our student body at SDSU in the early 1990s reflected a similar high percentage of Euro-American trainees and interns compared to a low percentage of diverse non-White ethnicities. Like the rest of California, we had a long way to go to have a more proportional ethnic representation within the mental health workforce. Therefore it was essential that we have a proportionally representative ethnic make-up in our trainee body. While we had been making progress on increasing the diversity and multi-cultural make-up of our trainee body, we needed to speed up this slow transformation as we prepared to work in the City Heights neighborhood.

However, by 2001 program at SDSU had not met the level of cultural diversity that we needed to make a success of moving to City Heights, an ethnically diverse community with a white population of less than 5%. While we were energized by moving to the new training facility, three of the five faculty were conscious of their white middle-class backgrounds. The energy and excitement was also accompanied by nervousness, and perhaps a floating unexpressed fear, about the extent to which we would be able to successfully serve this multi-stressed community. Not only was our own cultural readiness going to be a challenge; our program in many respects adhered to several conventions of middle-class culture, and we had been applying mainstream counseling and psychotherapy services congruent with middle-class cultural assumptions.

In general, there is little emphasis on the impact of middle-class values on counseling in counselor training programs. Like other programs, we were preparing mental health professionals to work with middle-class cultures, rather than with multi-stressed communities suffering serious social and economic disadvantages. It was not surprising that these cultural forces had captured us, as most universities in the West are shaped by the pervasiveness of middle-class culture.

Many mental health training programs are shaped and developed within middle-class culture. Graduate students, even if they were not raised in this culture, are drilled in cultural practices that require self-reliance, standard English, and the middle-class work ethic of delayed gratification. Graduate students raised in different class systems have distinguished themselves by succeeding amid the rigors of academia and have acculturated in a middle-class direction, with its emphasis on competing in an individualistic way. With our Master's program moving its clinical training site to City Heights, our students would have to adjust their expectations by working in a context that would probably not reward their middle-class standing and would not be commensurate with their middle-class grooming.

Committed to Making a Difference

The Department of Counseling and School Psychology in which our program had been housed had, for the last 15 years, made a commitment to train a new generation of therapists that would not be a continuation of a predominantly white middle-class student body. Instead, the department faculty targeted future possible applicants who wanted to enter the mental health services area who came with some para-professional experiences in delivering mental health and services in marginalized and isolated communities. As a program we began marketing ourselves as preparing mental health professionals to work in community agencies and in multi-stressed communities, instead of private practice. With the training facility in City Heights, our impetus for fulfilling this new mission was heightened. We wanted to contribute to changing the composition of the mental health provider workforce so that more and more therapists could speak in their clients' mother tongue and have some intimate ethnic understanding of the clients' backgrounds.

Culturally Competent Recruitment Strategies

By the late 1990s, two of our faculty had implemented an *equitable admissions model* to guide our professional programs when selecting applicants for training within multi-cultural contexts. This model applies nontraditional criteria to applicants based on three dimensions: academic readiness, professional readiness, and cross-cultural readiness. Our program at SDSU has used this admissions model for the last decade, which has led to a dramatic shift in the ethnic and linguistic composition of our students. At the beginning of 2012, the current majority of our 70 trainees continues to be from groups that are underrepresented in higher education; they are ethnically diverse, often first-generation college students, immigrants, and from diverse sexual orientations. We are now enrolling a student body that reflects the local community, with about 70–80% people of color in the current cohort, including both US-born, first-generation immigrants as well as international students.

Our success with attracting, recruiting, and then retaining culturally, linguistically, and ethnically diverse trainees is not based merely on the changing ethnic composition of the population of California. It is based on our department's tireless endeavor to train mental health professionals that have a passion to serve communities that are underrepresented in mental health. These trainees must have had lived experiences with these communities—either they are from these communities or they demonstrate a clear openness/commitment to service in particular underserved communities. A social justice mission has driven this effort conducted by the CSP Department and the faculty. Today the CSP Department's primary goal is to prepare culturally competent and compassionate professionals who provide leadership in marriage and family therapy and other mental health fields such as school counseling, school psychology, and community counseling.

Innovative Curriculum

Our program's commitment to social change and diversity has produced a dynamic and multi-cultural curriculum. In addition to specialized courses with multi-cultural content, the faculty work to incorporate cultural considerations into all coursework. Specialty areas within the curriculum include attention to relationships between families and other larger systems. We have courses such as

Multi-cultural Family Therapy and Eco-systemic Assessment in our department course offerings.

Walking the Tightrope in City Heights

Despite our success in recruiting an ethnically diverse student body, we continue to be confronted with significant obstacles in working in a multi-stressed community such as City Heights. By far the most consistent challenge we have had, and continue to have, is building trust with client groups that have a history of negative experiences with public and community agencies.

Some of our clients have viewed mental health professionals as untrustworthy, as we are associated with authority figures who have not brought a sense of wellness to the family. Another challenge we have faced is the client's expectations that the mental health professional won't listen to them, understand them, or place value on the things that they value. We often wrongly assess our clients' self-protective responses as poor motivation to receiving counseling.

One of the issues that has caused our neophyte therapists distress is that some families in high-stress circumstances are not concerned with people pleasing— especially when it comes to addressing authority figures. Therapists can become targets of angry and cynical responses directed at them by clients who have suffered from previous bad experiences, and family members can project their strong negative reactions, blindsiding new professionals who are expecting to be appreciated and welcomed.

Assembling a Diverse In-home Mental Health Team

One of the most important next steps for our delivery of accessible mental health services in City Heights is our assembly of an ethnically and linguistically diverse In-home Mental Health Team that visits families. The only way that some of our City Heights' families will receive mental health services is if our trainee and intern conduct home visits. As this book goes to press, our Center for Community Counseling and Engagement has mobilized the in-home team to provide services that are accessible in peoples' homes even though sometimes our trainee MFTs can feel reluctant to make these home visits, particularly in a neighborhood where they feel endangered. It takes great persistence to put together a professional team that can face the diverse needs of families in crisis in neighborhoods plagued by gang violence. Our team is up for the challenge. Some of our preliminary experiences have proved demanding. Our trainees are beginning to receive referrals from curfew sweeps, which are conducted in City Heights approximately every four weeks on Friday and Saturday nights. Children under the age of 18 who are out on the streets unsupervised by adults after 10 pm are deemed to have broken curfew. In an effort by local police to reduce the fatalities and injuries inflicted by gang-related shootings, which mostly occur between

10 pm and 3 am, the Mid-City police arrest young people—sometimes as young as eight or nine years old—and transport them to a local school and charge their parents with a misdemeanor. For the parents to be released from any pending charges, they must enter into a contract for psychoeducational, counseling, and health services. Many of our families become mandatory clients because of the curfew sweep process. Many of these families have chronic or acute physical and mental health issues. Since our trainees are often viewed as an arm of law enforcement, they begin their therapeutic work under a cloud of suspicion. Our trainee therapists have to be persistent in meeting with family members who distrust their motives and are apprehensive about the whole process of therapy. Persistent, respectful engagement is required to break through the mistrust and the angry responses that are sometimes generated by the multi-stressed demands the families are weighed down by, such as unemployment, finding food and shelter, grinding poverty, domestic violence, and fear of gang violence. If family members are undocumented immigrants, they also have a real fear of being deported. Dogged persistence, combined with respect for and responsiveness to the unique cultural environment of the clients, are vital to success. This persistence could be illustrated by being prepared to get on a bus or trolley and sit with a client in order to establish a relationship from which therapeutic work can be accomplished. It is pivotal to recognize the family's competencies and resiliencies in the face of their multi-stressed challenges.

Some economically poor clients anticipate adversarial interactions from middle-class professionals, expecting neither to be heard nor to have their strong feelings (which may likely include anger) validated. Many of the families we see

PHOTO 9.1 Gerald Monk and trainees discussing new intake procedures for the In-Home Therapy Program at SDSU

in City Heights have been exposed to professionals or quasi-professionals who work in organizations that are poorly run and poorly resourced. Some of the families have a low regard for punctuality, as they have had numerous experiences of waiting for hours on end in mental health centers, police stations, and various government agencies for just a few minutes of the professionals' time.

Many of our clients and their families, because of their day-to-day suffering, can exhibit a tough and invulnerable exterior where strong angry emotions serve a protective function. Whereas middle-class clients may be concerned with attaining beauty and perfection, many lower socioeconomic communities prize resilience, strength, perseverance, and outspokenness. We train our therapists to acknowledge the value of resilience, courage, determination, and the willingness to speak out. Economically disadvantaged clients may be more direct with verbal and physical expressions that may not conform to the middle-class cultural conventions of how to deal with strong emotions, which are exhibited in private (or not at all).

Acknowledging Privilege

For many trainee therapists, it is easy to overlook the constraining social factors that affect our clients pertaining to class and socioeconomic status. The isolation, self-loathing, and immobilization experienced by families struggling to survive in poor urban communities can be downplayed. When therapists understand the power of class and socioeconomic factors in shaping peoples' identities and aspirations, it can help the clients feel understood and accepted. Feelings of humiliation, remorse, guilt, and resentment can be alleviated, thus freeing the individual or family to draw on family and community resources that were not previously available to them. As Kliman suggests, "Deconstructing class relations in therapy both counters their shaming effects and helps therapists guard against falling back on privilege themselves" (1998). Families who are denied mortgages and loans can see, through careful questioning, that their problems may indeed be economically systemic issues rather than caused by their own failings.

If our trainee therapists come from a privileged background, we help them monitor how their own socioeconomic status differs from their clients and how this may affect the therapeutic relationship. We tell these economically privileged students that it is not wrong: the important issue is not *being* privileged, but how one *uses* one's privilege. If it is used to make a difference in the lives of others who are less privileged, then there should be no criticism of that. Our trainee therapists need to develop a consciousness of their own social class influences and refrain from imposing their own class-related assumptions on their clients' particular life challenges. Middle-class markers, which place value on such things as speaking standard English, can become barriers for therapists whose clients have not assimilated to look, speak, and act like the middle class. Our trainee therapists can, however, work to help minimize such barriers. This has been an ongoing challenge for me in engaging with clients and para-professionals that are of a different ethnicity and socioeconomic class than me. As a White middle-class professional, I can be perceived as being out of touch and not understanding or appreciating people who have come from highly oppressed circumstances. Worse still is the challenge laid before me that I am a member of a white oppressor class who can only, because of this membership, act and behave in oppressive ways. This reaction, which I cannot ameliorate, is sometimes tough to handle. There is nothing I can do, of course, to change from being phenotypically white and a member of the middle class. These untrusting dispersions cast upon me before I even begin to engage are understandable, considering the racist history of the United States and the immense suffering that has occurred for ethnic minorities or under-represented groups because of the harmful practices of many white people over the last few centuries. Not taking these negative reactions personally, and then demonstrating integrity, perseverance, and heartfelt respect for others, is the most helpful and workable response.

The need to make practical adjustments must to be taken into account by counselors working in multi-stressed communities. Many of our trainees and supervisors get very frustrated by the number of no-shows in the appointment roster. It is easy to move to a place of judgment that we have client groups that seem unmotivated and unreliable in addressing their own needs, while at the same time are disrespectful of the mental health professionals' time. We can overlook the struggles that many clients, who have no reliable means of transport, face to attend therapy sessions. Many working-class families also have great difficulty making sustained appointments. People on shift work can have constantly changing schedules and have little control over their working hours, which makes it difficult to schedule therapy services way into the future. Many of the families in City Heights are in a constant state of fear of losing their jobs from taking time off to attend appointments. Many clients are concerned with day-to-day survival, and a 50-minute therapy appointment can be a very low priority when an immediate crisis surfaces, such as finding a place to live or food to eat.

Some of the agencies in City Heights can have a high volume of personnel turnover. Families can start to build trust with a mental health professional of an agency or an organization who seems to understand their specific concerns and needs; the mental health professional may help the family let their guard down and reduce their suspicions. What often happens is the family, adult, teenager, or child feels that their trust has been violated when the person working in the agency or organization is reassigned to another role or moves out of the organization or the area. Our Center for Community Counseling and Engagement has worked on a semester system, and we have not been successful in maintaining therapeutic bonds over a substantial period. Our trainee therapists are often only present for a 13-week cycle. This format feeds into the high turnover of trainee therapists. It has been a great challenge to change the format to create a yearlong traineeship or a multi-year traineeship/internship. It takes a long time to build a therapeutic community when we have few financial resources, which are needed to pay supervisors to oversee trainee therapists who are able to provide services at the center for at least a year.

Encouraging Empathy

It can sometimes be difficult for our trainee therapists to understand and relate to the circumstances and day-to-day challenges people face in poor communities. It is easy for therapists to interpret the failure to overcome powerful systemic and discursive constraints as failures in client awareness or moral courage. In other words, it is easy to individualize the effects of social forces and ascribe a client's lack of action to a personal deficit of some kind. One of our challenges is to help our trainees understand the processes by which the poor come to internalize feelings of defeat, inferiority, and personal failure and become dominated by helplessness and hopelessness—not because of a personal failure, but because these are the interpretations that they are invited to make of themselves by the systemic events unfolding in the community in which they live. Slattery (2004) comments that sometimes lower-class and working poor clients feel so hopeless about the quality of their lives and their economic well-being that this hopelessness is transferred to their expectations about therapy. Our task is to help our neophyte therapists open opportunities in therapy for clients to challenge the negative identity conclusions they have internalized from the cultural and economic contexts of their lives. The strength-based therapies our students study and practice help them develop qualities and skill sets that build the resilience, strength, and perseverance necessary to survive in this tough (and sometimes unforgiving) community.

Remaining Positive

All forms of systemic change in organizations produce multiple challenges and pushbacks that inevitably come from people affected by changes in structures and new forms of service delivery. The biggest lesson I have learned in my work in inner city communities such as City Heights is the importance of demonstrating persistent, dogged determination and moving forward with bold plans, positivity, and flexibility. Most people who have worked for any significant period of time in any organization know that the greatest challenges and stresses come from colleagues and peers from within your organization, rather than from the organization's clients. I have been more vulnerable to challenges and unresolved conflicts from my fellow professionals than those heart-wrenching moments that arise when working with families in crisis. I have learned (and am still learning) to not take personally the challenges that arise when bold initiatives are proposed that change the way services are provided. Colleagues can go on the attack, and their personal exchanges can be disrespectful and designed to immobilize the proposed changes. Over the years, I have noticed that many personal attacks I have been subjected to often emerge from people who are threatened by the perceived losses and fears resulting from changes that should or must occur in the social order.

To be successful as a counseling center, we have to engender trust through our own persistence to stay connected with clients who lack enthusiasm for an appointment and become indifferent towards some mental health professionals. My challenge is always to keep an eye on the larger social order and macro-systems that affect our clients, who feel hopeless in the face of unemployment, the lack of safety in the community, and hidden violence in the home. There are so many pathways to defeat when working in a multi-stressed community. However, there are many pathways that open doors, build confidence, and inspire hope and promote community well-being and connectedness.

Building Trust and Never Giving Up

How do we stay involved in projects that threaten to engulf and undermine our persistence and determination? The following are strategies that we use when we are feeling like we are losing our way and encountering resistance that tells us that it is time to give up and go home.

1. *We must focus on small victories.*
    My greatest satisfaction about this project is the realization of a dream that my colleagues and I have held for nearly a decade: to provide accessible mental health services to the diverse community of City Heights. We have set up the infrastructure that allows our ethnically and linguistically diverse therapists to be supervised by ethically diverse clinical supervisors. We are rapidly moving towards having the majority of our client population represent the ethnically marginalized and underserved groupings. It is enormously gratifying to be part of creating this outcome as a team. The effects of ethnic differences and social class factors on the therapeutic relationship and therapy effectiveness cannot be emphasized enough. Our trainees and interns understand McGoldrick's (2005) point that therapists who are representative of dominant groups, such as the middle class, tend to view their own values as the norm, and therefore must be careful not to judge the meaning of client behavior they observe and impose their own methods and timetable for when change should occur. When client behavior does not represent a therapist's humanitarian or equitable values, we must understand the cultural context in which a behavior has developed, even as we try to change it. Respectful collaborative conversations about therapists' class dilemmas in therapy can guard against therapists imposing social class judgments on individuals from a different class. We have noticed that trainee therapists who have themselves experienced shame and humiliation pertaining to poverty and the prejudices against being working class can be immensely positive resources for poverty-stricken clients. Specifically, therapists can help clients locate the source of

their shame and humiliation within the wider cultural practices of the community, rather than within their character or personal foibles. Sometimes, poor or economically disenfranchised clients who are of a similar ethnicity as a middle-class therapist may perceive that the therapist has "bought into" Anglo-American middle-class values and cultural practices. Overtly naming possible distrustful responses from clients is a helpful way to proceed. For example, a middle-class therapist attempting to build trust with a client from a lower socioeconomic group might say:

> I notice that you look very uneasy talking to me. We have already established that we are of the same ethnic background, but I am wondering whether you distrust me because my way of talking is very different to yours and your family's. It would be really helpful to me if you can be really honest with me and identify any barriers that you think might be getting in the way of us working together.

2. *We must network with diverse communities to take advantage of local resources.*
In City Heights, where therapy is a foreign practice, there are significant barriers that stop families from taking advantage of counseling services. City Heights' families are more likely to take advantage of extended family members' help, if they can provide it, or seek help from a family friend or cultural healers, ministers, or priests in the mainstream traditional religions. Our therapists can play an important role in supporting families to take advantage of local resources when these resources are effective and accessible. In order to make this happen, it takes a dedicated effort to network with the full range of informal and formal support systems. Appointments and interviews with the directors and community outreach officers of Somali Family Services, The East African Community Center, The Horn of Africa, and The Nile Sisters are examples of just a few places we seek assistance to work with families in City Heights, which come from dozens of regions around the world. Some of the countries represented here in just one region include Eritrea, Ethiopia, Somalia, and the Sudan. Within those organizations there are well-known healers and community leaders who must be consulted when we have clients from these communities. To effectively build trust in this inner city community, we must also engage over and over with all of the other community organizations from Southeast Asia, Iraq and Iran, Mexico, and Central America.

In addition to problems with physical accessibility, linguistic differences are further barriers between clients and therapists. A therapist who knows the language and dialect of the client can be crucial in providing assistance. Therapists who know non-standard English and other language dialects can build strong empathy with their clients. There are almost always small, medium, or large differences between classes relating to dialect. For example, in some African American communities in City Heights, a therapist's fluency in Ebonics can be a powerful resource in assisting lower socioeconomic groups that often speak in non-standard English.

Understanding and respecting the speech patterns of different cultural communities is essential to building counselor-client rapport. When we are working in ethnically diverse communities, it is important to surround ourselves with mental health professionals who look and speak like the members of the community they wish to serve. The external and internal shared characteristics pertaining to language and ethnicity go a long way toward promoting trust and connection between therapist and client in the long term.

3. *We keep our eyes on the prize when the grinding poverty all around us becomes too much.*

One of the things I have noticed over the years, relating to changing the way we deliver services or improving current systems, is that innovation takes quite a long time to implement. It takes patience and hard work to deal with resistance from those who currently benefit from the existing systems. When resistance comes in the form of personal attacks, it can get tiresome and frustrating.

One of the unexpected challenges I have noticed is being around some members of the local community who have so little to survive on, and being aware of the considerable resources I have for day-to-day living. Privilege and poverty are difficult dynamics to manage over the long term. When therapists have class privilege, such as attaining the resources and mobility of the middle class, they must be watchful of how this privilege is managed with economically disadvantaged clients. Sometimes therapists want to distance themselves from poverty because of the level of struggle they witness their clients experiencing. Financial hardship may provide a depressing influence on client motivation and engagement with the therapeutic process. An overriding sense of hopelessness caused by the daily struggle to survive does not typically motivate clients to eagerly engage in therapeutic interactions. Therapists who have been subjected to poverty in their own lives may want to distance themselves from poor clients because it reminds them of the shame, humiliation, and daily grind they experienced in their own childhood. These internal processes are best exposed in supervision in order for therapists to move past these old triggers of shame and guilt. These emotions must be attended to if trust and connections are to be made with a suffering client.

Conclusion

I learned a long time ago that there is very little I can do by myself to support or help a multi-stressed community; the people I teamed up with, however, could truly make a difference. This has been proven again and again. Perhaps the most surprising reason why I do this work and stay connected to it is the vicarious pleasure I receive in witnessing extraordinary feats of resilience and endurance from those extraordinary human beings who live at the margins. My colleagues, clients, students, and community members inspire me with their acts of leadership and courage in the face of the most ugly and insidious marginalizing social processes in our society. These people inspire me and give me hope.

References

Green, R.J. (1998). Race and the field of family therapy. In M. McGoldrick (ed.), *Re-visioning Family Therapy: Race, Culture, and Gender in Clinical Practice*, 93–110. New York: Guilford Press.

Kliman, J. (1998). Social class as a relationship: Implications for family therapy. In M. McGoldick (ed.), *Re-visioning Family Therapy: Race, Culture, and Gender in Clinical Practice*, 50–61. New York: Guilford Press.

Lok, V. & Chapman, S. (2009). *The Mental Health Workforce in California: Trends in Employment, Education, and Diversity*. San Francisco, CA: UCSF Center for the Health Professions.

McGoldrick, M. (2005). *Ethnicity and Family Therapy*: 3rd edition. New York: Guilford Press.

The New American Standard Bible. (2007). *The Most Literal is Now More Readable*. The Lockman Foundation, 12–14. Luke 12:48.

2000 Census of Population and Housing. http://www.census.gov/prod/cen2000/. Retrieved February 5, 2012

Population and Housing Estimates (2010). City Heights Community Planning Area, City of San Diego. http://profilewarehouse.sandag.org/profiles/est/sdcpa1456est.pdf. Retrieved *February 5, 2012*.

Slattery, J.M. (2004). *Counseling Diverse Clients: Bringing Context into Therapy*. Pacific Grove, CA: Brooks/Cole.

10

TWO ROADS LEADING TO ONE

Dallas Stout and Debbie Stout

Many people in our state and county today would seek to put us on a pedestal. Both of us have won numerous accolades and awards for our community service, but that was never the goal. In fact, there never really was a concrete goal. We both simply saw needs in our community and were compelled to step up and get involved. Writing this chapter has been much harder than either of us thought. We don't have a life-changing moment like a car wreck or a murdered child that drives our work. Both of us have been affected by things (who hasn't), but neither of us considers them as catalysts for our community involvement. "The work" truly has just been a part of our personal and professional lives since the start of our marriage. Probably not as dramatic as some other stories, but it is what it is. Looking back, we clearly have been at this a long time, but the time flew by and some days we wonder where it went. This is our story.

The Initial Transformation of Two

I (Dallas) have yet to find a good answer for choosing to spend so much time involved in community issues. It has been pointed out that many in the human services field have been helpers their whole lives, which is true for me. I have always been keenly aware of those around me who have less or need help. There is not a very good answer for what compels me forward in this work, but rarely have I left a community meeting, network, coalition, motivational seminar, or conference without feeling the urge to do much more to better this world. Those feelings often bump up against the realities of life and the constraints of available time. My career started with programs for troubled teens, which led to work with substance-abusing teens, then involvement in school and family issues, gangs, violence, and ultimately guns. My path more or less unfolded before me through work or community involvement each day. Some days felt like being on top of the world; others like spitting at a forest fire. Overall, I have had a good deal of fun, met some great folks, and had a broad array of experiences that might not have been available otherwise. Considering these payoffs, I often wonder why so many others are not involved in their communities?

One thing is for sure: the impact of my work in violence prevention really came to the forefront in 2004. In June of that year I stood on a stage with a prominent local Chief of Police with Father Gregory Boyle, who runs the largest gang prevention program in the nation right here in Southern California, and a couple of other well-regarded community leaders as we were all given the Ambassador of Peace award. While feeling incredibly honored, there was also the sense that I had not done enough to earn the award. I decided that day that I would do everything I could to live up to the title of Ambassador of Peace.

As for me (Debbie), I often lie in bed at night overwhelmed with deep respect for all the individuals who are making a difference: those who don't turn their phone off at night so they are available to the child who feels suicidal; those who have lost a child to violence from a stranger and—instead of reacting with anger at the world—decide to make a difference. Instead, I am the individual who lies in bed each night torn between her family, her faith, and her ability to really "change the world" like her childhood idol, "She-Rah … Princess of Power." To that girl within, I call for strength while listening to clients' life stories. My obligation is to make a difference for my three-year-old daughter. Her world can be a better place, and it deserves to be better.

The Transformational Journey (Dallas)

Although I had been involved in social causes and prevention work since high school, my first professional involvement in community-based work came during my junior year in college. As an unpaid, undergrad intern, I was asked to attend a meeting of the Orange County Substance Abuse Prevention Network (OCS-APN) on behalf of our agency. Walking into a meeting of strangers that first day was daunting, but everyone turned out to be warm and friendly, and genuinely happy and grateful for my service to the group. Since that day about 20 years ago, I have continued to be involved in coalitions and networks in communities literally from one end of the county to the other: gang meetings, drug meetings, school attendance meetings, tobacco-use prevention meetings, a gang prevention project with KOCE public television, after-school program meetings, violence prevention meetings, meth task force meetings, and many others. A lot of work seemed to be needed in these communities, and I had the time and energy to be involved.

As my involvement in some gang prevention work with KOCE public television was ending, a movement arose to create a violence prevention coalition in Orange County, patterned after one created previously in Los Angeles

County (Evans & Weiss, 1995). This effort was a very interesting and enlightening process, considering that at the time, people in the county widely refused to admit that any kind of violence problem existed at all. While I had nothing to do with the founding of the Violence Prevention Coalition of Orange County (VPCOC), I was lucky enough to be involved in some of the very first meetings. Attendees at those early VPCOC meetings discussed the needs in our county and then formed committees to get to work. In these meetings and trainings, we learned more about the science of community activism and the Public Health Approach (PHA). The PHA model focuses on dealing with diseases, their conditions, and the problems affecting health and then aims to provide the maximum benefit for the largest number of people. The main concerns are to prevent health problems and to extend better care and safety to entire populations. The PHA examines the problem of violence from three different levels of prevention: primary prevention focuses on actions that prevent violence before it occurs; secondary prevention involves the immediate responses to violent action, such as hospital care or other emergency services; and tertiary prevention focuses on long-term care issues, such as rehabilitation and treatment. Cohen and Swift (1993) showed that in order to reduce violence, it is first necessary to understand it epidemiologically; that is, to determine the underlying causes and contributing risk factors. As we learned more about the PHA and its application to violence prevention, we also practiced speaking at city council meetings and writing letters to our elected officials, all of which was a great learning experience.

Many times over the years, people have noted my work in Orange County and questioned why my involvement did not extend to prevention efforts at the state level or in Sacramento. My answer was always the same: there is no lack of problems or kids in need right in my own backyard. Truthfully, serving those youth and the related programs over the years left little time to do much at the state level other than write an occasional letter to elected officials about one piece of legislation or another. So I just kept plugging away, thinking that maybe someday I might be more involved at a different level.

The Transformational Journey (Debbie)

At the age of 12, I moved to Orange County, California from an Idaho town with a population of less than 5,000, which had sheltered me from violence. But when I was 16, my family came face to face with violence. A 15-year-old boy brought a .22-caliber semiautomatic pistol to school and shot another classmate. He had a "hit list" of students he was planning to shoot, and my younger sister was on the list. My parents decided to move out of California three months later, citing other reasons. However, it is easy to believe that this incident pressed the case for leaving. In some regards, my initial reaction to social justice was similar: run away from the problem, and perhaps someone else can take over.

Entry into this whole community involvement thing came a little later for me than for Dallas. I was a business major with a lucrative management career in the teen retail clothing industry when we met. The start for me came as a result of the synergistic effects of watching Dallas in action, being affected by a few key professors, and practical experiences in the community. I decided that I needed to make a stand and get out of my comfort zone.

My professional advocacy first began while working for the Orange County Department of Education (OCDE) under a grant aimed at a low-income and high-violence community in Orange County (OC) (yes, OC does have violence) to make micro-level shifts using the youth resiliency model. This was my first experience attending city and county meetings with community youth. They made a difference in their immediate community and increased the availability of resources for youth, which was very empowering to witness. Shortly after starting at OCDE, the chair of the VPCOC asked me to chair the annual Ambassador of Peace Awards luncheon. After coordinating this event for two years, Dallas and I were named co-chairs of the VPCOC. My understanding of how to make policy changes at the state level was growing, and I also began attending the monthly OCSAPN meetings. Before long, Dallas and I were on the board. We enjoyed doing this work at the county level together. We were probably the busiest couple we knew, balancing our education, jobs, marriage, faith leadership roles, and our advocacy. However, because we frequently attended the same events and shared a passion for making a positive change in our world, our involvement brought us closer together.

The VPCOC, along with several other county agencies, was happy to support the creation of the OC Safe from the Start (OCSFTS) Coalition. Patterned after a similar state-level program, OCSFTS works to reduce children's exposure to violence. The coalition created a tool kit and a training program, and then proceeded to provide training across the county for anyone who was interested. While at OCDE, I was involved in the implementation of this program from the beginning.

Our Chrysalis

We initially agreed to become the co-chairs of the VPCOC for one year, but we would ultimately serve for eight. Our goal was to help VPCOC build a stronger, more diverse board of directors in order to enhance the coalition's effectiveness and ensure its future. We set about adding board members, with limited success at first, as some just could not commit to the work. With others moving on, the board was shrinking. Building outside involvement for special committee work was also difficult.

With a countywide organization to run and a dwindling number of board members (who themselves were stretched for time), we faced some real challenges. In fact, we had become a group that was very good at coming up with

ideas for things to do, but with no one around to do the work. We found ourselves repeating the mantra: "That's a good idea, but who is going to do it?" After
many months, Dallas started to wonder whether the organization had outlived its
usefulness, and ultimately posed the challenge to the board at an all-day retreat.
We all left that event with the firm understanding that if we wanted to stay
around, we either needed many more board members or a staff person. Without
any kind of real budget, a staff person was out of the question. We did decide to
keep operating and to work toward progress.

Once we decided to keep the VPCOC going a little longer, good things began
to happen. We looked for interns from local universities who might be able to
help us out, and we were lucky enough to find one right away. In addition, Debbie was able to enlist a student who was interested in doing some research, and
together, we investigated what people wanted from the VPCOC. After a couple
of failed attempts at grant writing, we were introduced to someone at a large
foundation who was very impressed with what the VPCOC had accomplished
for so long with next to no budget. The foundation invited us to submit a letter of interest and then a request for a grant. Armed with our recent research,
our intern helped us pull this grant together, and the VPCOC was awarded a
three-year capacity-building grant, the first in its 14-year history! This was a huge
accomplishment, as being funded by this particular foundation will make it easier
to secure funding from others in the future.

The grant allowed the VPCOC to hire a part-time employee, who began
doing much of the background work that we had handled in the past. To be
honest, having a staff person lifted a huge weight from our shoulders. This new
beginning and time of excitement also felt to us like a good time to plan an exit.
Realizing that we had been in the leadership position for a long time, we sought
to provide the group with six months' notice to ensure a smooth transition. We
also asked the board to create both an emeritus position and an elect position,
which would guarantee three years of sustained leadership to advise the board. A
new chairperson was chosen, and she was tasked with finding a chair-elect. Stepping down created mixed feelings for us. On one hand, we were glad to get out
from under some responsibility, and on the other we had a "now what?" kind of
feeling.

After VPCOC

Today, as emeritus co-chairs of the VPCOC board, we counsel with the current
chair and provide continuity to the board. Within months of our stepping aside,
the board extended the term of service for the chair, emeritus chair, and chair-
elect to two years.

When the word was out that we were stepping down as co-chairs of the
VPCOC, some of the same folks who for years had been quietly asking Dallas to
get involved in Sacramento started asking again. Within just a couple of months

of Dallas' decision to become president of the California chapters of the Brady Campaign to Prevent Gun Violence, as well as their Political Action Committee in Sacramento, he had several new "firsts" in his life. One of these was appearing at a Los Angeles press conference to present the Brady Campaign's position about the open carrying of guns in parks and restaurants. Soon thereafter, he was meeting chapter leaders and members at the state Capitol for a lobby day. While talking to one state senator about sensible gun laws, Dallas was invited to return in a month to provide expert testimony before the House Committee on Education for a teen dating violence prevention bill. Now there is talk of possible service at the national level in the not-too-distant future.

Debbie continues her involvement with the OCSFTS Coalition as a consultant. She worked with a team of three individuals to write the course curriculum and has trained over 500 trainers in Orange County. The frontline workers who work daily with families amaze her. The stories they share and the changes they make at the micro level are astonishing. She feels fortunate to see the cycle of violence in children's lives begin to stop, even though at times, the impact she has had seems miniscule compared with all the negative messages some young children have had.

One opportunity this work has brought us that most people never have is the chance to be on TV and radio—something neither of us was ever trained to do. Someone simply said there was a need to go talk about what we do, and we went. It's a good thing that TV studios are kept cold, so that people are less likely to sweat when they get nervous. Of course, speaking about something that we are involved in and passionate about also helps. Radio is much easier than TV because you usually have a big red button in front of you that you can push to kill the microphone. Even if you never push it, the fact that you can is comforting. There is no such button for TV, and we have never seen them do a retake, either.

OC, California is a place with many misconceptions, which can be profoundly frustrating. A recent, highly popular, national television show that portrayed every one in OC as wealthy, White, or surfers who live by the beach really didn't help. In truth, OC is an area of great ethnic and cultural diversity. Although it is commonly thought to be uniformly wealthy, in reality, a wide range of socio-economic statuses exists. One of the biggest challenges in working in drug and violence prevention in OC has been the level of denial. Dallas has run into local politicians and other community leaders who actually publicly announced that there were no drug, gang, or violence problems in their communities. This attitude has changed, but there are still many who like to think that there simply is no problem. To this day, we are concerned that so much work remains to be done in our communities, county, state, and nation—and yet so few really ever step up and get involved. We would like to believe that people mean well, but are too busy and caught up in their own lives.

Very early on in this work, Dallas wrote a letter to the editor of the countywide newspaper about gun safety in which he asked why, at the time, it was

PHOTO 10.2   Debbie and Dallas preparing to speak at VPCOC event "Frustrations, Challenges, and Obstacles"

harder to import teddy bears than handguns. The night after the piece appeared in the paper, Dallas was at a class for his Master's degree program and Debbie was home alone when she got a threatening phone call about the article. The call was especially alarming because we had always had an unlisted phone number, and we questioned whether we were up to the challenge. Thankfully, a similar incident has never happened again.

One of the lowest moments for Dallas came when he was chatting with someone he admires in the gun violence prevention movement, excitedly sharing our plans to drive to Solvang for a murder mystery weekend. The individual responded that there was a time in their lives that they might have enjoyed that kind of thing, but they no longer supported such entertainment since their son had been shot and killed on the streets of New York City. The moment was awkward and profoundly uncomfortable, but also life changing. That was the day that really sealed his personal commitment to be the change in how our society supports and pays for violence in entertainment.

Another challenge was coming to terms with how casual our society has become in using terminology that can be upsetting or offensive to those who have buried a loved one. Our TV shows, music, and movies all glorify violence and violent lifestyles. Once we decided that we didn't want to support this process anymore, we worked to be more careful with our use of words, and stopped seeing what we call "shoot-'em-up" movies—those that end with everyone being shot or blown up. Violence in the United States began to increase dramatically in 1965, at about the same time that the first generation of children raised on TV began to reach the age at which most violent crimes are committed. Centerwall (1992) research indicated that similar effects were found in Canada and South Africa about 15 years after television was introduced in those countries.

Dallas is an anomaly in some respects among his fellow volunteers with the Brady Campaign, as most others have been personally affected by gun deaths; many have lost children and/or spouses. At times, it's hard to see their pain and not be able to do much about that aspect of the struggle. Again, the years of sitting with the survivors of violent crime and gun death has an impact on one's soul. Your views of the world, of humor, and of entertainment, all begin to change.

About five years ago, we decided that if we were ever going to have a family of our own, that we had better get with it—neither of us was getting any younger. But to raise a family, we needed another change of pace. We decided to transition much of our involvement in the county closer to our home, which meant becoming more assertive and practicing saying "no, thank you" more often than not. Pulling back was hard, as some people actually got angry with us. Maybe when you do as much as we were doing, people just assume it must be your job and someone is paying you to be there. We had to remind people on more than one occasion that we were volunteers. As part of this new focus, we joined a local collaborative, a network of concerned agencies and individuals that deals with issues facing our community.

Implications for Continued Social Justice Counseling

We suggest to all our students, as well as the professionals we meet, that they find a way to get involved in their communities. Even the best community has a plethora of issues to address, and more often than not, some group, program, or agency is trying to assist. Start by deciding on the area in which you want to volunteer: for example, homelessness, drugs, literacy, domestic violence, seniors, etc. Make some appointments with the people or agencies doing that work in your area and find out how you could best get involved. Ask about community networks or coalitions and other people to contact. After all that, tour a couple of agencies doing the work that interests you. Start attending one or more of the meetings you learned about. Ultimately, you will have to decide how to get involved in a way that best suits you. Keep in mind that you may have to spend a couple of years trying out several different things until you find a good fit.

A clear understanding of what "our issues" are has been important to us, because so much needs to be done. If you choose to get involved in an issue, you will often be approached to get involved in other issues. You could be spread very thin if you allow this to happen. Dallas recalls one time when he was invited to join a coalition that was forming in the county to assist gay and lesbian youth. When he declined, the person who invited him seemed almost offended, and questioned his commitment to troubled teens after all. Dallas pointed out that he could physically do only so much and he had to draw the line somewhere. Being aware of the research about GLBTQ teens, Dallas was concerned about these youth; however, he was also keenly aware that his plate of issues was already full. With that explanation, the individual understood why Dallas had to decline the invitation. There have been many times when both of us have had to make similar decisions. We remind ourselves often that saying "no" to one thing is ultimately saying "yes" to something else.

We have also sought to live the violence prevention we have preached within our new family. Our young daughter's brain continues to absorb a variety of information and experiences, much like a sponge. We know that she needs the positive, repetitive, predictable experiences in her life for healthy brain development. As we learned through our violence prevention research, experiences during the first five years of life are very critical in shaping the ability to form close and emotionally healthy relationships (Perry, 2001, 2004). In fact, a child raised in a state of fear will react differently in the world (Perry, Pollard, Blakley, Baker, & Vigilante, 1995). A young child's brain develops well when he or she is surrounded by a calm environment. We are continually challenged to create this type of environment in our home for our daughter.

We have gained much as a result of our community service. The work has made us better Christians and better people. We still don't have a good answer for why we do it, yet we are less concerned about that these days. Family and friends who really wonder where the fire that compels us onwards comes from will just have to wonder. The bottom line is that we all need to find a healthy balance of how we spend our time. We don't have any more time than those standing next to us; we just choose to spend our time in service. We also happen to believe that you could too. There is no lack of work to be done.

Sometimes we think we could be doing much more for our community and state, and yet we also clearly understand that with a very young daughter of our own at home now, we need to be OK with doing what we can and trusting the universe to take care of the rest.

References

Cohen, L., & Swift, S. (1993). A public health approach to the violence epidemic in the United States. *Environment and Urbanization, 5*, 50–68.

Centerwall, B.S. (1992). Television and violence: The scale of the problem and where to go from here. *The Journal of the American Medical Association, 267*(22), 3059–3063.

Evans, C.A. & Weiss, B.P. (1995). Developing a violence prevention coalition in Los Angeles. In B. Bradford & M.A. Gwynne (eds.), *Down to Earth Community Perspectives on Health, Development, and the Environment*, 34–48. West Hartford, CT: Kumarian Press.

Perry, B., Pollard, R., Blakley, T., Baker, W., & Vigilante, D. (1995). Childhood trauma, the neurobiology of adaptation, and 'use-dependent' development of the brain: How 'states' become 'traits.' *Infant Mental Health Journal, 16*(4), 271–291.

Perry, B.D. (2001). *Bond and Attachment in Maltreated Children: Consequences of Emotional Neglect in Childhood*. Houston, TX: Child Trauma Academy. http://centerforchildwelfare.fmhi.usf.edu/kb/ChronicNeglect/ConseqOfChNeglect.pdf. Retrieved February 7, 2012

Perry, B.D. (2004). *Brain Growth vs. Body Growth*. Houston, TX: Child Trauma Academy.

11

MOVING BEYOND THE PROFESSIONAL RESPONSE TO GENDER-BASED VIOLENCE

Community Organizing with Women Survivors

Loretta Pyles

I worked in the movement to end gender-based violence for about six years as a women's advocate, community educator, fundraiser, policy advocate, and trainer before returning to school to earn my Doctorate in social work and embark on an academic career. I have continued to engage in consulting, activism, and community-engaged research for the last 10 years, for a total of 16 years working on this issue. I originally came to the work after experiencing significant loss in my own life. I found myself searching for a way to make my life's work more meaningful than the academic philosophy career I was headed for. The anti-violence movement turned out to be, at least to some degree, a healing place, where I learned more about myself, my family of origin, and the patriarchal world that I live in than I had ever learned in a feminist philosophy class.

The anti-violence movement, as I—and, I believe, others—view it, has historically been grounded in survivor-led feminist social change work, whereby our analysis of the issue of gender-based violence is informed by an intersectionality perspective (Schechter, 1982). This perspective affirms connections between racism, sexism, and classism, and critically analyzes the cultural and social values and institutions that marginalize women, people of color, and poor people. Furthermore, we believe that the *ways* in which we go about organizing, advocating, and intervening around gender-based violence are as important as the end results achieved (Pyles, 2009). When engaging in this kind of organizing, one's access to, awareness of, and use of power is crucial. Finally, the movement embraces the idea that personal change and social change are intimately connected. In short, this paradigm and the feelings of solidarity and sisterhood have formed who I am as a practitioner, researcher, educator, and human being.

Of course, most responses to gender-based violence for the last 25 years have been informed by values and practices that have strayed from the feminist origins of the work I describe. Rather, domestic violence interventions have been dominated by professionally driven social services provision, largely a function of public social welfare and criminal justice policies and, by extension, their funding streams. Don't get me wrong. We live in a society in which people need social services. But social services are not the same as social change. Social service provision, as a general rule, perpetuates the status quo, offering triage for people in crisis. Social services do not get to the roots of social problems. These two competing tensions—radical social change work and professionally driven social service models—embody a dialectic that has interested and befuddled me throughout the years.

In 2008, I had the opportunity to connect with an advocate at a local domestic violence shelter. As a new faculty member working in the community, I had reached out to her, seeking her engagement on an advisory board for a community service program at the university that I was directing. After many conversations together, a partnership began to emerge; our connection has been grounded in a mutual interest in feminist social change work, a critique of the current social services model, and a specific desire to re-center the voices of survivors in the gender-based violence field and movement. We have both been driven by the conviction that survivors can move from being confined to a definition of themselves as "clients" to a more empowered definition of themselves as social change actors.

Drawing from the shelter's former client base, we began to reach out to women survivors to find out who might be interested in social change work, specifically survivor-led community organizing around the issue of gender-based violence. We were lucky to find a few women who were interested and held our first meeting in June 2009; we have held monthly meetings continuously since then. The group eventually decided on a name for itself—Building Bridges—with the following vision statement: "We are women working to create a world of peace and harmony within our community while offering a bridge of support to empower women and the community through advocacy and education to bring an end to domestic abuse." Our key areas of focus have been: 1) internal capacity building, popular education, and peer support; 2) community education about gender-based violence, and 3) systems change.

Building Bridges is somewhat of a hybrid organization. We are not completely grassroots, as we receive in-kind support from a large social services agency, i.e. the local domestic violence program that my advocate partner works for. But we operate differently than a social services organization. We are proactively attempting to do something that is an alternative to the traditional social services model. For example, the women survivors (with our consultation and support) make the decisions about our agenda, procedures for operating, funding, and all other activities. Conversely, in a social services setting, case managers, middle managers, and corporate executives make decisions about programming, policies, funding streams, etc., with occasional input from clients.

PHOTO 11.1 Building Bridges Headquarters

The matter of "who decides" gets to the heart of the ideas of power and empowerment. It is the difference between doing "for" or "doing on behalf of" versus "doing with." I am not interested in being "a voice for the voiceless." The social construction of a group of people who are "voiceless" is based on a false premise. People who are marginalized in society resist oppression all the time and often speak out in creative and resilient ways, so being a "voice for the voiceless," is built on a racist, sexist, and classist fantasy. The women in our group have fought back against their abusers, called the police on them, proactively protected their children, reached out for help, and articulated new lives for themselves.

Nonetheless, I do have skills to share that can help the group members strengthen their voices and be more strategic in how they use their voices to effect change. Furthermore, I am not too quixotic; I realize that my advocate partner and I have power in the group that others do not have by virtue of our professional positions, our historical knowledge as co-founders of the group, and our central positions as group facilitators. This is somewhat troublesome for me as I have always been a reluctant leader, feeling deeply uncomfortable with hierarchy and more naturally inclined to sharing power and decision-making responsibilities. Maybe it's a result of growing up with an overbearing mother, or just a deep-seated feeling that humans work better in a horizontal environment.

One of our current projects is a "Know Your Rights" campaign, the goal of which is to provide women in the community who are experiencing or at risk of gender-based violence with the knowledge of state and local laws, and police and court procedures. Our group is researching the current laws and local criminal justice policies, and interviewing other women who have experience with the police. We plan to transform this knowledge and these stories into an educational and advocacy campaign to help women get more benefit from the current system and continue to effect meaningful changes in local criminal justice practices.

Small is Beautiful

I am a believer in the idea that "small is beautiful" (Schumacher, 1999). I lean toward social anarchism, which affirms the values of collectivism and mutual aid in society, and savor the idea that small groups of people can create non-hierarchical alternatives to traditional hierarchical models of working. This is an end in itself. (We saw this with the Occupy Wall Street movement, which operated using consensus building as a way to make decisions.) The group's internal processes and experiences are just as important as the "outcomes" we achieve in the community. Thus, my vision for Building Bridges has never been one around growth. My vision is that it is sustainable and transformative. I relish the idea of a diverse group of 10 or so people sitting around, eating good food, sharing stories, making connections about personal and social change, being critical and creative, and plotting a different kind of world. That is my idea of success. It's what we've been trying to do, and it is a vision that keeps me motivated.

Thus, every month that we have a meeting and people attend; that is a success to me. Maybe that is just a sign of extremely low expectations. But the fact that women are creating safe spaces, speaking out against violence, telling their stories, creating plans for change, and affecting those plans, is a significant form of resistance. This is not just some kind of outdated 1970s feminist delusion; it is vitally important that women do this, since not all women are safe in their own homes yet. Furthermore, it is salient because the social services model tends to silence survivors' voices in favor of the visions of executive directors, funders, and the social norms of professionalism, all of which have the effect of excluding survivors from opportunities for creative and transformative social change. And, frankly, the shortsightedness of this social services model angers me.

Early on in the tenure of Building Bridges, we had the opportunity to hold a seat on a local domestic violence community response team. The community response team wanted to have survivors' voices represented at the table, so this has been a fantastic opportunity for the women to educate the community about gender-based violence and influence systems change. We continue to be challenged to get our members to attend these meetings, as they are held at 3:30 in the afternoon, which is a convenient time for the professionals who are paid to go to such meetings, but challenging for women with children and jobs and school to attend. Nonetheless, the fact that we have an insider's position within this system is most certainly a success for our young group. And recently, four members of

Building Bridges participated in a Domestic Violence Awareness Month panel, along with some of the professionals from the community response team. The women survivors shared parts of their abusive histories in powerful and courageous ways.

Organizing Myself Out of a Job (or Not)

One of the greatest tribulations of this work, as is often the case in social change endeavors, is coming to terms with my own expectations. I think the women in the group have had the same challenges. When I asked one of them what she has learned about social change from her experiences in the group, she responded, "it doesn't come overnight." My dream for Building Bridges has always been, to paraphrase Saul Alinsky (1971), "to organize myself out of a job." In my view, this would mean women facilitating the meetings, creating agendas and minutes, notifying each other of future meetings, taking leadership on community issues, implementing community change campaigns, and the list goes on as to what I see the women doing in my mind. But, of course, this has not been realistic; my advocate partner and I, along with student interns, continue to do many of these tasks. Is this a sign of a healthy social change organization? Maybe not, but it's reality. It is just par for the course in community organizing work. Paid union staff often grumbles about how they wish the rank and file membership were more active. We have tried to mediate some of this by offering facilitation training (an expression of our commitment to popular education) to the women so that they can feel more empowered and comfortable running meetings and creating agendas.

Though the women are actively involved and make key decisions, there are several reasons why I think we still do many of these tasks in Building Bridges. First, the women are still coping with a variety of issues, many of which are manifestations of the ongoing effects of domestic violence in their lives. This includes economic struggles, such as looking for work and pursuing educational opportunities. In addition, personal and family issues such as health and mental health, and the behavioral issues of children who have witnessed domestic violence, present significant hardships. We try to diminish some of these barriers by providing childcare, food, transportation, and a small compensation of a $25 gift card for their participation in monthly meetings. Still, sometimes it's not enough and women report just feeling too tired to come to meetings.

Second, not every survivor wants to wear a survivor's badge of honor on her sleeve. For many of the women, having experienced emotional, economic, physical, and/or sexual abuse, is, frankly, embarrassing. They see themselves as intelligent, strong women, and it's difficult to put oneself out there as a survivor—in effect, announcing it to the world. For some, they just may not feel safe enough to do that; for others, the abuse is ultimately something they want to put behind them. And for still other women, their participation in Building Bridges may just be a short stretch of the road on their long path to recovery and healing. So, we have found that continuing to recruit new members is important.

Third, community organizing is challenging work. Not many people do it; we are content to allow politicians to address the issues through public policy, or for paid professionals to pick up the slack through social services, even though we know it's not sufficient. Also, a majority of the social justice work in this country is conducted by large-scale advocacy organizations such as the National Organization for Women or Greenpeace. We pay annual dues to such organizations and get a good feeling, believing that they are addressing the issues at hand. But such groups are not directly accountable to a grassroots constituency. For many people, the daily grind of community building and organizing, including holding meetings, making phone calls, organizing events, bringing food, securing childcare, etc., is just not very appealing or glamorous. Some people love humanity but don't really like people very much.

Fourth, the women may still see themselves as clients. Recently, Building Bridges reached a low point, a genuine nadir in its existence. We had a couple of months in a row of having meetings with only one woman showing up. Generally, things were stagnant and we were just not moving anywhere. I felt frustrated and was teetering on making the decision to throw in the towel. One decision we made was to reach out for help from a local activist who has tremendous experience organizing women around welfare rights issues. This simple act of reaching out to someone for a cup of coffee really shifted things for Building Bridges. We shared stories about the realities of organizing and felt validated in our struggles. We also got some fresh ideas. We realized that we weren't accomplishing our goals very effectively, and that was likely why people had quit coming, just out of pure frustration.

One of the decisions we made after that cup of coffee was to hold our meetings in a new location. We had been holding our meetings at the administrative and outreach offices of the domestic violence program. But maybe, we surmised, that location left the women feeling like they were still social service users or clients, and not empowered community activists. We are fortunate to have a space in the community specifically devoted to convening women activists that is in a perfect location, right on a bus route. Though we can't be sure why, membership in the group has suddenly exploded since we moved to the new location. The new energy and new setting has created some fresh enthusiasm that feels more connected to the community.

The Lessons of Social Change Work

Here I offer some lessons learned from doing social change work. Many of the insights are years in the making and come from doing other kinds of social change work, including organizing teachers in union and organizing with peasants in rural Haiti. To be sure, my work with Building Bridges has solidified these lessons, which are a result of self-reflection, making mistakes, learning to let go, and swallowing an immense dose of humility.

Keep Your Eye on the Big Picture

I've seen it many times. The original intention or mission of a group of people or organization is to change the world—to alleviate poverty, to end violence, or to transform a neighborhood or community. But slowly, the big picture is obscured by the demands of boards of directors or funders. In addition, activists may get caught up in political juggernauting and make too many compromises. One might call this co-optation or selling out. Or maybe it's just not seeing the forest for the trees. At any rate, while an organization's mission is to end violence, in reality the practice devolves into just maintaining the organization itself—keeping staff on board, meeting grant deadlines, and responding to clients and the community. While these two courses of action are sometimes compatible, they can often be at odds with one another. So not losing sight of the big picture is key.

Enjoy the Details

This may seem like a contradiction from the previous lesson, but it is vitally important. Finding joy in organizing, or anything work related for that matter, is something that is silenced in our culture. In our Puritanistic, capitalistic society, to find joy and pleasure in our work is a disruption of the status quo (Shepard, 2011). Social change work should be grim; it should be drudgery, right? It should be a form of self-mortification and should feel like wearing a hair shirt, right? Ironically, to experience joy in organizing, I have to work hard at it. In our group, we eat dinner together at every meeting, which creates a more socially oriented environment and a sense of community. We are guilty of being too serious sometimes, and try to bring humor and laughter to our work. Last year, we participated in a community domestic violence awareness month event that was a scavenger hunt. We had a great day with lots of laughs. We try to celebrate all of our successes, even if they are small ones. When I find myself re-hashing a narrative in my head about the toils of going to meetings and creating agendas, I try to remember what an honor and privilege it is to do this amazing work with such inspiring people.

Use your Networks

You already have many connections—friends, acquaintances, and colleagues in high and low places. These contacts have skills and resources that can be leveraged to help your social justice work. Your connections also have other connections, and so forth. I have found that reaching out to colleagues, students, a neighbor, and others can provide our group with the exact information or resource we are looking for. Or they might know somebody who can help. A colleague introduced me to an amazing woman who conducts workshops on feminist meeting facilitation, and these workshops have had an important snowball effect on our group. In another instance, I had a student intern who had done a previous internship at the state assembly and was a tremendous asset to Building Bridges in our legislative advocacy work.

A corollary to this lesson is to strengthen your networks and your mission through the use of technology and social networking. Our group has a Facebook page, which is a good way to create interesting synergies and share information. Though this is a good time to point out that technology can also serve to isolate and marginalize people. Not everyone in the group has access to the Internet, is computer savvy, or even speaks English fluently for that matter.

Nurture your Relationships

It has not been uncommon to lose contact with some of our members for weeks, or even months, at a time. Reaching out to them personally has been the best way to check in and re-affirm relationships. This can be tricky because it is common for the members of our group to disconnect cell phones (change numbers), move residences, or avoid responding altogether. There are several times when just sending a simple text message to a member or chatting on the phone about how things are going has served to re-establish relationships in meaningful ways. Also, my advocate partner and I have found that checking in with each other and nurturing our relationship is fundamental, whether by e-mails, phone calls, a cup of coffee, or lunch. Creating time to reflect on the work we're doing together, as well as talk about our personal lives, has strengthened the relationship.

Set Boundaries and Stay Healthy

If you don't set boundaries about what you can and cannot do, your social justice endeavors won't be successful. Only when we are healthy can our communities be healthy. If you are stressed out, harried, or physically ill and you bring that to your social justice work, then that's the kind of community you will create. I have found that if I am feeling depressed or closed down before a group meeting, then that's the kind of meeting we'll have. If I am feeling full of happiness and abundance, then this can surely influence the course of the meeting. So I have to nurture myself in ways that will facilitate a more joyful and abundant outlook. In Eastern medicine, poor health is a function of imbalance. Our communities are unhealthy because we haven't learned to set boundaries as a society—too much greed and not enough sharing; too much work and not enough play. And the same goes for individuals: we are out of balance. On the other hand, we can start where we are, even if we are not very centered or healthy. The best kind of organizing work will nurture us toward well-being. It's taken me a long time to learn this, having gotten to several different points in my life when my own health and well-being were compromised. I now understand that my own spiritual connectedness and health always comes first. I can only achieve this through serious doses of regular yoga, meditation, and exercise.

When I am organizing, I've also found that I have to check in with my ego. What are my intentions with an action? A conversation? With this whole endeavor? It's an ongoing practice. If I try to define myself by this work, I find that I lose my balance every time. It's not that one can't be proud of one's accomplishments. Indeed, we should be proud of our successes. But our egos, and the romantic stories they tell about community organizing, can be antithetical to the kind of change one is working toward.

Organizing is Sacred

My organizing work can feel like a chore and something that I can, quite frankly, come to dread. But when my head is screwed on right, I come to realize what sacred work it is. When we come together as a community, we are doing something that is very ancient, something that is completely natural for human beings to do. In our individualistic society, we often find ourselves spending the majority of our non-work time alone in our homes, with our family, or isolated in front of an electronic screen of one sort or the other. Sitting in a community space with a group of people from all walks of life is rare indeed. As a group, we try to codify the sacredness of this time by incorporating rituals into our meetings. For us, this just means holding sacrosanct our check-in time at the beginning of the meeting, when people talk about what is going on with them personally. Besides food, we have recently added other kinds of rituals, something that we have called "soul feeding"—engaging in a creative activity such as an "ice breaker" or sharing a poem or song with the group.

Don't Go at it Alone

Our society is full of stories of heroes. We cherish the image of an individual who makes sacrifices on behalf of large groups of oppressed people. Think Mahatma Gandhi, Martin Luther King, Jr., and Nelson Mandela. Realistically though, the idea that people create social change single-handedly is pure fiction. Social change happens because groups of committed, connected people work together on specific tasks to achieve their goals. They change their minds and hearts, and make and implement plans. MLK, Jr. was a charismatic and effective leader who was passionately committed to civil rights and social justice. But he was part of an organizing tradition (he trained at the Highlander Institute in Tennessee) and he organized with many other people (for example, members of the Southern Christian Leadership Conference) to achieve his and others' goals. Cultural narratives of individualism notwithstanding, we are indeed an interdependent species residing on an interdependent planet. We need each other to survive; the corollary to this truism is that we need each other to transform our lives and communities. I would not have the skills I have today, nor would Building Bridges even exist, if it weren't for my mentors and teachers. Building Bridges wouldn't exist without my advocate partner and her mentors, or the women survivors and their mentors. Our group wouldn't exist without the people that built the buildings we meet in, or clean them, or pay the electric bills. Even our "enemies"—cops, judges, and welfare caseworkers—are part of this interconnected circle.

My point here is also linked to my earlier discussion about ego. It's not about you, and it's not about me. It's about us. So, find a friend and get them involved in your organizing work. Or get connected to a group of people that has been organizing for a while. Or go to an organizing training course. As I write this chapter, the Occupy Wall Street Movement is growing. If you're curious and not yet involved, do some field research and go out and wander around the nearest encampment and talk to people. It looks like this movement, which builds on older organizing traditions and innovates new ones of its own, will be around for years to come.

Social justice work is a living, breathing cultural (albeit sub-cultural) tradition in our society. Though Building Bridges is just a micro-sized blip on the social justice screen, I feel and believe that we are part of a larger tradition of feminist organizing. Though there are many challenges, we continue to give voice to a form of oppression that has been unmentionable for centuries. We seek solutions by inserting ourselves into community conversations about gender-based violence. Being a part of this movement is an honor that allows me to make my own and others' lives more equitable, healthy, just, and meaningful.

References

Alinsky, S. (1971). *Rules for Radicals: A Practical Primer for Realistic Radicals*. New York: Random House.

Pyles, L. (2009). *Progressive Community Organizing: A Critical Approach for a Globalizing World*. New York: Routledge.

Schechter, S. (1982). *Women and Male Violence: The Visions and Struggles of the Battered Women's Movement*. Cambridge: South End Press.

Shepard, B. (2011). *Play, Creativity, and Social Movements: If I Can't Dance, It's Not My Revolution*. New York: Routledge.

Schumacher, E.F. (1999). *Small is Beautiful: Economics as if People Mattered*, Rev. Ed. Point Roberts, WA: Hartley and Marks.

12

I AM YOUR FUTURE, YOU ARE MY PAST

Reaching Back to Move Forward

Selma de Leon-Yznaga

Because we were so different, I always asked my *abuela* (grandmother) where she was from. She would laugh heartily and tell me she was from the very spot on which she was standing. In the late 1960s, rural South Texas didn't look too much different than it had to her grandfather or his grandfather. They farmed the same land, whether it belonged to the United States or Mexico, whether it was subsistence farming of corn, sharecropping of cotton, or finally, in the 70s and 80s, government-subsidized sorghum. My Mexican grandmother didn't immigrate to the United States. She was always here.

I am far removed from my grandmother and her farm. Her day consisted of feeding the chickens, collecting their *blanquillos* (brown eggs), and cooking huge meals for her family, the farmhands, and anyone else who dropped by. My day consists of evaluating student writing for critical thinking, navigating the information highway, and attending endless administrative monologues. I sit all day in cold, conditioned air. I do not cook.

My grandparents knew the value of education in the United States because they didn't have one. They worked with their hands, picking cotton to pay for my father's Bachelor's degree in education. They worked all day to give him an opportunity that would propel him out of the oppression of the Jim Crow laws and into mainstream America, brown as he was. After a few years of teaching and school administration, my father could afford to pay for his own Master's degree in business administration and start his own insurance agency. In turn, he paid for my college degree.

My paternal grandmother's eyes twinkle when she says it is Americans who should label themselves in terms of generational status. In 1845, when the Republic of Texas was annexed to the United States, *Tejanos* living there became citizens in their own land. For many years, Mexicans, Americans, and Mexican Americans moved freely between both countries in a symbiotic relationship. By the time my father and his siblings entered elementary school (in the segregated El Nopal Elementary School), Mexican-Americans were unwelcome and unwanted. Students caught speaking Spanish in school spent their free time removing rocks from the playground, or worse, were physically punished. In high school, Mexican American students and white students were integrated; the small town of Bishop, Texas couldn't afford to maintain two high schools. My father, an athlete with an easygoing personality and hearty sense of humor, had little trouble fitting in. The Jim Crow laws prevented him, however, from celebrating the victories that he heavily contributed to, because Mexican Americans weren't allowed into most restaurants. My father, the team captain and the only Mexican American to make the team, waited on the bus outside while his teammates rejoiced inside.

My father's recollections of his early childhood are full of pain and triumph. He was able to transcend ethnic barriers easily: he was a bright student who could masterfully mimic the South Texas accent of his classmates. He was a natural athlete, and his strong work ethic made him a star. Behind the façade of assimilation, though, his heart ached for his sisters, who frequently stayed after school to pick up rocks on the playground and who were constantly chastised for their accents, their dark hair, and their seeming unwillingness to leave their culture behind in favor of the dominant culture. My grandparents were partly responsible for this: they encouraged their sons to take advantage of educational opportunities, but their daughters were expected to find husbands and make homes for them. Neither of my aunts ever married or went to college, and they remained forever trapped by the farm life that lost its vogue soon after the 1960s. My father's discrepant, gender-based opportunities made him push his four daughters to pursue post-secondary education. He didn't want to see us caught in the same trap as his sisters.

Gaining Entry into My Own Community

Perhaps the generational distance in traditional values is what subconsciously drew me to the *Buena Vida* (good life) housing development. When The University of Texas at Brownsville's (UTB) Center for Civic Engagement (CCE) director invited me to participate in the university's initiative to revitalize the community, I readily accepted. The 2003 UTB Cross-Border Institute for Regional Development (CBIRD) report was intriguing: the Buena Vida community represents about 3,000 residents who are mostly Latino (91%), uneducated (50% of the adults have less than a 9th grade education), Spanish-monolingual (68%), and live below the poverty line (63%). The Buena Vida enclave is located directly across the street from UTB, and abuts the Rio Grande River. I knew that in addition to the challenging demography of this community, there would be assets. I wanted to be a part of UTB's outreach and the Buena Vida success story. Perhaps most selfishly, I wanted to immerse myself in a community of recently arrived Mexican immigrants. This population was facing the most notable racism and discrimination that the country had seen in years, and I wanted to experience it firsthand. My childhood, while saturated with my father's stories of discrimination and humiliation, was one of privilege. My parents both had graduate degrees, we lived in one of the most prestigious neighborhoods in town, and I rarely wanted for anything. I was generationally disconnected from my father's experience and pain. I wanted to pierce the bubble of my privilege and immerse myself in a community still very much vulnerable to discrimination. I wasn't aware of it yet, but it was a way for me to understand my father and my history in a more immediate and empirical way.

I met with the housing director and asked for permission to run a support group for immigrant women. I created some flyers, and the CCE staff helped me post them around the neighborhood. The following Wednesday morning, I showed up with *pan dulce* (Mexican pastries) and waited. Two or three women attended the session with four or five young children. We had an informal visit that lasted only as long as the *pan dulce*. The next week, I did the same thing. One of the women returned, and she brought a friend. The time passed as it had the week before. This went on for about three months. Two or three ladies would come, and we would talk about "here and now" issues with their children. I wasn't providing counseling services, but I kept returning every week, mostly because I hate to quit—and even more, I hate to feel like I haven't been successful.

One Wednesday, the president of the residents' association came to one of my group meetings. Years later, I learned that the perception of many residents was that university faculty came to Buena Vida when they had a grant or research project to complete. When the grant money was spent or the statistics analyzed, the faculty disappeared. Worse yet, the Buena Vida community was familiar with faculty on a mission to "help" them. In light of this, it's likely that the president only came to one of my group meetings because she was suspicious of my presence and wanted to protect her community.

I didn't have a grant, and I wasn't conducting any research. I explained to her that I was a licensed professional counselor and just wanted to offer my services to the community, pro bono. She immediately scoffed and replied that there had to be something in it for me. I figured I should be completely frank with her; she looked like someone who could see a do-gooder a mile away. I told her that part of my workload responsibilities at the university included service, and that I wanted to fulfill this obligation by doing what I love to do most, for people who I thought needed it the most. I told her about the CBIRD study that I'd read, and how "needy" her community was. As egregious as it was, I didn't recognize my second mistake right away. My first mistake had been to tell her that I was a professional counselor. In Mexico, counseling is still in the incubator; the mental health needs of individuals who can afford it are met by Bachelor's-level psychologists or practicing psychiatrists. For those without resources, a *curandero* (faith healer) prays and performs rituals over the afflicted. If the *curandero* isn't effective, the individual is relegated to being *loco* (crazy) or *malito* (sick). The extended family and community care for their *malitos*, and people with severe mental disorders are rarely institutionalized or medicated in Mexico.

What the president of the residents' association heard me say the day that I met her was that her community was sick and needed my expertise. I still cringe when I think about it. I respectfully asked for another chance to explain counseling, and she allowed me to try again. I described personal growth, catharsis, and support. I confessed my assumptions, based on the CBIRD report, that the Buena Vida community might be experiencing loss, anxiety, discrimination, humiliation, and above all, the isolation and fear of being undocumented. I used the word "*platicas*," which translates as dialogues or conversations, to describe the counseling process. She asked me if I thought the residents were crazy, and I differentiated between the wellness model and the medical model. I also disclosed that I periodically went to counseling myself, and asked her if she thought *I* was crazy. She laughed for the first time.

You are Never Alone

After this conversation, I was endorsed by Maria Calderon, the president of the Buena Vida Residents' Association. Things changed in my weekly meetings, albeit not as quickly as I thought they would. There was still a lot of skepticism about what I was doing. I didn't have grant money, I wasn't conducting research, and I wasn't offering any incentives, other than *pan dulce*, to talk to me. I wasn't a psychologist, and they weren't crazy, so what was the point? They enjoyed the *platicas*, though, and with Mrs. Calderon's approval, we continued to meet.

By this time, there were about 12 regulars and the group was growing. I was teaching group counseling at the university, and asked Mrs. Calderon if she thought we could offer more services, and if so, what kind. Mrs. Calderon had become a cultural informant for me, and I learned to consult her before trying to force new projects on the women. She gave me the great advice to poll the community about their needs. She helped my students and me design a needs assessment, and I sent my bilingual students door to door with it. Because Mrs. Calderon had told many of the residents to expect us, we were well received in most homes. That semester, my group counseling students offered four additional groups: a refusal skills group for adolescent girls, a social skills group for elementary school children, and two support groups for kids with an incarcerated parent. For the following two semesters, students in the group counseling class walked the Buena Vida blocks with a needs assessment, and then provided group counseling based on the response.

The room that we had been offered soon grew too small, and I went looking in the nearby community for another place for us to meet. Everyone wanted rent, and the university didn't have a regular funding source for me to offer any. I visited a soup kitchen called The Good Neighbor Settlement House, which was just around the corner from Buena Vida. I asked if I could address the board to ask for some space, and was granted the use of a large meeting room. The CCE heard about it, and provided modest funds for paint and furniture, and my students, the women, and I brought additional items to create a welcoming atmosphere in a room with plenty of space. Eventually, however, the director of the Good Neighbor Settlement House started asking me to pay either rent or utilities. I went back to the board, which voted to allow us to continue using the space because we were providing much-needed services in the community for free. Unfortunately, the director subverted the decision by failing to unlock the door for us on many occasions. After a few months of meeting outside, we were back to looking for meeting space. (Although the university is across the street, the counseling center is on the other side of campus and not within walking distance for the women and their children, particularly for the evening groups.)

We had now been in operation for almost two years, and the Buena Vida community's trust in us had grown considerably. Despite the lack of venue, the women were now heavily invested in the groups and were diligent in finding places for us to meet. At around this time, the CCE director again proved providential. He had applied for a grant that would provide communities surrounding the university opportunities to incubate small businesses. We met with the Buena Vida Residents' Association and brainstormed on ideas for business development. One of the women's greatest resources is their ability to cook. Tens of thousands of dollars later, a shed on the premises of the housing development was converted into a community kitchen with restaurant-grade appliances and a city permit. The back half of the shed was converted into a meeting room where we could hold counseling sessions. In 2005, the ribbon was cut on the Buena Vida Compassion Center.

For years we had been nomadic, going from one meeting place to another. There were times when we held our group on the lawn, in nearby coffee shops, or in private homes. We had received permission to use a housing authority van to transport residents to the university counseling center, but the numerous trips were cumbersome and gobbled up precious time. Through it all, the women were good natured, tolerant, and humorous. Finding a place to settle was something that they were familiar with, and they modeled patience and tenacity with grace. We all continued to show up for our group meetings, and although the venue changed almost weekly, our cohesion only grew stronger. By the time the Compassion Center opened, we were ready to work. This was a real turning point for this group.

It was an open group, and we met once a week. Women came in and out, and we talked about everything possible. The women were traditionally modest, and I suspected that there were some issues that they wanted to discuss but didn't feel comfortable enough to raise. One week I gave each of them an index card and asked them to anonymously write down anything they wanted to discuss. Whenever we had a lull in our group, I'd take one of the index cards from the basket.

PHOTO 12.1   Never alone: creating family from strangers

This was a safe way to approach topics like sex, domestic violence, deportation, humiliation, and the darker side of crossing the border "*bajo el agua*" (under the water).

I was prepared to talk about the effects of immigration that I'd read about: grief and loss, fear, depression, the effects of starting over with no resources, little understanding of the culture or language, and the lack of a support network. There was so much more that I didn't anticipate. The women were humiliated by the public housing system. Authorities had the right to enter their homes at any time and investigate if they suspected or had reports of drug use; they had often arrived home to find their personal belongings ransacked by housing staff. Space was limited and competitive, so neighbors made false reports to have them evicted. There were child abuse allegations for the same reasons. The competition for the limited resources was fierce. The fear that neighbors would call *la migra* (the Border Patrol) in order to have them deported was ubiquitous. All of this contributed to a lack of trust amongst each other. At a time when the women needed support the most, they were the most suspicious and reluctant to reach out.

From my first visit to Buena Vida, I'd had to readjust my understanding of who I was and what I was doing. I was taken to task many times by the women of Buena Vida. As a second-generation, relatively privileged woman, I thought

I had enough training and experience to do group work with recently arrived immigrants. Above all, I was a Latina. I wore this badge like the rapper Flavor Flav wears a clock around his neck. I assumed I had instant access to the community. I was wrong, and the women gently and patiently pointed it out to me. I had an education. I had an income. Most of all, I had the security and privilege of citizenship, which meant that I belonged here and didn't live under threat of being removed.

The trust was by now bidirectional. They knew that as a former school counselor, I could guide them through the school system that was foreign territory, and that I had a knack for helping them see themselves in new ways. But I made many mistakes about what I thought they needed and who I thought they were. I based my assessment of what they needed on my own values, and brought career counselors to talk to them, or tried to get them interested in vocational school. They felt safe enough with me to tell me when I had gotten it wrong, and I learned to listen carefully.

For our Christmas meeting one year, I planned a great event: the white elephant gift exchange. I'd had so much fun with this at faculty parties and other gatherings. I pictured us all, with our sharp wit and sophisticated sense of humor, sitting in a circle using the gift exchange as comic relief during the pressure of Christmas consumerism. I asked the women to bring a gift, hinting that it could be anything: used, valued, even kitschy. In the white elephant gift exchange, everyone picks a number and then gifts are chosen in succession, starting with number one. Each participant has the choice of taking a gift that has already been unwrapped or choosing one that is still wrapped. A few gifts down the line, I noticed that the women weren't taking each other's gifts. They each picked a new gift out of the pile. "No, no, no! This isn't how you play!" I explained. "Dora, I know you want that cookie cutter set! Take it from Luz!! That's the way you play!" Dora emphatically refused to play right. I sighed and we went on. Halfway through, I got frustrated because there was no usurping of gifts. Again, I explained the rules. The next woman, Julia, reluctantly went for the cookie cutter set and took it for herself. Luz, who had been holding onto it, started to cry. So did Julia. This started a chain reaction of confusion, anger, and distress. I didn't understand what had gone wrong. We put all the gifts back on the table and got in our circle. The women shared how wrong it felt to take something from someone else. It didn't matter that the baker hadn't gotten the cookie cutters. The original recipient was showing sincere gratitude for getting anything at all. To have given it up would have meant that she didn't value the giver's choice of gift, which would be perceived as rude and vulgar. To go after someone else's gift would demonstrate *envidia*, or envy, for someone else's possession. In the Latino culture, one must never show desire for possessions; it contradicts the value of collectivism and the desire for the well-being of others as opposed to self. In an effort to explain why I would expose them to such a cruel game, I told them how frequently the game is played and enjoyed in American culture. The women helped me process why it might be enjoyed by mainstream Americans: it's competitive and individualistic, two highly valued elements of American culture. Eventually, we did laugh—at my ignorance, however well intentioned. I came to these meetings with my mind as open as I could make it. It was always a little bit wider when I left.

After two years of meeting regularly and processing the multiple layers of pain and joy that the Buena Vida women experienced in their acculturation, we began to meet less frequently and our meetings took on a collaborative advocacy focus. Along with the CCE, the women of Buena Vida planned health fairs and other events for their community. I introduced them to a state legislator in their district. I had worked with this legislator while advocating for school counselors, and hoped that he would be interested in helping the Buena Vida community. I called his office to invite him to a breakfast prepared for him at the Compassion Center. I had an unusual caveat that might have ruined any chance the women had to talk with him: he had to come alone. No reporters, no staff, no entourage. We crossed our fingers and waited to hear from his office. I had a couple of reasons for wanting him to come alone. The women were still, and rightfully so, worried about their immigration status. Secondly, I didn't want the breakfast to be a photo opportunity. I had a good feeling that he would not exploit anyone in this way, but I still felt that we needed the safeguard. Later that day, the legislator's office called to confirm.

The breakfast that the Buena Vida ladies prepared for the legislator was simultaneously humble and fit for a king. About 20 women were gathered in the Compassion Center. The legislator was gracious and ate heartily among some of the poorest residents in the nation. He listened sincerely and was frank about how he might be able to help and what his limitations were. He spoke to them in Spanish, and shared his own experience of growing up in a housing development project. The women shared some of their stories about the humiliation of government-assisted living, as well as their success with the Compassion Center kitchen. It was a moving and heartfelt morning.

About two weeks later, I received a call from the legislator. He told me how touched he had been by the women that he met, and how unforgettable they were. He wanted to reciprocate their generosity, and invited us all to breakfast at his home. After I got over my surprise and delight (I knew the women would be thrilled, not only to see the legislator again, but to be guests in his home), I started worrying. Would he be at risk for hosting undocumented women in his home? Was he doing it for publicity? (I don't ever let my guard down when working with undocumented individuals—to put them at risk of discovery and deportation would be irresponsible and unforgiveable.) And finally, the sheer logistics wore me down: how would I transport 20 women to his home, located far outside of Brownsville? Who would care for the children during our visit? Children and extended family members are almost always part of the Latino immigrant equation. Comedians joke that Mexicans go everywhere together because they can't afford child care, but that doesn't convey the beauty of wanting to share important events with loved family members, the safety they feel when they are together, or the value of shared decision making. In addition, the Buena Vida women had few resources and didn't spend them on child care that they could easily provide themselves; that money was better spent on food or some other necessity that was valued above a mother's "alone time." In the end, we were able to procure a bus and driver, CCE provided childcare, and the legislator's staff treated the Buena Vida women like queens in his beautiful home. As we left, he gave each woman a 20-pound turkey (it was near Thanksgiving). For the last four years, the legislator has given the women turkeys at Thanksgiving, a luxury that they are always grateful for. When he is able to, he comes with me to deliver them personally and takes time to chat with each of the women. I know that meeting the women of Buena Vida has made the legislator even more sensitive to the plight of undocumented individuals, which has had an effect on the legislation that he files and supports.

Although I had clearly gained entrance into the community, there was so much I had yet to learn. I came to look forward to the *platicas* because I always knew that I would leave there changed somehow. I was empowered by the women's success and willingness to move forward. In our group meetings, we defined and refined each other's identities as mothers, as Latinas, and as women. We supported each other through difficult times; our work together gave us a sense of worth. Perhaps the most remarkable thing we did was to create a family out of strangers. Women who had felt isolated and alone in a foreign country now had other women they could count on as though they were sisters.

I Am Never Alone

I started my work in the Buena Vida community through the university's CCE, encouraged by the first dean that I worked for. It became the largest share of my time distribution, and I was advised by more than one chair and dean to reduce the amount of time I was spending in the community. I ultimately acquiesced. Every dean comes to campus with a new focus, and I've been lucky to serve under deans who have helped me balance my workload in ways that are commensurate with my professional goal to empower underserved populations and my personal quest to become a better human being through relationships with others.

I work less intimately now with the women of Buena Vida, although I am still in touch with most of them. We check in with each other, and when they have a particular project they want to work on, they call me and we plan for change. Most of the women have moved out of the Buena Vida housing development. They know how to advocate for themselves, and remain connected to each other for support.

Our relationship is synergetic. The women of Buena Vida see the fruits of my grandparents' labor in me. My success reminds them why they work as hard as they do, and although they might not live to see their grandchildren reach a higher level of education or income than they did, they have strong faith that it is possible and that it will happen. The women of Buena Vida remind me of the strong values that might have died with my grandparents had the women not come along to refresh them for me. I am a better mother, daughter, and sister because of them. My priorities have returned to family as opposed to work, collaboration as opposed to competition, and a collective, as opposed to an individualistic, worldview. I no longer feel estranged or different from my grandmother; the women of Buena Vida no longer feel isolated. We have traversed the borders of the past and the future, and we'll never be alone again.

My work with the women of Buena Vida now includes sharing what they taught me via presentations and workshops around the country. Foremost in what I try to teach others who work with any population that is different from their own is to resist the seduction of thinking that we know who others are or what they need. These assumptions are based on our own experiences and reflect our own, usually dominant culture, values. For example, women crossing the border without documentation frequently have to pay their way with sex. This appalled me until I learned that some women readily use their bodies as commodities when it means that they can bring another family along or avoid being abandoned on the dangerous trip north. There is no humiliation in this act; rather, the women feel a sense of empowerment at having access to a currency that is always in demand.

It took me years to gain entry into a community that I mistakenly assumed I already belonged in. Persistence and patience are what finally convinced the women of Buena Vida that I wasn't going to exploit them for research or missionary purposes. I just kept showing up, and this gave them the opportunity to teach me what they wanted me to know about them. I had to discard my assumptions, especially those that were subconscious and involuntary. I know that I've learned well. Recently, one of my colleagues at the university shared her acculturation to the community by telling a relatively large crowd that as a northerner, she'd had to get used to how people "down here" like to stand in lines. (She was referring to students who wait hours in line for late registration or for financial aid checks.) As respectfully as I could, I channeled the women of Buena Vida and told her that nobody here "likes" to stand in line for hours. It's something that people in this community are willing to do, however, to get the very limited resources available to them. My infinite repayment to the women of Buena Vida is to respectfully correct misconceptions that many, even those who are well intentioned, continue to have. Because this colleague had never had to stand in line for hours for anything, she mistakenly assumed that the only reason people here do it is because they must not mind it. She sent me an e-mail immediately afterward, admitting her lack of sensitivity and awareness.

In addition to abandoning preconceptions and being persistent, I recommend to anyone interested in working with a population that is different from their own to open themselves up to the idea that we are not there to teach, but to learn. As a professional, I gained much more than I could have hoped to impart. I went in to help, and became the helped. I don't doubt that my presence had an impact on the women as well. They connected me with my past, and I know that I connected them with their future. However, I am forever changed as a result of their generosity and willingness to teach me what I could never have learned in a classroom or from the literature. They most likely would have found their way forward without me, but I don't think I could have ever known my *abuela*, or myself, as well as I do now if they hadn't reminded me of what I had lost in my acculturation. For this I am eternally grateful to the women of Buena Vida.

13

"ILLUMINATION OF THE HUMAN SPIRIT"

The Evolution of an African-Centered Social Justice Counselor

Sharon Bethea

One of my favorite scenes in a movie called *Fridays* is a conversation that Mr. Jones has with his son Craig on the subject of how he got fired from his job on his day off. I remember chuckling, thinking, "wow, how do you get fired on your day off?" And then it happened to me. While I was Director of Children's Services at an organization for abused women and their children, I, too, got fired on my day off. Let me explain. I was very dissatisfied with the resources allocated for children in the program. To remedy some of these problems, I wrote and secured an $80,000 grant. After the money was awarded, the Executive Director (ED) informed me that the organization needed to use the grant monies to meet payroll. Understanding the laws concerning grant allocations, I challenged the ED's decision. The children's program received the money and my staff and I put in place much-needed services for children of abused women. I then took a much-needed and deserved vacation. However, as reprisal for my actions, while I was on vacation, I was summoned to the ED's office. The ED told me that I knew nothing about how an organization was run and fired me on the spot.

Introduction

I have spent the majority of my career serving and advocating for youth and their families in inner city communities. Having been a resident of these communities for a period of my life, the seemingly one-sided analysis of inner city life has always baffled me. The media overwhelmingly describe inner city neighborhoods as crime-ridden spaces inundated with social disorder. In addition, the social science literature states prophetically that youth residing in inner city communities are from disorganized families and are "at risk" for academic failure, juvenile delinquency, violence, and a myriad of mental health issues. Although some of the contextual descriptions espoused by the current literature exist in inner city neighborhoods, it does not adequately account for the majority of youth that succeeds in developmental tasks, stays in school, is not involved with drugs or crime, and accomplishes productive goals. What media and the social sciences fail to observe is the essence of the people who reside there, or the strength of the community that provides support for positive development. For me, these all-encompassing negative depictions misrepresent the neighborhoods where my family, friends, and I lived, played, loved, and felt nurtured, safe and secure.

Over the past 25 years I have worked with hundreds of youth and their families in numerous situations. Using some of these experiences as a backdrop, I will describe the evolution of my own particular style of African-centered social justice counseling. I will illustrate my use of cultural strategies (both my personal cultural strategies and those of my clients) and integrative approaches that merge psychotherapeutic skills, advocacy, and community resources to support the well-being of youth and their families.

My experience doing social justice work is extremely satisfying and has provided me with some of the most honorable moments of my life. However, as this chapter will further illustrate, social justice work is complex, demanding, and inundated with frustrations, obstacles, and personal sacrifices. But it is through the process of persisting and embracing all aspects of social justice principles that I have gained many rewards and learned life lessons. In discussing these experiences, I would like to share some practical social justice strategies that counselors may employ in their counseling process. I hope that I can motivate other counselors to integrate social justice ideologies and strategies into their own counseling practices.

Legacy and Culture: The Development of My Worldview

From a multi-cultural and social justice perspective, it is posited that clients cannot be viewed in isolation from the families, social groups, communities, cultures, and systems in which they are embedded. I believe this principle also applies to counselors and social service providers. In honoring that assumption, I would like to begin this narrative by putting my own evolution as a African-centered counselor who is committed to social justice in a socio-historical, familial, cultural, and community context; this contextual framework informs my worldview, values, and my perceptions concerning humanbeingness.

My cultural context and worldview is a culmination of my *spirit,* which directs me toward harmony with the universe, my *African ancestry* that grounds me in the values of collectivism, interdependence, cooperation, and the motivation to work for the survival of the group; *the Maafa,* the consequences of and conditions by which my ancestors arrived in the Americas; my *family,* for it is their collective love, nurturing, wisdom, guidance, and role modeling that protected and cultivated my genius; my *community* that provided context, support, role models, and resources; and *sankofa*, a predisposition to look back at historical events, learn from them, and plan for the future.

I Am Who I Am Because of Where I Come From

As I reflect on my life, it seems a bit cliché to begin a personal narrative about my work with my birth, but given the importance of the Civil Rights Movement in the transformation of the United States its seems appropriate to began my earthly journey in the midst of this socio-historical moment. Even though desegregation laws had been passed in 1954, prior to my birth, the stench of Jim Crow lurked in the very essence of the air I breathed. There were places that I was forbidden to go, and functions that I could not attend because of the color of my skin. Although these oppressive conditions loomed ugly in the history of the United States at the time, dominant among my recollections of my community were a climate and a character of resistance, revolution, and evolution.

In spite of the unjust consequences of segregationist policies, my community in Durham, North Carolina developed a thriving African American community. Grounded in the legacy of North Carolina Central University, the nation's first publicly supported Liberal Arts College for African Americans and Durham's Hayti district (referred to as "Black Wall Street"); university presidents, factory workers, college students, business owners, janitors, farmers, teachers, preachers, and CEOs reflected my culture, context, and worldview and served as role models for me and my community. In addition, the Royal Seven sit-ins in Durham played a preemptive role in a series of events that would alter the course of Jim Crow in the United States forever. The culmination of these experiences of social injustice and resistance began to formulate my understanding of social justice and guide the work that would later become my lifelong career.

The values of my family (my first teachers and preachers) affected my understanding of social justice in the most deep and meaningful way. My parents, grandparents, aunts, uncles, and fictive family taught me to respect and love family and elders, and to honor my ancestors, for it is their shoulders on which I stand. I grew up with my mother, father, and brothers in a segregated, close-knit neighborhood. My family and community taught me that education was the key to success, and to always be proud of where I came from and who I am. I attended well-managed, competent, community-segregated public schools. Our school song was *Lift Every Voice and Sing* (the Black National Anthem) and the historic and symbolic Red, Black, and Green flag flew proudly in my classrooms. The energy of the Black Power movement and African pride were a constant part of my day-to-day life. I remember early in my development wanting to be a part of this movement, wanting to right the wrongs and work for the betterment of my community, country, and world.

Education for Social Justice: An Alternative Perspective

In sixth grade, a major life event altered my world and worldview in a profound way. My parents divorced and my mother moved my two brothers and me to an inner city community in the Midwest. Not only did I experience upheaval, fear, confusion, and insecurity, somewhat typical of children of divorce, this move was my first introduction to integration. Although this integration experience expanded my knowledge about diverse populations, I also experienced personal racism and oppression from adults, teachers, and contemporaries, which I had been largely protected from in my homogeneous community. Eventually my mother remarried, and after high school graduation my family and I moved across the country to California, where I attended college, got married, had a child, and graduated with my Bachelor's degree in psychology from San Francisco State University 17 months after my child's birth. I believe it was around this time in my development and educational experience that I began to solidify my commitment to social service and test the convictions that I acquired in childhood.

During my tenure at San Francisco State University, I recall being very frustrated with the curriculum, mostly because of its ineffectiveness at addressing race, gender, and social justice issues. In my quest to experience at least one class that effectively addressed these issues, I took Black Psychology in the Black Studies Department. This course completely transformed my thinking about social service work. The tenets of Black Psychology gave me an alternative paradigm that not only addressed social justice and social change as its basic philosophy, but also provided me with a theoretical perspective that embraced the essence, cultural context, and strengths of human beings as a model for mental health and well-being. This prompted me to become a student member of the Association of Black Psychologists.

Totally captivated and fascinated with the knowledge that I acquired from my Black Psychology course, I continued to take courses in Black Studies. I am particularly reminded of a course called Psychology of the Black Child. As my professor lectured about the genius of African American children entangled within the social consequences of racism and oppression, I realized that I wanted to be part of a social movement that ensured a better life for children. It is also during this time that my interest in research manifested itself. I began to read with intention, passion, and enthusiasm everything I could about the conditions of children in America as it related to their development, culture, and the consequences of race and oppression.

Career Beginnings: "To Get Lost is to Learn the Way" (Swahili Proverb)

My first job out of college put me in the midst of social justice work. I became a case manager at a center that housed homeless and incarcerated women and their children. Seeing first hand the plight of women and their children overwhelmed and intrigued me at the same time. Being inexperienced and straight out of college, I had no idea what someone with my age and naïveté could offer. Nonetheless, I did understand I had to embrace my responsibilities and be of service to the women and children who depended on me for counseling and connections to resources to re-enter into their communities in a productive and respectful way. However, I quickly learned that school had not prepared me for this experience.

Even though school did not address the particulars of working with women and children in dire need of resources and community connections, it did teach me to think critically, ask questions, and conduct research. This experience afforded me the opportunity to translate my scholarship into action. As I continued to be committed to doing the best work possible to serve women and children, I found that these particular skills served me well. I read as much as I could about homelessness and the penal system that was specific to women and children. I embraced and understood the meaning of what had been, up to this point, abstract terms out of context: self in relation to others, human capacity and potential, empathy, active listening, and collective responsibility. Even though I was inexperienced, tapping into my humanity gave me a special connection, a human connection that helped me empathize with the particular circumstances that women and children were subjected to.

One of my first cases at the facility involved a middle-aged woman with a Ph.D. and four children. After graduation she was not able to obtain gainful employment, lost most of her belongings, and had to move from her home and seek refuge in the facility in which I was employed. She was assigned to me as a client and I recall the inadequacies that I felt. I often talk to my students about the old "tapes" in your unconscious that are activated by issues clients bring to therapy. For me, several "old tapes" were activated with this case. During my childhood many messages were given to me concerning respect for eldership and education. Part of that respect included not challenging anything elders had to say; I was reprimanded for challenging elders in my family. My client's age, education, and experience immediately activated that "old tape" and created a knee-jerk reaction that monopolized how my client and I negotiated our counseling relationship. I would have to say that the experience in the moment literally deskilled me.

At some point I felt very stuck in the therapeutic process and consulted with a more experienced counselor. We talked about my process, thoughts, and feelings and how they ultimately affect the well-being of my clients. We discussed experiences in which I felt those same feelings of inadequacy. In hindsight, I believe that my counseling demeanor (which was somewhat childlike) reinforced her behavior to parent me, which perpetuated my feelings of immaturity, inadequacy, and powerlessness—much like I felt when I wanted my voice to be heard amongst my elders. My clinical supervisor facilitated a process of self-exploration, during which I began to separate my feelings about my life experiences and make the therapeutic relationship about my client. That mentorship proved to be invaluable to me as a counselor, and ultimately (and most importantly) enhanced my relationship and therapeutic work with my client.

The Mother-Infant Care Program

Whereas I felt great pride and accomplishment at the organization at which I was employed, my real passion was to work with children and adolescents. I applied for and was offered a position as an educational specialist at a Mother-Infant Care (MIC) Program for incarcerated pregnant teens. The MIC program offered pregnant teenagers, or those with children aged birth to six years, the opportunity to complete the rest of their prison sentence in a residential facility in the community. Given the disenfranchisement of incarcerated teenagers, what became clear to me is that advocacy was an important aspect of my work. I began to understand the importance of integrative psychotherapeutic paradigms, community collaboration, and advocacy. To address the complexity of the lives of the teens in the program, a collaborative team of experts was necessary. My team consisted of parole officers, teachers, school counselors, doctors, lawyers, social workers, community organizations, and community activists. After doing a needs assessment of the teens in the MIC program, we hired a midwife, put together a nursery for their children, a parenting class for mothers and fathers, and a group that consisted of the teens' immediate and extended families. During this time, I was not armed with the definition of social justice counseling in a holistic cohesive way, but I now realize that my mode of working with incarcerated teenage mothers and their children embodied the very essence of social justice counseling (i.e., counselor, advocate, psychoeducator, change agent, and community worker).

I eventually became the Director of the MIC program. I still did individual and group counseling with the teens, but I understood that many of my duties, and the duties of my staff and the requirements of the residence, involved advocating for the rights of children in prison and the enhancement of community and educational resources for teen mothers. My tenure at the MIC program affected me profoundly and set the tone for my feelings about the need for a social justice component to social services. I was becoming more competent in advocating with and on behalf of my clients individually (client empowerment), systemically (community collaboration), and on a societal level (disseminating public information concerning teens in prison).

I also understood I needed more education and skills. While I was at the MIC program I began a Master's program in Clinical Psychology at John F. Kennedy University. A unique feature of this school was that it also offered a graduate degree in Consciousness and Transformative Studies. The curriculum integrated psychology, philosophy, spirituality, deep ecology, sustainability, and new science. I took a myriad of elective courses in that department, which also expanded my knowledge base and enhanced my ability to use alternative psychotherapeutic strategies with clients and engage with community activists and organizations.

I spent the next few years working part time while I was in graduate school. During this time I used social justice principles to work with and advocate for infants exposed in utero to drugs and alcohol and their families; teenage parents and their children; middle-school students; and youth in community programs. After I graduated, my experiences and social justice skills were further extended when John F. Kennedy University offered me a position as Director of Training for the Center for Parent Involvement. This job afforded me the opportunity to facilitate sessions with students, parents, teachers, and administrators to improve parent involvement in three inner city school districts. It also gave me an opportunity to collect research on the impact of parent involvement on the lives of children in inner city schools.

Working with families in inner city communities demonstrated the need for intervention and prevention. Drawing on the sheer courage and spirit of the children and families that I served, I began to understand their resiliency and strength of character, which far outweighed their present conditions. This illumination of human spirit and character prompted me to concentrate on ways to intervene and help clients prevent negative responses to the oppressive societal forces that children and families in inner city communities were subjected to. I began to concentrate on community organizations that supported the positive development of children. One such program that I became involved in was Oakland Freedom Schools (OFS).

Oakland Freedom Schools' Summer Youth Program: "We Desire to Bequest Two Things to Our Children: The First One is Roots, the Other One is Wings" (Sudanese Proverb)

PHOTO 13.1 Education is power: OFS annual drop everything and read day (photo by Reginald James)

I was sitting in on a community meeting at a local school that I was involved in concerning summer youth programs. The presenter was the Program Coordinator from OFS. He explained that OFS was the result of a collaboration of activities among a variety of individuals, youth-serving agencies, public housing authorities, and churches. OFS was culturally relevant, free, all-day six-week educational summer youth programs that required no testing or screening, so that every child who showed up in the neighborhood had an opportunity to participate. Given the inability of parents with limited income to pay for summer youth programs, being free initially attracted my attention. However, his explanation of the program ignited me into action. He explained that OFS was African centered in its orientation and philosophy, believed in the strength of the community to foster resiliency in children, and utilized *Nguzo Saba* (unity, self-determination, collective work and responsibility, cooperative economics, purpose, creativity, and faith) as a code of ethics and a set of guiding principles. Given that the OFS was located in a predominantly African American community, this cultural infusion was an important aspect of the program. It also resonated with the African-centered theoretical paradigm that I embraced during my time at San Francisco State University.

This presentation prompted me to speak with the Program Coordinator about the specifics of OFS, which seemed to embody social justice principles and adhere to an organizational framework of cultural competency. Its services were tailored to meet the needs of African American children by being responsive to their lifestyles, behaviors, language, attitudes, and beliefs. In addition, cultural relevancy was incorporated into the policies, infrastructure, and practices of OFS. Consistent with African-centered pedagogy, OFS utilized precepts such as *Harambee* (pull together) and chants to achieve unity, motivate students, and celebrate the spirit of OFS. Their "Righteous Reading Curriculum" strengthened reading skills and reflected the children's historical and cultural context. OFS used ancestral and cultural kinships, stories, tales, theatrics, raps, healing songs, rituals, recitals, play, games, and expressive movement to strengthen collective consciousness, interdependence, self-worth, and academic skills. In addition, social action projects were used to introduce social justice principles in the daily lives of students.

I was totally excited! Working with OFS seemed like a perfect fit for me; a project in which I could practice the culmination of my counseling and social justice experiences, in an African-centered organization that was about the business of prevention, intervention, and meeting some of the needs of African American inner city youth. After that meeting I was hooked; I wanted to learn more about the program and get involved. Some of my relevant areas of expertise were African-centered pedagogy, strategies specific to working with families in inner city communities, child development, and learning strategies of African American children (my Master's research project). After numerous conversations with the Executive Director of Leadership Excellence, I volunteered to offer workshops specific to the development of African American children in inner city communities.

Once the youth program started, the energy at OFS was contagious. I found myself spending countless hours participating in *Harambees*, listening and talking to administration, staff, and students, assisting in classrooms, chaperoning field trips, taking part in D.E.A.R, participating in sovereignty marches, helping with plays and video productions, and tutoring students. I also solicited African and African American restaurants to sponsor lunches; coordinated food drives and facilitated donations of healthy snacks, fruits, and vegetables for the students. Being an involved busy mother and fictive relative, I brought my son, my godchildren, and their friends to the program. This afforded them the opportunity to experience the OFS movement and spend time with each other and me. My godchildren attended the program for several years, and I recruited their parents to be on the board of directors.

Frustrations, Challenges, Obstacles, and Personal Sacrifices: "Smooth Seas Do Not Make Skillful Sailors" (African Proverb)

Throughout my tenure as a counselor, I have had many successes with using a social justice paradigm; I believe that social justice counseling is critical to doing great work with many of our clients. However, it is important to note that social justice work is much different than doing counseling for 50 minutes in a controlled situation. It is more time consuming, and it is inundated with its own set of challenges, frustrations, obstacles, and personal sacrifices, beyond the traditional counseling process. Although we can never contemplate all situations that might occur in the counseling context, I believe that understanding, reflecting on, and building strategies to deal with these constructs early in our counselor training will enhance counseling competencies and help students be more receptive to social justice principles. Most traditional counseling programs do not address these concepts in a meaningful or constructive way, which is a major challenge and a huge frustration.

For me, these obstacles manifest themselves on many levels. From an ecological systems perspective, doing social justice work in a society that has legitimized itself through injustice, racism, and oppression of human beings has been disheartening, and at times very painful for me. America's unmitigated institutionalization and perpetuation of racism and oppression (historically and presently) boggles my mind, and on some days rocks me to my very soul. As I described earlier in the chapter, social injustices have contributed in a positive way to my commitment to social justice counseling. But I have to admit that on a few occasions, my anger and pain around these issues have invoked hasty and angry reactions, especially when racist and oppressive policies have affected the well-being of my clients. Several times the consequences of my actions have excluded me from promotions to decision-making positions. This ultimately affects the work I do for my clients.

Another challenge to doing social justice work is dealing with the bureaucracy of organizations. Bound by traditional paradigms of the medical model, victim-oriented ideologies, and the promise of individual theories of counseling, many organizations that I was affiliated with discounted the importance of a social justice paradigm. In addition, the quality and quantity of programming and resources for clients seemed to be heavily dependent upon the ebbs, flows, and whims of the political climate of the moment. Educational Directors seemed to more interested in complying to rules, regulations, and constraints of governmental guidelines than following the mission of the organization or delivering the appropriate resources to the clients that we serve. I have butted heads with EDs, administrators, and colleagues about services for clients on numerous occasions, with varying degrees of effectiveness. I began this chapter with an example of one of those occasions. Although I would not change my reaction to the request of that particular ED, my actions affected my livelihood. The particular strategy that I used to resist injustice (a lawsuit) eventually got rid of the ED (she got caught embezzling funds), but because of the lack of funding, and the amount of money that the ED stole, the board decided to close a much-needed resource for abused women and their children.

One of the biggest challenges for me in doing social justice counseling was juggling personal life and the demands of the work. Earlier I mentioned that I married and had a child during my senior year of undergrad. The challenges of getting married young, being co-parents, the developmental agendas of young adulthood, the stress of being a student, and embarking on new careers took its toll, and our marriage ended. Although we had a great parenting partnership and I received lots of support from family and the community, being divorced and a mother multiplied an already hectic schedule tenfold. In addition to the day-to-day activities associated with being a co-parent, I was a basketball mom. I carpooled, hosted team sleepovers, tutored, ran my son to African boot dancing, piano, and saxophone lessons, karate, and basketball practice. And I rarely missed recitals, tournaments, games, work, or class. And I absolutely loved every minute of it.

However, my two worlds collided on more than a few occasions. My son slept in my office many times while I worked late hours. He attended events, meetings, rallies, and marches or played video games and read books at the desk next to me in my classes. I was sleep deprived, and on occasion I sacrificed my own health and well-being to attend to my family, advocate for my clients, and keep up with my studies. In social justice counseling, 40 hours a week usually meant 50 plus hours a week, and working nine to five with weekends off (even if that was my schedule) was non-existent for most of my career. Professors expected me to attend classes and turn in my work on time. And I had high expectations of myself. At some point this hectic schedule began to take its toll on my health. My doctor explained to me that I had to make some hard decisions or my health issues would get worse. So I took a vacation, made a very hard decision to step down as Director of the program, changed my lifestyle, eating, and exercise habits, and I got some sleep. Making these changes not only helped my state of mind and improved my counseling effective-ness, but I eventually achieved a clean bill of health.

I would be remiss if I did not discuss the frustrations, challenges, obstacles, and personal sacrifices that relate to my work with clients. We are often taught that we must have altruistic, non-judgmental, and unconditional positive regard for our clients. As much as I love working with my clients, doing so has involved some of my most challenging and frustrating moments. If I am to live in my authentic self, I will admit that my clients have filled my life with happiness, pride, joy, and light. They have graduated, gotten married, had babies, stayed sober, become great parents and partners, gotten jobs, started businesses, and purchased homes. But they have also made me oh so angry, sad, and disappointed—and have made me think very hard about a career change. Clients have lied to me, hid from me, cursed me out, hurt their children and partners, gone to jail, showed up to ses-sions drunk and/or high, and not showed up at all. When counselors are taught that neutrality is required in counseling, it sets them up for failure. It doesn't even make sense to me. I am human, my clients are human, life happens, and we are in a relationship. That is not neutral.

However, I have to be cognizant of my reactions to clients and how that affects my relationship with them. I have to reflect on my reactions of anger, sadness, happiness, joy, and pride to discern between my own human issues and those of my clients. Knowing that this is a normal part of the counseling process helps me understand that these emotional reactions will happen, and that I must have safeguards in place to help me manage my emotional investment and do what is best for my clients. I do this by taking care of myself, listening (in the therapeutic sense) to my clients' narratives, paying attention to my visceral reactions, remem-bering that the counseling relationship is a partnership, and being intentional (not haphazard) about the therapeutic process and any interventions that I negotiate with my client. I must attend to my responses to my client as soon as possible after the session, talk to a supervisor or colleague about my reactions, and if need be, discuss with and/or apologize to my client if it is in their best interest. Oh yeah, and take my days off and vacations.

Given the constraints associated with social justice efforts, I would imagine that readers are curious about my willingness and ability to continue to do this work. For me, that is easy to answer. This case illustrates why this work is so important, satisfying, and worthwhile. I was working at a community center that offered free after-school programs and counseling services to the surrounding community. While I was sitting at my desk, a probation officer introduced me to a beautiful young girl. The police picked her up because she was sitting on a bench in the park during school hours. Apparently this was not the first time this had happened, and she had run away from home several times.

During our first few sessions she was non-responsive. I read a short narrative about an Asante Queen mother named Yaa, which seemed to pique her interest.

Noticing that she enjoyed coloring, I gave her a picture of Queen Yaa to color. This prompted me to engage her in art therapy. In describing her art to me, I found out two important things that were going on in her life. Her mother was homeless and addicted to drugs, and every once in a while she would see her in the park and they would sit on the bench and visit. She was also being teased and bullied in school, so she hated going there. After listening carefully to her personal narrative, I found out that she received great joy when she spent time with her mother. To avoid being bullied, she would go and play with some of the children who had disabilities in her school. I contacted the school to address the bullying, which led to me facilitate a group for boys at the local school and a group for girls at the community center.

After several months of working with the girl I was able to facilitate her formally volunteering with disabled children. We continued to read narratives about famous African American women. In addition, after sessions with her grandmother we signed a contract to stop her from running away to the park and worked on a long-term plan to talk about her relationship with her mother. Her grades improved, she did not run away from home or ditch school during the period that I worked with her, and she gained great confidence and self-worth through her volunteer work. The happiness and smile on her face when she bought me her first report card with As and Bs: this is why I do this work. During our final session I gave her a copy of a book of famous African American women that we both signed.

For me, witnessing the successful transformation of the human spirit is an amazing, fulfilling byproduct of doing social justice work. So what keeps me going in the face of all the frustrations, challenges, obstacles, and personal sacrifice? I will end where I began: *Spirit, my historical past, to honor my ancestors, elders, and family, my responsibility to give back to my community and to leave it a better place for our children, my commitment to the populations that I serve, and I believe it is right thing to do.*

Lessons Learned: "We Become Wise Through Experience"

I have also learned many life lessons throughout my journey as an African-centered social justice counselor. First and foremost I would like to take the opportunity to honor the mentors and teachers who have held me up along the way. My teachers and professors have challenged me and set high expectations and goals for my character and intellect. Being associated with the Association of Black Psychologists for 25 plus years has afforded me the honor and privilege of being raised, nurtured, and mentored by some of the greatest minds in the world, and I have garnered ancestors, friendships, and allies that support me and keep me honest. And I would like to thank my ancestor, Dr. Asa Hilliard, who told me with genius, joy, light, and laughter that it was time for "ya'll" to be passed the baton cause you were getting tired. Feeling anxious, fearful, and definitely not worthy, I laughed. I now understand my responsibility to pay it forward to the next generation.

Although I cannot change the oppressive policies of American society, I have learned that I can affect change in my community. By attending rallies, voting, mentoring students, giving workshops, and providing strategies concerning social justice issues to clients, students, and the community, I realize and model for others that one person *can* make a difference in the lives of people. Understanding that for me to advocate for my clients I must be present at the table, I have learned to be more patient and have worked hard to be in leadership roles. I have learned that by listening, observing, gaining more education, skills, and experience and being more solution focused, I can maneuver myself into key positions where I influence policies and procedures that affect my clients.

I am also grateful for the many lessons the work has afforded my family. Although social justice work was time consuming, the time that my family spent with me in my various jobs gave them the opportunity to witness many of the values associated with social justice, i.e., dignity, human rights, equity, hard work, giving back, positive regard, persistence, dedication, and positive role modeling. I have also learned some of my best lessons from my clients: empowerment, courage, respect, tenacity, patience, the power of spirit, and the true meaning of reciprocity and propriety. And through the culmination of these lessons I have learned, and continue to learn, a lot about myself.

Strategies for Social Justice: "She Who Learns Teaches" (Ethiopian Proverb)

In my evolution as an African-centered social justice counselor, I have learned and created a myriad of strategies. It is important for counselors and therapists to reflect on their awareness and commitment to social justice. Critically reviewing the American Counseling Association's advocacy competencies is an initial process counselors can use to understand where they fit in this paradigm as a counselor. It is important to understand that becoming a social justice counselor is a process, and that part of the process of doing social justice work is experience, so be patient, study, listen, learn, model, act, and teach. It is essential for counselors to research (formally and informally) and reflect upon their own culture, heritage, and privilege. Although every individual incorporates these concepts into their identity in their own unique way, it is essential for counselors to reflect on how these constructs affect their counseling practices.

To enhance awareness, counselors can read social and historical literature and scholarly research concerning social injustices and issues of oppression perpetrated against various populations. Clients can also learn (formally and informally) and develop alternative counseling paradigms and strategies that address social justice and cultural issues. To enhance their knowledge, counselors can visit, have conversations with, and use as referrals traditional healers (e.g., preachers, *curanderos*, herbalists, shamans). In addition, it is essential to understand the sociopolitical and economic barriers that affect you and the lives of your clients. Being informed about how contextual and cultural environments influence clients' lives, mental health, and livelihoods is critical to doing competent counseling with diverse populations. The counselor that uses this information in an honest, appropriate, and skillful way has a better chance of gaining trust and forming much-needed human connections with their clients.

Advocacy is an integral part of social justice counseling. As a counselor it is important to realize that social justice counseling happens outside the office. I would imagine that this aspect of social justice counseling seems a time-consuming and daunting task. But every goal has a beginning. Counselors can begin by adding small actions to their counseling practice. For example, it is important to garner relationships in the community of the populations you serve. If you are working with clients who have limited income and no health insurance, fostering relationships with varied personnel at the county hospital or community clinic is important. I have often in my own practice acquired these relationships, which have saved my clients and I time. I have collected bus tickets and taxi vouchers for clients who need transportation, and made connections with organizations that distribute book bags, school supplies, and save spots in after-school and summer programs for the children of families that I work with. I always have the client go through the process with me so that they are empowered to continue seeking services themselves.

Earlier I told the story of a young girl that I worked with in a community organization. I would like to illustrate how social justice principles enhanced my work. By employing skills such as cultural knowledge, listening, empathy, and my knowledge of narrative and art therapy, I engaged myself in my client's reality and identified issues that influenced my client's social and academic functioning. Understanding the socio-historical, social, political, and economic factors that affect my clients' culture (race, economics, age, and gender) and recognizing the marginalization of my client (bullying) prompted me to coordinate services with her school and family. I relied on my knowledge of advocacy to identify the strengths and resources available to my client (working with disabled children) and used advocacy counseling skills to empower my client to advocate for herself (volunteering). I also expanded the advocacy process and shared information through community collaboration with the system that my client felt subjugated by (offered workshops to the school and community concerning bullying). And in doing so, I shared information and interventions with individuals and systems concerning some of the very human circumstances that my client was experiencing.

Conclusion

It is my hope that this story provides inspiration for counselors to become more actively involved in social justice counseling beyond their 50-minute sessions.

Although it is hard work, in my experience the rewards, lessons learned, and client outcomes far outweigh the challenges and frustrations associated with doing social justice work. The literature supports that counselors who have an understanding of the various contextual variables (i.e., socio-historical, political, social, distributive justice, oppression, and marginalization) that affect their clients' lives and invest in working holistically with them feel more confident and competent in their abilities to facilitate favorable outcomes for their clients. Given the relative scarcity of social justice philosophies, theories, and interventions in most counseling programs, it is also my hope that counselors and trainees advocate for more training in this area. If you were not given the appropriate tools to engage in social justice work, I hope that the experiences I have shared will provide you with the inspiration to begin to incorporate these principles into your own work.

This chapter is dedicated to Javad Jahi: Rest in Power Javad

14

WHEN YOUR LIBERATION IS TIED UP WITH MINE

Social Justice Work as a Tool for Resistance, Empowerment, and Nation Building for African-Descended Peoples

Jamila Codrington

When and Where You Enter

Only the black woman can say 'when and where I enter, in the quiet, undisputed dignity of my womanhood, without violence and without suing or special patronage, then and there the whole Negro race enters with me.' Anna Julia Cooper, 1892

Over a century ago, Anna Julia Cooper envisioned the unique position that black women play in a racist, male-dominated society (Lauter, 2002). In *A Voice from the South* (1892), she professed that black women, as they enter the world as a double minority and are caught in a web of multiple oppressions, bring an invaluable perspective on the struggle for justice and liberation. Cooper boldly positioned black women at the center of the movement for progress for African-descended people. She fulfilled this vision in word and deed. A contemporary of W.E.B. Du Bois, Cooper committed her life to serving and improving the conditions of the black community through her work as a scholar and activist within education and social service organizations.

Countless women of African descent have carried out Cooper's vision by confronting and fighting against injustice throughout the diaspora. Consider female warriors like Yaa Asantewaa, who in 1900 led the Ashanti rebellion against British colonialism in modern-day Ghana, and Nyabinghi, who fought to free enslaved Africans from English rule in Jamaica. The great warrior, Queen Nzingha, was a brilliant military strategist of modern-day Angola who fought against and defeated the Portuguese during the Atlantic slave trade in the early 17th century. Closer to home, Harriet Tubman and Sojourner Truth rose from the shadows of slavery to prominent leadership roles in the freeing of enslaved Africans within the United States. Cooper's vision was fulfilled after her lifetime through the work of Rosa

Parks, Assata Shakur, Angela Davis, and other powerful black women whose strong political, economic, and social convictions were the driving force behind the Civil Rights and Black Power Movements of the 1960s and 1970s.

Cooper's quote emphatically illuminates the reality of many women of African descent: *when* and *where* you enter matters. As a psychologist, I am first a woman of African descent. My sociopolitical history is marked by multiple, unforgettable layers of oppression. When and where I enter the work of a psychologist, there and then the whole community of African-descended peoples enters with me. I stand on the shoulders of my ancestors, whose spirits as freedom fighters remain alive in me and guide my work. As I reflect, I am increasingly aware that the seeds of my social justice work were planted by my ancestors well before I was born. In his scholarship on Bantu spiritual systems, Dr. Kimbwandende Kia Bunseki Fu-Kiau proposes that each living human being is "a seed of a seed of a seed of a seed of a seed of a seed of a seed of a seed ..." Dr. Fu-Kiau reminds us of what is inherent in many traditional African spiritual systems: the continuum of the past, present, and future, and the central role that ancestors play—as their energy never dies.

Within all of us is a stance, a way in which we can (and do) position ourselves in our work and make determinations about how we use our skill set. This stance can be shaped by many influences, particularly when we have the freedom to choose how we make a living. Often, the influential factors are people's orientation toward money, dreams, and ambitions, and/or their desire for power, status, or achievement. On a more existential level, this stance can be distinctly shaped by one's cultural history, lineage, identity, ideological beliefs and values, spiritual "calling," and/or life purpose. I have come to understand that my own commitment to the social justice agenda is primarily a result of the latter set of factors. I believe that there are no accidents in life.

Life Purpose as Service

We do not come to this world on vacation. We come here for service, and we have to remember what that service is. The nature of our service—our purpose—was configured already in the Spirit World before we came here. Malidoma Patrice Somé, 1998

We all have journeys to travel, opportunities to leave a special mark with every action we take, and individual and collective contributions to make throughout our lives. I recognize that every human being has a life purpose—one that is divinely shaped and intricately woven into all of his or her experiences. What if we lived our lives with the conviction that our purpose in this world was to serve others? Our greatest existential question would not be "what is my purpose in life?" but rather "what is the nature of my service to others?"

My journey in serving my community through African-centered social justice work began at the beginning, with my birthplace. "Being born into this world in a particular place is like having the signature of that place stamped upon you" (Somé, 1998). I am Brooklyn born and bred. Except for my college, graduate school, and post-doc years, I've resided all my life in my beloved Brooklyn neighborhood of Bedford-Stuyvesant (also known as "Bed-Stuy"). Bed-Stuy has many claims to fame, some positive and some negative. It's a historic black community in New York City (NYC) that contains one of the oldest free black settlements in the United States, founded by emancipated slaves in the 1830s. Since then, with the influx of Caribbeans and Africans, Bed-Stuy has been the cultural Mecca of Brooklyn, in which blacks have owned land, created institutions, and built a thriving cultural community. Its local prodigies run the gamut, from Shirley Chisholm and Chris Rock to rappers Biggie and Jay-Z.

My memories of growing up in Bed-Stuy are marked by its vibrant and artistic cultural life. The strong base of block associations, churches, community organizers, social activists, and grassroots organizations created a close-knit community and breeding ground for many social and political movements. Yet ironically, I journeyed many miles outside of my neighborhood just to go to school each day. My mother was committed to making sure I had access to high-quality education in safe schools, and the public school system in my Bed-Stuy neighborhood often did not offer this. Bed-Stuy, affectionately dubbed "Bed-Stuy Do or Die" by locals who didn't take crap from anyone and had a genuine respect for the way they survived the rough street life, had many impoverished sections plagued by gang wars, community violence, and drugs during the late 1970s when I began childhood. Education was not to be messed with. I came from an achievement-oriented family with roots in the Caribbean, and education was a strong cultural and family value.

My maternal grandmother, whom we all affectionately called "Mother," hailed from the small, still-colonized island of Montserrat in the Caribbean. She migrated to the United States by boat and ultimately settled down in Bed-Stuy, where she raised her children and grandchildren. My grandmother took pride in doing for others and embodied the "it takes a village to raise a child" African proverb in her day-to-day movements. She swept neighbors' yards when she swept her own, prayed for children on the block as she did for her own grandchildren, greeted all passersby, and made delicious cold drinks during the summertime for thirsty children exhausted from play. She was, in essence, a caretaker of the community, the unofficial ambassador of the block. She created an indelible imprint on my life.

In her own right, my mother, like my grandmother, is a caretaker of the community. She worked until retirement in the NYC public school system with a specialization in Black history and behavior management. As Dean of her school, she was known for her unconventional tactics of making weekend home visits to speak with parents of struggling students and hitting the streets to mediate between rival gang members who attended her school. I grew up bearing witness to this. Influenced by the philosophies of the Blank Panther Party and Black Nationalism when she was coming of age, my mother has always possessed a strong political consciousness and raised me and my brother to be no different. Both my mother and father are heavily steeped in African culture, and to this day are committed to passing on our history and boldly expressing a positive African identity. I am deeply grateful for this.

In my senior year of high school, I took an Advanced Placement (AP) psychology class—a course that I likely would not have had access to if I went to my zoned school in Bed-Stuy. Right then and there, I fell in love with the field of psychology. While much of the content of this class escapes me, I do remember having an epiphany that I had never seen or heard of anything mental health-related in my own neighborhood. In fact, I had many things "missing" in my neighborhood, and I became increasingly aware of this the more exposure I had to life outside of *the hood*. I soon learned and grew concerned about limited resources and systemic factors that contributed to poor conditions within neighborhoods like mine. My commitment to making a difference in my community through the field of psychology began to crystallize. The AP psychology class served as a *kairos* moment—a passing, opportune instant when an opening appears that must be driven through with force if success is to be achieved. After completing the class, I decided to become a psychologist and thereby serve the mental health needs of disadvantaged communities like mine.

Straight from high school I pursued "higher education." Ten years later I wrestled with the decision of what to do with the institutional learning that earned me my Bachelor's, Master's, and Doctoral degrees in psychology. Those blessed to pursue, survive, and complete higher education must not take such accomplishments for granted. Particularly, students of African descent who climbed the rungs of success did so by standing on the shoulders of others. They stood on the shoulders of parents, freedom fighters, and ancestors who lived, died, and paved the way for the right of African-descended peoples to be educated in this country. Part of this remembrance entails not succumbing to the lures of working merely for financial gain. Although financial gain is often the world's yardstick of success, we must consider the larger spiritual picture. Are we good stewards of the educational blessings bestowed upon us as graduates of higher learning?

Again, I ponder, what would our careers look like if they were a reflection of a sacred, divine purpose to serve? Our careers are often central to our lives—not only because they provide a source of income for the necessities and niceties of life—but because they are an outlet for our divine gifts to be used in the service of humanity. When our careers are connected to both our life purpose and the community around us (through service), we can live a meaningful, powerful, and fulfilling life.

African-Centered Social Justice Work

If you have come to help me, you are wasting your time. But if you have come because your liberation is tied up with mine, then let us work together. Lill Watson, aboriginal activist

Social justice work covers a broad spectrum of deeds, activities, and efforts that are as varied as the individuals who engage in it. As a woman of African descent, I understand that my own social justice work is not merely a good gesture or community service act of a well-intentioned person. Rather, it is an unquestionable personal responsibility to my community in an interdependent struggle for liberation and resistance against the status quo. A social justice agenda takes on great personal significance in my professional life, given the unrelenting hands of oppression that have historically served to destroy, dehumanize, and disenfranchise my ancestors and global African community.

Reflecting on my career, I realize that my social justice work began to manifest naturally through an affiliation with a professional organization that shared my commitment to addressing the serious social problems affecting the larger Black community. I joined the Association of Black Psychologists (ABPsi) and its New York chapter (NYABPsi) after the completion of my post-Doctoral program and my long-awaited return home to Bed-Stuy. The seeds that had been planted many years prior began to quickly germinate, as I was able to partner with like-minded comrades and kindred spirits in the struggle for liberation for people of African descent. I became increasingly involved in social justice agendas by planning community programs, collaborating with grassroots organizations, attending our national conventions, and receiving greater exposure to the critical consciousness and commitment of other social activists, scholar warriors, and elders.

These agendas emerged quite organically once on common ground, as there are endless openings to social justice work when you are driven by a collective spirit of self-determination and self-preservation as a people. By virtue of the applicability of psychology to nearly every aspect of human functioning and the benefit of a psychological perspective in understanding the plight and liberation of an oppressed people, these openings to social justice work cut across numerous social and political issues. I share below some aspects of my journey to help illuminate key lessons I've learned about creating openings for social justice work.

Creating Openings for Social Justice Work

Lead in With Your Heart, Not Your Head

I am deeply disturbed by the educational crimes being disproportionately committed against children of African descent in this country. I worked for several years as a service provider in an outpatient mental health center for children and families in a low-income NYC neighborhood, where I have witnessed the injustices of the educational system through the lives of my clients. These injustices include the overrepresentation of black children in special education, their lack of educational resources, abysmally poor and unsafe school conditions, and exposure to a curriculum that often does not reflect their culture or adequately prepare them to successfully participate in the global marketplace or to solve their own problems as an oppressed people.

Within this educational domain, my social justice efforts have involved planning and participating in free public forums in the community that raise awareness about inequities and racism within the educational system; parents are taught ways to advocate for their children, educational resources are shared, and solution-focused dialogue is facilitated among stakeholders. I have also taken on the fight for culturally relevant curriculum inclusion in the NYC public education system with the John Henrik Clarke Workgroup, provided free child development and advocacy workshops to unemployed mothers in the "Welfare to Work" program, and co-authored a position paper for the Association of Black Psychologists addressing the overrepresentation of African-American children in special education. The latter project evolved into developing a policy brief used to take further legislative action—an important step in dismantling structured inequalities.

The leap between facilitating personal- and community-level change as a counselor is not a broad one. Personal concerns can easily become seeds for social change. We are more likely to take social action on an issue that already evokes disturbing emotions. Further, as we begin to face the challenges of social justice work, we are more likely to maintain a commitment if we have some passion behind it, rather than if it is an intellectualized response to a problem from which we are disconnected. Your heart might be saddened by a client's narrative about childhood sexual trauma; you might worry about an immigrant family who is at risk of deportation; you might be incensed by a school that has misplaced your young Spanish-speaking client in special education after the use of culturally biased testing. You can take action on these issues by connecting your emotion to the larger social issues of human trafficking, immigrant rights, and disproportionality in special education, respectively. Are you passionate about treating clients with depression? Consider the social context in which depression occurs. You can shift from providing tertiary intervention (e.g., cognitive behavioral therapy for symptom reduction) to primary intervention by recognizing and challenging some of the social factors contributing to your clients' depression (e.g., unemployment, inadequate housing, racial and gender inequalities in income, immigration stress).

In essence, counselors can use their emotional connection to clinical issues to magnify their impact. Each individual client is a member of a larger community. We can use social justice work to facilitate the empowerment of disenfranchised communities, rather than helping a sole representative of that community through individual counseling.

Look for Serendipity

I became quite concerned about racial disparities in the access to, and quality of, health care for people of African descent in this country. Interestingly, this concern and my related social justice work evolved inadvertently through a partnership that existed between the NYABPsi and the Sickle Cell Thalassemia Patient Network (SCTPN). Understanding the prevalence of depressive symptoms in persons living with sickle cell disease and the overrepresentation of this medical condition in people of African descent, SCTPN reached out to NYABPsi several years ago for help. SCTPN sought the expertise of black psychologists to help educate those with sickle cell (and their caregivers) about depression and to decrease the stigma of mental health treatment. A formal partnership was eventually established. One day, the NYABPsi member who customarily provided the psychoeducational workshops indicated that she was unavailable for an upcoming SCTPN forum and requested a replacement. I volunteered for the job to help NYABPsi keep their commitment.

Given my lack of experience in working with individuals living with sickle cell, I prepared for my first presentation by questioning a few of the leaders within SCTPN to learn about their life experiences with managing the condition. In addition to common medical symptoms and psychosocial stressors, narratives reflected themes of the stigma attached to having a "black disease," disparities in grant funding for sickle cell research (compared to other autoimmune disorders), the closing down of comprehensive sickle cell treatment centers around the country, and inadequately trained physicians providing treatment to this special population. I began reading up on these systemic issues within the treatment of sickle cell disease and hearing more stories of suffering and injustices from forum participants.

Consequently, my presentations now go well beyond psychoeducation about depression to include a focus on the racism associated with the treatment of sickle cell disease, the social injustices that contribute to general health care disparities, and the critical need for advocacy. I have also collaborated with the SCTPN president to pursue grant funding to support the public forums and the creation of pamphlets aimed at decreasing the stigma of mental health treatment within the sickle cell community.

Through consistent participation over the years, my role has become the liaison between the two organizations and the primary service provider in the partnership. What began as a one-time volunteer effort with an unfamiliar group of people has serendipitously evolved into an ongoing social justice project with a newfound community. Serendipity often plays a major role in unfolding and shaping our career paths. Look for those unexpected encounters and significant "left-field" events in your professional and personal life that can be ripe opportunities for social justice work.

Create Collaborative Partnerships

Another line of my social justice work focuses on the longstanding epidemic of the mass incarceration and criminalization of the Black community in this country. While growing up in Bed-Stuy and moving through many other pre-dominantly black neighborhoods of NYC, police brutality, unlawful arrests, and racial profiling rippled through my community. My family members, friends, and clients have personally encountered these challenges and shared with me stories of poor treatment and injustice. There is much to do to fight against the structured inequalities within the criminal justice system (e.g., Rockefeller drug laws, stop and frisk policies, racial disparities in arresting, sentencing and probation practices, etc.), which have served to rip black youth, men, and women away from their families and communities for the purposes of capitalistic gain and social control.

However, as a psychologist, my opening to address this social justice issue came in the form of collaborative partnerships that focused on developing new models of re-entry for this disenfranchised population. Offender re-entry programs typi-cally involve an unsuccessful case management approach and an over-reliance on referrals to help the incarcerated transition back into the community and stay out of prison. To increase effectiveness, re-entry programs must confront the inter-section of racism, incarceration, and recidivism and be culturally responsive.

Initially I participated in the African-Centered Re-Entry (ACRE) Project think tank launched by the Association of Black Psychologists in 2010. With over 20 experts from various disciplines, elected officials, and representatives from the California Institute for Women prison, this collaboration confronted the prison industrial complex and the disproportionate number of African Ameri-cans affected by the dilemma. A close colleague who I've collaborated with on other projects encouraged me to participate and facilitated my involvement as an expert. I tapped into my experience in African cultural arts and trauma work to offer innovative ideas about creating a culturally congruent, psychologically informed re-entry program tailored to women of African descent.

Shortly after ACRE, I began collaborating with Hope Lives for Lifers in NYC—a small interdisciplinary group working to develop a reintegration pro-gram for locally incarcerated women from social justice, psychological, and cul-tural perspectives. I worked alongside the formerly incarcerated, other social service providers, educators, religious and community leaders, and victim rights advocates. As a psychologist, my contribution involved developing a model for a decompression group to address the psychological impact of incarceration—par-ticularly for people of African descent, given their history of bondage, oppression, and intergenerational trauma. I also conducted outreach to explore the possibility of introducing anti-racism training (by community organizers) into the prison as part of a pre-release program.

In doing social justice work, there are many concentric circles of like-minded people that have a common center: a commitment to social and political change. When you place yourself within these circles, one door always seems to open another and provide a continuous flow of social justice opportunities. Sometimes all it takes is being present in a network and being open to exchanges. Once counselors are exposed to a meaningful issue of concern, they can garner support by plugging themselves into groups/movements with which they can form alliances/collaborative partnerships.

Many professional organizations have committees, divisions, listservs, and various activities (e.g., writing policy briefs and position papers, lobbying, grassroots community projects, and submitting letters, e-mails, or testimony to Congress) that focus specifically on social issues and legislative agendas. If joining a professional organization does not interest you, your time is limited, or you are in an isolated area with limited support for your concern, consider using online activism platforms to create social change. For example, you can visit www.change. org and learn how to write or start an online petition to garner support from mutually concerned individuals within a global network, or connect with powerful opportunities for social change that you might not have considered. Psychologists for Social Responsibility (PsySR; www.psysr.org) allows for psychologists, students, and other advocates for social change around the world to join program listservs on various social issues and receive updates on related activities/opportunities, engage in topical discussions, and help plan and implement projects.

Go Beyond Your Immediate Community

At 4:53 pm on January 12, 2010, a devastating earthquake shook the ground of Haiti and sent reverberating effects through the hearts and spirits of Haitians throughout the diaspora. While the island nation of Haiti struggled with thousands of lives lost, missing people, displaced families in tent communities, illegal child trafficking, and shortages of food, water, and medicinal aide, the Haitian community in NYC suffered a great deal of vicarious trauma. News of the devastation in Haiti (through graphic videos, pictures, radio programming, phone calls, and text messaging) spread throughout the world minutes after the earthquake hit. Some cable networks provided prolonged exposure through 24-hour coverage of the quake. For people of Haitian descent living in NYC (and other places outside of Haiti), such television, radio, and Internet coverage of the destruction of their homeland and depictions of hundreds of people dead and suffering left lasting impressions that were emotionally and spiritually draining. Anxiety about missing loved ones who could not be contacted or located was widespread among those living off the shores of Haiti. In the wake of the earthquake, a wave of Haitian migration began as survivors were desperate to escape the devastation and seek a safe haven elsewhere. Many came to NYC (mainly Brooklyn), already home to one of the largest Haitian populations outside of Haiti.

With a commitment to Pan-Africanism, it was clear that the NYABPsi had to respond and work toward being at the forefront of the humanitarian efforts addressing the mental health needs of the Haitian community in NYC. We asked ourselves what could be done to help people manage the powerful emotions triggered by this disaster, heal from the deeply painful loss, and cope with the host of stressors that come with migrating to a new land with limited (or no) resources.

PHOTO 14.1   Dr. Jamila Codrington posts pictures drawn by children at the Haitian Family Resource Center in Brooklyn, NY to be included in the *Art from the Heart For Haiti* Calendar—a fundraising project to raise funds for NY-based Haiti relief efforts and the Restavek Foundation in Haiti

As President of the organization at the time, I facilitated the mobilization of a Haiti Relief Committee to offer sustained support to the Haitian community in NYC that was affected by the earthquake, particularly those survivors who had migrated to the area since the disaster. To build our committee and expand our reach, we formed a collaborative partnership with the New York chapter of the National Association of Black Social Workers. The committee turned out to be a small cadre of devoted mental health professionals from both organizations, along with non-affiliated Haitian mental health professionals and students who were sought out to help culturally tailor relief and recovery efforts. Our mission was simple: to promote holistic health and healing for NYC-based Haitians who were dealing with the long-lasting effects of the Haiti earthquake. In carrying out this mission, I have stumbled onto quite a few lessons learned about engaging in social justice work.

Lessons Learned

Meet the People Where They Are

Our committee's Haiti relief and recovery work began with more of a conventional disaster response and grew increasingly political once we set aside our own mental health agenda and prioritized the voiced concerns of the Haitians themselves. Initially, our committee focused on providing psychoeducation about trauma, secondary trauma, and grief through the circulation of fact sheets (in English and Kreyol). The committee then engaged in ongoing outreach efforts to individuals and organizations that could be a resource to the Haitian community in NYC, and created and disseminated a Haitian Community Resource List that housed all of the information. During the cold calls to mental health professionals, committee members particularly advocated for the provision of pro bono services. Most of the Haitian earthquake survivors were uninsured, unemployed, and therefore unable to pay for mental health services. The list included individuals who agreed to provide translation and mental health services at no cost, along with community-based organizations serving the Haitian community.

Attuned to the spiritual and religious strengths of the Haitian people as a source of resilience, the committee focused much of its efforts on partnering with Haitian churches throughout the NYC area. We believed the church would be a safe space for Haitians to process how they were affected by the earthquake disaster, learn about trauma and stress reactions, build on cultural strengths, and receive guidance and resources for coping with the disaster (all with the help of prayer, song, and food). Our first thought was to offer this psychoeducation as a stand-alone service—*straight up, no chaser*. However, we understood the importance of consulting with Haitian leaders in the community and were fortunately diverted from this plan. A ministry leader from the first Haitian church we partnered with anticipated that the stigma associated with mental health would result in a low turnout from the Haitian community. She recommended that we embed the mental health focus between other social services that were non-stigmatizing, and that addressed the serious challenges in surviving as recent immigrants.

With the goal of "meeting the people where they're at," we held a more comprehensive program at the church, which headlined immigration and employment support against the backdrop of stress management. It was a collaborative effort with presentations from several social service, advocacy, and community-based organizations. The program opened up with prayer, song, and food. Although our committee was ultimately able to discuss the invisible scars of earthquake survivors and the culture of silence around mental health issues in the Haitian community, we would have never had this opportunity if we had bulldozed our way through with a pure mental health focus. Providing holistic relief and recovery efforts that met the Haitians where they were—rather than at the typical "go-to" place for mental health professionals—was much more effective. When we listened and remained open to the voiced concerns of the Haitian community, we were able to transform our conventional disaster response into powerful social justice work.

Commit to Causes, Not People

During this event at the church, I had the opportunity to talk with a representative from a Haitian advocacy group who shared my table. She informed me about a new initiative to address the deportation risk faced by recently migrated Haitian earthquake survivors, and emphasized that the initiative could use the help of mental health professionals. Mindful of the inequitable treatment historically faced by Haitian asylum seekers, I was interested in finding out how I, and the larger committee, could assist. A few phone calls later, the opportunity arose to partner with pro bono lawyers in advocating for Haitian earthquake survivors to receive a rarely used immigration benefit known as Deferred Action, which could allow them to stay and work in the country for a fixed amount of time rather than get deported. From my prior experience at the Haitian church, I learned that for many Haitian earthquake survivors, the fears and anxieties about being deported back to the devastation and surviving in a new land can far outweigh those from the actual experience of the disaster. I came to understand this immigration dilemma as a mental health issue within a political context, and after careful deliberation with the committee, we agreed to move forward with the project.

The project aimed to conduct pro bono psychosocial assessments of Haitian earthquake survivors without legal status in NYC and determine the extent to which they experienced any mental health issues related to the earthquake disaster. Those assessments would then be considered for use with affidavits prepared by the lawyers in support of the Haitians' Deferred Action applications. We got off to a good start in the partnership, as we organized and implemented the first training session for committee members with a local psychiatrist who specialized in conducting assessments for asylum cases. However, shortly after the training the psychiatrist announced he was unable to continue his involvement in the project. Despite numerous outreach attempts, we were unable to find a replacement trainer and our project eventually fizzled out. Unfortunately, the psychiatrist became the lifeline of our project and when his commitment ended, so did our project. This is a dangerous pitfall. I've learned that while collaborative partnerships are an important element of social justice work, partners can fall out of the mix. We must prepare for the unexpected and sustain our social justice work by committing to the underlying causes, not the people or organizations with which we partner.

Consider Small Social Justice initiatives

There's no one right way to create a social justice agenda. While some may be inspired to think big, others may want to focus on a smaller sphere of influence.

I've taken on social justice projects outside of my day-to-day job; however this may not be the path for everyone. Counselors can consider taking smaller social justice initiatives within their own clinical practices, which can also be a powerful method of transforming the lives of others. Although social justice issues are unlikely to be resolved through therapy alone, therapists can take some first steps through a simple commitment to creating egalitarian relationships with their clients. Through self-reflection and openly processing our relationships with clients, we can raise our consciousness about power dynamics in our own clinical work and begin to equalize power inequities that exist within client-therapist relationships.

Regardless of our cultural identity or that of our clients, we can routinely ask ourselves: Who holds the power and privilege in my relationship with my client? How do I negotiate this from session to session? What values and intentions inform my work? Do I challenge institutional policies that punish individuals for systemic problems (e.g., terminating clients for "noncompliance" without considering barriers to transportation, child care, and flexible work schedules that are faced by low-income, disadvantaged, and under-resourced families)? How do I function as a gatekeeper to much-needed services? What are the social and political factors that influence where I position my clinical practice? Can I do more to help underserved populations? Am I searching for openings to honor the wisdom of my client (versus pushing forward with my own clinical opinion)? Do I collaboratively draw out and utilize my client's cultural assets to achieve treatment goals? How can I effectively engage in advocacy to give a voice to disempowered clients or help them develop their own advocacy skills? Are there times when I operate under the guise of neutrality (Prilleltensky and Nelson, 2002), assuming and communicating objective interpretations of client behavior when I am in fact influenced by stereotypic notions?

Such questioning (common within liberation psychology, community psychology, and narrative, feminist, and multi-cultural counseling approaches) helps integrate a social justice philosophical framework into our day-to-day office work, and serves as stepping stones as we become social change agents within the community. Counselors taking on a social justice agenda in their clinical work can also engage in what Frantz Fanon (1986) referred to as "conscienciser," the process of bringing the unconscious to consciousness in order to free clients from their unconscious desires and orient them towards social change. In line with Fanon's thinking, therapists can also ask themselves: How does my use of the colonizer's language and concepts affect oppressed clients' consciousness? To what extent do I conceptualize client problems in relation to their sociopolitical history (e.g., of oppression) and incorporate this understanding into therapeutic conversations?

When counselors' conceptualizations and/or interventions with clients focus solely on the self and not on debilitating systemic factors, they inadvertently perpetuate the status quo as they "medicalize" the behavior—a concept discussed by Dr. Amos Wilson (1983). Wilson professed that one of the most powerful methods of maintaining the status quo (i.e., oppression) is to medicalize behavior by moving the definition of the behavior away from social and political systems and onto the clients themselves (i.e., mental illness). When this is done, whether consciously or subconsciously, the demand for social and political change is taken away and the status quo is maintained. Counselors must be careful to avoid participating in this process by engaging with the aforementioned questions.

One does not have to have a radical social justice agenda that is played out on the big stage. Taking small social justice initiatives within counseling work that are based on an underlying commitment to equity, empowerment, and social responsibility can undoubtedly make an impact. Additionally, with a true commitment, momentum may build over time and create a natural pull towards involvement in greater social justice works.

Sustaining Factors: What Keeps My Fire Burning

Social justice work is something I care about deeply. It gives my life meaning and helps me fulfill the responsibility I believe I have to care for my broader community, continue the work of my ancestors, and create a better future for the unborn. Though over the years, I have come to realize that passion and commitment are not always enough to sustain me. There are many challenges to and complexities in doing this work. It is important to name these obstacles so that those who are considering taking on this work can have a more balanced picture of all that is entailed. Unearthing the collateral damage of social justice work can also assist those who are already engaged to develop a game plan to buffer the stress and prevent future burnout. So I share the challenges and sustaining factors that have helped me stay the course in hopes that these reflections will help others create a sustainable practice of social justice work.

Stay Present to Your Interconnectedness with the Community

One of the greatest threats to social justice work is a stance of autonomy. We must remember that we really are our brothers' and sisters' keeper. However, diffusion of responsibility sometimes creeps in, and we leave the work to someone else or believe it is the job of social institutions to take care of disempowered communities of people. For those who question whether social justice work should be an individual civic responsibility, consider the words of Dr. Martin Luther King, Jr., who sat in a narrow jail cell in Birmingham on April 16, 1963 and wrote a lengthy letter to his fellow clergymen. In that letter, Dr. King professed that "oppressed people cannot remain oppressed forever." Rather than "emulate the do nothingism of the complacent," he discussed his drive to engage in social justice acts—based on a firm understanding of the interconnectedness between communities of people:

Moreover, I am cognizant of the interrelatedness of all communities and states. I cannot sit idly by in Atlanta and not be concerned about what happens in Birmingham. Injustice anywhere is a threat to justice everywhere. We are caught in an inescapable network of mutuality, tied in a single garment of destiny. Whatever affects one directly, affects all indirectly. Never again can we afford to live with the narrow, provincial 'outside agitator' idea. Anyone who lives inside the United States can never be considered an outsider anywhere within its bounds.

Dr. King's sentiments so passionately reflect his profound sense of interconnectedness with the community and understanding that, "in community, the needs of one are the needs of many" (Somé, 1998)—or in Caribbean colloquial terms, "what hurt nose make eyes run." If we can stay present to this sense of interconnectedness with a community of people, remembering that we are individual threads woven together in the fabric of life, social justice work becomes a natural act in the maintenance of our own civil liberties.

Remember That Objectivity is a Myth—All of Our Work is Political

Sometimes my social justice work is questioned by others who believe I'm too radical, and too political. I don't let this deter me. For those who argue against helping professions (such as psychology and counseling) engaging in political acts and question whether it is in line with the origins of the field, I suggest they recall or further investigate the history of psychology. The profession has always been political. It's just a matter of what the agenda has been and whose needs and interests have been served by the agenda. For example, psychology played a critical role in promoting the Eugenics movement in the early 1900s, which was used to segregate, institutionalize, sterilize, discriminate, and commit genocide against groups of people deemed genetically inferior. More recently, the field of psychology has had an active hand in the CIA's abuse and torture of detainees at US military prisons. Complete objectivity and political neutrality are myths.

As counselors, we frequently promote some form of value, belief system, or political agenda—often without realizing it. Failing to name and discuss the impact that racism, poverty, discrimination, or neighborhood disadvantage have on mental health functioning—and focusing solely on individual change and maintaining a "value-free" stance of "neutrality"—are all political agendas (albeit unintentional) that perpetuate the status quo. In this way, acts of omission are just as damaging as acts of commission. As counselors, we must increase our critical consciousness so that we can be aware of the political nature of our work and determine on which side of the fence we will stand, rather than pretend that political issues do not exist or that we can be effective without delving into such issues.

When we can do this, social justice work becomes a natural investment of time. Acts of oppression in the world are illuminated and we are no longer caught in the web of ignorance, confusion, neutrality, apathy, or complacency that prevents us from positioning ourselves along political lines and taking a stand. We experience a deep, often irreversible shift in thought, feeling, and action that dramatically transforms our way of being in the world. We develop a critical understanding of power relations and the interconnection between power and oppression. We gain vision and the courage to stand against injustices.

Develop a Network of Support

In doing social justice work, one comes face to face with thick layers of injustice and oppression, fortified by every social system around you. Social justice work often requires you to stand with victims of poverty, racism, genocide, psychological torture, trauma, violence, abuse, unjust imprisonment, etc, and hear their stories of pain. Being "in the struggle" can, over time, lead to a loss of hope, feelings of intense anger, vicarious trauma, and a sense of being overwhelmed by the problems and powerlessness over one's environment. It is critical that those who take on a social justice agenda surround themselves with others who also do such work. Even if it's a small cadre of like-minded people, such a support network can be the difference between burnout and staying the course.

Make it Personal

A sense of interconnectedness with the community is a powerful motivational force for social justice work. However, social justice work—which often comes in the form of pro bono community service on top of one's regular job responsibilities—can be immensely draining. It requires ongoing personal sacrifices of time, energy, and (at times) even one's own financial resources. Given that many professionals are not willing to make such sacrifices, a social justice commitment can also leave one feeling isolated. A true devotion can at times interfere with personal relationships, as there is less time to nurture relationships with family, friends, and romantic partners. Self-care can be affected by burning the candle at both ends. Over time, even the most powerful sense of interconnectedness with the community may not be enough to sustain oneself.

Perhaps the only motivational force greater than this is the fight for one's own survival and liberation. When we can bind social justice work together with our own liberation struggle, we might get weary, but we can switch gears and catch a second wind as we enter a mode of survival and self-preservation. When I recognize that people of African descent around the world continue to be systematically oppressed and annihilated through neo-colonialist strategies, my commitment to social justice work as a counselor of African descent becomes deeply personal. I push harder because there is no other decent option. Either I do the work, or I have a hand in my people's own demise through a stance of "do nothingnesss" and complacency (as warned about by Dr. Martin Luther King, Jr.).

Certainly, there have been many benefits to my social justice journey. I have been fortunate to form meaningful partnerships (on both personal and organizational levels) with educators, public health professionals, elected officials, religious leaders, community organizers, and others on the front line. My natural interest in and commitment to social justice eventually led to a leadership role as Chair of the Social Action Committee within the NYABPsi and membership of the Public Policy Committee at the national level of the organization. To my surprise, I received the 2010 Bobby E. Wright Award from the Association of Black Psychologists for my commitment to community service and empowerment—an honoring and deeply humbling experience. After a year and a half of investing a great deal of time and energy into the Haiti relief and recovery work in NYC, the sacrifices paid off through a few thousand dollars of funding from a grant that I wrote. Yet what sustains me the most is the community of people that I carry with me in my social justice work. They are my own community, ever present and consistently reminding me of what is important and the obligation that I must fulfill in the name of collective self-preservation. How can you make your social justice work deeply personal? Can you bring it back home to your community? Can it be tied up with your own liberation struggle?

Specific Implications for Counselors of African Descent

It is my intention that the reflections I've shared have yielded some meaning and value for those in the counseling field, in ways that inspire and promote a social justice agenda. I recognize though, that my journey in social justice work has focused particularly on communities of African descent. I am driven to stand with brothers and sisters in my own community—whose liberation is bound up with mine. As such, my social justice work has specific implications for counselors of African descent. Whether or not to engage in social justice work cannot be decided until we ask the fundamental question that many African scholars have addressed over time: what does it mean to be African?

The basic principles of communalism, interdependence, and collective responsibility are found in many traditional African philosophical frameworks. *Ujima* (meaning collective work and responsibility in Swahili) teaches us to recognize that our own well-being is derived from that of our family and community and that above all, we must be concerned with the overall health of our family and community. In essence, the lives of each individual, family member, and that of the community are bound together. Menkiti (1984) and many other African scholars remind us that the community takes precedence over the individual in traditional African ontology and epistemology. This is in contrast to Western views, which generally value independence and autonomy, and position a person as a lone individual versus part of a collective whole.

Communalism, as a fundamental African value and guiding principle for human interaction, is reflected in many African proverbs across the diaspora.

Consider the popularized proverbs "It takes a whole village to raise a child" and "I am because we are, and since we are, therefore I am." Among the Zulu there is a saying, "one is a person through others." This proverb reflects *Ubuntu*, a fundamental concept in the African thought of the Bantu-speaking people. What does the embodiment of *Ubuntu* look like? According to Archbishop Desmond Tutu, "A person with *Ubuntu* is open and available to others, affirming of others, does not feel threatened that others are able and good, for he or she has a proper self-assurance that comes from knowing that he or she belongs in a greater whole and is diminished when others are humiliated or diminished, when others are tortured or oppressed" (1999).

If personhood is defined by community, and taking care of others is the essence of what it means to be human in traditional African thought, then what does this mean for how African-descended healers shape their career? If we are in alignment with the ethos from which we emerged, then social justice work should be a defining characteristic of our professional lives. To be authentically African, African-descended counselors should be known and identified in, by, and through our community. Hence, we must go where the community goes and be caretakers of the community, not merely helpers of individuals in separate and distinct 50-minute sessions. There should be a common thread that weaves through the fabric of our individual work and is inextricably tied to the needs and goals of the community with which we identify. Together, principles of communalism, interdependence, and collective responsibility should be the guiding light or internal compass that directs our movements as counselors of African descent.

In order to do the necessary liberatory work within African-descended communities, the healers (counselors) of the community must find ways to bridge their careers with social justice work. This type of sustained and transformative work will honor our ancestors and promote our own humanity. We cannot fail our ancestors. Neither can we fail the unborn—those to come who will continue our legacy.

It is my hope that by reflecting on my lineage, upbringing, journey to pursuing a career in psychology, and my own social justice efforts I might provide some inspiration for others to look within and find their own social action passion. Indeed, it is an honor to use our divine gifts and talents as counselors for the purpose of taking a stand in the world. To those already engaged in social justice work: stay the course. Continue to be a flame. Burn and shine light on issues that disenfranchise others. Be steadfast in serving people whose lives have been so torn apart by oppression and whose voices have been silenced. Experience the power and fulfillment of this liberatory work.

References

Cooper, A. J. (1892). *A Voice from the South*. Xenia, Ohio: Aldine Printing House.

Fanon, F. (1986). *Black Skin, White Mask*. C.L. Markmann (trans). London: Pluto Press.

Freire, P. (1990). *Education for a Critical Consciousness*. New York: Continuum.

King, Jr., M.L. *Letter from a Birmingham Jail*. http://www.africa.upenn.edu/Articles_Gen/Letter_Birmingham.html. Retrieved September 3, 2011.

Lauter, P. (2002). *The Heath Anthology of American Literature*, 4th ed. Vol. 1. Boston: Houghton Mifflin.

Menkiti I.A. (1984). Person and community in African traditional thought. In R.A. Wright (ed.), *African Philosophy: An Introduction*. Lanham, MD: University Press of America.

Prilleltensky, I. & Nelson, G. (2002). *Doing Psychology Critically: Making a Difference in Diverse Settings*. New York: Palgrave MacMillan.

Somé, M.P. (1998). *The Healing Wisdom of Africa*. New York: Penguin/Putnam Books.

Tutu, D. (1999). *No Future Without Forgiveness*. New York: Random House.

Wilson, A. (1993). Special education: Its special agenda unhooded. [video recording].

15

NO ONE GETS LEFT BEHIND

Cyrus Marcellus Ellis

It has been 26 years since I got off a bus in the darkness and cool air of Fort Leonard Wood, Missouri. I was a young 18-year-old kid from New Orleans, Louisiana trying to grow up and become a man. I had made the decision several months before to enlist in the US Army. Many of my friends did the same. I am sure I joined the Army to be like my father; he was in the Army in the 1950s and he always said it was the thing for a young man to do. I wanted to be like my father so much that if he said I ought to do it, then I was going to do it. I was not sure what my experience was going to be like. I was excited about being in the Army, but I had no idea what being a soldier meant or felt like.

All the new recruits were greeted by an old, square-chinned, menacing sergeant standing in front of a little welcoming hut. He used choice words to usher us into the hut, to tell us to take a seat, and to shut up! It was the first of many instances when I began to realize that I was no longer in the comforts of my teenaged world and that my journey to becoming a soldier was well underway. Over the course of the next eight weeks my body and my mind began a transformation into learning the traits, duties, history, and essence of being a soldier. It was a transformation that would guide my life for the next 20 years and that still guides my life today. The lessons taught to me such as self-sacrifice, selfless service, and military family life, serve as pillars in my conduct as a counseling professional. It is for these reasons and countless others that my activities as a professional counselor are directed to the needs of veterans and their families.

Responding to the Need

Over the last 10 years, the US military has been under siege, with multiple deployments fighting two wars in two different theaters of war. Military families, in the reserve forces as well as the active forces, have been stretched to the limit as soldiers are deployed for extended periods of time and are re-deployed to meet wartime needs. Military members and their families have not been able to keep pace with the demands of operations overseas. As a result, military members and their families are experiencing undue hardship in every area of their lives. Physical scars and injuries, compounded by intrapsychic concerns, have crippled the ability of veterans from Iraq and Afghanistan to reintegrate into society adaptively. Veterans' concerns and needs are well documented, but what many people do not realize is that their issues go beyond the need for counseling in a traditional context. As many veterans are losing the battle of coming home and re-adjusting to life, it became clear to me that I had to get off the sidelines. I had to take command of my feelings and of my ability to use my professional skills and position to help military members and their families beyond personal and familial counseling.

Military members and their families are a tight-knit group that depend on each other for survival. Sure, in recent years the military has been getting a lot of good press and respect. They deserve it. But the reality is that military families have always been in need, and seldom get the support they need from outside of their military environment. It hurts me personally and deeply when I hear of military service members on food stamps in order to feed their families. I get offended when I hear of military members and their families being disregarded, not for their service, but for their approach to life, which often tends to be logical and task oriented. At the height of the war in Iraq, service member suicides rose dramatically. In January 2009, more soldiers had killed themselves than were killed in battle. I knew it was time to stop talking, and like a good soldier, *move out!*

I have been a professional counselor for about 16 years, and a counselor educator for 11 of those years. I retired from military service in 2004. The wars in Iraq and Afghanistan were raging at that time, and the cost of war was rising significantly with regard to soldiers' lives and the lives of military family members. In those days, deployments for active duty troops surged to 15 months while Reservists and National Guard service members had a one-year commitment. It was not only the extended deployment time that was affecting troops; it was the multiple deployments that also put increased hardship on military members and their families. The results of prolonged combat began to show themselves when an overabundance of service members were being killed and severely wounded. The large number of physically and psychologically wounded soldiers began to strain the health care systems that service members counted on when they returned home from battle. Returning service members often did not receive the kind of care that was promised to them, and they encountered multiple barriers to receiving their benefits. This phenomenon came to my attention as I met with veterans and veteran groups in and around Chicago. I became angry and fed up with my brothers and sisters in arms being denied their due from their service. I decided to reach out and join the crusade to make sure that no one was left behind once they returned home.

As a retired soldier I carry a sense of guilt for having benefited from multiple years of service and never having given back to my nation by using all that I have been taught and trained to do for the nation in a time of war. I have a long service record and I don't have a scratch on me. I do not wish for war, nor would I enjoy it, but I owe this nation for what I have received and I do not believe I have given it back yet. I decided to use my talents to fight a system that created barriers for service members and kept them in the dark and separate from what they earned and what they were promised by the sacrifice of their service.

No Fight is Easy

While it is admirable for any veteran to assist his or her family of soldiers, the task is quite difficult to put into practice. The culture of the military is strong on ability, dedication to duty, strength, courage, and self-sufficiency. Military members work hard to project strength and confidence in everything they do. Soldiers are trained, from the very first day, to find solutions to problems and work through them. Service members are evaluated by the depth of their sacrifices for mission completion. Service members understand mission completion, and the success of the unit involves an "all in" attitude from every member of the unit. For a certain group of service members, known as "lifers," this attitude permeates every aspect of their personal lives. The attitude of overcoming obstacles, setbacks, and ambiguity extends beyond military service; for many veterans it becomes a standard that is very hard to maintain in their personal lives. As such, emotional issues, which they were formally taught to repress, causes difficulty in the lives of veterans who have been exposed to combat for extended periods of time.

Military members are cautious about letting down their guard and displaying any vulnerability. Those who seek help (or who are asked to seek help) tend to have a low tolerance for helpers who do not understand the explicit and implicit dimensions of military service, deployment, and combat. Veterans tend to suffer in silence or only talk to other veterans. I was banking on the latter premise to give me access to help my comrades. The greatest struggle was finding an entrance point that would allow my desire, training, and service to assist military members and their families.

I was able to overcome this obstacle by connecting with my university's veterans affairs representative. She was not a veteran, but she knew where many were and she was a great resource. As I was new to the area, my knowledge of advocacy groups and veterans groups was low and she was able to connect me with many people. As usual, many numbers were old and some were no longer working; some had moved on and others, sadly, had passed away. It was becoming difficult and frustrating to make real connections. I was able to work through this issue by convening a meeting with the veterans affairs representative and a member of a veterans group that was interested in providing veterans an array of services in the south end of Chicago, where no services were being offered. It took about a month to get together with the right people. We met in different locations around Chicago and finally cemented our ability to work together in the parking lot of my university. The reason for meeting in the parking lot was metaphorical. Soldiers like to establish an area of operations (AO) when there is a mission to be completed. When we were organizing our approach, my university was closed, but that did not stop us! We established an AO and kept moving forward! Once I was on the inside with this veterans group, which was housed at Jesse Brown VA Medical Center in Chicago, things were a lot easier.

The Veterans Program

The central idea behind helping veterans in and out of traditional counseling sessions involved recognizing the needs of veterans and their families. These needs involved not only their psychological readjustment to life outside of a war zone, but also their ability to find places of respite that did not necessarily meet the standard of needing counseling or therapy. Reviewing the data collected from the veteran's groups, I discovered that a major source of stress and frustration was veterans' inability to apply for and receive their benefits upon discharge from military service or return to reserve status. What emerged is a program that began to focus on the tangible aspects of helping veterans claim their benefits through the Department of Veterans Affairs or other entities, and help those who needed it receive support in transitioning to civilian life.

The veterans program, involves a grassroots approach to providing veterans in the area with a constant resource for all pieces of information that can aid them in working through re-deployment, family, educational, and benefit issues. The program operates as an arm of the counseling program and is not within the formal hierarchy of the university. I serve as the point of contact between our counseling honor society and the student counseling organization. The program involves holding all-day training and information seminars in the fall semester with veteran groups from the south suburbs and in and around Chicago. The Illinois Department of Veterans Affairs, the Department of Veterans Affairs (Federal), and the Jesse Brown VA Medical Center and VetNet (a nonprofit veterans group) all descend on the university to provide the latest information on benefits, new legislation affecting veterans' health benefits, educational benefits, employment assistance, and peer support programs. The program yields an audience of concerned counseling professionals and other helping professionals, as well as students and campus administrators who come to get in touch with veterans on campus and in the community. The greatest personal joy for me is to meet and greet so many veterans that span our nation's history. We have veterans of WWII, Korea, Vietnam, Grenada, Operation Just Cause, Desert Storm, and of course, Iraqi Freedom and Noble Eagle (Afghanistan). The program is based on veterans assisting other veterans. As veterans tend to talk to other veterans, we were banking on our peer support program being one of the most important elements of our program. I explicitly targeted veterans to assist other veterans through peer support. I wanted to emphasize their sense of common stories and experiences and make this the focus of the self-help approach. Veterans who are able to talk about their experiences can use their shared culture to communicate their stories and not feel as though they are weak or in a weakened position by talking about their struggles.

The peer support program is a self-help group format of facilitator-trained veterans who lead groups with other veterans in order for them to begin discussing their issues in an environment made up only of other veterans. Each facilitator is trained to assist each veteran respectfully, and to carefully process military experiences in a caring environment. The groups are like other self-help groups and are independent and operate without professional facilitators. The peer support program meets at various locations on campus, and their location and time are not posted or advertised in any way. Veterans inquire about the program through the veterans representative and the information is passed anonymously by word of mouth. While this dimension of the program has proven to be successful, the real social action arm, and most vivid example of how this program grows beyond the counseling hour, is at the core of this project's meaning of *no one left behind*.

The Iraq War Vet

As the point of contact for this program, many calls are referred to me from the veterans affairs representative on campus and the counseling department for the university. My colleagues also ask questions and provide referrals of veterans who need assistance from time to time. This is one such example of receiving a request for help from a colleague.

A colleague caught me in the hallway and said that friends had asked her about where veterans can go for help. My colleague is a psychologist, and I am sure that is why she was asked about programs that assist veterans. She had visited my veterans program and knew what services we had available, and quickly provided me with the veteran's contact information. This is the tricky part. Gerald is a 21-year-old Iraq war veteran. He had served two tours of duty in Iraq and was having some difficulty living at home. He had been discharged seven months prior, but he wasn't staying at home because of difficulties with his mother and siblings. In fact, I learned he was staying at a local motel and was in need of help.

Veterans understand action, so I began to formulate a potential plan. As this was a young veteran and I consider myself an old soldier type, I knew this would involve a lot more than just talking. This would involve determining what are this veteran's logistical needs (i.e., food, clothes, shelter). Entering into this call for assistance meant not only doing the best I could but also living up to the creed that veterans have when working with each other, which is exemplified by the phrase "all the way." In a traditional counselor role, many of my thoughts about Gerald could have taken the form of referrals. I could see contacting many agencies in the community and getting him in touch with others who were prepared to do specific outreach for Gerald's logistical needs. In my traditional role I would not have entered Gerald's day-to-day life, but maintaining a traditional role with Gerald falls short when approaching this as a veteran helping another veteran. I did not reach out to Gerald as a counselor; I approached him as a soldier who was willing to go as far as necessary to provide this soldier with what he needed. The boundaries for a professional counselor did not reach as far as they needed to for Gerald. As such, I proceeded to help him within the boundaries of an Army Officer seeking to secure one of his soldiers from harm.

I went to the hotel where he was staying (I don't endorse this practice for everyone) to pick him up and take him somewhere neutral to assess his needs. Along the way we stopped for "chow." We began discussing his needs. We talked about his two deployments and the job he had while inside Iraq. This is where most veterans feel comfortable. He was able to speak in military terms and I could question him about his narrative by using other military terms if I was unclear about any part of his story. This all took place over chow. You could say I was using "war stories" as the vehicle. It became clear he was in need of more social support than traditional counseling services. He had little money, inconsistent housing, and lacked a basic means of support. He had very little in terms of personal belongings (i.e., basic hygiene items and other personal items) and lacked social support. Moving into action for this veteran meant bringing together a great deal of resources to prevent him from falling through the cracks as he attempted to reintegrate into peacetime and civilian life.

Years ago I presented a daylong workshop on how we can address issues in economically depressed communities; it was called the A-P-C approach. I spoke of how the resources of academics (A), professionals (P), and the community (C) can be aimed at aiding individuals in the community.

I applied this model to the social justice format for the veteran I was assisting. I brought him to our counseling lab and assessed him initially to make sure there were no signs of trauma and that he was not in any immediate psychological danger. I prepared a referral list for pro bono psychological services for him if the need arose. I acquired a gym membership for him at my university. What would a gym membership do for him, you ask? A gym membership for this veteran was not to give him an opportunity to bulk up or to feel the burn, rather it was to accomplish one of his logistical needs: hygiene. One Saturday morning the veteran called me and said he had slept in his car and was very cold and in need of a shower. I was teaching a class that morning and instructed him to come to the university. I worked it out where he could have a membership that gave him access to the locker room. This gave him a place to shower and address his hygiene. I brought him to the university library so that he could have access to the Internet to follow up on veterans services and find information about military records, VA employment, government service ratings, and medical center information. Because there is a network of veterans as a result of the other dimensions of the program, contacts at the VA Medical Center helped Gerald find housing. The veteran was able to secure some basic needs, develop a supportive network, and find housing through other veterans in the program.

Programmatic Struggles

Working outside of the counseling hour in this program presents many challenges and frustrations. In traditional counseling sessions, a great deal of the work is done within one hour and is usually followed up on in consecutive sessions. In this program the work is not limited to one hour a week, but rather continues through each day.

This program is built on the premise that we will not leave veterans behind. When we began to work with Gerald, it was necessary to share contact information. In the beginning of our working alliance we would talk by phone. The veteran, having inconsistent housing, was rarely in the same place on a daily basis. As I was his advocate, he would begin to call me on a regular basis, sometimes four and five times a day. I was usually engaged in any number of normal work activities, not to mention my family responsibilities. He was like a thirsty man who finally found water; he was constantly bringing his needs to my attention. I would get messages during my classes, I would get messages during down time with my family, and while trying to relax. His needs grew from basic living to issues of physical health, needing a car, and other things. The demands of this veteran seeking reintegration became enormous and quite challenging. As I worked with him I began to realize that his needs were in many cases greater than those of my clients when I was a case manager back on the East Coast. It soon became necessary to put some boundaries in place in order for me to balance my desire to assist veterans and my professional responsibilities on campus and around the nation. Complicating this realization was the code of being a "lifer" as a soldier.

Soldiers understand that when we make a commitment to each other that it goes *all the way*. We recognize that the sacrifice of serving in a theater of war requires a commitment that is not common among all people. When developing our working alliance there was (and quite possibly always will be when vets work together) an unspoken and undocumented understanding between us that we will be there for each other. This understanding may come from our shared experiences as soldiers, who are knowledgeable about combat training and being deployed and separated from family and loved ones. This sense of connection drove me to be readily available to him, not just because of our alliance, but because he was a soldier and I gave him my word. In many cases when I was tired and needed to find a respite from the stress and strain of my daily routine, he would call and I would resist the temptation to let the phone call go to voicemail; I needed to take the call and do my best to assist him. I soon began to realize that this would extend to evenings and weekends. It is the price we pay to sustain the valor of the veteran seeking reintegration into civilian life. Their sacrifice in a theater of war ought to be matched by the intensity of our ability to help them when they come home. This view may be self-imposed, but it does match the sentiment of many veterans when working with soldiers when they return home.

The greatest frustration for me was the incongruence of people's attitudes when it was time to put up! People tend to give a lot lip service to helping veterans and thanking them for their service. That's good, but it is not enough. Veterans work all the time when in service, especially in combat. I used to pull 20-hour days and fatigue was as normal mosquito bites and cold food. I was dismayed at how people, when pressed to do extra on behalf of the veteran, would return with statements like, "this ain't the Army" or "I know he is a veteran, but I am not, I work until 4:30." I would like those who have not served to do one week of Basic Training to learn the lesson Duty, Honor, Country and the cost of it. Perhaps it would change their attitude.

Personal Satisfaction

The greatest joy of establishing this program for veterans is that it is in direct line with the values of being a soldier: selfless service. The frustrations that I addressed earlier are real, but they do not decrease my desire to serve a group of women and men that has sacrificed so much for other service members in theaters of war, and for our nation as a whole. My sacrifice must meet their standard of sacrifice and devotion to duty. Sacrifice is discussed when veterans assemble on campus and we begin talking about our experiences in service, no matter what era we served in.

I keep going because I owe my nation a debt I cannot repay. Much of my sense of self is rooted in the fact that my adult life has been spent in uniform. I have benefited from a decision I made when I was an adolescent, and I cannot rest until I give it back. My passion and drive must equal their sacrifice. For me, it's that simple.

Soldiers and their families are among this nation's best assets, and seeing families reconnect and begin to repair their lives gives me personal satisfaction. It is hard to put into words the internal sense of pride I feel when fellow veterans give me a particular glance, shake my hand a certain way, or salute me in thanks for helping them. It is, without a doubt, the greatest feeling one can experience. It ought to be noted that much of this occurs without public knowledge. We thank each other in the aforementioned way in parking lots or in meeting rooms when civilians are not around, and when there are no cameras around to capture the moment. It is a private, respectful exchange that is likened to our service, which was far away from civilian eyes and outside of the public's view.

Moving Forward With Your Own Plans

If anyone desires to replicate any portion of a veterans' program, there are a few things you might want to consider to make it a success.

First, make sure you have veterans as a part of your program. Veterans like to talk to other veterans. They can provide insight into the language and culture of the military so that the experiences that are talked about have a degree of normality to them for non-service members. Veterans can explain rank structure, family life, and issues that tend not to be discussed in mixed company but which will affect a soldier's ability to reintegrate into society.

Second, you need to do your homework. Veterans don't like it when they choose to seek help from non-military people and the helpers seem unprepared to address the issues of the military member or their family. Doing your homework means knowing the difference between a Marine, Soldier, Seaman, and Airman. This can be accomplished by some simple Google searches or by asking the veterans working with you about their branches of service and the other services. You could also decorate your office with flags and other paraphernalia to give it a "veteran friendly" appearance.

Third, be sincere. If you don't know something about being a veteran, you can ask. This work is not just about helping a special population or providing services to collect data to get a publication. This is about helping a special group of people who, by the way, were always special even before the wars in Iraq and Afghanistan. Veterans can tell if you are sincere by your actions, not your words. If you are serious about going all the way, it will show in your behavior toward them.

Veterans want and deserve the real deal. They have earned a 100% effort from us because of their 100% sacrifice for our nation and our protection. Fulfilling our promise to them, and doing whatever we can to help them regain their lives back home, is an obligation that we have and one that must be done.

16

COUNSELORS WITHOUT BORDERS

Community Action in Counseling

Fred Bemak

For as long as I can remember, I have been involved in community work. As a student activist in the Civil Rights Movement and the anti-Vietnam War movement, involvement in community action is familiar terrain for me. Thus sitting in the Association for Counselor Education and Supervision (ACES) national convention's opening session in 2005—where the entire national body of professors, supervisors, and leaders in the counseling field were together in the main convention hall three months after Hurricane Katrina—I found myself shocked by the lack of response to the devastation on the Gulf Coast. The President of ACES asked the room of 800 people how many had been to the Gulf Coast, and three people raised their hands. It was well known that the federal government and Red Cross had failed miserably in responding to the dramatic mental health needs after the hurricane, making it even more astonishing that some of the leading professionals in the country had not stepped up to the plate.

At that moment while sitting at ACES, Counselors Without Borders (CWB) was conceived. Inherent in the CWB conception was how to move quickly and decisively while being culturally responsive and unhampered by the red tape and rules that had bogged down the Red Cross and the federal government. These organizations had long-established policies and regulations that required certain types of licensure (for example, school counseling licensed counselors were not acceptable), two-week minimum stays (not everyone willing to help could block out two weeks), prior specialized training, etc. These rules, which had served post-disaster counseling work well in other less severe situations, fell alarmingly short in response to the devastation of Hurricane Katrina. CWB was organized to respond quickly and effectively with high-quality services and intensive supervision while circumventing the prohibitive requirements that banned other organizations from being effective in such unique circumstances.

To create an efficient and fast-responding team, I developed an internship-like experience through CWB, forming teams of advanced highly skilled graduate students who could provide on-site counseling under the supervision of experienced and licensed mental health professionals. Given the demand and need for psychosocial support and the serious lack of qualified personnel, this seemed like a "no-brainer" that would help meet the overwhelming mental health needs and lack of human resources. Thus with all these thoughts spinning around, CWB was conceived at the national convention opening session, without a great deal of planning or forethought. Rather, it was created based on an acute counseling need, and dovetailed with my decades of action-oriented, community-based work throughout the United States and globally. Essentially CWB was an extension of 40 years of counseling that began when I was 18 working in an anti-poverty program as a summer counselor.

Greatest Satisfactions and Personal Transformation

When I first began as a summer counselor working with high-risk impoverished youth, I was learning on the job. Exposure to counseling skills, theories, establishing trust and rapport, being open, learning how to not be judgmental ... all of these new dimensions were eye-opening moments about how to support and help other human beings in times of deep difficulty. These novel ideas and skills were seeping into my personhood. Gradually, as I became more trained and learned about the philosophy, values, and skills involved in counseling, these qualities started to become second nature, building on and deepening who I was as a person, and becoming embedded in my personality. Almost unknowingly, I experienced a gradual amalgamation of self and counselor. My synthesized self evolved, which incorporated my counseling and complemented my work experiences in the community. I soon became the youngest director of an Upward Bound Program (established by John F. Kennedy as a cornerstone of his War on Poverty) in the United States at the age of 26, finding myself with a peer group of directors at least 10-30 years older than me. I soon went on to direct a national pilot deinstitutionalization community-based program for adolescents with a school, residential facilities, and clinical services, once again being on average 20 years younger than my professional peers. My work continued to expand, branching into global consultations, and eventually led to a position as the Clinical Director for a National Institute of Mental Health grant based at the University of Massachusetts Medical School Department of Psychiatry, which provided national consultation and training for community mental health programs.

As a consultant and trainer, I had to see things "differently" and incorporate vision, creativity, and alternate viewpoints. My daily work required me to introduce new perspectives, new knowledge, and innovative alternative clinical and organizational solutions to any issue or problem that was presented. Part of

PHOTO 16.1   Post-disaster staff training after Cyclone Nargis in Myanmar

my ability to direct various human services programs and do consultation work successfully was the amazing transformation that happened while integrating counseling and my growing sense of self. Regardless of whether I was in senior-level meetings with state or federal directors and administrators, or whether I was sitting in the living room with a family, I was continually becoming comfortable with who I was and who I was becoming: a culmination of my various roles as a family member, administrator, community worker, social activist, supervisor, clinician, consultant, and trainer. This metamorphosis through these experiences was instrumental in conceiving CWB decades later sitting in a national convention hall, generating a completely new idea with a dramatically different perspective. As unusual as the idea of CWB sounded to everyone else, it came naturally to me and made perfect sense. My job history had helped me understand how to work effectively within complex organizational systems, so I viewed existing structures, rules, and regulations as merely deeply rooted structures and challenges that could be changed for the better rather than barriers.

Altruism, or caring about the fate of others and the common good, has been identified in counseling as a critical element in healing and transformation (Yalom, 2005). I would also add love, a healing component that I have written about in the past, as another critical component (Bemak & Epp, 1996). In its purest form, CWB embraces these concepts and is an absolute giving back to the community.

There are no personal gains, no financial gains, or any external rewards that would contribute to one's career or lead to a job promotion or advancement.

Participating in CWB has been challenging. It requires time-consuming and widespread organization. Participants in each of our trips needed to be trained about post-disaster mental health in advance, and required an extensive orientation to the geographical area's culture, history, values, customs, etc. It necessitated coordinating logistics—booking plane flights, transportation to and from the departure and arrival airports, sleeping arrangements, food arrangements, coordination with host agencies and organizations, on-site transportation, arranging for responsibilities to be taken care of at home while on-site, fundraising, etc. Once on-site, living conditions are primitive—electricity is often unavailable, transportation is difficult, food and water may be limited, and sleeping arrangements are inevitably complicated to coordinate. Yet I continue to do the CWB work, and receive a number of queries every month from people around the world who are interested in volunteering, and have five times more advanced graduate students who want to participate than can possibly be accommodated. Interestingly, I have never had to market CWB—the concept of giving back to the community markets itself.

Why Do All This Work?

Why endure the difficulties and complications planning CWB trips and the intensity of the challenges that are faced once on-site? When I reflect on these questions, I realize that I rarely think about the obstacles. This may be because my experience has taught me that rules are helpful and reasonable guidelines in certain instances, and unhelpful and unreasonable minor impediments in other instances. Subsequently, institutional challenges *never* pose insurmountable obstructions, but are rather organizational structures that must be redefined and reordered to reach positive social action goals. This outlook, combined with the belief that the rewards help to promote change, mental health, peace, personal and community growth, etc., provide a deep intrinsic satisfaction related to giving, helping, and transforming our world. A good example of this can be seen during the CWB trip to Mississippi after Hurricane Katrina. After an intense 10-day work period, the team of 18 advanced graduate students departed from Mississippi to return home the day before Thanksgiving. When the day of departure finally came after a demanding 12-hour per day work schedule, the entire team expressed a great sadness in leaving the site. Amazingly, *every* member of the team wished they could stay to help the disaster survivors on Thanksgiving Day and return to their families and loved ones later.

An Example of Transformation

Southern California was burning. The papers splashed stories of wildfires throughout the San Diego region. The television news had graphic pictures of large homes and buildings being destroyed and roads closing as out-of-control fires jumped over freeways, destroying everything in their path. As the stories kept coming in I was struck by one continuous theme in the media: the only things that seemed to be burning were large homes and properties of the wealthy and predominantly White population. "Does fire discriminate?" I asked myself. "Are there no people of color in San Diego County who are affected by the fire?" "What about poor people—has the fire reached them? Are their homes still there?" Concerned about these unanswered questions, I asked a colleague in San Diego about the impact of the fire on poor communities and people of color. She commented that her information was the same as mine—only the wealthy communities seemed to be affected by the fires. We wondered whether there was a media bias, and she agreed to check with some of the surrounding communities in Southern California. Not surprisingly, within 24 hours she responded that there was tremendous devastation in the poor communities and Indian reservations, where many low-income people of color had been affected. This confirmed that there was a lack of attention or news coverage about poorer communities in the San Diego region. Only large homes and business properties seemed to be burning, according to the local and national press coverage. I proposed that a CWB team join her in San Diego to address the "forgotten" groups who were devastated by the fires and were receiving little or no support. During the next week we quickly developed a work plan, and within 10 days I was in San Diego with a CWB team of nine students and two supervisors.

Logistics were difficult to work out. Plane tickets had to be secured from Washington D.C. to Southern California, and transport to and from the airports had to be arranged at both the departure and arrival sites. I immediately began scrambling for funding to cover these expenses. At the same time, team members had to be selected and attend orientation sessions, advanced training had to be put in place, housing needed to be arranged, and team members needed to make arrangements to leave their homes and employment that included child care, pet care, watering plants, transport for children, etc. Even so, with the intensity of preparation and the goal of helping, in the excitement and intensity of the moment everything was put in place. Team members were excited, eager, and nervous about the upcoming work and helping the survivors following such a devastating situation.

Once in California, we established a "command headquarters" in my colleague's home as a base of operations. We linked with the team of nine advanced graduate students from San Diego and two faculty supervisors. With the nine CWB team members from the East Coast and the nine CWB members from San Diego, the joint CWB team was comprised of four supervisors and 18 students. Based on the assessment of our San Diego colleagues it was determined that the areas of critical need were a number of San Diego schools and communities in low-income areas located in the southern part of San Diego County and two Native-American Indian reservations and schools.

The work took on a life of its own. We began sending teams to five sites in San Diego County using the model we had developed for post-disaster group work and group supervision (Bemak & Chung, 2011). One place the CWB team worked was in a Latino community, where we walked the neighborhood handing out water and asking people how they were doing. At a Native-American reservation we met with the Council of Elders and asked if there was a need for counseling and social support following the fires. When they replied that there was a great need, we asked their permission to enter the reservation and help in the healing that was so much in demand following the devastation. Our request resulted in a three-hour meeting with the Council in a highly reflective conversation that involved historical abuses and violations of the Tribe, cultural insensitivities of people from other cultures, and questions about our ability to provide culturally responsive counseling services. After careful deliberation it was decided that CWB could enter the reservation and provide assistance for the Native community. San Diego County Schools also asked us to visit two highly affected schools close to the California-Mexico border. A Head Start program with a predominantly migrant population also requested that we work with their children, parents, and extended family members. Clearly, there was a tremendous need; each day, as the word spread about our work, generated more calls and requests for our services.

Each night we brought the entire team together for supervision, which provided an opportunity to share each others' personal pain in hearing survivors' stories and develop additional clinical skills. As the additional requests for urgent help came in each day from communities and schools, we were faced with the choice every evening about which sites we should deploy teams to the next day based on who had the greatest need and where we would be able to serve most effectively. Given our limited resources these choices were difficult, and we were always cognizant of the fact that some of the sites would not receive any counseling services. By the end of our 10 days we had provided training and supervision for the San Diego School District Migrant Office with about 70 senior staff and supervisors; numerous elementary, middle, and secondary schools; Head Start programs; a Native-American school; and two reservations.

Trying to describe the day-to-day activities, emotional highs and lows, and personal responses to the suffering the CWB team witnessed is difficult. Organizing and having ultimate responsibility for the CWB program required significant clinical, organizational, leadership, and administrative, and interpersonal skills, as well as patience and the ability to take risks and make split-second decisions. It also was essential to be highly attuned to the work we were doing with clients, who were experiencing high levels of crisis and suffering and had histories of mistreatment and devaluation. In fact, Border Patrol was on high alert because there was the heightened concern that undocumented immigrants would illegally cross into California to receive the free resources available due to the wildfires. The result was that Border Patrol personnel would indiscriminately stop people based on their appearance to check documentation. The fear that was perpetuated in the migrant communities was also evident in our team; many of the Latina/os, who were all documented, were afraid of being stopped at random even while working on the CWB teams. All of this created a highly charged atmosphere, and CWB team members needed to be "recharged" every evening.

The recharging involved intensive nightly supervision. The supervision focused on four main areas: 1) cultivating and supporting teamwork so that each assigned team was running smoothly onsite the next day; 2) discussing the team members' deeply painful, personal reactions to the suffering and stories of the survivors, to help them attend to their own healing in order for them to be effective in their work; 3) improving clinical skills to work more effectively with survivors who were severely affected; and 4) understanding the social justice implications of their work with marginalized and unserved groups. In addition, supervision included sharing the other aspect of my role, which included working with administrators in the region who were trying to design and develop the most appropriate service intervention system to meet the dramatic needs in the community. Having responsibility for these multi-dimensional issues required my full attention, and tremendous stamina and energy.

Being the final authority and responsible party was not new to me. I had done similar work many times before. However, this was the first time I had included members of a team (the California CWB team members) that I didn't know. The need to be consistently "on," the need to be a role model at all times, and the responsibility of assuming a leadership role with local authorities was—as always—highly demanding. At the same time, since I had experience directing federal and state human services programs, followed by administrative roles in four universities over the course of my career, the challenge was welcomed and somewhat familiar. I found myself once again in a leadership position that was very recognizable to me—dealing with a high-stress situation, maintaining calm in the midst of a heavy storm, making on-the-spot emergency decisions that affected people's lives, handling others' personal crises: all of this was familiar territory, and I found myself easing into the role without much difficulty as we moved ahead to provide services to those in need and those who were marginalized and forgotten. The clarity was all about the overarching goal: helping those in need. My job was to ensure that the entire CWB team remained focused on this goal and to help cut through the team members' personal difficulties and concerns about modern conveniences (which are always absent during a natural disaster) and daily disruptions in scheduling and the heightened need for flexibility. Essentially there was an important reaffirmation about life's continuous transformation that was underscored by a critical need to keep one's eyes on the prize (the goal of helping and serving), while tending to the process of reaching that goal.

Greatest Frustrations, Challenges, and Obstacles

Community work is not easy. People get in the way, and institutional obstacles are inevitable. Not everyone will share your perspective about the benefit, quality, and goodness of the work you are doing. To further complicate matters, there are often turf issues that result in territorial conflicts with other organizations and individuals. Being effective in community work requires a rigorous focus on the goals of the work and a profound understanding that the process of achieving these goals may be fraught with challenges and complications.

There have been four major challenges with CWB's work. The first challenge relates to the major professional organizations that have longstanding linkages with well-established organizations such as the Red Cross or the Federal Emergency Management Association. Even though many credible organizations were either overwhelmed or not offering services in low-income or marginalized areas, and at times were not adequately providing culturally responsive services, the belief was that these were the "go-to" organizations with track records. This conviction about service providers was well ingrained into the institutional thinking, which creates significant barriers to entering the playing field for a newer organization, even though the organization had, in a short period, demonstrated it could deliver culturally responsive and effective services.

PHOTO 16.2   Counseling in Uganda

The second challenge is professional jealousy. It is human nature that when one succeeds or stands out from the crowd that some others may experience jealousy or resentment. This is always the case, regardless of whether it is a community-based social justice project or a professional accomplishment. Although the overwhelming majority of colleagues have been supportive and appreciative of CWB's work, some have been critical and have taken umbrage with it. I have always maintained that the antipathy that comes with standing out from the crowd is just "part of the package." The response requires a combination of an open mind to any helpful criticism of or objections to the work, along with a "thick skin" that can discount concerns that simply have no merit. Again, with CWB the focus has always been on the work and goals of helping without personal gain.

The third challenge is having the leadership skills and a personality that is conducive to "standing alone" for what one believes is right and just. My leadership style, whether as the director of large human services organizations, in the capacity of university administrative roles, or heading up a CWB team, is founded on the principle of democratic collaborative decision-making processes. However, at times in a crisis situation you have to make split-second, independent decisions. Having to live with those decisions, and explain them later when the intensity of the crisis subsides, presents a challenge for any leader. In addition, if the outcome of the work is highly positive it is important to able to articulate the benefit and results of this type of social justice work, which inherently challenges the status quo.

The fourth challenge is related to one's perspective about the world and having the ability to balance respect with the challenging and questioning of hierarchical structures, the defined order of systems, rules, and roles, and one's responsibility and relationship within the context of the personal and organizational authority. Being a leader of and consultant for numerous organizational systems, institutions, agencies, and schools always requires a unique perspective. Thinking and viewing situations in distinctive ways upsets the balance and norms that perpetuate the "same old, same old," and inevitably forces hard questions about "what," "why," and "how." In finding the right balance I would often offer perspectives that were outside the mainstream way of thinking. Inexorably the viewpoints and recommendations were beneficial, such as the CWB organization, and led to a very robust national and international consultation practice. One example of challenging convention was with an article I co-authored a few years ago about what we were calling the "Nice Counselor Syndrome" (NCS). The NCS criticized school counselors who were more concerned about collegiality and harmonious relationships than advocating for or helping their students (Bemak & Chung, 2008); we presented a framework for challenging the conventional role of school counselors. The article was for the most part received very positively, but it also generated anger and animosity from a small group for challenging the status quo. Weighing the merit of the hostile comments (interestingly, from what seemed like nice counselors), I still felt strongly about the efficacy and message of the publication. The article offers a good example related to CWB about how important it is to keep in mind that although you may receive negative reactions to your work, it is critical to maintain your convictions, carry on, and not be swayed by or sidetracked from reaching important goals of service and community support. In my opinion there is really no other way to be a professional than to live and breathe and act on our passion and convictions.

Why Keep Going?

Even with all these challenges, there is a tremendous reward to doing social justice-oriented community work. The rewards are both extrinsic and intrinsic. Counselors are healers, and healers work with those who need help. In post-disaster situations there are inevitably greater numbers who need support than receive assistance, and it is well documented that the poor, the marginalized, and those of color are frequently underserved or unserved. Helping people who are unserved or underserved heal and surmount their pain brings tremendous satisfaction. Clearly, there are also personal rewards. As I mentioned, my career began in anti-poverty work, with poor inner city youth from culturally diverse backgrounds. It has followed a path that continues to serve similar disenfranchised populations throughout the United States and globally. I became excited about this work early in my career and cultivated it through extensive national and international opportunities. The combination of passion and counseling, in my opinion, provides an essential foundation for a full and rich professional career. CWB was simply an extension of a long-term career that feeds that enthusiasm— something I think each of us, as professionals, should actively cultivate. I wouldn't change my career trajectory at all, and I feel a deep and heartfelt commitment to continue this work. Hopefully you will be able to say the same.

Advice for Other Therapists

Why are we therapists in the first place? What brought us to this work: what was our passion and motivation when we decided to train in counseling or psychology? I co-edited a book in which we asked 14 leading counselors and psychologists to discuss how they became involved with social justice and multi-cultural work, with the aim of capturing the essence of their transformation (Conyne & Bemak, 2005) and providing advice for upcoming therapists. In a new book another colleague and I did the same, outlining both senior-level mental health professionals and counseling trainees' perspectives on mental health and social justice (Chung & Bemak, 2012). The theme of each of these books, which is constantly repeated, is that we were drawn to the field to become healers, helpers, supporters of others. The purpose and vision of our lifetime goal may recede as we face the political and organizational realities of doing our work, yet the leaders in the field consistently describe how they *keep the focus*. My very strong recommendation is to always remember why you entered the field and to keep your eyes on the prize. If we maintain our passion and commitment to why we became therapists, then we will hold a vision of the world in a certain way, despite the challenges and obstacles that will inevitably arise in our work. Colleagues, who may be supervisors or bosses, sometimes focus more on their own power and advancement than on helping others or benefiting society, which may present difficult obstructions to our vision and passion for being therapists. Organizations that are more concerned about their funding and struggle to survive may forget or neglect the importance of their client's well-being, which also has the potential to interfere with the quality and integrity of our work as therapists. Pressure and demands that limit our ability to think ahead, to be creative, to cultivate innovation, and to speak up with new ideas all combine to restrict our enthusiasm and excitement as therapists. Keeping the focus helps us enjoy our work and life, and is important in helping us deal with life's pressures and challenges.

In managing these difficulties, it is important to *take risks* and stand up for what is fair and just. If you don't take chances, you will never know what you might have accomplished or created. When I see a great need for therapy, when there are underserved or unserved populations, I see opportunities. These opportunities do not fall into my job description; there is no road map made by others about how to develop these initiatives, and yet I continually take the step to meet these needs despite the challenges and obstacles. Each of us as therapists has skills that we can carry into multiple situations, and sometimes we must step to the fore to use those skills more effectively. The challenge for each of you becomes your willingness to step forward and take the chance to serve, above and beyond, using your passion and commitment to improve our world.

References

Bemak, F., & Chung, R. (2011). Post-disaster social justice group work and group supervision. *Journal for Specialists in Group Work, 36,* 3-21.

Bemak, F., & Chung, R. (2008). New professional roles and advocacy strategies for school counselors: A multicultural/social justice perspective to move beyond the nice counselor syndrome. *Journal of Counseling and Development, 86,* 372-381.

Bemak, F., & Epp, L. (1996). The 12th curative factor: Love as an agent of healing in group psychotherapy. *Journal of Specialists in Group Work, 21,* 118-127.

Chung, R., & Bemak, F. (2012). *Social Justice Counseling: The Next Steps Beyond Multiculturalism.* Thousand Oaks, CA: Sage Publications.

Conyne, R. & Bemak, F. (Eds.). (2005). *Journeys to Professional Excellence: Lessons From Leading Counselor Educators and Practitioners.* Alexandria, VA: American Counseling Association.

Yalom, I.D. & Leszcz, M. (eds.). (2005). *The Theory and Practice of Group Psychotherapy,* 5th ed. New York: Basic Books.

PART IV

Global Outreach

17

LIFE TASKS IN A LIFETIME

Tipawadee Emavardhana

A lot of what I write reflects what I have learned. This chapter explores what I've done outside the therapy room, and why. It is important to note up front that many of my views might be the opposite of Western thinking. So I invite the reader to consider my cultural roots as background for understanding this chapter. It might help if you read with contemplation. You will see both surface phenomena and underlying viewpoints to help understand the cause of my life's actions. A lot of my beliefs come from Buddha's teaching (i.e., to purify and carefully look inside yourself, then focus on how we can change others). I learned at a young age to mindfully choose my actions among so many chances. Whatever we select, we are responsible for. The choices I select are intended to bring good deeds for others, which is why I selected this career path as a psychologist: teaching and training in helping areas. While most people's focus in selecting a career is to make money, my focus is to make merit. The experiences shared in this chapter show how merit-making determinations can be achieved even when the road is rough. For me the counseling field is more than a career: it is life task.

Begin with a Strong Spark of Inspiration

The work I do always begins with a spark of inspiration. Enthusiastically doing any piece of work that I love ignites a feeling of happiness in me. Even in writing this chapter I also feel happiness in sharing my experiences that may give you some inspiration.

I also realize my motivation may be different from that of many other people. It is important to explain this so that you can understand how I created my many projects, which are unique to Thailand. This inspiration has characteristics of bright light that leave me feeling relaxed, but grounded and energetic. It has current expectations, but is not aimed necessarily at the outcome. I often imagine a vague image of what an end result could look like if I were able to continue my work. Most people normally aim to achieve outcomes, but I focus more on getting to do good deeds. This focus influences my internal motivation to pursue my goals enthusiastically without a fear of failing. I am not afraid, because I know that whatever results I achieve will only be good ones since I begin with good intentions. If I began with conditions, I would only push myself to aim for achievement, not to aim at just doing what is good. This is what I mean by starting with the right inspiration. For me inspiration is being aware and cultivating at the first step of any piece of work. I apply this to my clients and it always works. I have inspired and helped many people through teaching and transforming their lives for the better. Inspiration work has become my routine tool and it is the foundation for all cases, regardless of the type of work (e.g. prevention, intervention, or development and growth aspects) in counseling and psychotherapy. I have learned that the process of inspiring people involves helping them become aware of their own inspiration.

Every time I design a new project, it works well if I begin by touching my own inspiration. It flourishes more as my work progresses. I feel more energetic and can easily work long hours. I get back more than I expected. The inspiration remains high throughout the process, and even more toward the end. I expect myself to continue doing good deeds, as is the belief in Buddhism. Not every athlete should think of going to the Olympics, but should think of practicing for one's own good health. This way of thinking keeps my inspiration forever growing because I believe that the results of doing good deeds will help me reach a state of spiritual perfection.

Developing the Unconscious Determination to Help and Empathize With Others

One way for you to understand me is by sharing an early memory from childhood that relates to this spirit inside me. When I was a little girl I lived in a remote, northeastern region of Thailand that was a drought land. My schoolmates were all very poor. In the cold season my schoolmates, except my sister and me, wore uniforms that were suited only for warm weather. We were the only two students in school who had sweaters on; the rest wrapped their arms around their chest to protect themselves from the cold wind. I saw them shaky, with bluish-purple lips that showed the cold's effects on the body. My sister and I unexpectedly had the same thought, and we took off our sweaters and put them into our school bags. We were now in summer uniforms like the other girls. We now felt more like our peers. I remember that the cold air did not affect me at all. My intention to be like the others was stronger than the feeling of coldness. This memory seems to be the basis of where I developed my empathy and tendency to help the disadvantaged. The byproducts from this experience helped me naturally learn to practice using faith and strong intention to control my emotions: I self-hypnotized to fight against feeling frozen in the cold weather. Later on I studied and practiced more of this meditation to help others.

I received my doctoral degree in counseling psychology in the United States, but then came back to Thailand to work. People often ask me often how the Western psychology that I learned could be applied to Thai culture. My answer is simple. Psychology is developed in whatever form is appropriate for human-kind, wherever they are. Minor adaptation is an art that each psychologist must consider in his or her own context. It's my privilege to be one of the very first Thai to graduate in the psychology areas of clinical and counseling, way back in the early 70s and 80s. I was determined to bring psychology back to Thai society. My strong intention to help never leaves my heart and my soul. I found that this rooted loving kindness (*metta*) and compassion (*Karuna*) inside keep lighting up my soul never-endingly; my creativity persists through obstacles until I reach my goal.

Today my work covers diverse areas such as teaching, training, providing counseling services, education, consultation, supervision, and coaching. Target groups include drug abusers, those with HIV/AIDS, health care workers (physicians, family physicians, psychologists, social workers, nurses, nurse-aids, community workers), probation officers, monks, university lecturers, students, and laymen.

It might help the reader if I explain the characteristics I developed to perform my life work here. I don't reveal these characteristics to be egoistic, but only to humbly share what other colleagues and friends observe in my person, which I agree with in relation to the activities I have achieved in Thailand. These have included helping people unconditionally, creative, future thinker, playful, trustworthy, scrupulous, community minded, modest, ethical, sincere, flexible, persistent, activist, encouraging, and a Type T personality (a really big T!). The negative side is that colleagues noticed I sacrifice my own self-care and can be a little too forceful towards other colleagues. I often get verbal and nonverbal feedback from my colleagues and students that they feel exhausted and cannot drag on days and nights with little sleep. (In other points of view, my colleagues and students feel that I am an overachiever and a little pushy). In Thai society this is normally unbearable to hear, but I do not see it this way. Once I knew this, I tried being more mindful and changing my style when working with others. I have to practice more *metta*-loving kindness. I have to also remember that in Thai society, we value friendship, easygoing and relaxing attitudes, respect, a sense of humor, and playfulness while working. It is not easy to develop a style of work that integrates these opposite ends of the spectrum to be balanced enough to get the work progressing.

PHOTO 17.1 Leading a workshop on self-development

Various Sources of the Layout of Characteristics

I ask myself where I derived my characteristics. It is interesting to share that they came from various sources. I read extensively like my oldest brother, I liberated my thinking like my father, became creative like my grandfather, and of course, playful like most Thais. I have vision and think ahead of time because of the impact of a book that I read when I was very young: *Cheaper by the Dozen* (Gilbreth & Carey, 2002). I learned about Western culture from watching movies and reading. I honor moral conduct because I am aware of behaving appropriately to maintain the reputation of our family dignity. My last name was given by King Rama the sixth to my great-grandparents, who lived a very long life—over 100 years—and my grandfather was the governor of a small province near Bangkok. I inherited ideas of collecting a minimum amount of property from my parents. I have used the money from selling properties to support my projects. Thai salaries are very low compared to the average standard of living. It is only barely enough to live on each month, but not enough to pay for the extra activities that I have created alongside my main work.

Beginning my Life's Work

Without any questions, I took my first job working with a disadvantaged group as a consultant to a joint drug abuse program between Thailand and Sweden. This was my first piece of work outside my university lecturer position and being a consultant to other university graduate programs. When I look back to ask why I did this, my decision came from my feeling for the underprivileged. So I got involved in a drug rehabilitation, community, and social reintegration program that was a new model to help drug abusers in Thailand. This program was developed around the time that a greater awareness of the HIV outbreak was forming. Soon after this drug counseling work, I was assigned to head the design of a culturally appropriate approach to Thai HIV counseling. I had been a scholar at the University of California, San Francisco's Center for AIDS Prevention Studies in 1992. I became one of the first Thai AIDS awareness activists who was trying to promote and design a prevention program.

Since then I have been involved with multiple drug abuse and HIV/AIDS training programs. I do staff training on AIDS education, treatment, prevention, blood test counseling, and rehabilitation. These cover individual, group, family, and community services. I have worked in the drug abuse area for more than 20 years and have written three books on the topic.

I began to enjoy this kind of work and study due to the people it touches. I have created more projects in addition to working as a university lecturer and counselor. In order to manage all the work, I hired three assistants from my personal budget. I decided to spend my personal money to keep my academic, helping career, and my own spiritual work continuously functioning at full capacity. I am willing to spend personal money to do social justice work so that I do not need to be distracted by trying to earn extra paid work. I only concentrate on work for spiritual wealth. The more I give, the more I get. It is relevant to the King's speech given to the audience of well wishers on the Royal Birthday Anniversary, "Our loss is our gain" (H.M. King Bhumibol Adulyadej, 1995). This was His Majesty's response to foreign reporters about what kept him spending His time, effort, and personal money on his thousands of projects for the well-being of His countrymen.

The Emergence of the Rice Abstinence Program

In 1989 I was asked by a physician to help train staff on intensive drug counseling. In our discussions I was stunned by her lack of understanding of drug addiction. I felt that drug abuse personnel needed to be trained to understand drug addiction before they were trained in counseling skills. That afternoon, while driving home, an idea popped into my head: get them to abstain from rice! So I created a strategy to teach them experiential, in-depth learning about addictionology, drug dependence, craving, abstinence, contextual support, individual, group, family, and community counseling all in one program. The first group of trainees started with eight health personnel that consisted of physicians, nurses, a psychologist, social workers, and a researcher. The program looked to tie drug addiction to a traditional Thai way of life: rice is standard daily food, eaten three meals a day.

Nobody thinks that we are addicted to rice. But during my experience when I was an exchange student in high school in the United States in 1964, I realized how deeply addicted to rice I was. I integrated my early life experience and my behavior modification knowledge and skills of psychology into this design. I used the counseling process to teach these staff members to metaphorically experience a similar way of life to that of the real abusers (rice vs. illegal drugs like heroin, marijuana). Family counseling and therapy was used on the staff who then acted very similarly to the real drug abusers. The drug counselors, while abstaining from rice, could then understand lots of valuable work about the process and prevention of drug addiction.

The outcome of the rice abstinence program was successful. Participants reported that they felt more competent working with drug addicts and that they experienced an increase in professional commitment. They appreciated being treated as professionals, and they reported an expansion in their clinical reasoning abilities as they derived innovative solutions to difficult problems. A heightened sense of autonomy arose in a surprisingly short time as issues concerning the psychodynamics of addiction, relapse prevention, behavior modification, cognitive behavior therapy, and case management were examined. The program increased awareness of the importance of environmental and social factors in sustaining addiction rehabilitation. Many participants found the training program both potent and delightful, and as a result, greater interest was manifested in personal and professional growth activities that would allow them to better understand their professional roles as health service providers for addicted persons. For example, one counselor decided to quit smoking and another one committed himself to both cigarette and alcohol abstinence.

The idea behind this rice abstinence pedagogy was to train those who were serving drug abuse clients within the health system to provide counseling services within a context of understanding the depth of drug addiction. Their professional development is a critical necessity for them to work effectively with drug abusers. This project also developed a manual for drug abuse counselors to prepare them to provide the high standard of care demanded by society in the treatment of drug abusers. There is a great need for training manuals in the Thai context for Thai drug counselors. In general, Thailand's recruitment of drug counselors differs in many respects from that found in Western countries, where initial rehabilitative treatments for addictive disorders were developed. To be effective, the treatment models and manuals used for addicted Thai clients must be culturally appropriate.

Eventually, the model and manual were collated and constructed from the Thai context to be used by Thai drug counselors for drug abusers. The manual has been tested with Thai drug counselors and proved to be user friendly, sustainable, and cost effective. This rice abstinence program has extended to other groups of drug workers in other locations. Some health workers gain the byproducts of being mindful about what they eat at least three times a day.

Learning Through Lives

I feel fortunate to work in this area, which brings me into contact with so many lives. I have valuable experiences that I would count as spiritual wealth. The truth of what life is means that we have a primary duty to always cultivate a good body and mind; we have to prevent evil from coming near.

Believe it or not, I never charge for counseling services held in my university office or by private arrangement. I only get paid by organizations to conduct training programs or other relevant services including individual, group, and family sessions. I feel that they already have enough problems, and they do not need another (financial) one. I also feel that my life task is to be able to give gifts to those who seek them. I appreciate their kind opportunity to let me be part of this process of great giving, which in Buddhism we call *Dhana*. *Dhana*, intentionally sharing material and nonmaterial things or actions, is one of 10 ways to make merits.

Life Change After Natural Disasters

I went through two big disasters, the Asian Tsunami in 2004 and the Bangkok flood in 2011–12, when my seaside wooden house in Phuket was hit by tall waves higher than the roof and my house in Bangkok was soaked by a nearly two-meter-high flood for three months. The tides damaged lots of material things, which led to good lessons learned for life (i.e., to let go, be free from attachment). I had to flee from Bangkok to rent a place in an eastern province and lived with minimal daily facilities. When I came back to Bangkok, I found that I had to discard most of my belongings. The house now looks spacious, just like when I first moved in 35 years ago! It is back to the original philosophy: we were born with a bare body; we will leave everything behind at the end of life. We can carry nothing with us. The only precious thing we can take with us after this life is our good or bad karma. I have learned to let go now, after two big disasters in less than one decade. I also learned to give more of my extra material and nonmaterial wealth (i.e., knowledge and skills). I shall be more careful and more mindfully select actions that fit this philosophy. This is not only learning from others' lives, but from my own life as well.

I used these opportunities to share my knowledge with the victims (including myself) by organizing a team to be *Dhamma* friends with the tsunami and Bangkok flood victims and to hold a few training workshops for volunteer groups (Emavardhana & Kititvipart, 2008). There is a great lesson to be learned in accepting and letting go of external belongings. I collaborated with international psychologists to bring in professional help to the survivors and health workers, community leaders, and volunteers.

There was one tsunami survivor child custody case that stood out for me. A seven-year-old Muslim girl lost her mother in the 2004 tsunami. She had lived with her grandmother her whole life, since her deceased mother had separated from her father when she was pregnant. The father only showed up to claim fatherhood and take some donated money from the girl's account. The grandmother wanted to keep the girl because of bonding, but so did the father, but for different reasons. He sent the dispute to the court to gain legal custody. The grandmother was under a lot of stress after the loss of her niece and out of fear of losing the girl. She showed signs of anxiety and depression, and startled easily from loud noise. She remained haunted by the smell of the deep sea that came with the tide and waves of the tsunami. She had difficulty sleeping and developed a rare symptom of bleeding from the navel. People who are under stress usually throw up or bleed from the mouth or nose, but this woman bled from the skin of her stomach.

I wanted to help, so I reached out to 12 national and international organizations, schoolteachers, local government, NGOs, cousins, Buddhist monks, etc. But the agencies said that legally, the father would obviously win the dispute. I used at least three of my personal characteristics, i.e. inspiration, persistence, and determination. I encouraged the grandmother and the child, who felt so desperately hopeless and had no strength to continue. The girl refused to go to court on the appointment date, but eventually she went. During the court session she moved away and cried when the father touched her. Finally the judges saw the close relationship behaviors between the grandmother and the girl in the courtroom. The judges gave custody

PHOTO 17.2 Tipa leading a workshop with Jon Carlson

to the grandmother for workdays and weekends for the father. I had regular follow-up sessions with the family for three years after the tsunami and I observed positive changes in the girl. She is now more self-confident, happier, hopeful, and stronger both physically and mentally. The last time I spoke with her, it had been seven years since she had had any of her old symptoms.

A School Without a Building

After all the experiences I have had, I have the intention to help my colleagues, students, psychologists, and other interested paraprofessionals gain knowledge and skills of counseling at international standards. I started teaching counseling psychology in advanced programs so that I can be sure that those around me have decent counseling skills to serve the needs of society in Thailand. Learners are supervised after intensive training in the building (workshop venues). The learners have homework and practice their skills on the job and come back for periodic supervision. In this era of high technology, we can easily have access to Internet or long-distance learning. I run a few long-term training programs at my university, which has a physical building, letting technology serve as the delivery medium. Our programs include a one-year counseling certificate and training for facilitators and parents on parenting and study skills. We even formed a group called the Thai Adlerian Parenting STEP Network. In regards to parenting, we now have a (virtual) parenting school, a column in *Real Parenting* magazine (in Thai), parenting groups, and work to introduce group parenting training into Thai society.

My latest project is designed to train healthy thinking, spiritual development, and physical health. I designed this program when Thailand was marked by unrest because of differences in political concepts among people. We offer short three-contact workshops: a half-day recruitment meeting, a two-day workshop with very well-prepared modules, and a three-day *Dhamma* learning taught by a Buddhist monk. This project had a very strong impact on people after it was launched in various villages in the north and northeast, where there are big political conflicts that cause physical, mental, and societal discomforts. The project helps participants calm down their emotions of hate, anger, misunderstanding, and unhappiness. After two days of workshop, many begin to feel better. They feel the love of people, showed a significant change in the way they and others were perceived, reduced aggressive emotions, and had a greater appreciative interpersonal sensitivity—*metta* (loving kindness) to all living things (Emavardhana & Kititvipart, 2008). They were friendlier and felt an enhanced self-esteem and self-concept. With this success, we have had many requests for this program. Within one year we distributed our program to over 1,300 people in the community. The school without a building will support the training of all facilitators to expand all the projects mentioned.

Summary of My Life Task

The holistic summary of all my life tasks is presented in Figure 17.1. I realized that I have three main life tasks: to conduct myself morally, which includes refraining

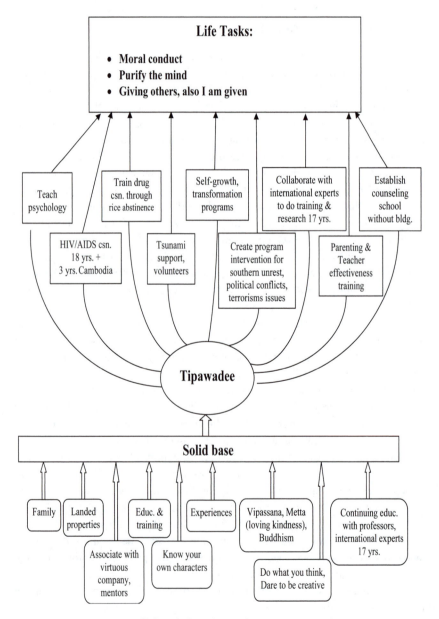

FIGURE 17.1 Summary of life task foundation, key concepts, and outcomes

from evil; to purify my mind; and to give charity, including forgiveness. My work as a psychologist or university lecturer is a part of my main life mission. My background from my family upbringing, personal traits, past education, career path experiences, culture, and landed properties give me the foundation to do more innovative projects. The more I give, the more I get. My remaining properties seem to go up in price every day, and I can use those increases to give back more to others. This proves to me that my spiritual life task is in line with my career, and this is the best choice for real happiness. Now I ask you: What is your life task? What do you care about? I recommend that each person should know this as early in their career as possible.

References

Gilbreth, F.B. Jr. & Carey, E.G. (2002). *Cheaper by the Dozen*. New York: HarperCollins.

H.M. King Bhumibol Adulyadej. (1995). "Our loss is our gain." Royal Speech, December 4, 1995, 112–113. http://www.youtube.com/watch?v=dWz-Om91mQ8. Retrieved on February 17, 2012.

18

COUNSELING INTERNATIONALLY

Caring for the Caregiver

Keith Edwards and Rebecca Rodriguez

Social justice counseling is an activist process. The activist/interventionist is typically involved directly with the people and social structures that affect a constituent's experience of justice or lack thereof. Our work is at least one step removed from activist involvement. Our short-term work is to support and empower the "activists" who have some form of social justice or compassion service role in their culture of residence. In this chapter, we will refer to them as cross-cultural workers. Often, they are expatriates who have committed to living in a foreign culture and working with nationals toward their justice or compassion goals.

Our primary goal is to support, restore, and strengthen such frontline workers so they can be more effective and sustain their work through frustrations and disruptions. Such workers are at high risk for burnout. They are usually living and serving in a culture that has limited resources, overwhelming need, and a limited social infrastructure to cope with and mitigate the social repercussions of injustice and poverty. We provide a compassion link and social support for these workers so they can receive restorative support and care for a brief period of time. Our work frequently comes at a crucial time of stress and impending burnout for these workers. We are able to help some of them, in our brief intervention, to return to their places of service encouraged and empowered. Some are too exhausted to recover, and therefore ultimately return to their passport countries. We help them assess their situations and make strategic decisions about getting the necessary resources for sustaining their recovery and facilitating their return to service or home.

Volunteering with Nationals and Cross-Cultural Workers: A Father and Daughter's Journey

We are a father and daughter who have valued practicing generosity throughout our lives toward those who face the struggles of poverty, injustice, and social darkness. Our volunteer work, whether as laypersons or professionals, has been with non-governmental organizations (NGOs) and cross-cultural workers who are employed by them. I (Keith) am a practicing clinical psychologist and a full-time faculty member. As of this writing, I (Rebecca) am a stay-at-home mom and a student in a Master's counseling program enrolled in my first yearlong practicum. I was a certified elementary teacher with a degree in Intercultural Studies. We worked together for the first time as professionals with a team of counselors conducting an intensive seminar in Interlaken, Switzerland for NGO workers employed in a number of nations in Africa, Eastern Europe, and the Middle East. This chapter describes our separate journeys as international volunteers and our collaborative effort, and provides some reflections on our experience.

Over the past 25 years we have traveled to foreign countries on many occasions to do a variety of short-term volunteer work. Our first involvement in cross-cultural activity began as a family affair. Throughout my (Rebecca's) high school and college years, we traveled yearly to Mexico during Easter breaks to do construction projects for a medical center and conduct educational programs for children of migrant workers. My wife, Ginny, and I (Keith) helped lead teams of young people who had volunteered to spend their Easter breaks working and teaching in poor communities. The primary "expertise" we provided during these ministry trips was our willingness to travel during our vacation time, raise funds within our faith community for needed resources, work hard for a week, and live in relatively primitive conditions. Although these were the challenging aspects of the trip, the experience of giving to others always proved very rewarding. I (Rebecca) especially enjoyed getting to know another culture and learning how to connect relationally within the Latin culture. This growing exposure to the Latin culture led me to learn a second language and inspired me to later live in Latin America.

In the years since our family trips, we have had many opportunities to travel separately and together to foreign countries to do volunteer work. I (Rebecca) lived in Mexico City for a summer, did semesters abroad in Europe and Latin America, have led teams of volunteers for various short-term projects in poor communities in Mexico and the Bahamas, and lived in Ecuador for two and a half years. I (Keith) have conducted short-term mental health counseling and training for cross-cultural workers over the past 12 years in Europe, Africa, South America, and Asia. While Rebecca was in Mexico and Ecuador as a cross-cultural worker, I visited her and volunteered my counseling services to the cross-cultural workers and nationals in both countries.

Life as a Cross-Cultural Worker: Gaining Empathy and Credibility

A desire to work with the population of cross-cultural workers grew out of my (Rebecca's) own personal experience as one. My husband, Osvaldo, and I, both fluent in Spanish, lived in Ecuador for two and a half years and served with an NGO mission hospital. Osvaldo worked as a physician in Medical Education, Health Care in Remote Villages, and several other health-related needs. I developed a tutoring program for children in a public school in a local squatter community. The children were behind in their studies and suffered from malnutrition. Twice a week I would go to this impoverished community on the side of an active volcano to do tutoring and provide hygiene and nutrition services. Because of the overwhelming poverty and difficult social circumstances, human suffering was common (and accepted) among the Ecuadorian poor.

I loved my time of service in Ecuador and was deeply saddened when it became clear that we needed to return to the States to support members of Osvaldo's extended family who were going through a medical crisis. Three months before leaving Ecuador, I had survived a pulmonary embolism in my eighth month of pregnancy and the birth of my second son by C-section. When it came time for us to leave, we sold many of our belongings, packed up the rest in barrels, made sure we made time for thoughtful goodbyes, and left with our toddler and infant in the span of a month.

It took a while for us as a family to reintegrate into our community in the United States. We needed to live with family for six months while we saved money for a place of our own. We had to adjust to the long hours of Osvaldo's demanding medical practice, reintegrate into friendship circles, experience reverse culture shock, and process the disequilibrium caused by our rapid change in environment. In retrospect, I realize I could have benefited from personal counseling to help me through this stressful period. But at the time, I was just trying to survive being a new mom of two in a time of massive transition.

I share my experience because my story is not unlike that of most cross-cultural workers. The stressors may vary, but it is not uncommon for cross-cultural workers to experience several stressors at once. Unfortunately, they often have to deal with them alone, due to the lack of mental health professionals in their locations. This isolation and lack of mental health resources contribute to the preventable attrition of cross-cultural workers and the social and religious services they provide to nationals. My personal struggle upon my return to the States made me acutely aware of the struggles cross-cultural workers face and how few services are available to this particular population. I felt great empathy toward this population and decided to become professionally trained as a marriage and family therapist to better serve them.

Our Strategy: Leveraging Our Impact

There are thousands of English-speaking people working in foreign cultures all over the world in a myriad of roles providing services for the purpose of enhancing the personal, social, and economic well-being of nationals. Most of the cross-cultural workers with whom we have worked are Christian missionaries who have dedicated their lives to serving others as an expression of their spiritual beliefs. They are earnest people seeking to live out the core values of their faith in the world, including compassion, sacrifice, justice, respect, and effective action in seeking to help the poor, marginalized, vulnerable, and needy. They are living out a central tenant of their faith as summarized in the Biblical text Psalm 82:3: "Defend the cause of the weak and fatherless; maintain the rights of the poor and oppressed". The services they provide include health care, food, clothing and shelter, community development, clean water projects, education, mental health and social services, micro-enterprise development, farming, and rescue/protection from sexual exploitation. They make a long-term commitment to live in the culture, learn the language and customs, provide resources, conduct training, and empower nationals to create programs to address the needs of their communities. These are the types of people with whom we have had the opportunity to work.

Cross-cultural workers face common struggles that threaten their holistic well-being: compassion fatigue, family and marital stressors, raising third culture kids who feel they do not fully belong in the home or foreign culture, feeling alienated from the American experience and therefore not understood by their home community, having to say good-bye to friends regularly, dealing with many transitions, and having to re-enter into different cultures, along with many other stressors (Taylor, 1997). Our short-term work over one- or two-week spans has therefore been to provide mental health consultation and training designed to enhance what the cross-cultural workers do over a longer period of time. Our strategy has been to leverage the worldwide impact of our skills by working with these cross-cultural workers so they can continue to function as agents of mercy to the oppressed and impoverished around the world.

I (Keith) experienced this type of empowering relationship on a very personal level when Rebecca and her family moved to Quito, Ecuador. My wife (Ginny) and I provided financial support, emotional encouragement, and social support to our children as well as counseling services to the NGO community, as we traveled to Quito on several occasions. My work with the expatriates in Ecuador provided needed relational support and training so that they could continue to be effective in their ongoing service to the Ecuadorian culture. It was of great benefit that I was outside of the NGO community, as I could provide the non-judgmental, confidential atmosphere the cross-cultural workers desired. In this way I experienced a very rewarding sense of leveraging the impact of my skills on the culture in which my children were serving.

Member Care Conference in Switzerland: Serving as Professionals

The time finally came when my (Rebecca's) role shifted from cross-cultural worker to international caregiver and we could work together as professional colleagues. We, along with Ginny, had been asked to be staff members for a member care conference in Switzerland for two weeks in the summer. The purpose of the conference was to provide recreational, spiritual, and mental health services to cross-cultural workers. It was the third installment of an annual conference organized by a nonprofit group in California. We were going to provide counseling and Ginny was to provide administrative support. The conference was announced to cross-cultural workers through their organizations. Participants register for the conference and pay their fees for room and board online. There is no charge for the professional services provided. All the staff members working at the conference raise their own support and pay their own expenses. The conference program includes excursions, hiking, lectures, worship, counseling, medical consults, and massage therapy. All activities are meant to address the holistic needs of the attendees. Most of the attendees come to the conference with marital/family issues, burnout, trauma, discouragement, team issues, and/or disillusionment. Most of these workers are on the front lines, serving in leadership positions in which they are giving of themselves to others. Their family, their marriage, or their being becomes the casualty of their response to the overwhelming needs around them.

As noted above, I had partnered with Rebecca on many trips before, but never in a professional peer role. I looked forward to sharing this work with Rebecca and seeing her grow in her new profession. I (Rebecca) was humbled and thankful for the opportunity to join my father in counseling for the first time. I was also deeply grateful for the opportunity to work with those who had faced similar struggles as myself. Working with cross-cultural workers requires someone who is sensitive to their environment and the unique challenges of living abroad. While I felt confident in my level of cross-cultural awareness, I did feel the uneasiness and fear that comes with seeing clients for the first time. I was the only student on the counseling staff and therefore worked under the supervision of my father. Once I met my clients I easily settled into the role of counselor and began hearing their stories of pain, sadness, and confusion. My background in cross-cultural work, my own personal counseling, my graduate training, the sand tray technique (metaphoric work with sand and figurines), and my access to my father for supervision all helped equip me for the challenges of first-time counseling.

Using the sand tray technique, I (Rebecca) was able to facilitate a process of partial resolution of a client's unfinished business with a former business partner who had treated her unfairly. I had my client select a figure, construct a scene with the person in it, and dialogue with the figure that represented the client's antagonist. The client found the experience very helpful and freeing. I (Rebecca) used the sand tray effectively with my couple, teen, and child clients. As her

PHOTO 18.1   Rebecca is ready to use her sand tray with her next client

supervisor, I (Keith) was impressed with how effectively Rebecca used the sand tray to facilitate client processing. I (Keith) decided I needed to attain my own sand tray set and get some training for myself.

I (Keith) have two concerns as I anticipate engaging in short-term, intensive counseling experiences. The first is, "Will I be able to connect with my clients and earn their trust in the short time available for the work?" I have found the process-experiential focus of Emotionally Focused Therapy (EFT) to be particularly well suited for short-term, intensive work (Greenberg, 2002). EFT is a collaborative therapy in which the therapist's primary focus is to hear, feel with, and understand the client's self-processes in a way that facilitates deeper levels of client self-awareness. The crucial contribution of the EFT therapist is to help the client attend to and become of aware of (avoided or implicit) not-yet-formulated experiences that bring clarity and validation to their situation. The process of identifying, clarifying, and validating primary adaptive emotions can proceed rapidly during intensive counseling. Clients experience this process as "helpful," and being helpful is a major predictor of a strong therapeutic alliance. The couple version of EFT (Johnson, 2004) has been very helpful in working with marriage issues in an intensive format.

The second concern I (Keith) have working in the conferences is, "Will the client's problems be responsive to the brief, intensive format of our sessions?" Long-standing, developmentally rooted patterns of emotional functioning and behavior that are no longer adaptive present a major therapeutic challenge in short-term work. Again, the process focus and non-pathologizing stance in EFT is a major advantage. Clients derive benefit from validation, compassion, and understanding of their experience and their coping patterns. Even the more challenging cases experience relief and healing as they process their options for their future.

Having Rebecca on staff added a third concern for me. Could I formulate my supervision advice into strategies she could use in her therapy sessions? My supervision of Rebecca was an intensive experience that was a "parallel process" to the counseling we were both doing. Her concern about being a student counselor and how she would be received by her clients was understood, validated, and processed in our initial meetings. These fears dissipated after her initial sessions, during which her clients were very accepting of and responsive to her. As her supervisor, I (Keith) was very impressed with Rebecca's professional approach to her counseling. She was well grounded in the ethics of patient care and demonstrated a passion and commitment to their well-being.

We consulted before, in between, and after client sessions to make sure I (Rebecca) had the direction I needed. This proved to be a great resource and gave me (Rebecca) a focus for each session and the support I needed. By the end of the conference, I (Rebecca) had seen six clients for eight days. All had received some help processing their presenting issues, and all of them were able to experience being valued and cared for by someone. Knowing that someone cares about them and what they are going through is not trivial for this population, as so many of them feel isolated and alone in their struggles. I (Rebecca) experienced a unique joy, a sense of completeness, when my passion to help this population was tapped into and used. It was a tiring experience because of the schedule, since these attendees received an intense level of counseling (two months' worth in just two weeks, meeting daily), but it was very rewarding. A highlight of the counseling experience was when my dad and I had simultaneously ended our sessions one afternoon. Without saying a word, we gave each other high fives in celebration of the successful sessions we both had just experienced. We shared a successful professional moment, in Switzerland, doing the very thing we both had dreamed of doing.

PHOTO 18.2 Rebecca, Ginny, and Keith at the Breathe conference in Switzerland, June 2011

Reflections on Case Studies Abroad

During our two weeks in Switzerland, we had the experience of doing significant work with a number of our clients. At the end of the two weeks, all conference attendees met together in a session of reflection and thanksgiving, in which some of the participants volunteered to share about their experience and the impact of the conference. It was a powerful experience to hear how some of our clients were affected. We worked together on one case in which Rebecca met with the child and I (Keith) met with the parents. The family was facing a major transition and the counseling facilitated a deeper level of communication. In another case, I (Keith) began meeting with a couple, but it became clear that there were family dynamics that needed to be addressed. He then met with the family for several sessions in which the child was very responsive. In another case in which Rebecca saw the child and I (Keith) saw the parents, the clients were able to work through multiple traumas that they had experienced living in a war-torn country. This family went on to experience a very challenging season in their lives soon after they returned to their home country from the conference. In all of our cases, the participants said that the encouragement and help they had received was unique in their experience and would enhance the work they were returning to do. Volunteering to counsel those who experience injustice or poverty, or the cross-cultural workers who are working to provide social justice, can be a very rewarding experience. It definitely comes with a sacrifice of time, money, resources, and self. The reward comes from giving of ourselves to those in need, from investing in causes greater than ourselves, and from knowing we made a difference in the lives of others.

Reflections on Other Case Studies Abroad

When I (Keith) began my volunteer service doing mental health training overseas in 1989, I had no idea of the world that was being opened to me. I (Keith) find it especially satisfying that I have been able to do seminars in the same places over many years. In the fall of 2011, Ginny and I made our 8th trip to Chiang Mai, Thailand to be on staff at a two-week intensive training for cross-cultural workers. I (Keith) enjoy the familiarity I have established with the culture and the growing number of relationships that we have established. I (Keith) have the same sense of connection with Estonians through multiple trips to their country. Estonians have also come to California for visits over the past five years. In all of this work, I (Keith) have been training a diverse group of international workers in basic mental health skills. During one trip, I (Keith) had a clinical consultation with a woman who worked with young girls rescued out of sex trafficking. As she shared her stories, she broke into tears of grief about a recent girl who had not returned from a home visit and was not responding to inquiries. She was able to process her grief as she met for daily counseling with a female colleague who was a member of our short-term team. In the couple's group Ginny and I led, she and her husband shared about the stresses of their cross-cultural marriage. The husband had difficulty learning to listen empathically, but as he began to understand her needs he marveled at the essential simplicity of the approach. "Is this all I have to do? Is this what she really wants?" ("Yes," she said!)

On another trip, a young couple I (Keith) had worked with six years previously came out to visit us with their three children. We have been able to keep in touch with them over the years. When we first met them, the wife was severely depressed and her husband was struggling to find his place in his work. The couple participated in the intensive marriage group, where they were able to share the challenges of their work and the pain of disappointments and betrayals. Our intensive work with this couple six years ago set them on a journey of healing that has been deeply satisfying to witness. The wife has found ways to express her gifts by working in a new ministry and the husband has been working effectively in several countries in the region. The disappointments and betrayals they had experienced were real, and the pain they both felt was a natural response to their situation. They needed space and support to grieve and move on, but they were stuck. With the group providing caring support and validation, they were able to identify their negative patterns of interaction and learned to hear and respond to one another with compassion.

The continuity of my (Keith's) work over the past several years in Asia and in Europe has provided a sense of connection that enhances and deepens my sense of purpose and fulfillment. The fact that I was able to have my daughter join me on the journey in Switzerland was deeply satisfying. My wife and I (Keith) have had the opportunity to support many workers in the service of others. In the process, we have been deeply blessed.

Frustrations, Challenges, Obstacles, and Rewards

International/cross-cultural work demands flexibility and humility. One area that usually requires flexibility is the accommodations. In Switzerland, we had very unconventional offices—we had to see clients in our rooms, as every room in the four-story retreat center was full. I (Rebecca) used the extra bed and nightstand in my room to lay out the figurines for my sand tray and adapted fairly well to the space. I (Keith) found the room arrangements for consultation on these short-term trips to be one of the most frustrating aspects of the work. Over the years, I have had sessions outside, in libraries, reading rooms, and recreation centers. The clients have adapted well to the various venues we have had to use, but I (Keith) do find the arrangements a major source of stress.

Another area that requires flexibility is personal space. Time to be alone and regroup is often a luxury that is not available when volunteering for intensive work abroad. This was especially the case with us in Switzerland. When you are using central showers and sleeping on the same floor as your clients, hiking, and eating with their families at mealtime, you become part of an informal community. Boundaries regarding "dual-role relationships" are more blurred during these residential, intensive conferences. The organizers believe the socializing and informal community makes the attendees' experience very powerful. Counseling happened in our "offices," but relationships happened informally over breakfast, in the hallway, on a walkway, or over coffee. The staff was encouraged to be proactive in our interactions with the attendees so that they could feel known and that they belonged. This high level of interaction was physically and emotionally tiring, but the investment and impact made the sacrifice worthwhile. We found ourselves skipping out on a morning session a couple of times to check in with an attendee who was in tears or sit in on the kids' program to observe the behavior of a child who was a concern to her parents. We were counseling in a community, and these multiple contacts were natural and helpful. Every adult at the conference had at least one counseling session, and it was up to them to continue. So the fact that a person was receiving counseling was understood. The one professional value we stressed and honored was confidentiality about the content of the counseling sessions.

Flexibility and humility regarding cultural issues is also important. All of the people with whom we worked in Switzerland spoke English. However, some of them were from passport countries other than the United States. Most of them had been living in their countries of service for many years and spoke at least two languages. A number of the countries in which they served had experienced political instability and war. We needed to be sensitive to and learn about their unique cultural experiences and challenges. A collaborative stance toward the therapeutic work is essential in these contexts.

Getting Involved

When considering getting involved in volunteer counseling or volunteer work abroad, there are several things to consider. The first is getting connected to ongoing work. The reality is that volunteers will only stay for a short period of time; the nationals or cross-cultural workers will be in their countries long term and will continue to face their challenges long after the short termer leaves. In order to make the impact long term, it is advisable to make sure clients are connected to local resources and support systems. When more resources are needed, we try to stay in touch with the clients to facilitate the connection to their organization's resources.

Another reason to connect to a long-term presence is to ensure preparation in cultural awareness of the visiting professionals. One can try to prepare ahead of time for understanding the culture, but having someone in the foreign country who serves as a cultural guide would be prudent. When we volunteer internationally, we try to approach our task with a servant's heart. There is much we can learn from a foreign culture. Americans in many countries have been perceived as insensitive and arrogant. We believe that we are more effective and better received when we maintain an attitude of humility and openness.

One more issue to keep in mind is the potential for culture shock. It is very common for a short-term volunteer to experience an adjustment period when functioning in a foreign culture. The phases of culture shock in brief description are: the honeymoon stage, when everything is exciting and new; the crisis stage, when frustrations about the culture set in; and the readjustment stage, when the home and foreign cultures are integrated and adjusted to by the volunteer. It is also common for international volunteers to experience reverse culture shock when they return to the States. The values and worldview of the short-term volunteer may have shifted, and processing their trip experience with someone can help. The volunteer may need some time to readjust to being back in their home culture. This would especially be the case with any social justice counseling and aid, as exposure to the suffering of others deeply affects the human soul.

Our involvement in caring for those engaged in social justice that we have described in this chapter is embedded in a context that makes our work possible. We volunteer our services through churches and NGOs that organize and market the intensive seminars. For psychology professionals, traveling means a loss of income and the interruption of a counseling practice. This is the where we incur the most significant monetary and professional cost for our travels. I (Keith) miss counseling sessions for a few weeks during my time of traveling. I (Keith) usually lose a number of new referrals starting a few weeks before my trip as I let people know of the upcoming break in my schedule. The various costs incurred are offset by the rewards of having a worldwide (though modest) impact for good in and through the lives we touch. By getting involved in problems that plague our world, we are changed. We become people of compassion, people who are generous, people with a heart for the world.

I (Rebecca) have always valued giving my time and resources to others, mostly because it was a value instilled in me from a young age by my parents. My return to the States from Ecuador meant that I shifted roles from being on the front lines to supporting those who are. I (Rebecca) value how my past experience as a cross-cultural worker is being woven into my present journey as a counselor. I (Keith) look back on my international volunteer work with fond memories and professional satisfaction, and plan to continue serving this population in the future.

Such volunteer work, as stated earlier, is a sacrifice of time and finances. It is also professionally challenging. However, our lives are enriched when we step into another's experience of pain and suffering with the purpose of understanding and support. We have found it to be a powerful and deeply enriching experience to be able to provide otherwise unavailable intensive mental health training and services for cross-cultural workers. We have grown and are becoming people who are connected to the world, making a difference in and through the lives of the dedicated cross-cultural workers around the world that we have been privileged to know.

References

Greenberg, L.S. (2002). *Emotion-Focused Therapy: Coaching Clients to Work through Their Feelings*. Washington, D.C.: American Psychological Association.

Johnson, S. (2004). *The Practice of Emotionally Focused Therapy for Couples: Creating Connection*. New York: Routledge.

Taylor, W. (1997). Introduction: Examining the iceberg called attrition. In W. Taylor (ed.), *Too Valuable to Lose: Exploring the Causes and Cures of Missionary Attrition*, 3–14. California: William Carey Library.

Scripture taken from the Holy Bible, New International Version. (1984). International Bible Society.

19

FEMINIST BORDER CROSSINGS

Our Transnational Partnership in Peace and Justice Work

Kathryn L. Norsworthy and Ouyporn Khuankaew

We, Ouyporn Khuankaew from Thailand, and Kathryn Norsworthy from the United States, have cultivated a remarkable 14-year transnational relationship and partnership, during which we have learned and grown together in our evolution as activists. By sharing some highlights of our journey, we hope to inspire readers to pursue border crossings of their own in order to ally with colleagues from other cultures, countries, and contexts in social change work.

Synchronicity and Connection

Our paths crossed by accident—some might say synchronistically. We met before e-mail existed. After being introduced by a colleague from Thailand's Thammasat University, known for its activist history, we spent almost a year corresponding by letter and fax, getting acquainted and deciding to work together. On December 25, 1997, we met in person at a traveler's hotel in the backpack district of Bangkok. In retrospect, we noted that in planning our first project we fell into the template for the "global order," in which US knowledge is privileged over indigenous "ways" and wisdom—Kathryn, the white, US Ph.D.-level feminist counseling psychologist as the primary facilitator and teacher, and Ouyporn, Thai, woman of color, MA-educated, feminist activist and experienced trainer, as the translator. We were leading a three-day workshop on violence against women for an NGO in Thailand. Only a few hours into the first day, the power dynamics of our partnership began to shift, as it became clear that each of us had important contributions to make to the facilitation process, the content, and the planning. Further, as we later reflected, we both became uncomfortable with the original hierarchical arrangement, particularly once we were immersed in the realities of implementing our initial plan.

By day two, we were sharing our ideas about what to do and slowly shifting to a process of co-facilitation.

Because of our commitment to our feminist roots and to social justice values, we took our partnership seriously as we debriefed after the first workshop and made plans for future work together. During the long conversation, a plan emerged to restructure our relationship and our roles to share power. We have spent the last 14 years working out the details, engaging in dialogues, sometimes difficult, yet very satisfying as we have developed our relationships with one another and with the local groups and partners with whom we have worked.

Getting Acquainted

When we first met, even though we knew very little about each another, we felt a deep connection despite the fact that we had grown up on opposite sides of the world. On the long bus ride back to Bangkok after our first workshop, we took a chance by openly talking about our lives and the paths that led us to our commitments to social justice and activism. We both remember the delightful "aha" moments that kept arising throughout this particular conversation—it was as if each of us had found a long-lost sister as we discovered so much common ground within the sea of differences in our identities, social and cultural contexts, regions of the world, "psychologies" and worldviews, professional preparations, and career paths. During the bumpy journey, it was revealed that we both grew up in high-stress environments and working poor families, leading each of us to develop a strong appreciation for the injustices connected with social class. Ultimately, we both made a commitment to change society's attitudes and the systems that perpetuate oppression connected to classism and poverty. Each of us had anchored our lives and work in Buddhist values and practices. Ouyporn, of course, was born into a Buddhist society and family, while Kathryn had adopted Buddhism about 15 years earlier. Since there are many branches of Buddhism, we were amazed that we both practiced the same kind of Buddhist meditation and had become involved in the social justice-focused "engaged Buddhist" movement. Holding a strong commitment to feminism and to achieving women's equality globally and within our respective countries, we were involved in activism aimed at eliminating sexism and misogyny and building new, more socially just organizations and institutions.

Perhaps one of the greatest risks we took on that bus ride was to "come out" to one another as lesbians, a move that took both of us outside of our comfort zones. Since we both lived in contexts of homophobia and heterosexism, sharing this identity with someone from an entirely different part of the world, who we had just met, felt like a leap of faith on a whole new level! Kathryn's partner, Deena, was accompanying her on that initial trip, so Kathryn's technique was to let Ouyporn in on the nature of their relationship. Ouyporn, after wholeheartedly affirming Kathryn and Deena's relationship, simply blurted out that she too was attracted to women. We both laughed when we discovered that each of us had at one time been married to a man, thus coming out later in life than many of our lesbian sisters in the younger generations. In retrospect, this shared identity and our choice to come out seems to be a crucial part of the glue that bonded us in our journey and growth together. Over the last 14 years of our work, together we have faced many situations in which we have had to make decisions about when and whether to come out to local partners, while taking into consideration our own convictions about the importance of being true to ourselves and our values.

For all of our common ground, we recognize that we have many differences that have influenced our work and growth together. We are both keenly aware of the power of the United States in the "global village" militarily, economically, politically, and in terms of "privileged Western knowledge," and how Kathryn's identities as a white, US counseling psychologist place her in the role of "situated outsider" (Lykes, 2001). This involves occupying multiple locations of privilege and access to information and resources, particularly since US counseling and psychology, in our well-intentioned efforts to internationalize, have followed some of the same uncritical, colonizing, and expansionist methods used by the US government. This also means that Kathryn can be limited in her understanding of the worldviews of local partners and participants and periodically falls back into her culturally encapsulated role of the "expert" even

PHOTO 19.1   Ouyporn Khuankaew and Kathryn Norsworthy

though she certainly is not an expert on the lives, cultures, and experiences of the people of Southeast Asia.

As a Thai woman of color and an insider, Ouyporn deals with the mixed experiences of having cultural, ethnic, and national identities in common with the participants of our Asia projects. While she may be able to immediately connect with our local partners, she is often better educated and holds greater degrees of social influence and status than many of those with whom we work. Yet, side by side with Kathryn, some of Ouyporn's power can be overshadowed. This can happen in connection with our differing national and ethnic identities, education levels, how skillfully (or not) Kathryn uses the power she holds in the service of power sharing, and by the internalized psychological colonization of our project participants. Many of them have been enculturated to believe that a white person from the US knows much more than even someone from their own country with extensive expertise and experience. At any rate, the challenges we have faced in negotiating these differences have offered occasions for difficult dialogues as well as opportunities for tremendous growth and learning, at times testing our commitment to dialogue and power sharing.

Learning Together

Inherent in a relationship like ours are possibilities—for creativity, passion, individual and synergistic expression, novel ideas, and momentum—as reflected in the many directions our activism and social justice work has taken since we met so many years ago. This kind of intense, challenging, and fulfilling work also solidifies deep emotional intimacy: a very real gift that emerges through the context of a relationship in which one is really seen, heard, and supported for being fully human. And, of course, the strength of such a relationship sets the stage for the inevitable challenges.

Voices of the Women of Burma: Awakening to Our Privilege

For a number of years, we worked together on projects with the refugee women's communities of Burma. Over a million refugees have fled the "Myanmar" dictatorship into Thailand. Most of these refugees live without legal status after fleeing the oppression and politically based violence to which they were subjected in their home country. We intentionally use "Burma" rather than Myanmar (renamed by the military junta) in solidarity with the ongoing democracy movement that began in 1967. At that time, the dictatorship was installed after a military coup, which disbanded the fledgling post-colonial democratic government that was formed after the British withdrew.

A major issue identified by the women of Burma was violence against women—in their own homes, in the Thai community where they are vulnerable to exploitation, and in their home country, where rape has been systematically used by the military junta as a weapon of war and genocide, especially in targeting ethnic minority women. Shortly after we met, we began developing a "feminist liberation" process and methodology for collaborating with our local women-of-Burma partners. We wanted to use processes and practices that supported them in voicing their own problems and concerns, analyzing the root causes of the violence, and developing and carrying out action plans aimed at changing the systems of inequality that create and support the violence. Drawing on their indigenous wisdom and "ways," together we began to focus on building families, communities, and societies of peace and justice. As the work continued, we responded to requests by the women's groups to offer workshops aimed at understanding the traumatic effects of the violence and helping them develop community-based, culture-centered trauma counseling and healing skills. We openly discussed with the project participants our hope that the model we were using supported their empowerment, particularly since they came from contexts in which power was misused and abused on a regular basis, where they received ongoing messages that their voices and contributions as women were not important.

Several years ago, we were invited by women from one of the ethnic minority groups of Burma to ally with them as they started a women's organization using feminist principles. We spent considerable time prior to the first workshop developing a plan to facilitate this process, wanting to embody feminist principles ourselves as we supported the group in using feminism as a guide for engaging with one another. Early in the workshop, in our usual circle format in which we all sat on mats on the floor, we invited participants to brainstorm about feminist values and principles they could use as guides to develop their organization. Having located what we thought would be a useful list (written in English) of contrasting patriarchal values side by side with [Western] "feminist" values, we offered this list to the group for their consideration. One local partner was serving as a translator and "cultural bridge" so that we could all communicate with one another since there were several languages being used, including the local ethnic language of the group members.

As the participants reviewed the list we provided, we sat on the edge of their circle, observing the process. Within minutes, the 18 group members began to draw closer and closer together, leaning in, heads nearly touching, becoming increasingly more animated. Soon we (Ouyporn and Kathryn) were outside the circle, a bit puzzled about the change in energy and the intensity of the conversation. At some point, we asked our local partner what was happening. She reported:

> The list you gave the group ... There are many words on it that are not part of our local language or even Burmese (the language of the dominant ethnic group of Burma). There is no direct translation, and in some cases, nothing in our language that is even close, so they are trying to get the meaning through a discussion. A couple of the women speak English, so they are trying to help. The group is in the process of inventing their own terminology based

on our cultural values and experiences. Also, we are not even sure that we want a "democratic" organization [defined on the list as a "feminist" ideal]. In a democracy, people's voices get left out. Small groups of people who are not part of the mainstream are not represented. We have lived in a dictatorship—a totalitarian system. We want something better than "democracy!"

In that moment, astonished, we (Ouyporn and Kathryn) turned to one another, expressing our amazement and deep respect for these women, our friends and sisters. They were inventing their own indigenous feminism! We also noted that, had the group members not been strong, empowered women, and had we not been using a liberatory model for facilitating the workshop, they might not have felt so free to take charge and engage in this powerful process of self-definition. We could have been the instruments of yet another form of colonization by the "experts" from the outside.

Forty-five minutes later, the group informed us that they had decided to take a break for lunch. Upon their return, we all debriefed the morning. Participants shared their struggles, the first of which was that while they were all too familiar with models of "power over" governance, leadership, and organizational structures, and process, they could not think of examples of "power-sharing" models. So on the one hand, in the absence of models to emulate, they welcomed the "chart" we provided to them; on the other, a number of the concepts and terms were not translatable or even part of their cultural constructions of their world. Incidentally, some months later this reality was reinforced when one of our Thai colleagues, who worked closely with Westerners involved in the early "gender" movement, commented that the word "gender" was not originally part of the Thai vocabulary. Our colleague described how some of the foreign "gender experts" had become very frustrated with a Thai group when the group members took a considerable amount of time figuring out, and even inventing, the Thai concept of "gender" based on their culture and context.

As we continued the workshop, the women did create a "feminist" organization based on their mutually agreed upon articulation of an indigenous feminism and their understanding of "power-sharing" principles and practices. They decided on a more horizontal model of leadership and decision making by consensus. This was a radical departure from the social, political, and historical "Myanmar" context from which this group arose—one dominated by oppression, imperialism, and autocracy. This experience reinforced for us, particularly in our roles as "situated outsiders" entering the spaces of others, that the model, methodology, and process of "consultation" or "facilitation" we employ can either support a group in accessing its own wisdom and strengths or get in the way by creating tension and resistance, complicating the group's work, and replicating the dynamics of sexism, domination, and subordination that are so prevalent in the lives of women.

Ouyporn observes:

We need to bring a humble mind to the work—one that recognizes that local people are the experts on their own lives and that they have the knowledge and wisdom to solve their own problems. The facilitators provide the structure and the space for the participants to listen to themselves—to find and express their voices. We need to embrace the position that we are all teachers and learners together in order to be successful.

Kathryn adds:

Of course, the facilitators have something to contribute based on our backgrounds, experiences, and training. We bring ideas to stimulate more ideas. Effective, culture-centered, power-sharing-based facilitation is a delicate balance and often paradoxical. Our goal is to draw out or provide a frame for the participants to express themselves, to remember what they knew all along, to dream it into voice, and to resist the loud dominant voices of society that convey the message that what they have to say and what they do is not valuable.

As facilitators who are not part of the local communities represented in the group, we may see what they cannot readily see—how they have internalized the sexism and other forms of oppression, for example—so we also challenge members at various points, especially through experiential exercises, hopefully in a way that leaves room for each participant to make her own meaning based on her context.

Working Within the Margins

Over the years of our collaboration with one another and with local communities, our dominant and privileged identities are not always the ones that lead in a given moment in a workshop or project. Whereas our privilege (e.g. nationalities, education levels, status as trainers) offers us the power to challenge group members, there are times when our minority identities come front and center (sexual orientation, gender). These situations tend to arise when we work in mixed-gender groups or those predominantly comprised of male or heterosexual participants. One such instance arose when we were doing longer-term women's leadership and peacebuilding projects with the multi-ethnic Burma women's communities.

For a long period of time, we collaborated with one of the local activists from the community. Weyan (pseudonym) was a well-educated gay man who had escaped the country during the 1988 uprising led by the university students, who had been brutally suppressed by the military junta. Weyan lost his partner during that period and, since his arrival in Thailand, had been trying to establish himself as an activist and leader. As a gay man, this was challenging due to the significant homophobia that he encountered within the Burmese communities.

At the request of one of the local leaders, the three of us teamed up to conduct a series of women's leadership and peacebuilding workshops with a multi-ethnic group of women leaders from Burma living in exile in Thailand. At that time, we (Ouyporn and Kathryn) were not "out" as lesbians to the community and our colleague, Weyan, was in a marginal position. Interestingly, the foundational principles of the project in which we were engaged were social justice and diversity, so an exploration of power, privilege, and oppression was on the agenda. We planned to invite the group to analyze their experiences of oppression in relation to the Burma regime and their status as women, and to self-reflect on their group dynamics so that they could take their evolving awareness, knowledge, and skills back to their own community peacebuilding work. As the project unfolded, we all became aware that there were a couple of lesbian participants in the group who were also not completely "out," though it seemed that some of the other group members knew about and were somewhat disapproving of their sexual orientations.

Weyan held a complex position in this situation. He was an out gay Burmese man, highly educated, one of the workshop's leaders as well as the translator, and privy to the concerns of these lesbian participants who were not feeling welcome by many of their peers in the project due to homophobia and heterosexism. As we moved into the second workshop of the project series and more deeply into the diversity and anti-oppression focus, the three of us (Weyan, Ouyporn, and Kathryn) debated how to address the homophobia in the group. What experiential exercises might we introduce that would engage participants at the emotional and relational levels? How might we offer an experience that would loosen their current tightly bound constructions of gender and sexuality and opening their hearts and minds to one another and new ideas about sexual orientation and gender identity?

We decided to draw on our own power and influence as facilitators—our educational levels and the respect we had earned from this group and the larger Burma community through our ongoing work with them. Borrowing from Ouyporn and Kathryn's privileged nationalities and ethnicities and our status as group leaders and facilitators, we planned an exercise in which we would also participate and eventually "come out" to the group as gay or lesbian. We wanted to elicit the experientially based "ruptures" that create dissonance and active exploration (Worthington, Savoy, & Dillon, 2002) and often fuel consciousness raising.

The experiential exercise, which focused on increasing understanding and awareness of various forms of oppression and systemic inequalities, involved having the group members line up side by side at one end of the training space. We as facilitators "stood with" them so that we were essentially in an insider-outsider position—leading the activity while also participating. Out of the requested silence, one of us would say a sentence out loud and group members to whom the sentence applied were invited to walk out five steps, stand still for a few seconds, then turn, face the group, and walk back to their places in line.

We started with statements that allowed people to stay in their comfort zones. "Step forward if you have brothers and sisters." "Step forward if you speak more than one language" (which all group members did). Gradually, the statements began to tap into societal privilege. "Step forward if you had books available to read at home when you were growing up." A number of participants stepped out. Experiences of oppression were introduced. "Step forward if you have ever been discriminated against because of your ethnicity or culture." Nearly the whole group simultaneously stepped out, made their way forward, and then returned to their respective locations. Eventually we posed the big one. "Step out if you have been looked down on or discriminated against because you are gay, bisexual, or lesbian or because you love someone of the same gender." We (Kathryn, Ouyporn, and Weyan) all stepped out together, and then, hesitantly, two other participants joined us. Upon our arrival at the fifth step, we all stopped, looked at one another, and then simultaneously turned around and directed our gazes to the remaining group members. The facial expressions ranged from surprised, pained, compassionate, to deadpan. We took it all in and then walked back, rejoining the rest of the participants.

After a few more statements, this part of the activity concluded, and the debriefing began. We asked the group, "How did you feel, and what stood out for you in doing this exercise?" Eventually we got around to unpacking the feelings and thoughts related to stepping out in relation to sexual orientation, though the conversation was brief. We were encouraged that one of the lesbian participants who had taken the risk of stepping out during the activity shared her feelings of apprehension about doing so, though she also reported feeling proud, more herself, and more free after "coming out." Two of the heterosexually identified group members supported her as she shared.

From that point forward in the workshop, the topic of sexual orientation became as much a part of the conversation as sexism and cultural oppression, though there was certainly more work to do. That evening, in our (Ouyporn, Weyan, and Kathryn) end-of-the-day reflections, we discussed our own experiences in doing the exercise and how happy we were to have made the decision to "step out," though we felt it was a calculated risk. While it was unrealistic to think that the disapproval or homophobia had completely disappeared, the participants remained active and engaged, appearing to gain a greater degree of consciousness about the various forms of oppression, their impact, and about how to change the systems of inequality through social action and activism. Weyan felt supported by us (Kathryn and Ouyporn) and seemed truly empowered to be out and moving into greater degrees of leadership and organizing in the Burma democracy movement. Since that workshop, we have seen him build an organization devoted to human rights and justice and provide the spark for the LGBTQ people of Burma to found their own organization, which continues to be a powerful voice for their community.

Difficult Dialogues

We still remember facilitating a Bangkok project focusing on violence against women with a group of Thai women NGO staff and community workers. On one of the breaks during the second day of the four-day workshop, we had the following conversation.

OUYPORN: "Have you noticed what is happening?"

KATHRYN: "It seems to be going pretty well, don't you think? The participants are really speaking up and seem to be into it."

OUYPORN (serious facial expression and voice): "The group members are mostly speaking to you, looking at you when they respond to our questions or report on their small group work. I feel invisible."

KATHRYN (surprised): "I didn't realize this! And I think I am reinforcing their behavior because when they do it I respond back."

OUYPORN: "Yes, you are. How do we deal with this to change the dynamic?"

KATHRYN (embarrassed): "I am so glad you told me and I am very sorry. Let's figure this out before we start again."

This situation was particularly troubling because, as we mentioned at the beginning of this chapter, the issue of the "Western expert" was surfacing. Participants were ignoring the Thai facilitator, Ouyporn, who was quite experienced, skilled, and knowledgeable, instead focusing their attention on the white Western facilitator, Kathryn, who had fallen into the "expert" trap and was engaging with them to the exclusion of her Thai co-facilitator. In the ensuing discussion, we decided that Ouyporn would take the lead and Kathryn would step back, both in terms of facilitating and also by sitting down rather than standing (since she is a full foot taller than Ouyporn). We immediately got into a rhythm of Ouyporn setting up an exercise, supported by Kathryn's briefer directions and explanations, then together we invited participants to share their experiences and learnings. When Ouyporn invited a check in and participants directed their comments to Kathryn, Kathryn stayed quiet and turned her attention back to Ouyporn. After a few hours, we began to gradually and consciously shift into a "power-sharing" approach in which we deliberately worked to share the space so that neither of us was dominating the facilitation nor subordinating our contributions. The group members saw and experienced a Thai-US collaboration, in which a woman of color and a white woman were enacting values of mutuality, respect, and egalitarianism. We hoped this process would be empowering and offer a framework of collaboration for the participants to emulate when they returned to their own communities.

Caring for Ourselves

Another challenge we regularly face involves recognizing our limits and caring for ourselves so that we can be fully present for the groups with whom we collaborate. Both of us have struggled at times with the emotional overload of witnessing and holding the traumas and injustices experienced by our local partners. When we are in the midst of a workshop focusing on participants' lived experiences of community and state-sponsored violence, AIDS, family violence, oppression, and other forms of trauma, we need to really pull together to support one another by debriefing, listening for whether one of us is particularly affected by what we have been "holding" with the group, and encouraging each other to practice self-care as a way to inoculate against vicarious or secondary trauma. Each of us can remember times when we left a session and one or both of us began sobbing in response to the intensity of the experiences we had just witnessed. Sometimes there is not enough time to "metabolize" an experience before needing to move on to the next activity, so the emotions pile up. The times when we have not built in space at the end of a project to sit together, draw close, and offer the supportive space for debriefing because we have another project scheduled right away have taken an emotional toll. We both have had to be conscious not to schedule one workshop after another without a substantial break after learning the hard way in our early years of working together. Kathryn recalls:

> One year I went to Thailand for five weeks. During that period, we co-facilitated four projects, each ranging from 4–7 days. I started working immediately upon my arrival (in the midst of jet lag) and concluded the last project just a few days before I returned home. When I got back to Orlando, I was talking to some colleagues about the trip. Right in the middle of a sentence, I began to weep and it took several minutes to regain my composure. During that trip, we did not take time to rest between workshops or to debrief after a project. I remember feeling like I was in survival mode, just putting one foot in front of the other to "get through" all of my commitments. It was a hard lesson, but one that led me to be more careful about giving myself time to rest and recover from jet lag after the 28-hour trip and to take a substantial break between projects. I have found this challenging because, since I travel back and forth, I have to say no to projects that I would really like to support. Yet I know that my own mental and physical health are crucial in my effectiveness as a project facilitator.

Because there is so much to do, it is easy to take on too much and then to become fatigued and burned out because we have not taken care of ourselves adequately. This issue is particularly tough for us, because we can find ourselves feeling guilty for not doing more in the face of the tremendous hardships faced by those for whom we have come to care deeply. Yet, we recognize that the "frenzy of activism" (Merton, 1966, p. 73) and overwork can potentially extinguish our capacities for empathy, connection, and wise action.

Final Reflections

In our final reflections on our 14-year journey together, we again recognize that growth truly takes place "in relationship." While at this point in our lives we have each branched out, now collaborating with many second- and third-generation mentees, we continue to "return home" to one another for anchoring, support, and periodic collaboration on social change projects. We also serve as "wise council" for one another as we proceed on our respective, yet interconnected paths, always maintaining the deep and sustained connection that we forged, fought for, and to which we remain steadfastly committed. Through the sharing of our stories, we hope that others will be encouraged to take risks and to maintain the "beginner's mind" (Suzuki, 1973) necessary to learn when faced with uncertainty and ambiguity in the context of crossing borders. We encourage readers who are inclined to cultivate and maintain meaningful cross-cultural partnerships, since they are fertile ground for powerful work and learning to take place, particularly as each member of the partnership grows into herself in the process. Clearly, as interconnected beings, the peace and justice inherent in these kinds of power-sharing partnerships ripple outward and have the potential to contribute to the transformation of our communities, and indeed, our world.

References

Lykes, M.B. (2001). Activist participatory research and the arts with rural Maya women: Interculturality and situated meaning making. In D.L. Tolman & M. Brydon-Miller (eds.), *From Subjects to Subjectivities: A Handbook of Interpretive and Participatory Methods*, 183–100. New York: NYU Press.

Merton, T. (1966). *Conjectures of a Guilty Bystander*. New York: Doubleday.

Suzuki, S. (1973). *Zen Mind, Beginner's Mind*. Boston, MA: Weatherhill.

Worthington, R.L., Savoy, H.B., Dillon, F.R., & Vernaglia, E.R. (2002b). Heterosexual identity development: A multidimensional model of individual and social identity. *The Counseling Psychologist, 30*, 496–531.

20

BON KOURAJ

Learning Courage through Service

Chante DeLoach

I have no words. I haven't been able to write. The pain, the fatigue, the absolutely overwhelming emotion is just too much. Journal excerpt

The earthquake that hit Haiti/Ayiti[1] on January 12, 2010 was an unparalleled natural disaster. With an estimated 250,000 killed, millions displaced, countless children orphaned, and disease and contagion spreading, I felt compelled to respond. My own familial background, which is rooted in the Louisiana and Arkansas deltas of this country, connected me culturally and politically to the fight and plight of the Ayitian people. My own African ancestry and experience working with African people here in the United States and around the world necessarily motivated me to mobilize in the same way that I would if my own family were directly in need. So like many others, I soon volunteered to go and serve as part of a trauma response team. I wanted to use my skills and training as a psychologist specializing in trauma to aid the Ayitian recovery process in any way I could. Yet I wondered how I could do so, given my full-time job and an additional part-time job. I went immediately to my supervisor who, to my surprise, gave me her immediate support and told me I had the complete support of the department in whatever way was necessary, including covering my assignments. That provided tremendous relief, as I could focus on finding an organization that seemed to have a need for my particular skill set and expertise. I was surprised to find out that many organizations had a host of restrictions and even longer waiting lists. Yet, I was committed to going and resolved that this would not be another Hurricane Katrina, where I regretfully allowed the prohibitive restrictions on volunteer organizations to limit my ability to serve. Indeed, I contacted and signed up on the volunteer lists of several organizations and anxiously waited to learn if I would be selected to serve.

During this wait, my father passed away suddenly. My attention immediately turned to my own pain and grief. As I returned to work teaching and seeing my own clients, I recognized the challenge of balancing my own bereavement process and being fully present for my students and clients. It was at this time that I was finally contacted to go to Ayiti as part of a medical mission. I was asked to serve as the Chief Psychologist of my team, and I honestly wasn't sure if I was ready and prepared to do so, given the enormity of the challenge of my own personal pain and recent loss. Yet, with much prayer and the support of my friends and family I decided that going was really the only option for me. I hoped that I could use my own loss in the work in which I was about to engage.

It is noteworthy that I have avoided writing about this topic for over a year because I haven't been able to fully articulate what I experienced, what happened, and why I kept going back—why I still want and need to return. I didn't go to Ayiti with a missionary zeal to heal the "poor, suffering Ayitian people." When I saw the faces of Ayiti, I saw my own. I saw every resilient black child and mother that I have seen in pain from my birthplace in south Los Angeles, to Addis Ababa, to Salvador da Bahia, or Cuba. The strength and pain looked strikingly similar everywhere I have been. I promised myself years ago, especially following Hurricane Katrina, that I would no longer wait for direction or permission from others; I reminded myself that it's okay to act. In fact, inaction is a dereliction of duty, as negligence is an act of harm.

The Setting: A Makeshift Hospital

Allow me to first describe the setting and context of the experience, as this strongly influenced my experience, what I gained, and how my work and I have been transformed. The first time I went to Ayiti, I served as Chief Psychologist of a team of five mental health volunteers (which included a pastoral counselor and Master's-level counselors with varying areas of expertise). I immediately noticed that there were very few volunteers of African ancestry. In fact, the overwhelming majority of volunteers were white Americans, many of whom had never worked in this type of setting. We were working in a makeshift hospital, which was really a series of tents powered by generators located near the Port-au-Prince airport. All necessary amenities were lacking; there was no indoor plumbing and the electricity frequently went off and on. The triage area was beneath a mango tree and the emergency room was an unshaded outdoor area in the humid, unrelenting 100+ degree heat. There were limited abilities to isolate contagion, given the close proximity of patients. Despite the limited amenities and infrastructure, the hospital served close to 200 patients per day. Patients slept on small cots with little room for family members. It should be noted that while these conditions were minimal, many patients and their family members were residing in tents or were completely homeless. Therefore, while the conditions were not optimal, many patients adjusted well as it was slightly better than their housing options upon discharge. There was a small outdoor morgue in a tent (located in very close proximity to everything else), which lacked refrigeration; thus there was a strict policy that bodies had to be claimed by the family within a few hours because of the rapid rate of decomposition in the heat. Unfortunately, many families were unable to afford appropriate burials for family members; therefore, bodies left at the hospital were cremated at a public crematory, which was often devastating, as this is contrary to many cultural and spiritual practices in Ayiti.

These were the conditions of the hospital, but this is also where the volunteers lived. The physical conditions of living there were difficult for many, and some volunteers were unable to remain. The heat alone was too much of a challenge for some volunteers unaccustomed to such conditions and who did not remain sufficiently hydrated. Volunteers lived in a large tent that was also powered by a generator and slept on cots with mosquito nets. Some nights there was limited air conditioning, but many nights it wasn't functional at all. We also had limited water for bathing and were limited to brief (less than 1 minute) showers in outdoor wooden stalls and only had port-a-potties. The food was limited to sandwiches dropped off daily. My own dietary restrictions meant limited food for me, primarily the granola bars and peanut butter that I had packed. We worked long shifts and operated a 24-hour on-call procedure, particularly if a patient was expected to die during the night. Most patients only spoke Ayitian Kreyol (there were a limited few who could speak some French) and therefore most of us needed to use the assistance of interpreters. There were a few amateur interpreters available, most of whom were young (18–25) men who learned English from music videos and perhaps family members in the United States. This is noteworthy because much of the information that we needed translated was rather sensitive in nature, and it was emotionally very difficult for these young men to do so. Moreover, the translations were not always accurate, which complicated the provision of effective mental health care.

Working as a psychologist in this context took me far outside of my usual scope of responsibility. While I have worked in many countries and specialize in trauma, I ordinarily do so outside of the hospital context and with a more defined role. In this context, I found that there were few opportunities to engage in "counseling" as typically defined in a Western context. Once patients were discharged, there was no follow-up available, there were no community practitioners to whom we could refer, and there was limited privacy as patients had no rooms, only cots. Thus, we provided a lot of psychoeducation to groups in the waiting areas on topics such as trauma and coping. Much of our work focused on crisis intervention in the ER and providing death notifications and support to families in such instances. We also provided much-needed supportive counseling to the medical volunteers. I will focus primarily on my experience working with children, as it seemed particularly impactful.

Challenging Therapeutic Experiences

The neonatal intensive care unit (NICU) was a particularly challenging experience. First, none of the team members specialized in pediatric or child psychology. Second, we experienced multiple deaths during my first week there. This was particularly difficult for all of us. Given the lack of knowledge and experience of most team members in the local culture and spiritual ideologies, a brief one-page handout notwithstanding, this further impaired many providers' ability to understand the culturally embedded grief and loss process. Yet, the mental health team was used to help provide difficult diagnoses and feedback to patients and their families. In the case of the NICU, many of the mothers were unaware of the severity of their child's presenting condition, and therefore the news was often even more devastating. I had no experience in providing death notifications, so the experience of providing multiple notifications to unsuspecting mothers was overwhelming. In addition, I was often called in to be with the mother as the child was dying. Not only was this a far departure from my usual work, the process of watching a child die was unbearable. Being surrounded by constant death was even more difficult, given the recent loss of my own father. While these experiences were overwhelming and even discouraging at times, fatigue did not seem to be an option. The strength of our Ayitian patients felt contagious; just as they willed themselves to go on and supported one another, so did the medical and support team.

Reconsidering Competence and "Therapy"

I was stretched beyond comfort and beyond what I previously thought of as my "competence." Many of the ways in which I needed to engage with patients to provide comfort and healing are beyond that which is traditionally (by Western psychology) thought of as therapeutic or within the role of a psychologist. Holding and singing to a mother who is broken as she clings to me for three hours in the blazing afternoon sun is beyond what many of us may feel comfortable doing. Further, it may lead to questions about physical and emotional boundaries between "doctor" and "patient." Watching child after child die, I was often brought to tears. Yet I believe that authenticity is essential in joining therapeutically. I began asking myself after a day or so of being there: What is most therapeutic in the most excruciating of circumstances? In asking this question, I began to be led far more by spirit while still relying on the knowledge and skills acquired as a healing professional. This began to shift the way in which I made "treatment" recommendations and what part of me I relied upon to make "treatment plans." I believe the following example demonstrates this therapeutic flexibility.

I recall one particular mother who brought her son into the emergency room following a severe seizure. He had suffered from a seizure disorder for most of his life according to the mother. Like any mother, she seemed optimistic and certain that he would recover as he always did. Unfortunately, the effects of this seizure were particularly damaging and with limited resources there was little that the NICU doctors could do for this child. The treating pediatric doctor called me in and requested that I help talk with the mother about the state of her child's health and prepare them to remove the ventilator. While talking to this mother, I learned that she and her husband had recently separated since the earthquake and that they were both living in one of the proverbial "tent cities." The mother feared that the husband would blame her for the health of the child; she had been frantically trying to reach the father since the child had been admitted. Part of my role was helping to facilitate this process, which included working with our logistics team to reach the father so he could say goodbye. So we worked with logistics to get the patient access to telephone service, because many patients and their family members we were trying to reach did not have phones. This was a constant challenge. In addition, once someone was reached, transportation to the hospital was also lacking or very slow and could take a number of hours.

When the treatment team told this mother the severity of her son's condition and that it was not likely he would survive, she broke. She fervently expressed the pain, shock, and horror that any mother would feel in such circumstances. Many Western mental health professionals would categorize her response as "hysterical" or perhaps even "psychotic." Indeed, her response was not containable and the medical staff immediately restrained her physically and administered Haldol to suppress her. I must pause and note that this was perhaps the moment that I felt most ineffectual and powerless as a psychologist. Not only would the medical staff not listen to me, but one member of my own team actually asked if this was "some of that Voodoo stuff." To which I responded: "No, this is some of that pain stuff." It became clear to me that like in many hospitals, psychologists are not high in the power strata, and therefore my recommendations were not privileged in these circumstances. The deleterious impact of physician discomfort and biases around issues of race and religion also became painfully obvious. It was clear that grief and loss were to be expressed only in ways deemed most appropriate by the white American treatment team. Despite this, I was able to be therapeutic later in a surprising way. The mother was asleep for a few hours as a result of the administered medication, during which time the father arrived in time to say goodbye to his son. Unfortunately as the child began to pass away, the father was not emotionally able to be present with his son as he left his physical body. The mother was still out cold from the meds, so a NICU nurse and I were able to step in and hold the child during his final time. Words cannot describe what it was like for me to 1) have the honor of providing comfort to this precious child as he departed this realm in the absence of his parents, 2) how grateful I was to the nurse who stepped in without hesitation, and 3) what it felt like to have lost numerous children in similar ways that week. Yet in that moment I had to remain focused on the mother and her needs. While I was not in an emotional space (nor did I have the time) to journal much during my time there, I found the following statement from that day in my journal: *"Pain is too small a word. I can't even describe where I feel it."* I believe this statement still aptly reflects how I felt at that time, and perhaps how many therapists, physicians, humanitarian workers, and the like feel in bearing witness to and carrying such pain.

After this child made his transition peacefully, I consulted with the treating physicians to advocate for the mother's right to say a proper goodbye to her son, particularly given that she was in a medicated sleep when he passed away. Recall that given the extreme climatic conditions, there were strict policies about the amount of time a body could remain at the hospital. Further, most families could not afford to pay for the proper burial of a family member and therefore had to leave the body to be disposed of by the hospital administration. Moreover, the body needed to be removed from the NICU unit immediately in the interest of the other patients. I had to strongly advocate for this mother's right to view the body and say goodbye in the most humane manner possible. The logistics team finally agreed and said they would find a place outside of the NICU unit to do so. They came to get me to approve the arrangement. Much to my surprise, the place they selected for a viewing was on a table in the active operating room (OR). Indeed, it was currently in use for two surgeries! To even to get to this location, I had to walk through the entire surgical tent. (Note that I was not in any sanitized or appropriate attire to ensure hygiene and limit contamination.) I indicated the range of problems with such a location—the hygiene issues notwithstanding—namely that this mother was likely to be very emotional and expressive and that the OR with two surgeries underway was not appropriate. Further, such an arrangement may endanger all of the patients, surgeons, and staff involved.

So I arranged for a location outside on a makeshift concrete table under a nightlight and wrapped her son in a white sheet. I prepared our translator beforehand and explained the sensitive nature of what we should communicate and how the mother might respond. I underscored that it was completely normal for her to be in pain and that she needs to be allowed to express her pain, but that we needed to ensure she was safe and supported. With that, we were finally able to wake the mother and I disclosed the horrible news with the aid of the translator and we escorted the mother to view her son's body. She was able to say goodbye, at which point she again began to become very emotionally expressive and I encouraged the team to allow her to get this out since we were outside and away from other patients. But I encouraged our translator to stay close to ensure her safety. She began wailing and dancing in the street. I was told that she was saying something about not wanting to live and calling out the name of God repeatedly. She then took off running for quite some distance until she suddenly fell to the ground wailing. Another mental health professional and I were able to hold her and just sat with her on the ground, singing as she shook and cried. Another team member—a midwife who had been in Ayiti for some time—was able to talk to the husband and expressed the importance of putting their differences aside and the need to support one another though this pain. He was finally able to go to her and they embraced and cried together. This family, like many others, lost a child only to go "home" to a tent. They only asked us if perhaps we could give them a ride as it was now very late in the night, or if we had a sleeping bag.

Bon Kouraj: Have Courage

I recall a mother who, in the midst of her losing her daughter, asked me to take a picture of her daughter connected to a respirator fighting for her life. She said she never wanted to forget how she fought. She cried and begged to be bound up to protect her (physically and spiritually). She was having a difficult time providing emotional support for her son, as he was particularly upset about losing his big sister. He could only cry out "Bondye! Bondye!" (God, God!). After the daughter passed away, the mother had to be carried out by some of the male support staff. The mother was only consolable when her head was in my lap and I was holding her. I sat with her and held her in the blazing afternoon sun for hours. Her son, who had lost his sister, didn't know how to respond, and his mother was in no condition to help him. He cried to the mother and she could only lift her head slightly and respond without ever opening her eyes: "bon kouraj pitit mwen" which translates loosely to "have courage or good strength my son." Another member of the mental health team took him and provided support and was able

PHOTO 20.1   A powerful mural depicting both the pain and triumph of the Haitian people

to get him to calm down until the father was finally able to arrive. Unfortunately it was too late for him to say goodbye to his little girl. Before he left, the little boy said that he wanted to stay at the hospital with us where his sister was and where he could receive love from us. I was encouraged as the family left together. The mother paused and hugged me tight and walked off without a word, since she spoke no English. Yet words weren't necessary.

These are but two families' experiences. I share them because these experiences affected me in numerous ways. It struck me that I was at once able to feel the visceral pain and strength in these mothers. As a licensed psychologist, I have narrowly prescribed roles and tasks defined as therapeutic. As a woman of African ancestry, I know personally that such paradigmatically narrow definitions don't emanate from my own definitions of healing and therapy. From my own practice with Black and Brown people locally and globally, I know that I must be broad in my understanding of what constitutes healing.

I had to put aside the fundamentally limiting questions of liability, ethics (as defined by those whose values and politics are often contrary to my own), and professional boundaries. I learned that the *Ubuntu* or human[2] part of us transcends contextual issues and language barriers to that which is most therapeutic. I found that it was the part of me that *knows* pain and that fully understood the shrill of the mother's screams that could mobilize most effectively in an environment that was so antithetical to what I believe is therapeutic. I am reminded of the Zulu proverb: "*Umuntu Ngumuntu Ngabantu,*" which means "I am a person through other people; my humanity is tied to yours." Ironically, it was in the face of such pain and ontological desolation that I found myself feeling most life seeking. It was through the connectedness of my humanity and pain with their humanity and pain that mutual support and healing began. Outside of the therapy room and the safe confines of theory, my own therapeutic practice found liberation. I learned that therapy (and therapists) must be courageous. I have not been the same therapist or woman since then. Yet with all that I gained, this work was met with much frustration and many challenges.

Challenges and Frustrations

During my two subsequent trips to Ayiti, I had the opportunity to work with hundreds of health care volunteers. Most were well-trained and well-intentioned professionals who not only volunteered their time and expertise, but often paid out of their own pockets to do so. Without them, the hospitals in which I worked would have been inoperable, and thousands of Haitians would have not received often lifesaving medical care. Thus, my discussion of the challenges and frustrations of this work is presented in light of such acknowledgement.

As I mentioned previously, much of my work included advocating for culturally responsive and supportive care for patients and their families. This was necessary because of the clear biases that influenced decision making by other health care volunteers. We tend to think of medical volunteers as fundamentally altruistic and general "do gooders." Yet I am very clear that good intentions are seldom enough. The overwhelming majority of volunteers were white Americans with little or no experience of working in post-disaster contexts or perhaps more importantly, with African people, particularly Ayitians. I am reminded of the nurse who, when asked about any previous experience in the Caribbean or the developing world, responded with a description of her cruise to the Bahamas. While I am certain that she was a skilled nurse, cultural preparedness for such work is essential. Indeed, the cultural and religious biases the volunteers brought with them negatively affected the care they were able to provide. Such experiences also underscored that what we consider "cultural competence" is insufficient and may need reconsideration, particularly in work with traumatized and colonized populations where our efforts may only serve to retraumatize.

African people around the world are still suffering, yet they are still fighting for freedom and health. I exist because of that struggle and quest for freedom, and that motivates me to continue. I know there are relatively few who are interested and skilled in responding to the needs of African people, and that I must therefore continue forward in this work. I recognize that training in the Western context of mental health is inadequate to prepare a healing professional to engage in work in these contexts. It takes more than being a licensed practitioner and a "humanitarian" to provide competent and effective services.

Advice to Other Therapists

It is imperative that we move beyond the therapy office and the therapy hour. Pain and suffering are all encompassing; thus our healing initiatives must be similarly expansive. As I learned in Ayiti, not everyone is well suited or trained to work across contexts. I believe we must understand and honor that which we are prepared to do competently. I am grateful to my local colleagues who did not volunteer, but who instead provided a host of donations for me to take on all of my trips to Ayiti and other countries, and who assisted in my local responsibilities while I was away.

To become involved in social action, I believe it is important to identify issues that are personal and integral for us in some way in order for our work to be sustained. If the issue is temporal or lacking in personal meaning, we are less likely to remain engaged over time. The way in which we extend ourselves should feel like an extension of ourselves: we should be using our skills and gifts to do so. It is also important to remember that this work begins at home. While the work that I describe was within an international context following a natural disaster, recall that what motivated me was the familiar nature of it. I saw, and continue to see, my work in Ayiti as a continuation of my familial legacy and my work with African people in the United States, who are surviving the assaulting experiences of life in US inner cities. Without the personal nature of the work, I'm not sure that I would have been able to return another two times, given its intensity.

It is also important to note that while engaging in service and social justice sounds good in theory, it often costs us money, time, personal comfort, and familial sacrifice. We must ask ourselves whether we are willing to pay this cost. Such work is personally taxing and emotionally exhausting. The type of work in which I have engaged is also very emotionally and spiritually challenging. My work around the world has forever changed the way I see and experience the world and the people in it; I am blessed to have had these experiences, but I have lost a protective ignorance as well. Secondary and vicarious traumatization are real experiences. I dream of every child we lost. And I can still see the face of every child we lost, even after some time. I have great support and healing rituals for myself that are necessary for my own health. I was careful to assess when I was ready to return. I noticed that even as I wrote about my/their/our experiences, I wept—not out of pity, but because of the unforgiving perseverance of pain. I wept because of the unimaginable strength that I witnessed and that I gained as a result of my experiences there.

I completed three trips to Ayiti, working in different contexts. I recognized that I needed a short break, but I am resolved to return. I was struck by the politicized nature of service; there was clear money to be made. Many of the organizations and foundations that received large amounts of funding were politically affiliated, and given the complex history of politics and colonialism in Ayiti, this is particularly noteworthy at such a vulnerable time. The frequent cameras and scripted interviews with the most visibly injured patients not only compromised patient care, but was also disheartening to many volunteers who were there to serve. I am saddened by the decreased attention to the plight of Ayiti, particularly in light of the cholera outbreak and hurricane season. Much work remains to be done. During my break, I was able to travel to Zambia on three occasions and work with children living on the streets and in orphanages. I was also able to provide trauma training to child care workers who work with these children and their families. In so doing, I was able to use my experiences in what was most therapeutic, and not rely solely on trauma theory. Given the lived experience of life and chronic loss in sub-Saharan Africa, I was able to personalize the experience of trauma, death, and dying in a way that moves beyond theoretical imperatives. I believe that the work in which these professionals will engage will be better as a result.

Ultimately, what I learned most from my experiences engaging in social action are that even in the midst of the darkest moment, there is something life seeking within that sustains us. I learned that I had more courage than I imagined, and that showing authenticity and love in the midst of despair is often the most powerful intervention a therapist can offer. I am much more courageous, loving, and flexible therapeutically as a result. Personally, I am grateful that I was able to use my own pain and bereavement to connect with these families. I am honored to have had these opportunities, and I share them only in hopes

PHOTO 20.2 Having hiked a mountain to see clearer, more beautiful vistas of Ayiti, I am reminded of the mountainous sacrifices and accomplishments of Ayitians. Ayiti is truly a beautiful and strong country, if only we look from the right perspective.

that the suffering of the Ayitian people might not be in vain, and that others may feel compelled to act.

Notes

1 Ayiti is the Kreyol word for Haiti. Because I stand in solidarity with Haitian people, for purposes of the present discussion I will use their words and language as much as possible. Thus, Ayiti will be used in lieu of Haiti.
2 *Ubuntu* refers to the human soul that is inextricably connected to other souls. It conveys the idea that injury to you is injury to me. In transcending the Western notion of the disconnected therapist, their pain was my pain. Such a divine process defies the psychoanalytic construct of countertransference.

21

KICKING AND SCREAMING

My Social Action Journey

Cirecie A. West-Olatunji

When training for multi-cultural competence, I often ask participants to develop a one-page cultural biography about their early experiences with diverse individuals and how those experiences shaped their attitudes today. Recently, when working with early childhood educators, they asked to see my cultural biography. I was taken aback at first, then I rose to the challenge and constructed my own narrative. I wrote about how my parents had migrated from the South to upstate New York and bought a brownstone house. In this home, we temporarily housed a host of relatives on both my father's and mother's side, as our extended family also migrated from Alabama and Mississippi. During my early childhood years, as the youngest and only girl in my immediate family, I roamed our brownstone—three stories and a basement—and interacted with aunts, uncles, cousins, grandparents, and even non-blood "kin." The experience of constructing my own cultural biography was insightful for me; it made me realize that I had acquired my community competencies at an early age.

Community Engagement in (pre-Katrina) New Orleans

Early on in my professional career, I was offered the opportunity to take on a project in a local public housing community. I accepted the position with the caveat that I wanted to conduct a community-wide needs assessment prior to developing the interventions suggested by the contracting organization. The organization's leaders had stated what they believed to be the community's problems, such as violence, adolescent behavior problems, and substance abuse.

I solicited assistance from graduate counseling students at one of the local universities and had several goals for their immersion experience. I wanted the students to consider themselves counselors, rather than generic mental health professionals. This concept had been strongly emphasized in my Master's and Doctoral degree programs, and I wanted to infuse these students with the same ideals. I also wanted to discover a way in which social justice and advocacy could be integrated into their counselor identity. At that time (late 1990s), few publications in counseling journals discussed advocacy in counseling. So I broached this topic with graduate counseling students with whom I had interactions. They asked me how counselors' advocacy was different than social work. I thought this was a good question that required a sincere and well-thought-out response. I shared my belief that advocacy is the act of promoting the rights of individuals or communities whose liberties may be in danger.

This just seemed like common sense to me, for several reasons. First, I grew up in a working-class neighborhood where outsiders were constantly coming in to try out new approaches to health care, education, and civic engagement. However, the outsiders rarely asked members of my community what we wanted, what we needed, or what we thought the obstacles were to our intended ways of living. Second, as an outsider to the community in which I was to intervene, I knew that it would be socially inappropriate to presume that I knew what was best for the residents without first speaking to the elders and other key community stakeholders. So I decided to model the community assessment approach for the students.

Our first task was to enter into the community. Given that we were to work in a public housing development (a.k.a., "the projects"), my students asked questions such as, "Should I leave my car in another area and walk, or ride the bus to the housing development?" and "Should I leave my purse at home?" or "Should I ask my husband to come with me?" I think the most amusing question was, "Can I sit in my car and collect data?" I thought, "If this is the baseline for acquiring advocacy competencies, we have nowhere to go but up!" I observed that counselor education training had focused so intently on rehabilitation and the individual that we had overlooked individuals in context. My students were lost outside of the clinical interview room, and were thus over-reliant on physical structures rather than their knowledge and skills.

One would think that because these students were mostly African American, and attended a historically black college/university, they would have more compassion, understanding, and empathy for the members of this public housing community. However, I soon realized that these middle-class students had the same preconceived notions about people in impoverished communities as any other counseling students. They had internalized stereotyped beliefs about public housing communities that initially prevented them from wanting to make contact. They were fearful and anxious. They also wondered about my credibility as a professional. And to be honest, at the beginning of this journey, I also realized that I had stereotyped these students and did not see them as they were. Why did I expect that they would relate to the public housing community? Because they were African American? Because I am African American? I had to revisit my own cultural competence by not presuming I knew anything about the students or the community. Instead, we needed to start with curiosity.

Over several weeks, the students and I partnered with community residents and conducted behavioral observations and informal interviews. Later, after analyzing the preliminary data, we held focus group and semi-structured interviews. We also collected artifacts from the community newsletters, neighborhood meeting minutes, and news media from outside of the community. When debriefing about the experience, one student stated that she began the project by objectifying the members of the community ("those people"), but she later realized that they were very similar to individuals within her own social system. In fact, one student stated, "… there but for the grace of God, go I." Through direct contact as part of this immersion experience, students were able to break through their preconceived ideas about people in impoverished communities and begin to identify with them as just *people*. Once that happened, they became motivated to see beyond individual weaknesses to consider contextual influences and advocate on behalf of the community residents. Rather than seeing community violence, the students conceptualized the adult men and women as having relational problems that were, in part, due to the structure of the social services rendered to families. This familial conflict sometimes spilled into the public arena and looked like (or became) community violence. They subsequently developed and provided male-female relationship seminars in the public housing development that were well attended by both men and women. Instead of labeling the youth as having behavioral disorders or other diagnosable concerns, they conceptualized the adolescents' acting-out behaviors as extensions of the parental conflicts. They designed a rite of passage program for the middle school children that focused on the use of appropriate adult role models, cultural identity development, local and cultural history, and academic support. Substance abuse and other addiction counseling was offered in partnership with a local community agency in response to the needs articulated by community members.

Following the success of my work in the public housing development with the assistance of the students, I earned a reputation in the city for being able to enter communities and readily develop a rapport with the residents. I was later commissioned by the US Witness Assistance Program (formerly known as the Witness Protection Program) to gather survey information from young adult males (18–24 years old) in the public housing community. The government wanted to know what they could do to improve services for individuals in the Witness Assistance Program. Most of their service recipients were young adult males, 18–24 years old, from lower-class communities in large urban cities. Once again, I solicited the assistance of graduate counseling students and we were able to successfully survey a large sample of this population in the target neighborhood, using the survey instrument that they provided.

A year or two later, I was approached by a major insurance company to conduct a community needs assessment. To build a multi-purpose office building, they needed to tear down a city block of houses. The neighborhood residents were in an uproar about the loss of properties. Only one house remained on that block, and residents were resistant to having it razed like the others. The insurance company agreed to leave the house standing, and offered it for use by the members of that working-class neighborhood. The insurance company was not sure how best to use the house, and wanted us to communicate with the neighborhood residents to solicit ideas. Using the same methods as before, with a team of graduate counseling students, I was able to identify the desires of the community residents and communicate them to the insurance company. Through these activities, the students were able to not only provide a justification for advocacy in counseling, but also to engage in advocacy behaviors. I thought these experiences would culminate my social action and advocacy experiences. Little did I know what was in store for me.

Disaster Counseling in the Aftermath of Hurricane Katrina

When Hurricane Katrina hit New Orleans, I was devastated. Not just because I felt sorrow for the people affected, but because it was personal to me. I had lived in New Orleans for 14 years. This was where I had given birth to my last child, raised both of my children, and earned both of my counseling degrees. It had only been two years since we had packed up our belongings and moved to Florida. This disaster took my breath away. I felt an overwhelming sense of relief for having moved away, but I also felt the residents' collective grief and loss. I knew, firsthand, about the seven generations of family members buried in the cemeteries. I knew how important family is to New Orleanians, who grow up and build homes across the street and next door to their parents, siblings, and grandparents. The sense of loss would be great; I understood that.

Immediately after the flooding occurred and the images of stranded New Orleans residents were spread across the news media, I was bombarded with questions from students and colleagues about what was going on there. My e-mail account was filled with messages from family members and friends inquiring about lost and unaccounted for individuals. As the e-mails came in over time, I noted messages of relief as family members were accounted for in other parts of the state and in neighboring states. Within a couple of weeks, I was headed out of the country to provide consultation in the Pacific Rim. There I encountered even more questions about what was happening in New Orleans. Foreigners wanted to talk about the blatant racism and lack of humanity demonstrated by the US government. Why were people being left without resources, without assistance? I had few answers to provide, and felt ashamed about the way my government was responding. I knew that people—my people—were suffering and not enough was being done.

I had so many feelings about the disaster in the area that had been my home for 14 years. At first I felt the conflicting feelings of grief and relief. After all, I had been spared this tragedy. None of my belongings were lost. I had carefully packed and moved my family's belongings just two years prior. But I still trembled with the thought: "that could have been me." I also felt fearful for all the people I knew, and those I did not. Maybe there was a small voice inside telling me that I should return to help, but mostly I panicked with horror, fear, and relief. Initially, I just watched in terror like everyone else.

After returning home to the States, I continued monitoring the post-hurricane events in New Orleans. I even had several opportunities to speak with friends of mine. That gave me some relief, but I still felt that something was missing. I still heard that small voice inside my head, urging me to do more. Later, I received a call from a very close friend who invited me to join him as a deployed licensed professional counselor for the Substance Abuse Mental Health Services Administration (SAMHSA). As a relatively new staff person in my department, I was concerned that taking the time away from my job might jeopardize my position. Reluctantly I declined. Several weeks later, he called me again. His invitation was much stronger this time. He told me that he had already served for two weeks and, given his experiences, he knew that the people of New Orleans would be greatly served by my clinical skills and knowledge of the community. I still was not convinced that I could get away. In any case, as a single parent I thought, "Who would take care of my children?" and, "What would happen to my work?" It just didn't seem possible.

The third time my friend called, I was ready—emotionally—to hear him through. He told me that because I knew the people, the culture, and the city, I could make a significant difference in my service provision. He told me that my presence alone would be uplifting to the people who knew me. He told me that going would satisfy my own spiritual needs by participating in the healing of New Orleans. As I listened to his, I knew he was right. I needed to go: not just for the people of New Orleans, but also for myself.

Saying yes to my friend allowed me to speak truthfully. Saying it aloud, instead of in that small voice in my head, was like a breath of fresh air. I could breathe again. I felt whole. Thus, he was able to convince me that it was possible for me to get away from my work and spend time providing disaster counseling in New Orleans. Once I switched my thinking, I began to problem solve and think creatively about *how* I could serve. The first thing I did was talk to my mother about coming to visit for two weeks to supervise my teenage children. To my surprise, she said she would be glad to do it. Then I met with my supervisor to talk about the possibilities. This was a more challenging conversation. He admired my commitment and passion for disaster counseling, but was concerned that my deployment would derail my professional focus. He encouraged me to think about how going to New Orleans for two weeks would affect my work and the evaluation of my work. Yet my friend had convinced me that this was something that I needed to do and I had agreed. So I continued to discuss the possibilities with my supervisor and we finally settled on a compromise. I agreed to deployment during the winter holiday break.

As other people were preparing for the holiday festivities, I was organizing for deployment. I was a little nervous about seeing my former city in disarray, and also anxious about my disaster counseling skills. As a Red Cross Disaster Mental Health volunteer, I had been deployed to several local disasters and provided counseling, but I imagined that this deployment was going to be different. I was flown into New Orleans and taxied to the host hotel where the SAMHSA staff was housed. The first order of business was an orientation to the paperwork, procedures, do's and don'ts, and the doling out of the bright orange SAMHSA t-shirts. I was relieved to run into people I knew from when I lived there. They greeted me warmly and gave news of the whereabouts and status of their family members. I was glad to be home again.

My deployment consisted of providing clinical outreach to a community of first responders (such as law enforcement officers and firefighters), sewage and water board workers, and City Hall employees who were housed on the two Carnival cruise ships in the Port of New Orleans. I found myself excited to be back in the clinical realm. I realized how much I missed having direct contact with clients. I also found the interactions with other mental health professionals invigorating, stimulating, and informative. My first day of training was with a social worker *extraordinaire*. He was phenomenal! In the two weeks he had been in New Orleans, he had developed connections with area residents and had discovered resources in the community. He had developed such a rapport with the people that they greeted him warmly by name. As I watched him work with the members of the community and the deployed medical professionals and other first responders, I hoped that I could maintain his level and quality of responsiveness. He had learned a lot about what services and resources were up and running that could be accessed, and had acquired knowledge about who were the key stakeholders in the communities. He had also spent time talking with people about their concerns, likes, and dislikes. He was listening. I also observed that he was cheerful and had a tremendous sense of positive energy that was infectious.

During my deployment, I felt so alive! I was back at home in the brownstone, flitting from floor to floor and room to room, engaging in conversation, visiting with people and hearing their stories. I liked and enjoyed the immediacy of the moment, the here and now of every day. There was no time for boredom or gossiping. There was only time for the now. I was faced with the daily challenge of assessing and addressing clients' issues in any and every setting, and in very short periods of time. I had to think about how I was going to say hello each morning. I thought to myself, "What would be the best intervening, 'hello'"? I brushed up on my assessment skills so that I could discern dispositions in passing and adroitly stop someone and inquire about their situation. I learned how to quickly find an out-of-the-way corner in which to conduct a brief counseling session with the spouse of a police officer or the parent of a firefighter. Each day was filled with a "newness" that is rarely experienced on an ordinary day. I created interventions for children. I consulted with other mental health professionals. I solicited giveaways from storekeepers and restaurant owners (and provided counseling in the process) for our community-wide interventions, and admired colleagues who I may never see again. Mostly, I learned from the people I met who, despite their losses, still stood united. They continued and went on. As did I.

My Current Path: Use of Global and Local Outreach

Until Hurricane Katrina (and the subsequent flood of water from the levee breeches) destroyed what had been my home in New Orleans, I had thought that I could not conduct any work that took me outside of my office, away from my desk. Since 2006, I have led disaster outreach projects to different parts of the world to provide counseling services to survivors of natural and human-made disasters. No matter where I go, I am still that little girl in the brownstone who learned how to make sense of multiple systems through her extended family networks. And I have brought with me a conviction that, when entering communities, we need to be respectful and maintain a degree of curiosity to keep our stereotypes and other preconceived notions at bay. Now I make contact and work toward real solutions in communities.

Southern Africa and Haiti

In 2007, I organized and directed an outreach trip to Botswana and South Africa for practicing counselors, counselor educators, and graduate counseling students as an immersion experience. The primary purpose of the trip was to offer the opportunity for US scholars and those in southern Africa to exchange information about multi-cultural counseling practices and research. Botswana was chosen as the primary site because of its recent establishment of a Master's-level counseling program, and because one of the instructors at the University of Botswana was entering into our Doctoral program in the fall. The 2007 trip was so successful that I organized a return trip with another group of US scholars in 2009. Included in that year's experience I organized a three-and-a-half-day conference that represented speakers from Botswana and surrounding countries as well as the United States. That exchange of knowledge significantly contributed to advancing our understanding of culture-specific interventions, indigenous healing, and African-centered counseling theory.

The 2007 trip to southern Africa did not evolve as easily as it is written here. This idea was not my own. Following my post-Katrina outreach to New Orleans, the participating students approached me with the challenge that, if we thought our model for increasing cultural competence during disaster response was effective, wouldn't we want to test it in an international arena? I responded quite flippantly that if they (the students) wanted to organize an international outreach trip, I would take them. To my surprise, they did, and off we went to Johannesburg one year later. By then, we had a well-articulated model for culture-centered disaster counseling and were able to apply it to international outreach. For these students, it became a natural option.

As a result of my global outreach initiatives, I have been able to further articulate the concept of counselor advocacy, as well as model and describe counselor advocacy behaviors. I have also been able to engage in a dialogue about counseling as a profession with my colleagues across the Atlantic. I have also learned about culturally specific interventions that can be applied to socially marginalized individuals in the United States. Finally, global outreach has allowed me to remain humble and provide a humanistic perspective within the academy.

No matter how much I enjoy my work, some aspects are particularly challenging. First, carrying the weight of clients' issues can be stressful even when I am doing a good job. Second, the day-to-day grind of the clinical paperwork can be … well, boring. However, when I have just come back from an international outreach trip to South Africa or Haiti, for example, life's everyday demands can seem small and insignificant. When I have returned from a trip where I have provided counseling to an AIDS-infected individual who bids farewell to me knowing that he will be dead the next time I return, I am not significantly affected by or concerned about minor work or personal items. Issues such as scheduling a training session and what's for dinner tonight have new meaning for me after an outreach trip.

I often find myself daydreaming about people I've met in remote villages or intense urban settings. I wonder if they have been able to access clean, running water or if they were able to buy food for their families. Sometimes I wonder if they are still alive. Most recently, I met a 15-year-old girl in Haiti who lives in one of the tent cities. She lost both of her parents in the 2010 earthquake and now lives with her aunt. She was rescued by a community agency that focuses on sexual violence against women. This young girl had been prostituting in the camp for money to buy food. Since being rescued, she has helped other girls to get away from sexual predators in the community and make better choices. I admired this adolescent girl for her resilience and courage. I don't know what I would have done at her age. She is hoping for a miracle to somehow earn enough money to be able to return to school one day.

I try to serve as a vehicle for communicating the voices of these individuals in my work. I want their voices to matter, to make a difference in the way we counsel—maybe even transform the way we (as counselors) live. Lately I have been using my leadership position to bring attention to social justice and advocacy in counseling on the international level. My outreach to southern Africa has become the first step in developing a global conversation among counselors. Much of the current conversation in counseling is in the Western hemisphere and reflects Western ideals. Given the developmental youthfulness of counseling as a discipline, we are still discovering its applications to individuals, communities, and organizations. Moreover, our identity has not yet crystallized. Thus there is room for non-Western concepts and beliefs to be integrated into how counseling is defined. I believe that inviting a global conversation among counselors can aid in the identity crystallization process. This is particularly important when considering non-Western ideals that focus on communalism, interdependence, and collaboration. While we in the Western world are struggling with integrating social action into counseling, many of our colleagues in other parts of the world see counseling and social action as integral to our work with clients. There is much that we can learn from our counterparts around the globe. Eventually, I hope to organize outreach trips in several global sectors while folding in key stakeholders from other regions I've visited in order to—hopefully—achieve true dialogue. However, not all of my work has resulted in an international focus.

Sharing My Story

So far, I have had the opportunity to provide keynote addresses at global conferences and have been invited to write book chapters related to outreach, advocacy, and social action. All of these activities remind me that it is always beneficial to "do what you do best" and all the rest will follow. This is important because I had a junior colleague approach me one day and ask how did I determine what would be the *magic bullet* for my career. I was a little taken aback, and responded by saying that I did not search for the magic bullet; it found me, and even then I resisted—kicking and screaming.

If I started this journey kicking and screaming, then my supervisor was ranting and raving. When I came to him and shared my desire to go to post-Katrina New Orleans as part of a SAMHSA-deployed team, he objected vehemently. Looking back, I think it was because he was concerned about my professional development. My supervisor was sure that my social action would become a distraction to my work. Perhaps that was sound advice, at least generically. Yet I knew at a deeper level that social action was something I needed to do. Fortunately I was encouraged by other, informal mentors within and outside of counseling who encouraged me to explore why social action resonates with me. This is where I am now.

What is my compassion satisfaction? I remember giving a keynote in Bucharest, Romania; as part of my presentation I shared a video clip of an outreach experience in the suburbs of Johannesburg, South Africa. The women of the village were singing a song and moving in a circle, clapping their hands. The women sang with voices that resounded, "Never Give Up."

When I was there as a participant, I believed them, despite the challenges of HIV/AIDS in their community, which was killing off mothers, fathers, grandparents, and children. I still believed them whenever I replayed the video in my office, in class, or at a conference. This conference was no different. What surprised me was looking into the audience and seeing that the Romanian counselors were crying. I asked them what the tears meant, and they said it reminded them of their grandparents in the villages out in the countryside. They said that out in the

PHOTO 21.1   Working in South Africa

countryside, when people have problems, "They dance and they dance and they dance until there are no more problems." This is why I am working toward a global conversation. There are similarities in the ways people define healing that are not covered in our counseling books. And we won't know about them unless we open up the dialogue and cross-pollinate the discourse. Moreover, if we involve students in this dialogue, we can ensure that the future of counseling is more inclusive and more effective in facilitating transformation for diverse clients.

Shortly after Hurricane Katrina hit New Orleans, the pictures of abandoned citizens were aired on CNN and other news media around the world. Try as I might, I could not explain why these people were not receiving help. In the end, I accepted what the world already knew: these people were being marginalized and treated unjustly. Perhaps the seed of deployment was set then, even before my colleague called to implore me to go to New Orleans and serve. Who knows?

What I Have Learned

Personally, I have learned that I am stronger than I think I am. I have also learned to believe in myself (to listen to that voice inside) and focus on what really matters in life. I realized that, materially, I have more than I need. Also, planning a successful outreach trip takes organizational skills. Not only is it important to plan the outreach itinerary, it is important to plan the travel details for the team so that the trip runs smoothly. As outreach director, I have also served as the clinical supervisor. Additionally, it is important to plan my courses, advisement, and research activities before, during, and after my outreach so that I can return to my professional life. And, of course, it is important to make arrangements for my (now) college-age children and home so that there is minimal interruption to my personal life while I'm away. Finding out that I can handle all of these things every time I plan an outreach trip has allowed me to see myself as both strong and capable.

Having survived the naysayers to follow that small voice tells me that I can believe in myself no matter what the outcome. Despite how scary it was initially, I have learned to trust myself and commit to those things in which I strongly believe. Associated with this lesson learned is the concept of risk and reward. Prior to making the decision to step out on faith and integrate outreach into my research agenda, I was afraid to take the risk for fear of losing the privilege of tenure. It was only when I took the risk out of belief in outreach as the right thing to do that I became creative in my research and writing, found my voice in my teaching and collegial interactions, experienced the greatest amount of compassion satisfaction, and was able to integrate my passion for research and clinical practice.

Ultimately, I experienced a form of freedom in which I was able to acknowledge what really matters in life. I accepted my humanism and reached out to other human beings within and beyond my own ethnic, engendered, and class-based lens. When I embraced the idea that people are living with or dying from AIDS, that idea became more important than others' perceptions of me or my work. Conducting outreach as a form of social action has been liberating for me. It also makes me think about what I really need in this life. If others are living with so much less, do I have more than I need? This is where I am now; I am transitioning to needing less, consuming less, and experiencing more.

My Future Path

Where do I go from here? I continue to work on my model for culture-centered disaster counseling. The second version of the model has been developed based upon more recent outreach experiences. I am encouraged to see that the 2009 accreditation standards by the Council for the Accreditation of Counseling and Related Educational Program (CACREP) require programs to provide disaster and crisis counseling training across the curriculum. Such a bold move will help to ensure that there is a cadre of trained professionals armed to meet the needs of disaster-affected communities.

I am also developing a culture-centered intervention model for disaster counseling that uses a psychosocial approach similar to that of India. During a People-to-People trip to India, I learned about their psychosocial model of disaster response. Due to the low numbers of mental health professionals in India, it would be imprudent to adopt the more Westernized psychological first aid model that is prevalent in the United States and Europe. Thus India relies upon community stakeholders to provide support. They are given minimal counseling interviewing skills and then trained using workbooks and activities to help community members following a disaster. This model has worked very well for them, and versions of this approach have been applied to other professions in countries with similar needs. The rationale is that it is easier to train a paraprofessional from the community about basic counseling skills than it is to train an outside professional about the community. I agree. In the next 3–5 years, I hope to develop a psychosocial model of culture-centered disaster counseling that can be used in the Western hemisphere.

To be sure, I plan to continue directing international outreach projects in various regions of the globe and include select participants from previous outreach experiences to facilitate a global conversation about counseling. Each region of the world offers its own unique complexities to disaster work and brings a host of pre-existing interventions and forms of healing that will inform how counselors conduct their work. Inherent in my outreach endeavors is a focus on international counseling. Rather than exporting a Westernized version of counseling to other parts of the globe, I seek bidirectional conversations in which counselors in the United States and Europe are informed by indigenous peoples' practices in Africa, Asia, Central, and South America.

I began this narrative by talking about how I started the journey toward social action as a professional counselor. Central to my narrative is the idea that I did not come willingly. Rather, I came kicking and screaming, unaware, lacking congruence, and (sadly) a bit narrow in my thinking. I was afraid that I would lose my focus on my work. In fact, I gained more focus; my vision is sharper. I thought I would be disconnecting myself from my personal and professional communities. Instead, I am more connected than ever. My interactions with peers and family members have become more authentic and enriched by my outreach experiences. Most importantly, I have found my voice. I have something to say, something to contribute to the profession that has roots in my early childhood experiences. I am empowered to take social action, one step at a time. To other counselors who may also hear a small voice inside their heads whispering the call to social action, I recommend that you abandon your excuses about why you can't step out of your office. Instead, try listing the reasons you can, and then noting *how* you can. No longer kicking and screaming, you can take your first step toward *real* social action.

22

PLEASE DO NOT FORGET ME

Heather A. Guay

> *When you are inspired by some great purpose, some extraordinary project, all your thoughts break their bonds. Your mind transcends limitations, your consciousness expands in every direction, and you find yourself in a new, great, and wonderful world. Dormant forces, faculties, and talents become alive and you discover yourself to be a greater person by far than you every dreamed yourself to be.* Patanjali

New Perspectives

Although two years in a Master's counseling program propagated a growth and individualization process in my personal development, a 16-day humanitarian visit to Nepal in 2007 was the catalyst that changed my life and me forever. Just two years before, as a new counseling graduate student, I listened in awe and was touched to the core as my counseling professor shared his story of how he helped save the lives of little girls by providing educational scholarships in Nepal. Little did I know then that two years later the entire course of my life would change on a clear October day, when I accepted my professor's simple but outrageous invitation to join his volunteer group traveling to Nepal only two months later. I felt petrified when I first read his e-mail message and itinerary. I really thought he was only being trivially kind by saying, "Maybe one day you would like to go to Nepal." It took me three days to reply to his e-mail because I was completely shocked by even the thought of traveling to Nepal, a fourth-world country located literally on the other side of the world. I thought, "Me in Nepal? I am a third grade teacher, what would I do in Nepal?"

Preparing

As a teacher, a therapist, and a mom I absolutely believed in the mission of saving girls' lives by providing educational opportunities. Improving the quality of life for others had always been my aim in life, but I felt terrified and apprehensive because it all seemed so unknown and foreign to me. I had traveled to Europe before and around the United States, but I had never been to Asia. For whatever reason, traveling to Asia had actually been one of my deep, secret fears because *everything* was *so* different. How would I handle it? Could I physically do it? How would it be to be away from everything and everyone I know? What would I see there? Was I ready to travel so far from home and my comfort zone? Not only was I afraid of how I would personally "handle" the trip, but I was working as a full-time elementary school teacher, going to grad school, and working as a counselor trainee. In addition, the trip was over the Christmas holidays and I had three children and a whole host of other "responsibilities." There were so many reasons NOT to go, but after searching within, my inner voice gently whispered: "go." So I hesitantly accepted the invitation to travel to Nepal on this humanitarian mission. I reasoned with myself that no matter how difficult the journey may be, I could extend myself for this important work of saving girls' lives. I knew I could "survive," although not really knowing how well, for at least the few weeks that I would be gone on the trip. Agreeing to go on the mission was a rather impulsive decision and completely different from my normal way of being. Once I bought my ticket I somehow felt very excited, because I knew "This is it!" "I am really doing this and there is no turning back!" I didn't know where this was going, but I knew that I had agreed to begin this journey of helping the girls in Nepal; I knew it was the right thing to do and I felt inspired as I began to walk down this unknown path.

I had only two months to prepare for the trip and to raise $5,000 to help provide educational opportunities for the "untouchable" girls in Nepal. It took only $100 a year to provide a scholarship for a girl and keep her safe from human trafficking. Without these scholarships or some other intervention, many of these underprivileged girls could find themselves one of the 20,000 girls who are taken, tricked, or stolen form Nepal to become sex slaves in the brothels in India or child servants in someone's home, all with the promise of a "better life" and the idea of making money for the family. Little did I know that when I began the work of helping to find a way to keep young girls from slavery around the world that I would also help free myself from my own personal bindings, and help many others grow in ways that would not be evident to me for some time.

Should I have taken the opportunity to move beyond my comfort zone and travel to Nepal? The answer was unequivocally "yes!" Since then, my service in Nepal and to the girls has directed my path to rich and challenging journeys that have extended in unimaginable ways. I am grateful for accepting the challenge of deciding to help in this humanitarian project, as my own humanity and purpose in life have been enriched beyond measure.

The Mission

The main purpose of my first trip to Nepal was to bring scholarships to the recipients from the Empower Nepali Girls (ENG) Foundation, but we also did many other projects and activities while we were there. The ENG group visited and worked with professors from the local college to help collaborate on possibly new programs for their university. We visited and honored many guests of Nepal within the Foundation; we offered support to families and local health care clinics in the areas of counseling and domestic violence. Our schedule was physically challenging and kept us moving through Nepal at a whirlwind pace. We were swept from place to place each day as we navigated the 12-hour time difference, culture shock, rough terrain, and a few intestinal upsets. We took in the magnificent Himalayan views, the abject poverty countering the rich culture and glorious architecture in many communities, and the warm and wonderful smiles of the children in each village.

There was no way to prepare for the constant visceral reactions that bombarded our senses and emotions. We had to just move through the day accepting what we saw and heard, only later having time to reflect on each experience and what it meant to us. Finally on top of the Buddhist Shrine, a sacred worship site overlooking the most splendid view of the Himalaya Mountains, I finally caught enough time to free myself from the day. As my weary body rested, my mind was still swirling from everything and I began to write about my experiences. As I began to pour myself onto the paper, I started to cry. This was a mourning reprieve. I could finally try to wrap myself around this new, beautiful, cruel world: a world that could be so peaceful and loving, and yet contain such harshness. I had yet to process such deep paradoxes. I could not stop my tears once they started, and I worried that others would hear my uncontrollable sobbing. I was so overwhelmed by everything I had seen, heard, felt, and experienced. I cried for the poor, dirty, and starving children I saw in the streets who I could not help. I cried for those who had obvious visible signs of illness or infections that could be helped by antibiotics or medical care who I could not help. I cried for the little girls and boys who could not go to school and had to work all day in the fields to help their families. I cried for those who would be sold and who were already being sold, raped, and brutalized day after day because they could not afford to go to school; they did not have the privilege of being born into the "right" caste, so they were forgotten, untouchable. I cried for the homeless orphans who ran the city streets in packs, huffing inhalants because they had no way to comfort themselves and decided to numb and kill themselves because no one cared for them. I cried for the injustice of life in which we had so much and they had so little. I cried because life was so unfair for some and they had no way to help themselves. Although I was *only* a teacher, a therapist, a mom, *I knew* I had to do something; I had to do more to help those who could not help themselves. There was no question in my mind: something had to be done, and although I really did not know what to do or how to do it, I knew that a very little bit could make a big difference in Nepal. If we could help at least one, it would be worth it; I saw clearly that ENG's work helped many and I knew I could do that, but I also saw that more must be done.

Inspiration

During the first visit to Nepal, each school I visited, each teacher I met, and each student I encountered reaffirmed my belief in the strength and inherent goodness of humans. I had the privilege of teaching in a variety of classrooms during the trip, and as I taught the Nepali children I felt transformed and renewed, just as I feel when I taught in America. These students *are* my students; all of these children are *our* children. "We are all connected!" I have always believed that, but that day teaching in Bandipur Class Five, *I GOT IT!* I understood this on a complete and deep physical, emotional, and intellectual level, and this moved me.

When I arrived in Nepal I felt sorry for the poor students and people I met and I felt that I had a lot to offer them, but through continued interaction with many of the gentle, loving, kind, funny, resourceful, intelligent, spiritually rich, and astoundingly delightful people, I began to realize how rich *they* were, and how much I gained from them as a result of our meeting! How can it be? I came to help the "poor" people of Nepal, but what I quickly realized was just *who* was *poor*. I realized how poor I had been in my own spirit, and how my life in America was missing something that I had received here in this beautiful fourth-world country. I became rich when Nepal held a mirror to me and I saw the world and myself with new eyes. Although I am not exactly sure what produced these changes, I returned a different person than the one who left a few weeks earlier. I was stronger, clearer, and more my authentic self. Months, or even years, of therapy could not have affected me as dramatically as this sojourn.

Since my first trip to Nepal I have returned many more times and done a variety of different "projects" to help the Nepali people. In the summer of 2008, I received a fellowship through Fund for Teachers to research different types of schools and educational environments in Nepal. I felt a strong need to share my knowledge, abilities, and passions with the teachers and students there. I began exploring ways I could share and support teachers and students in Nepal, in my school community, and with others from around the world as well. The answer came from the President of ENG with the proposal of providing a 12-day teacher training workshop for rural Himalayan teachers, teaching English, mentoring adults and children, and creating a library for children in the village of Bandipur, Nepal. The thought of leaving my family and friends for nine weeks over the summer of 2009 was heartbreaking to me, but I knew that taking on such service projects often involves real sacrifice not only for me, but for my family as well. The benefit of doing such meaningful work to enhance education, literacy, and connection with those who are so neglected created in me an unstoppable spirit, and I took on the challenge with the full support of my family and friends.

Working with Nepali women and girls from the rural villages to teach English and mentor was empowering for me. The experience and skills I gained through this endeavor challenged me as a teacher, and I had to adapt and adjust my complete teaching approach to fit into this new culture in order to be effective. This was challenging and a great learning experience for me both as a teacher and a student. I realized that I am able to adjust to any situation to meet the needs of my students. Teaching English and mentoring made me a better teacher and, more importantly, developed relationships with over 30 women and girls in Nepal. These relationships and friendships are still strong today, three years later.

Raising the funds and building the Children's Library in Bandipur fulfilled my ultimate dreams as a teacher to help bring literacy to those who did not have it before. Today in Bandipur there is a beautiful library for all the children and members of the community to use for free. Each day over 60 children from all levels visit the enriching environment to explore and read books written in both Nepali and English, and each day lives are being changed through education, literacy, and developing a love of learning. As a teacher, therapist, and global citizen I feel humbled and honored to have had the opportunity to teach and help others learn about the power of literacy and education.

Commitment and Change

I started my social justice journey with ENG Foundation and have since started a nonprofit organization called Namaste Nepal-Helping Himalayan Children (NNHHC) because I felt inspired to do projects that were different than the mission of ENG. The leadership and experiences introduced to me through ENG helped me grow and move into areas that used my own helping gifts that were aligned with my unique interests, education, talents, and skills of education and literacy. When we help others grow and reach their potential, we are also helped in these ways as well.

The mission of NNHHC is to continue the important work of helping to improve education and literacy in Nepal. NNHHC has connected with individuals from around the world through social media, which has led to social justice fundraising projects worldwide. A few examples of efforts from around the world include a couple who walked across the UK to build a library, and people in Spain, Canada, and the United States have completed marathons to help raise funds for NNHHC projects. We connect teachers and students from the United States and other parts of the world to provide cross-cultural experiences while raising funds to build more libraries and provide more teacher trainings. As I continue to work and teach in the United States and Nepal, I am forever grateful to those who provide opportunities to others that allow them to be challenged, to grow, and to experience new parts of life and learning. Together, truly, we can change the world and use our knowledge, our skills, and our passions to make the world a better place.

PHOTO 22.1 Together, we can truly change the world and use our knowledge, skills, and passions to make the world a better place. Bamboo School—Chitwan, Nepal

Challenges

My life since my first visit to Nepal has not been easy. As an educator in California, I have "lost my job" each year as school districts are suffering in the turbulent economy in California. Starting a nonprofit was not easy. I had no idea how to start or even run one, but I knew I needed to continue the work that had been started in helping to build libraries in the rural villages, so I knew I had to give it a try. With the support of two close friends and little money or knowledge of how to create a nonprofit, the Internet, books, and dedication I found my way through it all. It was a proud day when NNHHC was accepted as a 501(c)3 tax-exempt organization, as this brought a level of legitimacy to the organization as being recognized by the government, and people could then make tax-exempt donations. This entire process was challenging because it was entirely new and unknown, which made it a great struggle, but with great struggle comes a feeling of great satisfaction, especially when it is done on behalf of someone else with a spirit of pure intention.

I currently work part time in private practice as a therapist, as an educator at the elementary level and also at the local university in the Counseling and Human Services Department. I believe that my work in Nepal helps me be a better therapist, teacher, and human being. I am able to encourage my students and all people to find their service passion and follow it. When we use our gifts and talents to help others, everyone is blessed. When we help others we cannot help but to also help ourselves, and that is a win/win in any book. If each of us can tap into what type of service we are born to do, we will clear space in our life to do it—and ultimately leave this world better than when we found it.

It has been five years since I made that first trip to Nepal. Since then I have been to Nepal seven times and have helped to provide educational scholarships to underprivileged children, built two flourishing community children's libraries where hundreds of children visit each year, a computer lab, and a beautiful basketball court in a Nepali Bamboo School with over 2,000 children. These awesome projects were only made possible with the help of so many people working together. This entire process has been an incredible changing experience that has caused me to see my family, country, world, and my life completely differently. Even the simplest things have new perspective. Although we really have no concrete numbers or clear understanding of the impact of our work in Nepal, we are sure of the impact and changes within those of us who work together on these missions.

Some people think it's such an amazing thing to do volunteer work in a fourth-world country, and in many ways it is amazing. But there are also many frustrations, challenges, and obstacles involved in doing this work. Some of the greatest frustrations have been related to negotiating cultural differences when working with those from different cultures. It can be challenging to understand the in-depth cultural norms and political and social laws and mores of working in a different land. Some of the most challenging obstacles have come from trying to negotiate these differences. It takes great patience and understanding to view things from different perspectives than our own, and sometimes it is near impossible. During these times, when emotions run high, it is always best to hold fast to core values and the organization's mission, and to use them to keep working together to move ahead on a path that is beneficial to the goals of the organization and those we wish to serve. This work is not about fame and glory, it is about what is right and beneficial to those who are being served. It is about hard work, because at the end of the day, when you are the "leader" you are the one left with everything in your hands. There must be a strong commitment and sincere passion to your goal and to those you are trying to help; when you are beaten down by obstacles, you can look into the face of a child you've helped and find the courage to get up and do it again tomorrow.

As therapists and teachers, if you see someone in need, isn't helping the right thing to do? If it is in your power to do something, then do it. When we are in a place to help, we do. We help in ways that use our gifts, talents, and passions. We open our eyes, our hearts, and our minds to see fully and then move to make a difference, whether big or small.

Please Do Not Forget Me

Sometimes when you are leaving the villages in Nepal a child will look deep inside you sweetly and say, "Please Do Not Forget Me." As strange as it sounds, I could never forget them, as their sweet smiling eyes have left a mark of love on me. I carry the children of Nepal daily in my heart and with each step and action. It does not take much to make a difference in the world and to become inspired by some great purpose. Truly, if you allow yourself the opportunity to participate in an extraordinary project, whether big or small, you will find yourself (and the world) to be new, wonderful, and great. What will you do to make a difference in the world? I am sure it will be great, and I am sure you will be changed by the experience in ways that you could never imagine. Namaste ~ "I greet the place where you and I are one." I wish you well on your journey, and I beckon you to become inspired by a great cause and see where the road takes you!

PART V

Closure and Reflection

23

TWENTY INTENSELY PERSONAL MOTIVES FOR INVOLVEMENT IN SOCIAL JUSTICE PROJECTS

Saving the World or Saving Myself?

Jeffrey A. Kottler

It is a given that we became therapists in the first place, and got involved in social justice and service, because we want to save the world. We want to make a difference. We believe strongly in advocacy, and working on behalf of the marginalized and oppressed. We feel a strong commitment to make things better for our communities—and the world at large.

Now, put all that aside for the moment.

What are the *real* reasons (or at least the alternative motives) why you appear to care so much about helping people?

I've been teaching classes on social justice for some time, inspiring young people and beginners in the field to become actively involved in altruism beyond their professional responsibilities. Yes, I know it's part of our ethical codes and moral obligations. You'd have to have had your head in the sand not to know that this is a primary thrust of our organizations and mission statements.

We all know what to say about this: that it's important to care about others beyond our own worlds. Any helping profession has a strong mandate to do pro bono work, to volunteer our time, to reach out to those who need assistance the most. And most of us devote a portion of our time to seeing clients on a sliding scale, or to offer our services to those who would not ordinarily have access to help.

I get asked a lot by people (and so do you) about why I do what I do. Recently a student asked to interview me about my work in Nepal and why I devote so much time, money, resources, energy, and commitment to traveling so far, for so long, to work under the most challenging political, physical, emotional, and cultural challenges. I have lots of standard, boilerplate kinds of answers for that: "Because I care," "If I don't do it, nobody else will," "I have an obligation to give back to others because of what has been given to me," and so on. Usually that's enough for the questioner to nod in apparent understanding, or at least acceptance.

But this particular student listened politely, waited patiently, then cocked her head and said, "Yeah, yeah, I know all that. But tell me: why do you *really* do this stuff? Forget all that happy-helper crap. What in it for *you?*"

Okay, since I'm coming clean, she wasn't *quite* that blunt. But she did want to know about the personal benefits, or at least my private motives, for all my apparent self-sacrifice and noble good deeds. She was contemplating her own career and life journey, and was making some hard decisions about where to go and what to do, as well as what she was willing to give up for her choices.

After stalling for a bit, then stuttering, I did offer her a few of the reasons why I'm so involved in Big Causes beyond what I'm paid for. I finally admitted that I'm not really so interested in saving the world as much as I'm trying to save myself.

1. **Use my pain.** Perhaps like many others who entered helping professions, I suffered a lot early in life. Without getting into too much detail, suffice it to say that I was insecure, neglected, and lost throughout my childhood. Alcoholic parent on the verge of suicide. Family dysfunction. Learning disability. Depression. Feelings of social isolation. To add to the picture, I'm more than a little oversensitive, never really having learned how to stop taking things personally. I get hurt easily and spend *way* too much time thinking about past slights and injustices: this stuff adds up over time. I have a limitless reservoir of pain to access, and I try to use those intense experiences for some greater good. It gives meaning to the suffering and makes it worthwhile.

2. **Feeling worthless.** I never felt like I had much to offer the world. I was a terrible student and was told I was stupid. I couldn't get into college. I didn't feel very attractive or popular. I wasn't a good athlete. I had little direction and no particular ambition. I was going nowhere. Once I found my stride, even accomplished quite a lot, I still held onto the old script that I'm only as good as what I've done lately (why do you think I write so many books?). Whatever I do is never enough, so I try to do more. I feel best about myself when I am doing something for others.

3. **Immortality.** I want to live forever. At the very least, I'd prefer not to die anytime soon. This preference is becoming much more of an issue as I feel the ticking clock winding down. When I first entered this profession, I caught on very quickly that I can remain alive as long as someone remembers something I did or said that was memorable or useful to him or her. I quickly figured out that if I did *group* therapy, I could reach even more people and increase the probability that someone would remember something I did that was helpful. Moving into the classroom as an instructor increased my audience a hundredfold, then writing books a thousandfold, then being a presence in the media a millionfold. All this effort hasn't quite eliminated my fear of death, but I must say it does feel good to be able to talk to a lot of people and think that something I said might linger for awhile after I'm gone.

4. **Feeling better about myself.** As screwed up as I felt during most of my early years, it was reassuring to learn that my clients were a lot worse off than I had been. Most of all, I "enjoyed" working with people who were really struggling, because it put my own problems in perspective. The things I whine and complain about, and the things I feel disappointed and discouraged about, are nothing compared to what I see people struggling with in the most poverty-stricken parts of the world. I wish I could afford a car or a house I covet, and then I work intimately with people who are homeless or live in mud huts. I think I've just *got* to have a cool new pair of expensive running shoes that are beyond my budget, and then work with people who are barefoot. Every time I return from a service trip in South Asia I feel so incredibly fortunate for what I have, perhaps guilty about my position of privilege, but also so much more grateful. I just wish the feelings would last.

5. **Feeling grateful.** See above. The effects of feeling so, so fortunate that I have a house, and a car, and shoes, and a job, and discretionary time, usually last just a few weeks after I return from a service project. I feel a renewed sense of appreciation for the most simple pleasures. I swear off all materialism and consumerism. I remind myself, again and again, how amazing it is to live where I live and to do what I do. I tell my friends and family how much I love them. I notice things around me that I've taken for granted. I feel intense joy from the simplest pleasures. I wake up each morning incredibly grateful. Then the feelings fade; before I realize it, I'm smack in the middle of my ambition and desire and complaints. In order to regain that amazing sense of wonder I have to go back into the field, the more remote the better.

6. **Being important.** I don't like admitting it, but it does feel good to have power, to feel important and valued. Some of the places I work are so remote and isolated that they rarely get any visitors, much less anyone who wants to be helpful. I feel so appreciated in my work, 10 or a 100 or 1,000 times more so than back home. My clients and students take me for granted. I can easily be replaced; somebody else can do my job, maybe a bit differently, but perhaps just as well. Yet if I don't go to the places I go, nobody else will. I know that. The people there know that. And so I'm treated like royalty, if not as a god. Anyone who doesn't admit that's fun is lying. Sure, it's unnerving and uncomfortable to be considered so important and powerful, but I also quite like it, even if I feel guilty for admitting that.

7. **Distraction from my issues.** We're therapists, right? So we can be honest with one another? I know only too well that clients get themselves over-involved in things that so occupy their time and attention that they don't have to deal with the really difficult personal stuff that is too threatening and frightening. We see this pattern frequently with workaholics, or even during sessions when a client will talk and talk about the most mundane things just to fill the time and avoid some of the deeper issues. It's not like I don't

already have enough to do in my life, but I take on even more responsibilities and projects so that I don't have to address some of the things I've been hiding from most of my life.

Like what, you ask?

Well, like the absence of real intimacy in most of my daily interactions, the aforementioned sense of futility and worthlessness, the vulnerability I feel, not feeling liked or appreciated, the list goes on. Yet as long as I keep myself going, especially in places that occupy so much of my time and energy, I can successfully avoid looking at parts of my life that are still quite raw and empty.

8. **Feeling smug and superior.** There is a sense of moral superiority that I (and others) feel/display when the subjects of human rights and social justice come up in conversation. There is almost a competition in some groups to see who can come out on top with the latest and most impressive act of service. It is as if acts of generosity and self-sacrifice become their own kind of currency, which is used to gain status and approval. I get a lot of positive attention from my work and a degree of validation that isn't possible in any other way. I also get to walk around feeling special: aren't I wonderful that I'm sleeping on floors and eating mush while you sit comfortably in your homes?

9. **Hunger for intimacy.** Service projects are always forms of collaboration; it just isn't possible to do them alone since, by definition, they involve sharing pools of experience and skills. I love the planning that goes into this work. We're all so busy and scheduled that we need an excuse to get together. I love being part of a team with like-spirited people, in which we have these incredibly intense, emotional experiences and then get to talk about them afterwards. We get to commiserate about the hardships, compare notes about the annoying outliers, and pat each other on the back for our good deeds.

10. **Feeling like a martyr.** Who am I kidding? Doing this kind of work is hard; really, *really* hard. It is emotionally overwhelming, and frequently accompanied by feelings of despair. Someone is almost always crying. There is an undercurrent of futility, that anything we are doing isn't really making much of a difference. There are so many physical hardships, living in squalor, missing familiar food and conveniences, being exposed to disease. Sometimes we go a week without a shower. There are often squat toilets and no running water. Intestinal and respiratory disorders are frequent companions. Then there is the vicarious or secondary trauma of being so close to others who are suffering so terribly. All of this adds up to a big-time martyr complex: suffering for the cause. Yet I must say that the pain, annoyances, inconveniences, and sacrifices feel good in a masochistic, purging sort of way.

11. **Helper's high.** There is a body of research that supports the notion that altruism is good for the soul, if not for longevity (Post, 2005). People who routinely help others, especially for no intrinsic satisfaction, are happier and more content, and feel greater meaning, than those who only pursue per-

sonal ambition, kudos, and wealth. There is no doubt that I feel the most incredible buzz when I'm working in the field. I feel more intensely alive than anywhere else. I feel a kind of spiritual transcendence, a deep connection to people and the earth, that I have not experienced in any other way, or to this extent. I am so overwhelmed with feeling that it often flows out of me in the most unexpected ways. Sometimes I just start giggling or crying, or skipping or laughing; sometimes I am so filled with things I can't or don't understand that I can't hold it all in.

12. **Escape from the mundane.** I have a high need for stimulation, especially new experiences. I get bored easily; I am often bored with myself. I am constantly trying to reinvent myself. The way I do therapy now is very different from the way I used to operate a few years ago, much less decades ago. By the time any of my books are published (including this one) I've already moved onto something else. I read what I've written and wonder: "who *was* that person?"

Getting involved in social justice and service projects allows me to live alternative lives. I have an excuse to get outside the normal, predictable routines of my life and dive deeply into other worlds. Many of my usual habits are abandoned as I try to "go native" and immerse myself in the dominant culture of where I'm working. This is true whether it is in Little Saigon

PHOTO 23.1   Jeffrey conducting home visits with girls in the Everest region of Nepal who are supported by scholarships

in my home community or in the real Ho Chi Minh City. All the strange smells, new foods, novel sights and sounds, peculiar habits, and unfamiliar environments awaken things in me that I didn't know were there. I feel more fully present than I ever have in my life, because I am constantly confronting things that are beyond anything I recognize.

13. **Excuse for travel.** I am addicted to movement. I love going to places I've never been before, just as I enjoy returning to places that spark intense or complex memories. I love the idea that whenever I go somewhere new, I can be whoever I like and nobody knows it isn't the "real" me. As I'm writing these words, I'm sailing on a ship in the most remote place in the world, in the middle of the Pacific Ocean, as far from land as it is possible to be. For almost four months we have been traveling from place to place, diving into projects where we land—an orphanage in Cambodia, a school in Southern India or the Amazon, a leprosy center in Ghana. As stimulating as the settings are, there is none more interesting than the culture aboard the ship. "If you don't like who you are," a friend said to me, "then it's not too late to become someone else."

Wow. I know that, of course. I teach that, as do you. But when we are traveling there is an assortment of transformative opportunities that just aren't accessible back home.

I have written extensively in the past (Kottler, 1997, 2003, 2009) about how if someone came to me and said he wanted to change, and wanted to do it fast, and wanted the effects to last as long as possible, there's no way I'd ever recommend therapy for that task. What we do is too slow, too mild, passive, and benign an experience; too short acting and fleeting in its effects. What I'd really like to do for that person is to act as a travel agent—to plan a trip with certain features that might resemble what we do in therapy, but with a much more potent influence. Instead of just talking about stuff and making plans, hearing reports, and processing experiences, we would *co-create* the kinds of transformative events that would be the most powerful and enduring. This would mean taking risks, venturing into the unknown, exploring novel environments, developing new ways to solve problems and get needs met, and mostly just becoming more fully present. This can be done at home; it can even be accomplished in therapy; but it's a heck of a lot easier when traveling.

Service projects provide opportunities for me to visit new places and meet new people, but to do so with a mission rather than as a tourist.

14. **Access to the hidden and forbidden.** One of the clear benefits of being involved in a community project is that it virtually requires digging deeply into the nature of the culture and daily life. As highlighted in many chapters, we can't make any kind of constructive difference if we don't understand much about what is going on, what is most needed, and what is within acceptable bounds. Service projects give me an opportunity—make that a

license—to explore what is really going on in any particular environment or situation.

Girls are disappearing in rural villages. What happens to them, and where are they going?

Children aren't showing up to school. What is keeping them at home?

People are complaining of physical symptoms without any apparent organic cause. What is going on?

Conflicts and fights are breaking out with increasing frequency in the community. What has happened recently that changed things?

Violent crime is decreasing. What led to that change?

There are thousands of similar questions that we ask wherever we go, precisely *because* we are outsiders and strangers. We are able to look at situations with a fresh, if not a different, perspective, just as someone else can do so within our own world. Such access to the hidden and inner aspects of a culture makes immersion so endlessly fascinating.

15. **Something interesting to talk about.** Not only do I know cool stuff about a lot of really remote, inaccessible places, but it's really fun to talk to what I've learned. I love telling stories (can you tell?) about the places I've been, the people I've met, and the things I've seen. I've explored sexual abuse in a seal-hunting village in East Greenland, shamanic healing rituals among tribesmen of the Amazon or the Bushmen of Namibia, the effects of genocide on families in Cambodia, sex trafficking in rural Nepal, child disabilities among orphans in Ghana, alcoholism among Aboriginal Australians or Native-Americans, the list goes on and on. My life has evolved into a collection of narratives that are organized not by where I've been, but rather by who I tried to help and how it worked out. Suffice it to say that I've got stories I haven't yet even told myself.

16. **Learn new things about yourself and others.** Many of us became therapists in the first place because we are so hungry to learn new things—about others, about the world, but mostly about ourselves. Over the years I've become desensitized, if not immune, to the potential power of standard change agents—books, workshops, continuing education, even therapy or supervision as a client. I know how to hide. I know how to stay safe, or to take risks within comfortable parameters. But when I'm in the field, when I'm working in communities and unfamiliar environments, I am testing myself in ways that I could not possibly anticipate—or imagine.

There's the old expression about being careful what you wish for, because it might come true. I tell myself that I want adventure and new challenges. Then once I manage to create or find such opportunities, I end up complaining about how difficult they are, about how far over my head I feel. Like so many such transformative experiences, it's only afterwards that I realize how much I've learned from what I faced. Sometimes I don't like what I've seen—in others, but often in myself as well. That is what forces me to stretch and grow in new and wonderful ways.

17. **Get to be in charge.** Most of the projects I've been involved with are rather informal, spontaneous affairs. Sure there is some planning involved, but more often than not, opportunities for service seem to just evolve. I suppose one reason for that is that I'm actively searching for those experiences because they are the most stimulating, interesting things that I do. In some other aspects of life I feel like I have relatively little control over what I am allowed to do and how I do it; this is a common practice when working as part of any bureaucracy or large organization. But in my service-oriented groups, especially those that are grassroots and collaborative, I get to be the one who delegates tasks and makes the final decisions. The one great thing about power is that you get to spread it around to those you like and trust the most.

18. **Creative expression.** Let's face it: psychotherapy is a rather rigid, restrictive helping enterprise, defined by a bunch of rules that have been devised over the years, informed by consensual practice, research, political and social considerations, and our ancestors. The participants largely spend time sitting in the same places, talking about certain things that are fairly prescribed, and engaging in forms of communication that take place in familiar contexts. There is certainly room for some creative interpretation and application, but always within certain parameters. For instance, therapeutic activities usually take place in an office environment, mostly in conversation, rarely in accompaniment with music, dance, movement, or community involvement. You can tweak a technique here and there, personalize some treatment regimen, maybe even invent some new protocol, but by and large it all pretty much looks the same to the uninformed. When doing community service, or engaging in activism, there are whole new paradigms available to frame the experience.

19. **Act out rebelliousness.** In case you haven't already figured this out, I enjoy coloring outside the lines. Almost by definition, if not as a requirement, community service involves challenging the status quo. We are essentially taking resources away from those who have too much already and redistributing them to others in need. I love that a lot!

20. **See measureable, observable, immediate, dramatic results.** I don't know about you, but I've been frustrated with figuring out the impact of my work. Does it work? When does it work? With whom does it work? How do I really know if and when it ever works? And what does it even mean to say it "works?"

There are clients we see for months, even years, and we can't ever really be sure that we are being all that helpful. There are clients who consistently report how great we are, and yet we can't honestly say we see much difference. There are other clients who complain incessantly about how little we are helping them and yet they sure seem like something has taken hold, even if they won't admit it. The progress is often slow, intermittent, and filled with relapses. The results don't often last over time. In truth, much of the time we can't tell whether what we do matters or not. Even when we are pretty confident that we've done good work, we are sometimes surprised by what people choose to remember or report that was most useful. And then sometimes it takes such a long time to see any kind of measureable, sustainable changes.

I think the one reason why I so enjoy being involved in service projects in my community and abroad is because it often takes very little effort to produce such amazing results. There are places I go where $100 saves a child's life, where a single afternoon's workshop reshapes education in the community, where a meeting with community leaders can change the whole agenda. I have influence in these places that I can't touch back home. Hardly anyone ever listens to me in my normal staff meetings; and even if they do listen, I have remarkably little impact on what decisions are made. Yet I can go to a place off the beaten path, where nobody knows me, and voice an opinion or make a suggestion that is acted upon immediately, as if it were handed down from a mountaintop.

I don't mean to make it sound as if this is simple or easy. There are some communities I've been working in for 15 years, and although I can point to some significant changes in the lives of dozens of girls who would otherwise not have been able to attend school, it seems to me that little has fundamentally changed in the way women are treated.

Don't Try to Fix Me: This is My Normal State of Being

I realize, dear reader, that you are a therapist: you might have this uncontrollable desire to fix me. Please don't be concerned. As much of a basket case as I might come across in this confession, I manage to be remarkably happy, relaxed, and joyful almost all the time. I must also admit that a big reason for the relative contentment and satisfaction I feel in my professional and personal lives stems from the realization (or at least the hope) that I'm doing some good, doing my part to help those who would otherwise never receive any attention.

I know that the suffering I've experienced in my own life is a significant part of my motivation to reduce that pain in others. I also know that there were limitations to what I felt I could do in my therapy office. I always feel the clock ticking, counting off minutes in a cadence that seems, at times, artificial.

But this is *my* journey, my issues, my confession—not yours. The goal of this book is not to instill guilt or to be critical of therapists who don't have the time or inclination to become involved in projects outside their usual professional practice. Rather, we wished to highlight examples of the work that some therapists are doing, and I suspect for reasons that go way beyond pure altruism. Whether working in remote villages, the poorest neighborhoods of our own communities, or in our own offices, it is through service to others that each one of us finds meaning and fulfillment in our life's work.

References

Kottler, J. A. (1997). *Travel that can change your life*. San Francisco: Jossey-Bass.

Kottler, J. A. (2003). Transformative travel: International counselling in action. *International Journal for the Advancement of Counselling*, 24, 1-4.

Kottler, J. A., & Marriner, M. (2009). *Changing people's lives while transforming your own: Paths to social justice and global human rights*, New York: Wiley.

Post, S. G. (2005). Altruism, happiness, and health: It's good to be good. *International Journal of Behavioral Medicine*, 12(2), 66–77.

24

A LIFE DEVOTED TO SERVICE

Jon Carlson

It's been said that only when you face death do you discover what's most important.

Welcome to my life.

This is an interesting time for me to be looking back on a life devoted to service. I was diagnosed with a rare, nasty form of cancer that has invaded my bones and blood, fractured my vertebrae, and subjected me to chronic, agonizing pain. I've suffered through treatments that have been even worse than the disease itself, including chemotherapy, quadruple bypass surgery, and stem cell transplants. By the time this book is published, I may not be around any longer. But then, I suppose the same could be said about you.

When Jeffrey and I first spoke about doing this book, we talked about how there is so much talk in the field about service and social justice, but precious little *sustained* action. That's not to say that many (if not most) in the profession are not actively engaged in pro bono work and advocacy, and we wanted to celebrate these extraordinary efforts through the stories you've read in this volume.

Over the years Jeffrey and I have been working together as partners exploring cutting-edge issues in the field, whether related to clinical failures (Kottler & Carlson, 2002), seminal cases (Kottler & Carlson, 2003, 2008), creative breakthroughs (Kottler & Carlson, 2009), reciprocal influence in therapeutic relationships (Kottler & Carlson, 2006), spiritual transformations (Kottler & Carlson, 2007), indigenous healing methods (Kottler, Carlson, & Keeney, 2004), or lying in therapy (Kottler & Carlson, 2011). In each case we have been interested in looking at some of the most neglected issues in the field, or at least those that dig a bit deeper into phenomena that are least understood. We have also been huge fans of the power of narratives to illuminate major themes and inspire deeper exploration of some very complex issues.

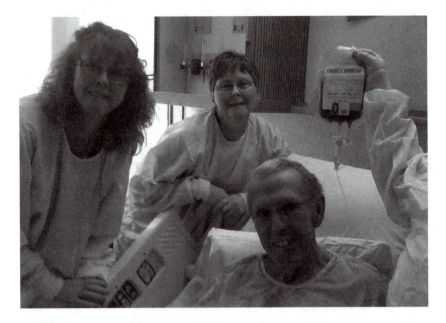

PHOTO 24.1 Jon receiving a stem cell transplant with the support of his wife Laura (center) and daughter Kirstin (left)

Our original discussions about this book centered on our concerns that, although academics and practitioners enthusiastically endorse the *idea* of social justice, we need more visible case examples of such advocacy at work. We wondered about ways we might look at how such a commitment would operate in daily life, or at least as a significant part of our identified professional roles.

The Meaning of Social Justice

The idea of social justice has always been an integral part of my understanding of therapy and the helping process. I was originally trained in Individual Psychology, or what is known as Adlerian psychology. For most of my professional life I have been a devoted scholar and practitioner of this approach, which has the idea of service at its core (Carlson, Watts, & Maniacci, 2006; Carlson & Maniacci, 2012). This system of understanding human behavior places a strong emphasis on understanding individuals in their social context. Alfred Adler believed that all behavior has social meaning. He equated having a high level of social interest with being mentally healthy.

The German word for this concept is *gemeinschaftsgefuhl*, which translates as having a commitment to community welfare as opposed to a life focus on one's own personal concerns or issues. This concept involves having a positive outlook on life with an interest in furthering the welfare of others. This fits quite nicely with the other major influence on my commitment to service, which is the study and practice of Buddhist ideas as they can be integrated into life and work. Buddhism emphasizes compassion and realizing that all work is important and can serve society.

Adler lived in the early part of the last century in a world that was in turmoil. His first scholarly paper was written on the physical injustices to people who worked in the tailoring industry (Ansbacher & Ansbacher, 1956). He described how poor lighting, poor ventilation, long hours without breaks, and other negative conditions created life-altering medical and emotional problems for the workers. Adler stressed the importance of looking at the entire context in which an individual lives to create a more complete understanding.

Adler differed from Freud in that he believed strongly in the golden rule and that we are "our brother's/sister's keeper." He stressed that healthy people treat others the way they want to be treated. Social justice is essentially doing something that is good for oneself, for others, and for the community. We each have a responsibility and obligation to work on behalf of those who don't have a voice—especially those who might never consider traditional psychotherapy to improve a life filled with suffering and despair.

Sometimes therapy is guided by Adlerian theory but, more often, the therapist works within a more complete context of the client's life. Social justice issues are one aspect of this process that involves living a more healthy life. For someone like me, whose life is in imminent jeopardy, this is more important than you can possibly imagine.

Walking the Talk

According to the Adlerian perspective, each of us has signature strengths and skills that can be used not only to further our own goals, but also to create a healthier community. I have found that most of the clients I see in therapy have a relatively low level of social interest, in that they are concerned (even obsessed) with themselves and not all that concerned with others. They wallow in self-pity, ruminate about their own problems, and see themselves as the center of the universe—to an extreme. As part of their treatment, I routinely ask them to look at what others might be thinking about their situation. I also negotiate homework assignments with clients that actively involve them in volunteer work in an area of interest. This has involved things such as highway clean up, cleaning cages at the humane society, establishing and staffing a local food pantry, coordinating the sale of girl scout cookies, volunteering to coach youth sports, and serving on community service boards. The main idea is to help depressed or anxious people to get *outside* themselves.

Since I believe that it is crucial for us to walk our talk, to become models of what we want our clients to be (and to do), I've tried to make service a visible part of my own daily life. Over the years I have created a countywide family education program, served on the YMCA board, coached Little League teams, created a summer running program for area athletes, spoken at most civic organizations in the county, served on church councils, and worked one morning each week at the local K–8 school as a counselor/psychologist. It has been much easier to encourage clients to become involved in service when they see me doing the same things. Since I have lived and worked in a small community for much of my life, such congruence has been even more important.

Social Interest as a Guiding Force

Most people who see therapists want to get rid of a presenting problem, believing that this will pave the way for ongoing health and happiness. Unfortunately, problems seem to follow one another. So much current therapy supports this faulty thinking by focusing only on problem resolution and not on living a healthy life. Without this component, clients often relapse, or at least continue to struggle with other issues.

The more I focus on others, the less time I waste thinking about my own ego and its survival. By focusing on others and their needs my own problems seem less bothersome. As a child I always thought that it was better to receive than give, but when I matured and became honest with myself, the happiest moments in my life have been those when I was giving and thinking of others and their needs. I know this is a familiar feeling in our field, and it is what led most of us to become therapists in the first place.

I was raised in a conservative Midwestern home. We attended a Christian church and my mother participated in and served as a leader of many social justice programs in our city. My parents were very giving, but lived in a segregated community that had a difficult time accepting the growing diversity. I believe that they were limited by the culture of our suburban Chicago community. The town was unofficially divided into areas such as Jewish, Hispanic, and African American. The unspoken rule was that of segregation, and people seemed to know and remain in their places.

I was the youngest of four children, all of whom preceded me to college. I attended college at state universities and began to realize that my upbringing was very different than that of my peers. So many of them had to struggle financially to be in school and were the first of their families to be attending college. For me, a college education that my parents paid for was something I took for granted. My doctoral work was at Wayne State University in the heart of Detroit, immediately following the race riots of 1968. I was exposed firsthand to the poverty and deplorable living conditions in which so many Americans were living, and had very little hope of getting out of without a major change in the system that created and maintained the marginalization. I felt completely overwhelmed by this situation. I didn't know what to do, but I knew that something different needed to happen. Privileged White people could not continue to turn our backs and ignore the hopeless lives that were created by our good fortunes.

After graduation and joining the faculty at Governors State University on the far south side of Chicago, I was in involved in two years of group work aimed at race relations. It was a powerful medium for me to understand and appreciate the inequity that exists all around, and how our thoughts, words, and actions perpetuate the ongoing injustices. Later I worked in Hawaii and gained a greater understanding of the complexity of cultural differences. I have also traveled to various parts of the world, from Africa to Asia to India, adding depth to my experiences of cultural differences.

Finding a Passion

I think what has interested me most over the years has been a focus on family education. I know this arose, in part, because of all the cultures in which I have worked and lived. Just within our own country I have worked at creating family education programs in the south side of Chicago, south Florida, Hawaii, and the community where I currently live in southeastern Wisconsin. At all of these sites I have provided educational programs focused on teaching people the skills they need to live as equals. These programs have involved training for parents, teachers, couples, as well children and teens. This type of intervention can change the psychological context to ensure that children are nurtured in positive ways. This was very similar to what Adler attempted to do in Vienna when he created Child Guidance Centers throughout the city. The programs that I created were housed in churches and schools and were open to the public at no cost.

The old adage that if you give a person a fish you feed them for a day, but if you teach them to fish you feed them for a lifetime was in operation. I believe these skills are essential to make a community function in a healthy manner. For example, the many parenting classes that I taught helped to raise future generations to have higher self-esteem and a feeling of courage to face life's challenges. Participants were taught how to communicate, to be positive and encouraging, to use education as part of discipline, to make decisions and solve problems, and to live in a community of equals.

Let's be honest: I am the prototype of the privileged. I am an older, White male who has been given every opportunity as a function of my socioeconomic class, race, religion, and gender. Even now, as I struggle for a cure to my cancer, I can afford access to the best medical care and cutting-edge treatments. I appreciate the good fortune that my birth and education provided me. My wife and I realized this after the birth of our third child. We didn't feel right about having more natural children when there were so many children in the world who needed good homes. We realized that we had resources that we could share with others and thought that this was one way to do it. With this in mind, we went through the rigorous process of foreign adoptions for our next two children, who were orphans in Korea. Being a multi-racial family was another eye opener for us, as we realized the prejudices that existed in our immediate community.

Spiritual Influences on Service and Suffering

The Dalai Lama, the exiled spiritual leader of Tibet, has inspired me throughout my life. He has lived a life based on consistent principles, which he has maintained even in the face of great sacrifices. His commitment to social causes, advocacy, and human rights has moved and influenced me profoundly. Even more than that, I now take such comfort in Buddhist ideas while struggling with my own mortality.

I have had the good fortune to meet the Dalai Lama on a few occasions, once in his home in northern India. Being in his presence, feeling connected to him through his words and physical touch, lifted a veil that I had hidden behind for 30 years (Love & Carlson, 2011). He triggered a process of self-honesty that forced me to look at how I had been hiding behind work and over-achievement, often to the neglect of other things that are far more important. This self-deception had been keeping me from the deeper connections I so desired but felt unable—or unwilling—to create. This was a turning point for me in choosing to live more authentically and make new choices about what is most important. Of course cancer has most recently played a significant role as well.

I remember asking the Dalai Lama to describe love in the context of social justice. He just looked at me with that incredible smile, cocked his head a little, and said without much thought, "Love is simply the wish to make others happy."

Wow.

That got my attention, big time. I realized that love wasn't about my own needs and satisfaction, but rather about focusing on the happiness of others. This

PHOTO 24.2   His Holiness the Dalai Lama blessing Jon in McLeod Ganj, India

was only one of his gifts; another was learning about the value of suffering, which has been a major task for me during my illness.

Jeffrey tells me that what he admires most about me has nothing to do with my achievements, but rather with the way I look at the best in people and stifle my own critical voice. That was another gift from the Dalai Lama: accessing greater compassion for others, regardless of what might be initially triggered.

My growth edge has been to learn how to better honor the worth and merit in each person that I meet. This strikes me as one of my most important accomplishments, especially considering how materialistic, competitive, and ambitious I was during earlier stages of my life.

Learning to become less critical of others was easier than I thought it would be: I just didn't like myself very much during those times. This took considerable work to connect this to my therapy and professional roles, because I just don't buy into the Diagnostic and Statistical Manual (DSM) and all the emphasis on diagnosing and labeling people in dysfunctional ways. I'd much rather talk to them about their positive characteristics, resilience, and strengths.

In so many ways, this reminds me of what it felt like to be with my grandparents, who seemed to overlook my deficiencies and instead to value what delighted them the most about me; this is the model for how I now strive to be with my own grandchildren. The truth is that I prefer hanging out with people who are most noncritical of others, and so that is what I have strived to become.

I don't mean to say that I'm a Pollyanna who overlooks problems and minimizes difficulties; I just view them in a different context. We tend to describe people by their least desirable characteristics and act like this is a healthy way to operate. We describe people as depressed or an alcoholic, but they are also so much more than that. At times, when I revert back to my old, critical self, I try to channel the Dalai Lama and imagine what he would do.

Re-Visioning Our Profession

This has been an incredible time in the development of our profession, as we have moved away from a focus on the individual, or even the family, and embraced a far more community, systemic, and global perspective. In some ways, I think individual psychotherapy is obsolete for so many intractable problems; at the very least, some of the entrenched systems of our profession have compromised greater effectiveness. I mentioned our over-reliance on the DSM as one example, but I'm also referring to other traditional ideas related to what constitutes legitimate research, political discourse, managed care, measureable outcomes, and curricula for preparing therapists.

Deep breath. (I'm trying to avoid being critical).

One of the major themes of this book, reflected in the title, is that we must do more to get out of our offices and the traditional ways we define our work. Private practices need to be significantly less "private." Mental health (actually illness) treatment continues to work in the wrong places. At least 25% of work needs to be focused on the positive and on creating an environment that supports and creates mental health. I know I am preaching to the choir: anyone who is reading this book, and its stories of action, cannot help but feel greater inspiration to reach beyond the normal parameters of our insular work.

I'd like to return to some things Bill Doherty said in Chapter 2 early in the book. The face of therapy is indeed changing, in which we broaden our roles as "citizen-therapists," using our skills and experience to not only help our own clients, but also to help change the world. We can no longer justify working with a few people who have health insurance when the level of mental and emotional health seems to be declining. We need to be more proactive and show others how to live healthy, well-balanced lives. We need to become models or exemplars of healthy living in the ways we walk through life and practice what we teach to others. We need to develop new models (such as those in this book) to reach out to others. It is not comfortable being a pioneer and having to live a life of daily uncertainty. Our new professional charge needs to become like the proverbial challenge: "comfort the afflicted and afflict the comfortable."

Metta-Psychology: One Project Dear to My Heart

It has only been in the last decade of my service career that I've been volunteering to work on projects abroad, as well as those in my community. About 12 years ago, about the same time that Jeffrey began his project in Nepal, I started offering training throughout Thailand. The original focus was on substance abuse, but the breadth of my volunteer work expanded as I learned more about the country and its most pressing needs. I worked with tsunami victims in the South, cadmium poisoning victims in the West, and those recovering from floods and mudslides in the North. The prevalent theme has been to teach people how to help one another in a positive, strength-based manner. We called this *metta-psychology*. "Metta" is a *Pali* word meaning "loving kindness."

Over the past few years it has become apparent that the traditional Thai family is breaking apart because of economic development, displacement, technological advances, and employment opportunities, but also due to other factors. Families have lived in the same communities for centuries, but that is now changing.

Thai people have always parented in a set way that involves deference to adult members in the family. With exposure to other cultures, media, and an influx of Western influences, this pattern has changed significantly, just as it has elsewhere. A program was created to teach Thai people the skills of effective parenting for a democratic world. Thai volunteers were trained in the first year of the program in the skills needed for effective parenting. The Systematic Training for Effective Parenting (STEP) program (Dinkmeyer, McKay & Dinkmeyer Jr., 2007) was translated into Thai by the workshop participants. This translation included making the ideas more culturally appropriate and relevant to their needs and interests. A participant handbook and leader's manual were also developed and translated, along with audio-visual materials to support the instruction. The second workshop involved training the volunteers in how to teach an effective parenting class. Representatives were sent from all of the 50-plus Thai provinces and materials were provided. The training, publishing of materials, and travel costs were provided for by a combined effort of many different public and private social service organizations. The representatives have gone back to their provinces and begun to train parents. Volunteers from the original group serve as consultants to those teaching the parenting classes. The program is operating at a grassroots level and is becoming very popular. The Thai people now want to offer similar skill training for school personnel.

I am so proud of accomplishments like this one, in which I was able to teach people important life skills that they, in turn, shared with others. This program furthers my belief that most people need training, rather than formal mental health treatment. Most people want to make better life choices and to be more satisfied, if only they knew how. This program results in the type of sharing that empowers others and leaves everyone feeling better. Long after I'm gone, it feels good to know that a part of me will still be alive as these programs continue to evolve.

Benefits of My Service Work

By working with such well-intentioned and good-hearted, giving people I have learned that a different way of life is possible. I have developed a deeper level of compassion for others and a way of communicating with others about what the alternative dynamics of a situation appear to be. My clinical work has become much more effective, and I believe I am reaching clients and students at a deeper level. This is a constant struggle and challenge, as voices from my upbringing continue to appear and to modify my good intentions. One example of this involves making choices that are personally fulfilling but perhaps financially stupid. It is all fine and good to advocate service and volunteerism, but we also have to earn a living! Putting all my children through college has been a major financial struggle, one that has only been made more difficult by the amount of time that I give away. Do I regret these choices? Clearly not! But I still hear scolding voices in my head: "Jon, why are you doing this stuff? Do you really think it matters?"

When I feel such doubts, daily meditation and supportive friends and colleagues help to put me back on my service path when I start to stray. This support has become even more important as my health deteriorates and I must confront the limits of the time I have left. I spend each morning in meditation before going over my plans for the upcoming day. I am a list maker, so I write down the things I want to accomplish each day. Some days everything is checked off the list, while on others the list looks untouched. It is important for me not to get discouraged when I can't accomplish much, especially when there are some days that I can hardly manage to get out of bed. More than ever, I reach out to friends, colleagues, and family to provide the encouragement I need to start again the next day. This has become much easier to do now that I have cut loose three of my five jobs. I am often amazed by how much human contact can change my day and increase my hopefulness and energy levels.

Growing up by a lake, I remember thinking and feeling how hard it was to untie the sailboat for fear I would never get back to shore. Too many of us talk the talk but don't walk the walk. It is hard to break the mold and go against what seems to be the usual, customary, and comfortable way of doing things. It takes energy that many people do not have to keep on working in this fashion. I believe that most people want to act in caring and compassionate ways but are afraid to spend time helping others when they could be using the time and energy to secure their present and future resources. Many Asian cultures do not feel or think the same way. It is a part of their cultures that people help one another on a daily basis, understanding the law of karma—you get back what you give. Even though Western Christian theology purports that when you help others you will reap blessings a thousand times greater, it has not been put into practice. This is probably at least partially do to with the underlying view in Western societies that everybody needs to look out for themselves, and that you can never have enough money and material goods.

I have realized how much of my life has been about creating security and maintaining my personal level of comfort. I find that I often go only so far and hold back if it involves investing too much of my time or energy that could be used to earn money or maintain my material comfort level: a comfort level that is far beyond what I need. I realize that if I could detach myself from so many material comforts and simplify my life, I would be able to provide more to others. If I don't do this, how can I teach or expect others to?

References

Ansbacher, H. & Ansbacher, R. (1956). *The individual psychology of Alfred Adler: A systematic presentation in selections from his writings.* New York: Basic Books.

Carlson, J, & Maniacci, M. (2012). *Alfred Adler revisited.* New York: Routledge.

Carlson, J., Watts, R. & Maniacci, M. (2006) *Adlerian therapy.* Washington, D.C.: APA Books.

Kottler, J.A., & Carlson, J. (2011). *Duped: Lies and deception in psychotherapy.* New York: Routledge.

Kottler, J.A., & Carlson, J. (2009). *Creative breakthroughs in therapy: Tales of transformation and astonishment.* New York: Wiley.

Kottler, J.A., & Carlson, J. (2008). *Their finest hour: Master therapists share their greatest success stories,* 2nd ed. Bethel, CT: Crown Publishing.

Kottler, J.A., & Carlson, J. (2007). *Moved by the spirit: Discovery and transformation in the lives of leaders.* Atascadero, CA: Impact.

Kottler, J.A., & Carlson, J. (2006). *The client who changed me: Stories of therapist personal transformation.* New York: Brunner/Routledge.

Kottler, J.A., Carlson, J., & Keeney, B. (2004). *An american shaman: An odyssey of ancient healing traditions.* New York: Brunner/Routledge.

Kottler, J.A., & Carlson, J. (2003). *The mummy at the dining room table: Eminent therapists reveal their most unusual cases and what they teach us about human behavior.* San Francisco: Jossey-Bass.

Kottler, J.A., & Carlson, J. (2002). *Bad therapy: Master therapists share their worst failures.* New York: Brunner/Routledge.

Love, P. & Carlson, J. (2011). *Never be lonely again: The way out of emptiness, isolation and a life unfulfilled.* Deerfield Beach: HCI Books.

25

PAYING RENT FOR OUR PLACE IN THE WORLD

A Reflection on the Personal Meaning of this Book and its Stories

Matt Englar-Carlson

I wasn't planning on writing this chapter. In fact, I really was not planning to be involved in this book at any level. And now, a bit over a year after agreeing to work on this project, it feels only fitting that I write some words to bring this rather remarkable project to a close. It's not that social action and social justice, as my three-year-old daughter Bea would say, are not "my thing." In fact, like many others in the helping professions, I think about social action and social justice all the time—and in so many ways it is why I do what I do. Rather, this was a project that my father and Jeffrey were all excited about; it was something *they* were doing. And then in a matter of a few weeks, all their projects were in jeopardy. My father's rapid downward health spiral and the vague, yet serious cancer diagnosis shook up all of our worlds. Though critically ill, my father was focused on finishing up many of his projects, perhaps his last acts. Jeffrey and I both suggested dropping this book as he took time to prepare for chemotherapy treatment, but my father really wanted to finish what he'd started even if it was literally his last act on earth.

Despite my inner voice telling me to say no, I reluctantly agreed, thinking this would not be a big deal (which, ironically, is a consistent piece of self-talk that I certainly could learn to challenge). Also, I was looking for a way to help my father, and keeping busy on this project could also help displace some of my own fear and uncertainly about his future. Then a few months later the chapters began to arrive. The first two chapters I read (Chapters 1 and 2 in this book) from Jeffrey (one of my best friends, who changed my life in innumerable ways) and William Doherty (whose book *Soul Searching: Why Psychotherapy Must Promote Moral Responsibility* changed my beliefs about my professional outlook) created a type of dissonance in thinking about social action, but also altered my understanding of what this book could be about. The juxtaposition of these chapters—from the gut-wrenching reality of the Nepalese girls whose lives can literally be saved for the equivalent of $50/year to the craziness of Out of Control Kids' Birthday Parties, where well-to-do parents compete in an arms race to see who can host the most expensive and lavish celebration for their five year olds—certainly made me pause.

I had seen both of these realities firsthand, and both created shifts in how I viewed the world and the ways I intended to navigate it. I had traveled with Jeffrey to Nepal in 2003 on one of the early ventures to rural Nepalese villages to present girls with scholarship money. More recently, I had been a parent at some over-the-top Orange County birthday parties with my eight-year-old son. So I could locate myself in those stories and find something meaningful with which to challenge myself. After reading those chapters I questioned whether both of these examples can be defined as worthwhile missions of social justice advocacy and outreach that truly help people. I mean, one chapter was about saving impoverished girls, but the other one was about wealthy adults that needed saving from themselves. Do they both fit under the social action rubric? Further, I wondered about the gauntlet that both chapters offered to mental health professions—namely, here it is, what are you going to do about it? How are you going to make sense of this? Here is a glimpse of how I made sense of those chapters and the book.

My Heroes Have Always Been More Than Just Fighters

I don't pretend to be a rebel. In fact, rebellion only feels meaningful if it has a focused cause. The stories in this book are all about being moved towards a particular goal: to improve people's lives. It seems impossible to read this book and not be moved, inspired, and challenged to re-imagine how your current life could be different. The stories in this book represent the types of narratives that have always drawn my attention. I grew up a child of the 1970s with young parents who certainly embodied the idealism and activism of the previous decade. But my parents were also finding their own way by leaving the comfort of their respective geographic homes and families. Social action was certainly a priority (though it was never called that) through political beliefs, causes, and conversations. Being the son of the only local psychologist opened my eyes to worlds I know most of my friends couldn't imagine. Though we lived in a rural middle-/upper-class community, I was exposed to some of the realities beneath the surface. Abuse, domestic violence, significant mental illness, alcoholism, poverty, marginalization from being different—all of these were not explicitly talked about as much as my parents helped guide me in making sense of it by encouraging me to develop compassion for pain, suffering, and those in need.

When I think back to my adolescent years, I now understand much of the context that I was missing. I marvel at the memory of my Aunt Mary. As the owner of a local ice cream parlor, she was really the only person who would hire non-White teenagers—and she fed those same teenagers who needed to eat, and she would drive them home at night if they worked late hours. In her own way, she was engaging in social action by providing opportunities. It is no big surprise that observing all of this inspired me to get into this field, that I initially chose to research social class in mental health, and that much of my current work is focused on social justice work with men.

The first book I remember reading about Martin Luther King, Jr. created a watershed moment as I marveled at his courage, righteousness, and love—and the way he helped change the world. That book led me to another one, about Malcolm X, and I am sure no one had ever read that book in my rural elementary school library. I marveled at a photo of Malcolm X and Muhammad Ali—after all, Ali was in the news as his boxing career was ending, but I did not know about his life as a social activist. That started a lifelong interest in Ali's life and his ability to help others understand and respect each other. I loved his career as a boxer, but adored him for being a social activist. I realize now that when it comes to all of my heroes, they have always been more than fighters (or authors, musicians, or athletes). For many years I carried a card with Ali's statement "Service to others is the rent you pay for your room here on earth" around in my wallet and used it as a personal mantra. When I read and edited the stories in this book I kept coming back to that mantra: all of the authors in this book are looking for ways to pay their rent. The impact or outcome of their efforts seemed unimportant, as each author was willing to *do* something and *paying the rent* helped make their time on this earth worthwhile.

Themes From Social Action Work

Reviewing the book as a whole allowed for a sort of thematic analysis to emerge. Some of these themes are alive in all of the stories, and others are prominent in only a handful. Above all, however, these themes represent some of the core ideas that locate the intersection of helping professionals and social justice and action. Below are some of those ideas that appeared to be most significant.

1. Helping professionals are already overwhelmed by responsibilities and commitments, with little discretionary time or energy for additional "jobs." Yet this totality of an overwhelmed life, and the awareness that this may not be enough, leads many to construct a different path or create new professional priorities. Both Jeffrey Kottler and Jon Carlson speak of their own developmental growth over their career, and how social action found a home and became their professional priority. Loretta Pyles describes how she needed to go deeper than the usual professional response and engage in community organizing.
2. Many authors find motivation from deeply held and felt connections to their cultural (and family) roots. Similar to higher levels of racial identity develop-

ment, many authors experience high levels of regard toward their cultural group, which leads to activism to eliminate marginalization and oppression. Both Jamila Codrington and Sharon Bethea eloquently voice how they felt the calling to empower African Americans in their own communities, and they knew they had to lend a hand.

3. Social justice and action *are* priorities for most of us, but we lack a clear vision or path to put the best of intentions to work. Many authors had the desire, but the pragmatic steps of what to do (and how to do it) were often vague. It took leaps of faith, encouragement from others, and solid role models to move into action. And sometimes we just stumble ahead. Sari Gold illustrated this sentiment: she knew there was something she needed to do, but she wasn't exactly sure how to do it; her story is about her commitment to make something happen.

4. Simply stated, social action work is tough. This work is too hard to do alone; we need collaborators and supporters to share the burden, to brainstorm ideas, and to keep the momentum going. These supportive and challenging collaborative relationships allow many social justice workers to keep moving ahead. Most of the successful and sustained programs are those not run by individuals but by cooperative groups that grow over time. Fred Bemak writes about the development of Counselors Without Borders and how the energy of new students and professionals keeps that organization alive. Cirecie West-Olatunji made social justice outreach part of her work with students—again, the flow of new people and energy created an established program with long-term viability.

5. Failure and incompetence are as common as success and positive outcomes. Many of the concerns targeted by social justice advocates have deeply entrenched contextual barriers and histories. We often fail to reach our bigger goals, so it is important to acknowledge what we can do, rather than what we cannot. Small victories are victories nonetheless. Byron Waller narrated his difficult attempts to create a racial common ground in his Chicago community. He did not reach his goal, but he still moves forward.

6. Although we tend to glorify and romanticize advocacy and social justice efforts, those involved pay a dear price in terms of the hazards and challenges they face; they jeopardize their health, safety, employment, emotional stability, and social relationships. This work is tiring; it can drain your available time and resources, and affect your ability to maintain stable employment. Relationships can easily become strained, since your work exposes you to experiences that others do not share, and you might grow (and isolate yourself) in ways that take you out of reach of others who once were close. Almost all of the authors experienced some hardship about the changes in their lives—they acknowledged taking the good with some bad. Henry Sibbing recalled how he was almost voted out of his municipal judgeship for trying to create meaningful change rather than only issuing punitive sentences.

7. There are many emotional and psychological hardships with this work—including confusion, chaos, conflict, uncertainty, despair, helplessness, vicarious trauma, and exhaustion. These stories provide some informed consent that there is indeed a price to be paid in how one experiences the world and oneself. Chante DeLoach vividly writes of her gut-wrenching experiences in Ayiti and how despite being overwhelmed, she found the courage to sustain herself.

8. All of the risks aside, this book is certainly a testament to the wonder of social justice and action. The satisfactions, joys, and benefits reported in the stories are profound—the feeling of really making a difference that is observable, dramatic, and clear—in ways that are quite different from doing therapy. There *are* clear differences, and that is what makes this work so exciting and stimulating—and actually balances our clinical work. Many authors wrote of a balance between their clinical and social action work; this balance creates energy and motivation.

9. The relationships developed with collaborators are magical and often transcend other relationships in our lives; in some cases the experiences with our colleagues deepen existing connections. There is an intensity and electricity to social action that creates quick, energetic bonds. The universality shared with others engaged in the same process becomes cemented in a way that seldom goes away. Kathryn Norsworthy and Ouyporn Khuankaew write about that magic. Of course, as father and daughter, Keith Edwards and Rebecca Rodriguez had the opportunity to connect completely new parts of their adult lives together by working side by side. Dallas and Debbie Stout marvel about how their lives have come together in the pursuit of social action around gun control and violence prevention.

10. Whether social action takes place in one's local community or halfway across the world, this work provides access to worlds that are usually not available to many people. We discover things about the world, about others, and about ourselves, that are remarkable. Selma de Leon Yznaga navigated new worlds in her backyard and discovered connections unlike any others. Leah Brew found herself at the podium at the State Capitol in California. New Zealander Gerald Monk found parts of his adopted home of San Diego that most lifelong residents would only quickly drive by in an attempt to avoid stopping.

11. This work teaches us a new definition of resilience so that our appreciation for it is on a scale that is unimaginable. Social action work illustrates the world of trauma, and we see the ways in which people have been so neglected, marginalized, and abused, yet they still manage to carry on, inspiring us in remarkable ways. We certainly see the pain of others, but we also learn to see their protective factors, hardiness, and resilience. Stan Bosch and Joseph Cervantes understand these ideas oh so well, as their work with adolescent youth in violent communities teaches daily lessons about death and loss—but also about survival, thriving, and overcoming deadly odds.

12. Love is tangible, real, and felt through social action. The love that we feel for others, feel directed back our way, and spread by the work and the relationships we create becomes an inner fuel. Cyrus Ellis certainly loves his fellow veterans—and that fuels him to not give up and continue to fight for them.

13. With love often comes some questions and doubts. Are we really helping anyone, or just ourselves? Will the effects really last? Are we instilling hope or greater despair? Have we actually been able to measure the impact of our actions? There is often no solid data about our work, and certainly not the type of data that might impress our academic colleagues. So we question whether we are doing enough. Heather Guay provides an honest account of her own wonders and fears about working with girls in Nepal.

14. One reason why we question our impact is because the gifts that many of our authors received from this work are so profound: life-changing transformations. And because of that, we might feel some guilt about not giving enough. Tipawadee Emavardhana examines her constant urge to do more for others as this is her life's calling, but she wonders if it will be enough.

15. If we want to keep the momentum going with all of the complexity outlined above, we have to acknowledge and look for the reciprocal changes that are inevitably occurring within our clients, our social action programs, and within ourselves. We have to honor these changes, talk about them, recruit others to our cause, or encourage them to begin their own. As we change, silence is not an option as silence dampens growth. Josselyn Sheer provides an exuberant example of this as she feels the almost addictive thrill of doing things she never imagined doing.

16. Of course, nearly every single author mentioned at least one time: get off of the couch, out of your head, and GO DO SOMETHING! NOW!

An Ending is Just Another Beginning

As we come to close, there is a Buddhist *koan* I want to share that goes something like this: "When the student is ready, the teacher will appear." It is safe to say that the teachers in our lives don't always look like the ones from elementary school or your professors in the classroom. Right now I interpret this *koan* as twofold. As the reader, if you are ready, then the teachers will appear in the pages and stories in this book. Yet in reading this book, you will quickly learn that the teachers in this book are really the students. The people served and helped within each story are the true teachers.

   I wanted to end this chapter and book with the words of novelist Toni Morrison, from her commencement speech at Rutgers University:

   I have often wished that Jefferson had not used that phrase "the pursuit of happiness" as the third right ... I would rather he had written, "life, liberty, and the pursuit of meaningfulness," or "integrity," or "truth." I know that happiness has been the real, if covert, goal of your labors here. I know that it informs your choice of companions, the profession you will enter. But I urge you, please do not settle for happiness. It's not good enough. Personal success devoid of meaningfulness, free of a steady commitment to social justice—that's more than a barren life; it's a trivial one. It's looking good instead of doing good. (Morrison, 2011)

Explore your roots, follow your compass, reach out to those in need, seek meaningfulness, and write your own story.